The Unity *of the* Church

Other works by Dr. Surrendra Gangadean & The Logos Foundation:

Philosophical Foundation: A Critical Analysis of Basic Beliefs

History of Philosophy: A Critical Analysis of Unresolved Disputes

Theological Foundation: A Critical Analysis of Christian Belief

Philosophical Foundation: Trivium Study Guide

The Logos Papers: To Make the Logos Known

The Westminster Confession: A Doxological Understanding

The Westminster Shorter and Larger Catechisms: A Doxological Understanding

On Natural and Revealed Theology: Collected Essays of Surrendra Gangadean

The Logos Curriculum: Grammar Catechisms: Philosophical, Theological, and Historical Foundations

The Contradictoriness of Sin: A Reading of Paradise Lost

Fundación Filosofica: Un Análisis Crítico de Creencias Básicas

DOXOLOGICAL REFORMED SERMON SERIES:

The Biblical Worldview: Creation, Fall, Redemption—Genesis 1–3: Scripture in Organic Seed Form

The Epistle to the Hebrews: Christ Is Superior in Every Way—Foundation to Persevere in Biblical Faith

The Person and Work of Christ: To Undo What Adam Did and To Do What Adam Failed to Do—A Summary Exposition

The Gospel of Matthew: The Person and Work of Christ—The Fulfillment of Redemption Through the One to Come

The Epistle to the Romans: The Righteousness of God Revealed from Faith to Faith—The Gospel According to St. Paul

The Book of Revelation: What Must Soon Take Place—Doxological Postmillennialism

The Natural Moral Law: The Foundation for Lasting Culture, Volumes 1–5

PHILOSOPHICAL FOUNDATION DIALOGUE SERIES:

Introduction to Philosophy: The Basic Things Are Clear to Reason

DOXOLOGICAL REFORMED SERMON SERIES

The UNITY *of the* CHURCH

That They May Be One
That the World May Believe

SURRENDRA GANGADEAN

A DIVISION OF THE LOGOS FOUNDATION
Phoenix, Arizona

The Unity of the Church: That They May Be One That the World May Believe

Logos Papers Press 2024
Phoenix, Arizona
logospaperpress.com
thelogosfoundation.org

Printed in the United States of America

Cover design: Beth Ellen Nagle
Typesetting: Matthew P. Hicks & Brian J. Phelps

Library of Congress Cataloging-in-Publication Data pending

Gangadean, Surrendra, 1943–2022.
The unity of the church: that they may be one that the world may believe
Includes index.
ISBN: 979-8-9898295-7-6 (hbk.)
ISBN: 979-8-9898295-8-3 (pbk.)
ISBN: 979-8-9898295-9-0 (e-book)

1. Unity of the Church 2. Ecclesiology 3. Theology—Doctrine of the Church 4. Theology—Reformed 5. Doxological Reformed I. Title

For those looking for
the city whose architect
and builder is God

Contents

Series Preface

THE *DOXOLOGICAL REFORMED SERMON SERIES*[1] is a collection of Pastor Surrendra Gangadean's sermons during his over two-decade tenure as the founder and senior pastor of Westminster Fellowship church. During this period, he delivered over 1,000 sermons, preserved through audio recordings, handwritten outlines, and congregants' notes. These sermons now form the basis of dozens of books, offering a Doxological Reformed exposition of the Scripture, the moral law, and foundational theological doctrines.

The significance of this collection lies in its pioneering nature—in seeking to advance the kingdom of God—providing the groundwork for future hermeneutical works. Pastor Gangadean developed and applied Rational Presuppositionalism[2] to general revelation in his work *Philosophical Foundation*,[3] addressing enduring challenges of the modern and postmodern world. Similarly, he tackled central questions concerning the content and application of Scripture. Recognizing the impracticality of writing full commentaries, Pastor Gangadean used sermons to engage the meaning of Scripture, foundational doctrines, and the moral law as applied to all of life.

Consequently, The Logos Foundation Editorial Board has unanimously decided to present the sermon series in its original form. Minor grammatical changes aside, the content remains untouched, accurately reflecting Pastor Gangadean's ongoing thought process. We aim to prepare the way for future generations to connect directly with the

1. Surrendra Gangadean, *The Westminster Shorter and Larger Catechisms: A Doxological Understanding* (Phoenix: Logos Papers Press, 2023), xv-xxxii.

2. Surrendra Gangadean, "Paper No. 101: Rational Presuppositionalism: Critically Examining Assumptions for Meaning," in *The Logos Papers: To Make the Logos Known* (Phoenix: Logos Papers Press, 2022), 521–526; "Paper No. 52: Common Ground (Part III)," 281–282; "Paper No. 2: Common Ground," 9–13; "Paper No. 95: Rational Presuppositional Apologetics," 503–506; "Paper No. 96: The Project of Rational Presuppositional Apologetics," in *The Logos Papers*, 507–508.

3. Surrendra Gangadean, *Philosophical Foundation: A Critical Analysis of Basic Beliefs*, Second Edition (Phoenix: Public Philosophy Press, 2022).

mind that shaped these doctrines. Preservation of the original will also aid the Editorial Board in capturing the diverse contexts in which his ideas were expounded. These sermons, coupled with foundational work in philosophy, theology, the humanities, and history, form the basis for forthcoming biblical commentaries. While each book is not exhaustive in itself, the series collectively reflects Pastor Gangadean's distilled wisdom throughout his body of work. As more books are published, a complete tapestry of his understanding will gradually unfold.

We regard the content of these sermons as invaluable contributions to the Next Reformation.[4] They illustrate how contextual thinking can illuminate the organic content of Scripture, reaching across every book and addressing even the most disputed passages that have troubled the Church throughout history. Through these sermons, the perspicuity of Scripture is meticulously brought into focus, shedding light on the clarity derived from general revelation, special revelation, and the cumulative insights of the Historic Christian Faith.[5] The convergence of the doxological focus, the doctrine of clarity and inexcusability, the knowledge of God as the good, and Rational Presuppositionalism collectively work to unveil the profound meaning of Scripture and encapsulate the essence of its truth.

Pastor Gangadean's preaching approach unfolds with a discernible progression. In the earlier sermons from 1993 to 2004, the emphasis rests on biblical exposition of the books of Scripture, laying a robust foundation by elucidating fundamental doctrines such as clarity and inexcusability, the divine image in man, the knowledge of God, church authority, and worship. Delivered with rapidity, these sermons were densely packed with content aimed at a comprehensive exposition.

From 2005 to 2014, a pronounced shift occurred in Pastor Gangadean's sermons, with a heightened focus on the need for sanctification within the context of discipleship. This period aimed to equip the congregation to grasp the interplay between foundational truths and personal application, fostering maturity. These sermons naturally evolved from the preceding foundational exposition of Scripture. After a decade of delving into the objective and subjective facets of biblical

4. Gangadean, "Paper No. 62: The Next Reformation," in *The Logos Papers*, 335–337.

5. Surrendra Gangadean, *The Westminster Confession of Faith: A Doxological Understanding* (Phoenix: Logos Papers Press, 2023); Gangadean, *The Westminster Catechisms*.

truths and their integration, the imperative to address remaining sin within the congregation became increasingly apparent.

The subsequent phase of preaching, spanning 2015 to 2022, witnessed a shift towards existential hermeneutics, emphasizing the moral law, the unity of the Church, public witness, and adopting a more deliberate and rhetorical expository style. While his pace slowed, his focus intensified on discerning how to apply truths to dismantle self-deception and self-justification among congregants and within the broader Church. The doctrine of repentance of root sin and an in-depth analysis of the doctrine of clarity and inexcusability assumed central significance.

The essence of these sermons constitutes the most profound exposition of the Word of God in its fullness to date. The expositor lived an exemplary life, building upon the cumulative insights from the three foundations, and endeavored to equip God's people with a clear understanding of Scripture amidst its myriad challenges, facilitating enduring responses.

Anticipating that this sermon series will serve as an essential source for crafting a biographical account of Pastor Gangadean's life and work, it becomes evident in these sermons how providence in his life, the challenges inherent in shepherding the flock, the practical application of doctrinal principles to the life of the Church, and a continuous response to the prevailing state of the Church and culture are interwoven. They stand as a testament to the life of a faithful servant who fought the good fight, finished the race, and kept the faith.[6]

These sermons, given initially to the congregants of Westminster Fellowship over the years, are deemed blessings that must be shared with the broader body of Christ. We consider it imperative to extend these blessings to our fellow brothers and sisters, and view it as our duty to contribute to the spiritual enrichment of the larger Christian community.

May the Lord bless the preaching and hearing of His Word, and may this compilation serve as the foundation for the contextual interpretation of Scripture for generations to come, and persist until

6. *2 Timothy 4:7–8.*

the fulfillment of the dominion[7] and mission[8] mandates in the earth being filled with the knowledge of the glory of the Lord as the waters cover the sea.

—THE LOGOS FOUNDATION
EDITORIAL BOARD
Phoenix, Arizona
February 2024

7. *Genesis 1:26–28.*

8. *Matthew 28:18–20.*

Introduction

On the Necessity for the Unity of the Faith

WHAT IS THE UNITY OF THE FAITH?

THE UNITY OF THE FAITH IS ABOUT THE *basic* beliefs of the Christian faith—what is foundational—about God and man, and good and evil.[1] The unity of the faith is not about making converts. It is not about what is fundamental for initial conversion, for being saved, or for entering into the kingdom of God. It is about what is foundational, which is necessary for maturity in Christ.[2] Foundation is for fullness, and what is maximal includes what is minimal. Unity of the faith is not to be equated with the unity of the Spirit in professing one Lord, one faith, one baptism, which already exists among believers and is to be preserved in the bond of peace.[3] Unity of the faith is about the fullness of Christ to be attained, as mentioned in Ephesians 4:13. It is not about ecclesiastical unity, that is, church government, which comes naturally if there is unity of the faith. It is not about what is less basic, the outward before the inward, whether in piety, in law, or sacrament. If we agree on what is more basic, we can and will agree on what is less basic. This is a theme I will emphasize—always getting the more basic in place—and then we can address what is less basic. Unity of the faith is about *basic* beliefs that are clear from general revelation

1. "On The Necessity for Unity of the Faith" was a public lecture presented at the Unity of the Faith Conference held at Arizona Christian University, April 18, 2015, and originally published in Surrendra Gangadean, *On Natural and Revealed Theology: Collected Essays of Surrendra Gangadean* (Phoenix: Logos Paper Press, 2023), 107–118.

2. *Hebrews 6:1.*

3. *Ephesians 4:3–6.*

(philosophical foundation),[4] from Scripture (theological foundation),[5] and from Church history (historical foundation).[6]

The unity called for is the unity that is in the Trinity. As Jesus prays in His High Priestly Prayer, "that all of them may be one, Father, just as you are in me and I am in you. May they also be in *us* so that the world may believe that you have sent me" (Jn. 17:21).[7] This is the most comprehensive and deepest unity possible. All diversity originates in God, who is one. This includes male and female, rich and poor, bond and free, barbarian, Scythian, and all the nations. All of this is in God, and God is one. The unity called for is the unity in Christ himself. Paul's response to the divisions in the Corinthian church is to ask, "Is Christ divided?" Christ, in his office as prophet, priest, and king, is not divided. Yet, note, the division between prophetic, priestly, and kingly may penetrate within any church, even those that profess the same thing. We are not to say, "I am of Paul, or I am of Apollos, or I am of Cephas" (1 Cor. 1:12–13 NKJV). The unity of the faith is unity in the Truth, capital T. Truth is attained by the work of the Holy Spirit, through the work of the pastors and teachers in Church history.[8] This is where the historical foundation comes in. Unity of the faith requires unity in the good, which is the philosophical idea corresponding to "eternal life"[9] in Scripture, and to the words in Historic Christianity, "man's chief end."[10] Unity of the faith is a unity in the meaning and purpose of life, in man's chief end, which is to glorify God. Jesus prays for this at the beginning of his High Priestly Prayer, "Glorify your Son, that your Son may glorify you" (Jn. 17:1b).

---

4. Gangadean, *Philosophical Foundation;* Surrendra Gangadean, *History of Philosophy: A Critical Analysis of Unresolved Disputes* (Phoenix: Public Philosophy Press, 2022).
5. Surrendra Gangadean, *Theological Foundation: A Critical Analysis of Christian Belief* (Phoenix: Logos Papers Press, forthcoming).
6. Gangadean, *The Westminster Confession;* Gangadean, *The Westminster Catechisms.*
7. Emphasis added.
8. *John 16:13; Acts 15; Ephesians 4:11–13.*
9. *John 3:15; 17:3.*
10. *The Shorter Catechism Question 1.*

IS THE UNITY OF THE FAITH NECESSARY AND URGENT?

We come to the crux of the matter. The necessity for unity depends on one's view of the good. There are two views. In one view, unity is not necessary; in the second view, it is necessary. We will need to decide where we are in our thinking, taking into consideration the background from which we are coming. In the popular view of knowledge by direct experience, regardless of what has happened on earth, when you die, in heaven you receive the fullness of blessing by direct experience. It is regardless of the idea that creation and history are revelation, and that through the work of dominion, the revelation is exposed. This is one view. It is often correlated with other beliefs, such as the view that only by Christ's return and direct rule on earth can evil be removed. Rather, it is by his rule through the curse of toil and strife, and old age, sickness, and death, that moral evil is removed. Christ restrains evil, he calls us back from evil through regeneration, and he further sanctifies us through the Truth. In the popular view, unity of the faith is not necessary for attaining the good.

On the other hand, in the view that knowledge of God is by understanding God's self-revelation in creation and history, the fullness of blessing is received only by Christ ruling through the Church to complete the work of dominion given to man in the Garden of Eden. In this view, unity of the faith is necessary for the good. This is the crux of the matter, depending on one's view of the good. If we do not have the good in common, we cannot go on to speak about unity of the faith being urgent, and there is no point in considering proposals.

Is the unity of the faith urgent? Consider this: without foundation (understanding basic things, beginning with the meaning and purpose of life), we do not thrive. We do not go on to maturity, fruitfulness, unity, and fullness. We remain infants rather than become teachers, "In fact, though by this time you ought to be teachers, you need someone to teach you the elementary truths of God's word all over again. You need milk, not solid food!" (Heb. 5:12).

Without foundation we have meaninglessness. We not only do not thrive, we shrivel and fade, and we lose meaning. Meaninglessness is a state in which we continue to lose more and more meaning of every word that we speak and profess. Consequently, with the loss of meaning, boredom (with transgression to overcome boredom), and with that, guilt, we are in a state of spiritual death.

Without foundation, the family breaks down. Not just families, but the very idea of the family breaks down. Christ said, "I have come that they may have life, and have it to the full" (Jn. 10:10b). Have it to the full. He said, "If anyone is thirsty, let him come to me and drink. Whoever believes in me, as the Scripture has said, streams of living water will flow from within him" (Jn. 7:37–38). We will be like "a tree planted by the water that sends out its roots by the stream. It does not fear when heat comes; its leaves are always green. It has no worries in a year of drought and never fails to bear fruit" (Jer. 17:8). "And in old age, when others fade, their boughs with fruit shall bend" (Ps. 92:14).[11] Life more abundantly. We need it, our children desire it, and without it, they will try to find it in the world through cheap imitations—it is not there. The world is full of emptiness. Foundation is needed for the family—it is not only individual, but it is corporate.

By divisions and apostasy in the Church, the Church ceases to be the pillar and ground of the Truth. It is taken captive and it does not take thoughts captive. We are to demolish every pretension that raises itself up against the knowledge of God[12] and yet we are in captivity. Foundation is for fullness, to prepare us to do this work. Currently, the Church is not salt and light. It is the tail of the culture, not the head. The universities that lead the way, Princeton and Harvard, are hotbeds of unbelief. The culture without God, in education, in economics, and in politics, decays and collapses. How far along are we? We may differ, but the cup appears to be nearly full. Not being salt and light, we will be cast out and trampled underfoot. If this is so, then unity is urgent.

WHAT PROPOSALS ARE THERE FOR PROGRESS TOWARD UNITY?

My proposal begins with five areas of basic agreement and seeking to be more conscious and consistent. By taking a step-by-step approach

11. *Psalm 92b, The Book of Psalms for Singing* (Pittsburgh: The Board of Education and Publication, Reformed Presbyterian Church of North America, 1998).

12. *2 Corinthians 10:4–5.*

to unity, I hope we can identify where differences arise and address those differences. I will speak of five areas.

The Knowledge of God: Man's Chief End, the Good, Eternal Life

The first source of agreement, something I believe all Christians affirm, is that "Man's chief end is to glorify God, and to enjoy him forever" (SCQ. 1). I am going to try to show this step-by-step and reach towards fullness. We will also do this for the other areas. Let us see how much we can agree with as we go step-by-step.

Man's chief end, also referred to as "the good" in philosophy, and "eternal life" in Scripture, is the knowledge of God. According to Westminster Shorter Catechism, Question 1, "Man's chief end is to glorify God, and to enjoy him forever."[13] This is part of the ABCs—the milk. The Catechism goes further—we are to glorify God "in all that whereby he maketh himself known." This is how Question 101 of the Shorter Catechism is answered, connected to the first petition of the Lord's Prayer, "Hallowed be thy name." How does God make himself known? He makes himself known in all his works of creation and providence.[14] This is comprehensive. Through everything that comes to pass, we are to glorify God.

Jesus said eternal life is knowing God.[15] Putting these thoughts together, relating them, and connecting the dots, we come to infer that the good is grounded in human nature and, therefore, never changes. Human nature is established by God. The good, which is the knowledge of God, has been the goal from the beginning. God said, "Let us make man in our image . . . and let them have dominion."[16] The goal then was the knowledge of God—it was knowledge of God through dominion. The good was given to man from the beginning, and the good never changes. The work of dominion now extends, after the Fall, over sin. "For sin shall not have dominion over you, for you are not under law but under grace" (Rom. 6:14 NKJV). We are to overcome and have

---

13. *SCQ. 1;* Gangadean, *The Westminster Catechisms,* 321–325; Gangadean, *The Westminster Confession, 88–90;* Gangadean, *Philosophical Foundation,* 171–177, 208–211; Gangadean, *History of Philosophy,* 61–64.

14. *The Westminster Confession of Faith, 4.1, 5.1.*

15. *John 17:3.*

16. *Genesis 1:26–28.*

dominion; we are to take thoughts captive. Dominion extends over sin, and the program has always been, always, to move from the Garden of Eden to the City of God.[17] What is said in the first two chapters of Genesis is completed in the last two chapters of the Book of Revelation. Fully and clearly there—Jesus is the Alpha and the Omega who will bring this about.

From the beginning, we are told that the work of dominion will be completed, as God completed his work and hallowed the Sabbath. The Sabbath signifies the completion of the work. Christ, through the Church, will rule to complete the work of dominion in place of Adam. He will do what Adam failed to do—he will rule through the Church. Christ is to rule through mankind, and mankind together must do the work of dominion. The result is that "the earth shall be full of the knowledge of the LORD as the waters cover the sea" (Is. 11:9).[18] Through the rule of Christ, the curse will be removed, consummating in nothing less than the resurrection of the dead. "For he must reign until he has put all his enemies under his feet. The last enemy to be destroyed is death" (1 Cor. 15:25–26). This is the Christian mission; this is the fullness of life. By believing it, understanding it, and giving our lives to it, out of our innermost being will flow rivers of living water.[19] Remember the picture of the water flowing out from under the threshold of the temple in Ezekiel,[20]and it became greater and greater until it could not be crossed. It is the same river that appears in the last chapters of Revelation, the river of life and the tree of life on either side, bearing fruit in twelve seasons.[21] Fullness of life. This is the goal. How far did we get in agreeing?

Common Ground

The second source of agreement is Common Ground. It is a necessary condition for thought and discourse for all human beings—all thought,

17. *Revelation 21–22.*

18. Gangadean, "Paper No. 104: Eschatology (Twelve Points)," 539–544; "Paper No. 118: Eschatology (Seven Points)," in *The Logos Papers,* 603–607.

19. *John 7:38.*

20. *Ezekiel 47:1–12.*

21. *Revelation 22:1–2.*

all discourse.[22] It begins with what is self-evident—that we are thinking beings, having been made in the image of God. We are thinking beings, and reason in itself is the laws of thought, which is more self-evident than what Jefferson said and, therefore, more certain.[23] Reason, as the laws of thought, is most basic. It is, therefore, the test for meaning, and it is self-attesting and authoritative.

Next, we should be committed to *reason* as rational, thinking beings. We should have *integrity*, a concern for consistency, both logically and existentially. An argument has premises and conclusions, and premises are more basic than conclusions. We have assumptions, and we should be aware of our assumptions—critically aware of them. We should be aware of the assumptions of others, be able to address them, and test them for meaning using reason. There must be something eternal—we can know this with certainty. Only some is eternal—we can also know this with certainty.[24] There are many basic things we can know with certainty, and we should have these things in place.

A third feature of Common Ground is *Rational Presuppositionalism*, which says thinking is presuppositional. We think of the less basic in light of the more basic. If we agree on the more basic, we can agree on the less basic. Rational Presuppositionalism tests basic beliefs for meaning. This is what I have been involved with for 45 years in philosophy and teaching. I was aware this was not going on as I went through undergraduate and graduate school, and I said to myself, "If I ever teach philosophy, I will always consider assumptions and address those assumptions." By the grace of God and the opportunities given to me, I have been giving myself to this for 45 years with the added benefit of Historic Christianity, as that came into focus, and the riches of the faith became so much more beneficial.

---

22. Gangadean, "Paper No. 2: Common Ground," 9–13; "Paper No. 50: Common Ground (Part I)," 275–276; "Paper No. 51: Common Ground (Part II)," 277–279; "Paper No. 52: Common Ground (Part III)," 281–282; "Paper No. 53: Common Ground (Part IV)," in *The Logos Papers*, 283–286.

23. "We hold these truths to be self-evident, that all men are created equal, that they are endowed by their Creator with certain unalienable Rights, that among these are Life, Liberty and the pursuit of Happiness." Declaration of Independence, https://www.archives.gov/founding-docs/declaration.

24. Gangadean, *Philosophical Foundation*, 3–5, 287–292; Gangadean, *The Westminster Confession*, 1–13; Gangadean, "Paper No. 53: Common Ground (Part IV)," in *The Logos Papers*, 283–286.

The fourth feature of Common Ground is the *Principle of Clarity*, which states that some things are clear; the basic things are clear; the basic things about God and man, and good and evil are clear to reason.[25] The Principle of Clarity is opposed to skepticism, which dominates the thinking of the world, and fideism—believing in God without being concerned to prove the existence of God based on understanding the basic things. By faith we understand. Both skepticism and fideism fail to see that basic things are clear. As the apostle Paul said, what may be known of God is clear so that men are without excuse. The lack of clarity ends eventually, sooner or later, in nihilism, the loss of all meaning. Understanding clarity, we can see why unbelief is inexcusable and why Paul says this.[26] One has to neglect, avoid, resist, or deny reason not to see what is clear. Understanding the Principle of Clarity is necessary to understand sin and spiritual death. If there is no sin and death, there is no need for Christ and him crucified. This is where Paul begins: "For I resolved to know nothing while I was with you except Jesus Christ and him crucified" (1 Cor. 2:2). If we cannot account for the crucifixion of Christ by going back to sin and death, we cannot begin our witness. If we do not get to clarity and inexcusability, we will not get to Christ crucified.

The Moral Law

The third source of agreement is the moral law. The moral law is clear, comprehensive, and critical, and the law is basic. It is given in special revelation from Mount Sanai, it is in the ark under the mercy seat, and Jesus says, "Therefore go and make disciples . . . teaching them to obey everything I have commanded you."[27] The moral law is also given in human nature as stated in Romans 2:14–15 and Deuteronomy 30:11–14. Moses says:

> Now what I am commanding you today is not too difficult for you or beyond your reach. It is not up in heaven, so that you have to ask, "Who will ascend into heaven to get it and proclaim it to us so we may obey it?" Nor is it beyond the sea, so that you have to

25. Gangadean, *Philosophical Foundation,* 3.

26. *Romans 1:20.*

27. *Matthew 28:19–20.*

> ask, "Who will cross the sea to get it and proclaim it to us so that we may obey it?" No, the word is very near you; it is in your mouth and in your heart so you may obey it.

This is the law that is in the heart of all men—this is what makes it *clear:* it is grounded in human nature. We should be able to derive the moral law—the Decalogue—from human nature.[28] The law, therefore, is universal for all men and it is perpetual for all times. The law is *comprehensive:* it is total for all choices, it is spiritual for all levels, and it is summed up in the commandment to love. Love is not higher than the moral law, but is expressed in obeying God's law. The moral law is *critical:* its consequences are a matter of life and death. Spiritual life (the knowledge of God in the kingdom of God) or spiritual death (both personal and cultural). In the first four moral laws is revealed the real meaning of autonomy, idolatry, hypocrisy, and hope in connection with the Sabbath.

The moral law as given in human nature is neither arbitrary—merely posited by divine command (as in the divine command theory), nor is it strange to us (foreign to human nature) as if we are being imposed upon. Rather, it is in our nature. The moral law is teleological—it is aimed at the good. It is not deontological—aimed at virtue. We have to be careful about this—virtue is the means to the good. And the law is not consequential—aimed at happiness. Happiness is the effect of possessing what is the good.

The moral law, aimed at the good, is corporate, cumulative, and communal. This was so from the beginning: "Be fruitful and multiply; fill the earth and subdue it; have dominion over [it]."[29] This work is *corporate:* it is going to take all of mankind to complete. It is throughout history, so it is *cumulative* and it is *communal*—it involves active cooperation and sharing. The moral law is for oneself as well as for others. It is personal as well as cultural. We achieve the good through the kingdom of God, which is the City of God.

The moral law is over all institutions of culture; no institution is total—over any other. I mention this because when we talk about the law we tend to fall into theocracy. I am not talking about theocracy.

---

28. Gangadean, *Philosophical Foundation,* 171–284; Gangadean, *History of Philosophy,* 61–69; Gangadean, *The Westminster Catechisms,* 215–267.

29. *Genesis 1:28* NKJV. Emphasis added.

Sanctions differ according to the form and function of each institution. We can and should be able to distinguish each institution—the family from the Church, the State, business, education, etc. Civil law only applies to crime, which is but one distinct aspect of moral evil, so we do not criminalize sin. We understand the difference between crime and sin and apply the civil law appropriately, so we do not fall into a theocracy, which is a common objection when talking about the law of God.

Foundation in Scripture: Creation–Fall–Redemption

The fourth source of agreement is the foundation in Scripture. This foundation is creation–fall–redemption. Foundation consists of elementary truths of the faith. It is milk, not meat.[30] It is the ABCs. It is necessary for a lasting culture in the City of God. Abraham was looking for a city with foundations.[31] What we find at the end of history is a city with foundations in Revelation 21:14 and 19–20. Foundation is necessary, as we said earlier, for maturity, fruitfulness, unity, and fullness. It is possible not to have the foundation in place. Hebrews 5:12 speaks about this, and so it has to be laid again. Or, it is possible to hear about the foundation but not build upon it, as Jesus said, not building on the rock but on sand.[32] Paul says, let every man take heed how he builds—gold, silver, precious stones or wood, hay, stubble—every man's work shall be made manifest.[33] Jesus said we should have fruit, much fruit, fruit that will last.[34] It is by having the foundation in place that we can go on to maturity and fruitfulness.

Foundation from Scripture is found in Genesis 1–3. Creation–fall–redemption.[35] We do not have to wait until the New Testament to know this foundation. It is there from the beginning. The account of creation reveals God's purpose for creating man in the image of God. We see

30. *Hebrews 5:12–14.*

31. *Hebrews 11:10.*

32. *Matthew 7:24–27.*

33. *1 Corinthians 3:10–15.*

34. *John 15:8, 16.*

35. Surrendra Gangadean, *The Biblical Worldview: Creation, Fall, Redemption—Genesis 1–3: Scripture in Organic Seed Form* (Phoenix: Logos Papers Press, 2024); Gangadean, "Paper No. 14: *The Biblical Worldview* (Expanded)," in *The Logos Papers,* 81–89.

the good and the means to the good through the work of dominion, and the Sabbath hope that the good will be attained. The account of the Fall reveals the covenant of creation—there is a covenant that is corporate. We see clarity and inexcusability, temptation and sin, and spiritual death in meaninglessness. Adam was not thinking when the serpent said, "you will be like God, knowing good and evil" (Gen. 3:5b). We are to understand that God knows good and evil by determining the nature of things by creation. Adam could not possibly do this. He was not seeking and was already lapsing into misunderstanding. When confronted, he was in a state of self-deception—they used the coats of leaves to cover sin instead of facing it—and then self-justification in blaming his wife and God instead of accepting responsibility. This is the condition revealed in the Garden.

In the account of redemption, the curse comes with the promise—the seed of the woman will crush the head of the serpent, and, cursed is the ground because of you. The curse is imposed, not as punishment, but as a merciful call back to repentance. We also find the teaching of vicarious atonement in God providing the coats of skin (the animal was killed), and also, we see justification—we are covered through the death of another. Finally, they are expelled from the Garden to live under the curse so that we might, through suffering, come to seek God diligently and understand. The doctrines are there—justification and sanctification—from the beginning. Christ in the place of Adam will undo, as the Lamb of God, what Adam did, and he will do, as King, what Adam failed to do—that is, exercise dominion through his people.

Historic Christianity

The last source of agreement is Historic Christianity. Historic Christianity is the work of the Holy Spirit leading the Church into all Truth,[36] according to Jesus, in John 16:13. This work is through the pastor-teachers, in response to challenges, and it is after much discussion. As in Acts 15–16, they come to agreement, and this agreement is summed up in the creeds and delivered to the churches for the unity of the faith. The process is depicted in the first council in Jerusalem.[37] The Council of

36. Gangadean, "Paper No. 16: The Historic Christian Faith," in *The Logos Papers,* 103–114.

37. Gangadean, "Paper No. 60: The Spiritual War (Part II)," in *The Logos Papers,* 329–330.

Jerusalem (A.D. 51) addressed the question of sacraments, specifically, the question, "Is circumcision necessary for salvation?" The answer was, "We gave no such command."[38] We have to draw the implications of this ruling for the history of the Church.

Next, the Apostles' Creed (*ca.* 180) addressed Greek gnosticism and otherworldliness, which minimized the value of creation as revelation, and all that went with that view—our failure to engage with the world, and withdrawal from the world in many ways. Then, Nicea (325) addressed the Trinity and the unity and diversity in God. The Council of Carthage (397) particularly spoke about the New Testament canon. The Old Testament was addressed by the Church in the Old Testament, based upon what the Jews included, and only what they included, as Scripture. The Council of Chalcedon (451) addressed Christ as both God and man. He is fully God and fully man, two whole natures joined together in one person, without conversion, without composition, without confusion. The Council of Orange (529) addressed the question of Pelagius and semi-Pelagianism on the topic of free will. The Reformation built on the previous councils, continuing each—this is the holy, catholic, and apostolic faith. Finally, the Westminster Confession of Faith (1648) built on the six earlier creeds of the Reformation.

The councils, creeds, and confessions are the work of the Holy Spirit leading the Church into all Truth. We can say the work of the Holy Spirit leading the Church into all Truth is continuing and will continue until the end of history. A base was laid in the first five centuries of the Church. It needs to be, but has not yet been, developed. There is much more to say, but in closing, thanks be to God for the measure of unity that we do have as His people. May this unity increase.

38. *Acts 15:24.*

The Unity of the Church

1

The Word of the Lord

A Perfect Unity Through the Fullness of the Word of God

2009

John 17:1–23

1After Jesus said this, he looked toward heaven and prayed: 2"Father, the time has come. Glorify your Son, that your Son may glorify you. For you granted him authority over all people that he might give eternal life to all those you have given him. 3Now this is eternal life: that they may know you, the only true God, and Jesus Christ, whom you have sent. 4I have brought you glory on earth by completing the work you gave me to do. 5And now, Father, glorify me in your presence with the glory I had with you before the world began.

6"I have revealed you to those whom you gave me out of the world. They were yours; you gave them to me and they have obeyed your word. 7Now they know that everything you have given me comes from you. 8For I gave them the words you gave me and they accepted them. They knew with certainty that I came from you, and they believed that you sent me. 9I pray for them. I am not praying for the world, but for those you have given me, for they are yours. 10All I have is yours, and all you have is mine. And glory has come to me through them. 11I will remain in the world no longer, but they are still in the world, and I am coming to you. Holy Father, protect them by the power of your name—the name you gave me—so that they may be one as we are one. 12While I was with them, I protected them and kept them safe by that name you gave me. None has been lost except the one doomed to destruction so that Scripture would be fulfilled. [13]"I am coming to you now, but I say these things while I am still in the world, so that they may have the full measure of my joy within them. [14]I have given them your word and the world has hated them, for they are not of the world any more than I am of the world. [15]My prayer is not that you take them out of the world but that you protect them from the evil one. [16]They are not of the world, even as I am not of it. [17]Sanctify them by the truth; your word is truth. [18]As you sent me into the world, I have sent them into the world. [19]For them I sanctify myself, that they too may be truly sanctified.

[20]"My prayer is not for them alone. I pray also for those who will believe in me through their message, [21]that all of them may be one, Father, just as you are in me and I am in you. May they also be in us so that the world may believe that you have sent me. [22]I have given them the glory that you gave me, that they may be one as we are one: [23]I in them and you in me. May they be brought to complete unity to let the world know that you sent me and have loved them even as you have loved me.

THAT THEY MIGHT BE ONE AS WE ARE ONE

THE WORD OF THE LORD HAS SUCH RICH connotations and such fullness. While recognizing the fullness that is in the Word of God, we need to recognize how we come short of this fullness and what we are to do to attain fullness. The context in which I want to open this up is in John 17. There Jesus prays three times, or in three different ways, or three utterances, **"that they may be one"** (v. 22b). The oneness He is speaking of is a perfect, complete unity because He says, **"as we are one"** (v. 22b). We can say of the oneness in the Godhead between the Father, the Son, and the Holy Spirit, that it is perfect in every sense.[1] God wants us to come into this perfect unity, this complete unity.[2] Three times He says, **"that they may be one as we are one"** (v. 22b) in His High Priestly Prayer before He goes to the cross. Three times the Lord prays this; He speaks His Word explicitly. Before this, three times in the same prayer, He speaks about protecting them. In verses 11–12 and 15, the word **"protect"** is used three times, **"protect them by the power of your name"** (v. 11). He prays to protect them from harm and from turning aside while praying for them to attain a complete unity.

1. Gangadean, *The Westminster Catechisms,* 122–127.
2. Gangadean, "Paper No. 47: The Unity of the Church," 263–265; "Paper No. 22: The Unity of the Faith," in *The Logos Papers*, 139–145.

If "**protect**" has a negative tone, "**that they may be one**" (v. 22b) has a positive tone. There are two parts: "**that they may be one**" is about unity, and "**that the world may believe**" (v. 21) is about fullness. We want to keep in mind that there is a connection between unity and fullness.

In Christ's prayer, He says, "**Sanctify them by the truth, your word is truth**" (v. 17). There are three things we should notice: The word sanctify means holy, to be devoted. It comes from the word *sanctus,* sanctify, to be made holy, to be not divided, particularly within ourselves. This sanctification, or holiness and devotion comes through the truth. The Bible does not see any tension or discrepancy (far from it) between knowledge and holiness, between truth and holiness. Rather, it sees a perfect unity between the two as there is between the Father and the Son. "**Sanctify them by the truth,**" and then He adds, "**your word is truth**" (v. 17). There is no question or ambiguity about what He means. We can say from this that all divisions at every level, in every aspect, in every way, are due to sin. This is not the way the Lord made the world, with divisions and tensions within it. God created the world good as it was emphasized seven times in Genesis 1; it says, "it was good" (Gen. 1:4, 10, 12, 18, 21, 25), and the last time, "it was very good" (Gen. 1:31).[3] Divisions do exist due to sin at every level, starting within ourselves, within our nature, and in the fallenness of our human nature. Divisions manifest, or give proof of, a lack of the Word of God.

In this message concerning the Word of God, we will discuss how the existing divisions manifest and prove the *need* for the Word. The spiritual war takes place at several levels, beginning within ourselves in our fallenness, and in believers between the old fallen nature, called 'the flesh,' and the regenerated nature.[4] "For the sinful nature desires what is contrary to the Spirit, and the Spirit what is contrary to the sinful nature. They are in conflict with each other so that you do not do what you want" (Gal. 5:17).

Sanctification has particular reference to the flesh: the old nature. Paul speaks about the old nature by saying, "And they that are Christ's have crucified the flesh with the affections and lusts" (Gal. 5:24 KJV).

---

3. Gangadean, *The Westminster Confession,* 75–79.
4. Gangadean, "Paper No. 58: The Spiritual War (Part I)," 317–322; "Paper No. 60: The Spiritual War (Part II)," 329–330; "Paper No. 109: The Spiritual War," in *The Logos Papers,* 573–575.

He is not referring to the physical body per se; he is referring to the old nature, the fallen nature, the heart turned away from God, the self-life. He says, "Crucify." You have heard the phrase, 'Just say no.' I suppose it would apply here. Denying the cravings of the self is not all of it, but that is a significant part of where to begin the struggle. God is able to sanctify us in an instant—and He will sanctify us at death completely. In the glorified state, all sin will be removed. God wants sanctification now, after conversion and justification. He wants sanctification by using the ordinary means in which we engage in struggle against the flesh, in which we engage in the spiritual war, in which we engage in dominion—remember, Paul stated, "For sin shall not have dominion over you: for ye are not under the law, but under grace" (Rom. 6:14 KJV), and Christ wants us to overcome. The purpose of having us struggle through sanctification in this life is to enlarge our activity of dominion and rule, which is necessary to know God in the fullness that He is revealed. Apart from sin, dominion was necessary to know God. Now, with sin in the world, dominion is all the more necessary to know God.

There are divisions among us—and I want us to reflect on this; we have named the levels of the spiritual war in the past,[5] the first level being within ourselves, our double-mindedness, our going back and forth, saying, "For what I do is not the good I want to do; no, the evil I do not want to do—this I keep on doing" (Rom. 7:19). We are all aware of the internal struggle unless we are in self-deception. In any case, we are aware in some measure of internal conflict within ourselves, although there is much that we do not recognize, and that division reveals a lack of the Word of God. In this message, we are bringing the Word of God into focus to say that through the Word of God, we can overcome. This is the first level.

The second level of division is with those round about us: "And I will put enmity between you and the woman, and between your offspring and hers" (Gen. 3:15a). This enmity is between believer and non-believer, and within families: "with pain you will give birth to children" (Gen. 3:16). There is sin within the family passed from parent to children and from one generation to the next. Scripture often says

5. Gangadean, "Paper No. 58: The Spiritual War (Church and World)," 317–322; "Paper No. 60: The Spiritual War (Part II)," 329–330; "Paper No. 61: The Present and Future State of the Church," in *The Logos Papers*, 331–333.

that we ought to teach our children diligently: "Impress them on your children. Talk about them when you sit at home and when you walk along the road, when you lie down and when you get up" (Deut. 6:7). Talk about and remind them of the Word of God and the law of God.[6]

Divisions also exist between husband and wife. All married couples know the reality of sin remaining, and when you live in close quarters with another, sin cannot be hidden. Paul says they will have trouble in the flesh because of the old nature remaining, and God wants us to overcome the old nature.[7] The division in marriage reveals the lack of the Word of God. Every source of tension with your spouse reveals a lack of knowing that Word. If you wonder, 'Do I have need for the Word of God?' Ask yourself, 'Do I have tension with my spouse?' If you have tension, that shows the need for the Word of God in our lives.

Divisions extend within the Church, including this church. Imagine that.[8] Paul says, "One of you says, 'I follow Paul'; another, 'I follow Apollos'; another, 'I follow Cephas'; still another, "I follow Christ'" (1 Cor. 1:12). Paul says, "You are still worldly . . . Are you not acting like mere men?" (1 Cor. 3:3). Christ is not divided, and there are many other ways in which sin manifests, and it is here within the church. We acknowledge sin and the need for sanctification when we take membership vows, and we are pressing on by God's grace. There are divisions among the churches. The divisions among the churches reveal a lack of the Word of God. I think you would agree.

There is a significant and serious divide within the nation. The divide is spoken of in political terms between conservatives and progressives; there are many ways to describe it. We see the divide every day in the news and on social media. This speaks of a lack of the Word of God. Because believers are not united, the world does not hear and believe. Scripture says, "All the kings of the earth shall praise thee, O LORD, when they hear the words of thy mouth. Yea, they shall sing in the ways of the LORD: for great is the glory of the LORD" (Ps. 138:4–5 KJV). The kings of the earth are not hearing the Word because the Church is not what it should be; it is not salt and light in the earth. But we can be, and we will be. Christ has prayed for it. The work will be completed. We will make progress. We will struggle, but we will make progress.

6. *Deuteronomy 5, 6:4–9.*

7. *1 Corinthians 7:28.*

8. This statement is referring to Westminster Fellowship church, located in Phoenix, Arizona.

We will overcome, and the Church will be one. Can you believe that? Can you fail to believe that? Or does it seem like such a far-off dream?

Christ prayed, **"that they may be one"** (v. 22), which entails that we can overcome and come to unity among Episcopalians, Presbyterians, Baptists, Methodists, Charismatics, Roman Catholics, Eastern Orthodox, and all other denominations—**"that all of them may be one . . . that the world may believe"** (v. 21). I think we can all say in our hearts, 'If the Church can be one, the world will believe.' When we stop and think about it, we can say this. The question is, can we be one? Can we talk to each other? Can we learn how to talk with each other? The same process involved in husbands and wives learning to talk to each other is also involved between parents and children; the same process is involved in settling disputes in the Church. Sin is one and the same; it is the self-life in place of God.

Divisions are manifest, and we said there is division within the nation. The Church should be salt and light; it should be the head of the culture and not the tail.[9] We were the head, more so, at one time. We lost it. Just as a reminder, the leading educational institutions were in the hands of the Church: Harvard, Princeton, Yale, and Brown, among many others, were Christian colleges and universities. The leading lights were Christians, and we were taken captive because we did not know the Word of God sufficiently. We did not hold onto the Word of God. We did not witness to it and thus became the tail of the culture.

Not only are there divisions within a person and among persons, within the Church and among churches, and within the nation, but there are also longstanding divisions among nations, cultures, and worldviews, and each is seeking to make its claim once again, to find meaning and glory, and go back to the old days. It used to be Iraq under Saddam Hussein, Iran under Mahmoud Ahmadinejad, China under Mao, so with India, Russia, and many other nations and cultures. Everyone is seeking some meaning, some identity, some purpose, and fulfillment. All of these nations, cultures, and worldviews have to be brought to the Lord. Christ commanded us, "Go and make disciples of all nations . . . teaching them to obey everything I have commanded you" (Matt. 28:19a–20a). The discipling of the nations is the purpose of the Church. The Word of God must be spoken to the nations, and

9. *Matthew 5:13–16; Deuteronomy 28:13.*

the Word of God in its fullness must be spoken. Let us give heed to what that Word of God is.

WHAT IS THE WORD OF GOD?

We read from John 1, and I have gone over this a number of times, so I will go over it rather quickly now.[10] We speak about the Word of God in a fivefold sense.[11] I emphasize this because the Word of God is often spoken of as Scripture and Scripture only. This is not the teaching of Scripture. The Word of God is very full. The Word of God is the Son of God, eternal, co-eternal with the Father, by whom all things were made.[12] This is the first sense of the Word of God. The eternal Son of God is the Word of God.

The Word of God Makes God Known (John 1:1, 18, 17:6, 26)

"In the beginning was the Word, and the Word was with God, and the Word was God. He was with God in the beginning" (Jn. 1:1–2). The Word is God the Son. The Word then comes to all men. The Word of God reveals God. The Word of God makes God known. Our word makes ourselves known to others. This word may be simply the straight spoken word, but speaking may be done through actions of many kinds, symbolism in art, and practice in many ways. Our word expresses what is in our innermost being. The Word of God makes God known, and the Lord Jesus knows this, and He states it. The Scripture states it as well in John 1:18, "No one has ever seen God, but God the One and Only, who is at the Father's side, has made him known," and in John 17:26, "I have made you known to them, and will continue to make you known in order that the love you have for me may be in them and

---

10. Gangadean, "Paper No. 30: The Word of God," 179–180; "Paper No. 56: The Gospel (Summary)," in *The Logos Papers,* 303–313.

11. After further development, the five senses of the Word of God were expanded to seven senses. The sixth sense of the Word is the work of the Holy Spirit leading the Church corporately into all truth in the Historic Christian Faith. The seventh sense is that the Word is in each believer by regeneration and sanctification. For a fuller exposition, see: Gangadean, *The Westminster Catechisms,* 113–114; Gangadean, "Paper No. 45: The Logos Theses," in *The Logos Papers,* 257–259.

12. *John 1:1.*

that I myself may be in them." There should be no doubt about it: The Word of God makes God known.

The Word of God is spoken of as the light. "In him was life, and that life was the light of men" (Jn. 1:4). The life of the Logos is in all men, made in the image of God, as the light of reason; man's life is rational life. The light is that by which we see. The light in man is not a physical light, but the spiritual light of reason by which we understand all the forms of the revelation of God. "He was in the world, and though the world was made through him, the world did not recognize him" (Jn. 1:10); the world knew Him not as a general revelation. The Logos, by whom all things are made, is revealed in all things made. "He came to that which was his own, but his own did not receive him" (Jn. 1:11). The Word of God in redemptive history came to His own people called by God. This is the prophetic word, the Word coming through the prophets embodied in the Scriptures, the written Scripture.

Man has rejected the Word of God as reason, as general revelation, and in Scripture. So, that Word of God, the Son of God, became incarnate and dwelled among us: "The Word became flesh and made his dwelling among us. We have seen his glory" (Jn. 1:14a). We beheld His glory, and He is the one who makes God known. John 1:18 says, "No one has ever seen God, but God the One and Only, who is at the Father's side, has made him known." John also says, "We have seen his glory, the glory of the One and Only, who came from the Father, full of grace and truth" (Jn. 1:14b), to make God known. This is the initial sense of the Word of God in its breadth and fullness.

The Breadth and Fullness of the Word of God

We are to reckon with the fullness of the Word of God because when we do not, when we have a truncated view of the Word of God, it is the source of so many of our divisions. We have to enlarge our minds concerning the Word of God. I am bringing and setting before us the teaching of Scripture from John 1, calling us to hear this word, to believe this word, and to acknowledge it—the Word of God in its fullness.

In John 17:6, Jesus Himself says: **"I have revealed you to those whom you gave me out of the world."** The Word of God reveals God. Then, at the end of this prayer, He says, "I have made you known to them, and will continue to make you known in order that the love you have for me may be in them and that I myself may be in them"

(Jn. 17:26). The Word of God makes God known, and we have to be established in that. If we do not acknowledge the Word of God in its fullness, if we reject the Word of God, we will be rejected. This was certainly said of Saul.[13] There was a particular application for Saul, but the principle applies to us.

I want to emphasize the idea of fullness to help us see this is a Scriptural notion. It is not an idea that a few of us came up with in our spare time. Ephesians 4:9–10 says, "What does 'he ascended' mean except that he also descended to the lower, earthly regions? He who descended is the very one who ascended higher than all the heavens, in order to fill the whole universe." The one who descended is Jesus, the Son of God, Jesus Christ, Our Lord. He ascended in order to fill the whole universe. When He ascended, He gave gifts to men—to enable them to do the work through the Spirit and accomplish the work of dominion so that he might fill the whole universe. The work of the pastor-teachers will be continued "until we all reach unity in the faith and in the knowledge of the Son of God and become mature, attaining to the whole measure of the fullness of Christ" (Eph. 4:13). There are three words that are used: unity, maturity, and fullness, to be attained to the whole measure of the fullness of Christ.

Ephesians 1:22–23 says, "And God placed all things under his feet and appointed him to be head over everything for the church, which is his body, the fullness of him who fills everything in every way." The Word of God, by whom all things were made, who sustains all things, is to fill everything in every way. "For from him and through him and for him are all things" (Rom. 11:36a). The Scripture speaks of the Word of God in its fullness; lack of holding this view of the Word of God is the source of divisions.

Colossians 1:15–20 speaks of fullness in Christ, the Word of God:

> He is the image of the invisible God, the firstborn over all creation. For by him all things were created: things in heaven and on earth, visible and invisible, whether thrones or powers or rulers or authorities; all things were created by him and for him. He is before all things, and in him all things hold together. And he is the head of the body, the church; he is the beginning and the firstborn from among the dead, so that in everything he might have the

13. *1 Samuel 15:26.*

> supremacy. For God was pleased to have all his fullness dwell in him, and through him to reconcile to himself all things, whether things on earth or things in heaven, by making peace through his blood, shed on the cross.

Colossians 2:9–10 says: "For in Christ all the fullness of the Deity lives in bodily form, and you have been given fullness in Christ, who is the head over every power and authority."

Hebrews 1:1–3a says,

> In the past God spoke to our forefathers through the prophets at many times and in various ways, but in these last days he has spoken to us by his Son, whom he appointed heir of all things [fullness], and through whom he made the universe [fullness]. The Son is the radiance of God's glory [fullness] and the exact representation of his being, sustaining all things by his powerful word [fullness].[14]

Matthew 28:18b–20 says,

> All authority in heaven and on earth has been given to me. Therefore go and make disciples of all nations, baptizing them in the name of the Father and of the Son and of the Holy Spirit, and teaching them to obey everything I have commanded you. And surely I am with you always, to the very end of the age.

In Revelation 1:8, Christ is spoken of as the Alpha and the Omega of the Word of God. "I am the Alpha and the Omega," says the Lord God, "who is, and who was, and who is to come, the Almighty." In Revelation 1:14–17, we see the vision of Christ and His glory before whom John fell as a dead man when he beheld the glory of Christ, a manifestation of His glory.

> His head and hair were white like wool, as white as snow, and his eyes were like blazing fire. His feet were like bronze glowing in a furnace, and his voice was like the sound of rushing waters. In his right hand he held seven stars, and out of his mouth came a sharp double-edged sword. His face was like the sun shining in all its brilliance. When I saw him, I fell at his feet as though dead. Then

14. Emphasis added.

> he placed his right hand on me and said: 'Do not be afraid. I am the First and the Last.'

Revelation 5:9–12 speaks about all the creatures in heaven and earth worshiping the Son of God, the Lamb of God who takes away the sin of the world. There is fullness there.

> And they sang a new song: 'You are worthy to take the scroll and to open its seals, because you were slain, and with your blood you purchased men for God from every tribe and language and people and nation. You have made them to be a kingdom and priests to serve our God, and they will reign on the earth.' Then I looked and heard the voice of many angels, numbering thousands upon thousands, and ten thousand times ten thousand. They encircled the throne and the living creatures and the elders. In a loud voice they sang: 'Worthy is the Lamb, who was slain, to receive power and wealth and wisdom and strength and honor and glory and praise!'

The fullness of the Word of God is spoken of in Revelation 21 and 22 in the form of the City of God: It is vast. It is vast beyond our imagination: full, strong, and beautiful. It is the completion of the mandate God gave to man in the Garden. Christ, in the place of Adam, will *undo* what Adam did and will *do* what Adam failed to do. In these chapters of Revelation, we have a picture of that work completed. He is the Word of God in whom all fullness dwells. Of course, in Isaiah 11:9, which we have used so often, the whole earth will be full of the knowledge of God as a result of Christ's rule. As a result of the rule of the son of Jesse, the son of David, Jesus, after the flesh born of David, incarnate in due time. He will rule. As a result of His rule, "the earth will be full of the knowledge of the LORD as the waters cover the sea" (Is. 11:9b). This is another way of speaking about the completion of the work.

Christ is the Word of God, and the testimony of Jesus Christ is spoken of in Revelation 1:2, 9, 6:9, and other places through the Scriptures—"the word of God, and the testimony of Jesus Christ." The Word of God is vast, and it is full. He is a person, not just a principle. He is the Son of God, our Lord and Savior. This is the one we worship. This is the one we bow before. Angels and all the heavenly hosts adore Him.

God the Father was pleased to exalt His Son in this way, and He has given glory to the Church, His body, to each member a particular glory, that He may dwell in the Church, the fullness of Him who fills everything in every way. Let us put aside these weak and beggarly elements that hinder us from the fullness that is in Christ. Let us remind ourselves in many, many, many ways of who Christ is and what the Scripture says of the Word of God.

The Foundation Is Necessary and Sufficient for Maturity, Fruitfulness, Unity, and Fullness (MFUF)

If we have the foundation in place, the cornerstone,[15] and Christ Himself is the cornerstone,[16] as Christ is spoken of—as we have just seen through these several Scriptures—there is fullness. He is by whom all things were made and for whom are all things. This is the Lord Jesus Christ, who is the cornerstone, the Word of God incarnate. He is not someone whom we may greatly diminish and whom in our piety we may say, 'This is the one to whom I am devoted.' A diminished view truncates the Lord; through it, we do not worship Him as He is in His glory.

We must have the foundation in place, starting with the cornerstone. We must have the basics in place, which is necessary and sufficient for maturity, fruitfulness, unity, and fullness.[17] We must understand good and evil as we should. Evil is in light of the clarity of general revelation and failing to seek and understand (root sin). We must understand the good, eternal life, knowing God, and the earth being filled with the knowledge of God.[18] This is what is necessary and sufficient for unity and fullness.

We express this many-faceted teaching through the basic terms used in the Garden: life and death, good and evil. If we had the Word of God concerning good and evil in place in our minds and in our hearts, we would have unity instead of all the divisions that we spoke

15. Gangadean, "Paper No. 4: The Cornerstone: Good & Evil – Life & Death: The Beginning of the Foundation," in *The Logos Papers,* 21–25.

16. *Psalm 118:22–23; Mark 12:10–11.*

17. Gangadean, "Paper No. 54: From Foundation to Fullness," in *The Logos Papers,* 287–292.

18. Gangadean, "Paper No. 6: The Good: The Source of Unity," in *The Logos Papers,* 329–330; "Paper No. 106: The Good and Heaven," in *The Logos Papers,* 547–556; Gangadean, *Philosophical Foundation,* 171–183, 208–214; Gangadean, *On Natural and Revealed Theology,* 9–39.

about earlier. We must consider how we will come to this knowledge of God, the Word of God.

THE WORD OF GOD VS. WHAT IS NOT THE WORD OF GOD

Some things are raised up in the place of the Word of God, and we have to examine those things. There is a war going on, and it is a spiritual war. In that war, the Word of God will triumph. The only question is: On which side will we be in that war? The side that minimizes, neglects, avoids, and diminishes the Word of God, or the side that embraces the Word of God in its fullness, where we ride with Him in the spiritual war to take everything captive that is raised up against the knowledge of God?[19]

Ephesians 6:17 says, "Take the helmet of salvation and the sword of the Spirit, which is the word of God." Gideon said, "If Baal really is a god, he can defend himself" (Judg. 6:31–32). The Word of God, truly, is able to defeat us or defeat what is opposed to the Word of God. We are told that the sword of the Spirit is the Word of God. Notice the connection between the Word of God and the Spirit of God, the sword of the Spirit. It is the Spirit that enables us to know the Word. I will summarize again briefly that the Word of God comes to us in several senses: in man as reason, in general revelation, in Scripture, incarnate, and in the Historic Christian Faith summed up in the creeds and confessions.[20] The Spirit of God enables us to understand the Word more and more. God wants us to use the ordinary means to come into maturity, unity, and fullness. Ephesians 6:17 describes the Word of God as the sword of the Spirit.

Hebrews 4:12 says, "For the word of God is living and active. Sharper than any double-edged sword, it penetrates even to dividing soul and spirit, joints and marrow; it judges the thoughts and attitudes of the heart." The Word of God can discern in all the short swordplay of counseling. In all the twists and turns of self-deception and self-justification, the Word of God is able to discern. It is sometimes a struggle

19. *2 Corinthians 10:4–5; Revelation 19:13–15.*

20. Gangadean, "Paper No. 16: The Historic Christian Faith," in *The Logos Papers,* 103–114; Gangadean, *The Westminster Confession,* 1–13; Gangadean, *The Westminster Catechisms,* xvii-xxxii.

to get to that point, but once you get to the Word of God, we put that point, that sharp edge of the sword on it, and it becomes clear what is of self and what is of God. The Word is able to do this.

2 Corinthians 10:4–5 says,

> The weapons we fight with are not the weapons of the world. On the contrary, they have divine power to demolish strongholds. We demolish arguments and every pretension that sets itself up against the knowledge of God, and we take captive every thought to make it obedient to Christ.

Every thought raised up against the knowledge of God is to be taken captive. We are in a spiritual war, fought through the Word of God, against everything raised up against the knowledge of God. In Revelation 19:11–13, we have a picture of Christ riding forth in His robe:

> I saw heaven standing open and there before me was a white horse, whose rider is called Faithful and True. With justice he judges and wages war. His eyes are like blazing fire, and on his head are many crowns. He has a name written on him that no one knows but he himself. He is dressed in a robe dipped in blood, and his name is the Word of God.

This is the Armageddon that people speak about. It is a spiritual war going on throughout history. The Word of God is abundantly able in its power to oppose, discern, and overcome everything in our hearts that is set up against the Word of God.

THE WORD OF GOD IS KNOWN THROUGH SUFFERING

We come to know this Word of God through much suffering and trials because we are not seeking as we should. The trials reduce us to nothing. We are brought down; we are brought low until we are forced, in a sense, by the trials, to cry out to God. We may have cried out to many things, but we come to the point where we cry out to God. God reveals Himself to us more. "You will seek me and find me when you seek me with all your heart" (Jer. 29:13). "He is a rewarder of them that diligently seek him" (Heb. 11:6b KJV). We do not seek

Him as we should, and the trials are brought upon us to get us to stop and think. We should understand and know that it may take 20 years to get the point across.

We are not to put our feelings first in the place of the Word of God. Our feelings are not the Word of God. We do not go by our feelings. After going through fire seven times, like silver purified in an earthen vessel seven times,[21] we say, 'Oh, yes.' God is able to do it. He will do it. We belong to Him; He loves us and will do it. He will bring us through trials of faith to come to know Him. He will not let us stop. We may cry out to the Lord, 'Stop, Lord!'

I have been in a place where I have cried out like that. Working a knotted muscle out of my body, the guy took his elbow and went deep down. I literally cried out. 'Stop!' Sometimes, we cry 'Stop!' in the trials. As the Hound of Heaven[22] who will not stop or let us go, think of what the Lord our God did with Job. At the end, Job said, "now my eyes have seen you. Therefore I despise myself and repent in dust and ashes" (Job 42:5b–6).

James says to remember the patience of Job and the kindness of God.[23] God is gracious. The Word of God is abundantly able to make Himself known, to sustain Himself sovereignly. Christ says, "If you abide in My word, you are My disciples indeed. And you shall know the truth, and the truth shall make you free" (Jn. 8:31b–32 NKJV). The Bible knows nothing of anti-intellectualism and nothing of a balance between the head and the heart. There is an order. There is not a balance between the Father and the Son, as if their intention has to be balanced. There is an order, a unity in God, that we might be one—**"that they may be one as we are one"** (v. 11b). There is a prophetic, priestly, kingly order within human beings and in the Church and the world.[24] We must reckon with this and not play the 'balance game.' The balance game is because we do not have the basics in place. We do not balance left against right. It says, "Do not turn aside from any of the commands I give you today, to the right or to the left" (Deut. 28:14a). It is not a matter of balance. It is a matter of going to what is more basic. It is not

21. *Psalm 12:6.*

22. This is a reference to Francis Thompson's poem, *The Hound of Heaven.*

23. *James 5:11.*

24. Gangadean, *The Westminster Catechisms,* 133–135; Gangadean, *The Westminster Confession,* 79–83; Gangadean, *Philosophical Foundation,* 43–45.

a balance between communism and capitalism to inter-socialism. God is the absolute owner of all things, not man individually or collectively. It is not a balance. Balances are due to antinomies.[25] Both polar opposites are wrong because the basics are not in place. We are to come to the Word of God, for the Lord is abundantly able. If the Lord has to take 2000 years and another thousand years, He will do that. God wants us, one way or another, to use the ordinary means to exercise dominion, to overcome in this process of sanctification.

THE WORD OF GOD VS. THE FALSE PROPHET

Consider some specific applications about the Word of God. Modern society has put science in place of the Word of God. 'Science says this,' and 'science says that,' and in the name of science, these are the things that are given credit, and these are the things that get grants and recognition and honor. The whole educational system is presently dominated by empiricism summed up in science. This is put forward as the Word of God. It is not! Not as it exists now.

Science within its limits is God-given, God-ordained, and a great blessing. Science without God, not grounded in God, not recognizing the limits of empiricism in relation to reason—between the visible and the invisible—is not the Word of God.[26] The educational system is set on this course. Many other things have been set against the Word of God, generating antinomies.

There is skepticism that comes from the failure of the many attempts to know God without the Word of God, or to know reality without the Word of God. Skepticism has been with us historically because we have not known and acknowledged clarity. The Church has not given itself to affirming the first and most basic thing about evil: clarity and inexcusability. We need to come back to affirm clarity and inexcusability. It is there in the Scriptures, the historic creeds, and the Westminster

25. Contrary positions, both of which can be false at the same time because both share a common assumption—capitalism and communism; this-worldly and other-worldly; all is eternal and none is eternal; skepticism and fideism; virtue is the good and happiness is the good—a source of recurrent conflict within and between cultures.

26. Gangadean, *Philosophical Foundation,* 26–27.

Confession's opening words. Seek God to know what is clear about God, and do not simply go by faith that is without understanding and proof.[27]

Postmodern skepticism[28] is another response from the failure to know God. This response comes out of multiculturalism and all the havoc going on in the name of multiculturalism—there should be a unity of diversity, not a mere multiplicity. There should not merely be a celebration of the alternative in the name of 'otherness,' and a reaction to subordination in the name of alterity, and all the language that changed because of this view—this is not the Word of God.

The Word of God stands against the present educational establishment. All the accumulated teachings need to be hauled off like a Herculean task, cleaning out the Aegean stables. A lot of 'stuff' was collected there. These teachings did not bring us to God. The world, in its wisdom, did not know God, and divisions remain. Over and against the false prophet and many things that lead us away from God, we are to bring the Word of God. The things that are known by the Word of God as reason—the invisible things of Him—are understood, inferred, from the things that are made.[29] We are not to allow science to say, 'We cannot speak about what cannot be observed.' Alright, if you cannot, then limit your talk to what can be observed; do not say, 'It cannot be known.' We know a lot of things by the Word of God—the necessary foundation. We know there is no being from non-being;[30] we know that nothing can violate this. All things are made by the Word. We know there are no square-circles. We know there are no uncaused events. If quantum physics tries to make that move, we say, 'No!'[31]—as Gandalf stood before Balrog, the fire demon, and said, "You shall not pass!"[32]

We will stand our ground. Having done all, to stand.[33] We will reveal the meaninglessness that comes in once you try to do away with God's

27. Fideism is holding a belief without proof; proof is seen either as not relevant or not possible or may not actually be present; belief may be either theistic or non-theistic; fideism assumes basic things are not clear; belief without proof based on understanding loses all meaning.

28. Gangadean, *Philosophical Foundation,* 18–21; Surrendra Gangadean, *History of Philosophy,* 163–174.

29. *Romans 1:18–20.*

30. Gangadean, *Philosophical Foundation,* 61–65; Gangadean, *History of Philosophy,* 40–44.

31. Gangadean, *Philosophical Foundation,* 27–31.

32. J. R. R. Tolkien, *The Lord of the Rings* (London, England: HarperCollins, 1991).

33. *Ephesians 6:13–14.*

Word, which is so clear. We reduce it to silence. As it was said by Calvin, "I should not find it difficult to stop their obstreperous mouths."[34]

THE WORD OF GOD VS. THE FALSE PRIEST

The Word of God speaks of the false prophet, but there are also false priests who go by feelings in the name of holiness. This does not bring us to God. I have encountered much by way of being led by one's feelings and not by the Word of God. I can list eight persons I have had contact with in the near past where I see this at work. Now we are feeling self-conscious, 'Oh no, he is talking about me. He went so far as to say that. He had contact with me recently, didn't he?' I am concerned about the common pattern of going by feelings rather than the Word of God. Feelings or intuition are, at best, a negative guide, like conscience regarding danger. We are not to violate our conscience, but conscience is not a positive guide. Some try to make it a positive guide. The self-life can affect the way our intuitions operate. Feelings could be from self-life, the Spirit of God, or a mixture of both. Did intuition lead to belief in God for many who rely on intuition?

What God? God without Christ? Did intuition lead to the foundation and getting the foundation in place? A person can create conflict based on the deliverances of intuition. Our intuitions may conflict with another person's intuition. Intuition may be influenced by our personality, our body, or our feelings of right and wrong. Sensations may be influenced by our bodies. Serotonin levels may affect the way we perceive things. A person may be taking drugs that affect their feelings. We have to let the effects of drugs, alcohol, or other influences clear the system before we continue to talk and not allow feelings to prevail. Intuition may be influenced by one's gender. Men and women have intuition, and difference in gender can affect feelings. Feelings are not the Word of God.

We cannot make intuition the Word of God or our guide. It is a negative guide in terms of danger, similar to conscience, but it is not a positive guide. Our background can influence how we feel—this includes our personal history and our ethnic background. We can

34. John Calvin, *Institutes of the Christian Religion* (Peabody: Hendrickson Publishers, Inc. 1845), 33.

be influenced by our unique personality. I have seen the attempt to collapse all of the differences in our personality into one. Our power of explanation can be distorted. We misunderstand and think we know by intuition, and this is not the Word of God.

We have spoken about what the Word of God is and the order we can and should have regarding general revelation, Scripture, and Historic Christianity. Basic truths are about good and evil, and when clearly in place, are used to understand our experience—this is where the Word of God comes in.

THE WORD OF GOD VS. THE FALSE KING

Lastly, we can speak of not only false prophets and false priests but also false kings and laws that are made by false kings. Righteousness in the Church can be legalism.[35] We have a very narrow reading of what the law of God requires. It is a very narrow reading of what stealing, lying, murder, adultery, truth-telling, and discontent are. We have a very narrow reading of the law and a very narrow reading of the Sabbath. Remember, the Sadducees had a narrow reading of the Sabbath, and they persecuted Jesus about it, but Jesus spoke the truth.

We can have a narrow understanding, and we do have it. We fall into legalism quite easily—this is not the Word of God. We have a whole system of laws in the public realm and within institutions, sometimes where they ought not be, and we ask, 'What are the boundaries and limits of government?'[36] Rather, can we ask, 'What is the Word of God in this?' Can the Church speak the Word? We are called to do this. We are to know the Word of God and speak it.[37]

We are up against the Beast using force to get its way and persecuting according to its own laws rather than the righteousness of Christ in His fullness. We are to look to our Lord Jesus Christ in His obedience,

35. Legalism is conformity to the law in an outward form without understanding its meaning. It is an expression of deontological ethics, concerned with duty and virtue rather than the good. On the contrary, the Law of God is spiritual—it reaches to the thoughts and intents of the heart. It is summarily comprehended by the commandment to love God with the whole heart and love one's neighbor as oneself.

36. Gangadean, "Paper No. 27: The Limits of the State," in *The Logos Papers,* 165–169.

37. Gangadean, *Philosophical Foundation,* 171–284; Gangadean, *History of Philosophy,* 61–69; Gangadean, *The Westminster Catechisms, 215–267;* Gangadean, *On Natural Revealed Theology,* 127–139, 166–178.

His walk, His way, how He engaged with others, and the way He took thoughts captive. Remember the four questions asked toward the end of His ministry: He took those thoughts captive then and throughout His ministry. Jesus, the Word of God incarnate, our Lord and Savior.

We worship Him in spirit and the truth. He is the Word of God. He is against everything raised up against the knowledge of God and the Word of God. He is abundantly able to subdue everything to Himself by His Word and Spirit. He gives us the privilege of suffering for Him and with Him in bringing that Word of God into the world. May God grant us grace to hear the Word, be faithful to the Word, and love and serve Him as He is worthy.

2

Unity of the Spirit and Unity of the Faith

Diversity and Unity in the Body

2004

Ephesians 4:1–16

1As a prisoner for the Lord, then, I urge you to live a life worthy of the
calling you have received. 2Be completely humble and gentle; be patient,
bearing with one another in love. 3Make every effort to keep the unity
of the Spirit through the bond of peace. 4There is one body and one
Spirit—just as you were called to one hope when you were called— 5one
Lord, one faith, one baptism; 6one God and Father of all, who is over all
and through all and in all.

7But to each one of us grace has been given as Christ apportioned it. 8This
is why it says:

"When he ascended on high,
he led captives in his train
and gave gifts to men."

9(What does "he ascended" mean except that he also descended to the
lower, earthly regions? 10He who descended is the very one who ascended
higher than all the heavens, in order to fill the whole universe.) 11It was he
who gave some to be apostles, some to be prophets, some to be evangelists,
and some to be pastors and teachers, 12to prepare God's people for works
of service, so that the body of Christ may be built up 13until we all reach
unity in the faith and in the knowledge of the Son of God and become
mature, attaining to the whole measure of the fullness of Christ.

[14]Then we will no longer be infants, tossed back and forth by the waves, and blown here and there by every wind of teaching and by the cunning and craftiness of men in their deceitful scheming. [15]Instead, speaking the truth in love, we will in all things grow up into him who is the Head, that is, Christ. [16]From him the whole body, joined and held together by every supporting ligament, grows and builds itself up in love, as each part does its work.

WE WILL LOOK AT THE PASSAGE IN EPHESIANS 4, which concerns itself with the unity of the Spirit and the unity of the faith. We are talking about the subject of unity. There were events in the past week that characteristically became of concern. You should know ahead of time that this has been on the burner for several weeks. People often say, 'Oh, he is preaching that at me.' If it seems to apply to you, it is not at you particularly; if you are included, please heed it, but it is for all of us. Think about whether we need this concern for unity.

TEAMWORK:
Marriage, Church, Dominion, and Divisions

First, by way of preparation for this subject, think about our need for teamwork. The most basic place for teamwork is in marriage. Many of us struggle in this area; we struggle for husband and wife to be a team. Some of us hesitate to enter into marriage because we think it is going to be difficult. We know some basic things need to be there to be a team: to work closely together, in the most intimate way, in the smallest detail, and to be together. It is not teamwork to be fighting, straining, grieving, and saying things that harm each other. Teamwork begins first and foremost in the first relationships of life on the human level between husband and wife.

Then, there is a need for teamwork in the Church. We know that there are strains within the Church as there are within marriage; there are strains in personal relationships in the Church. We will be looking at this in some detail. There have been strains, there will be strains, and we need to know how to deal with these in a godly way. We need to know how to *maintain* the unity of the Spirit in the bond of peace while we *work toward* the unity of the faith.

There are two aspects to this unity: a present unity and a progressing unity. Both are equally real and equally vital for our attention. We must learn to hold to this. We confess that we are sinners, that sin remains in us, and that we are being sanctified. We say this theoretically, we say this with our mouths, and we say this off the top of our heads, but it has not worked itself into the details of our lives. It has not become a habit of mind with us (as we will be reading in Great Books this Wednesday).[1] That is, we need the process by which we go through a struggle to come to a new place of unity and being established in Christ.

We need unity in the Church. We need it in the area of dominion, the work given to the first man, "Be fruitful, and multiply, and replenish the earth, and subdue it: and have dominion" (Gen. 1:28a KJV). We certainly need it under Christ, the last man, who is ruling until all His enemies are made His footstool,[2] who is to fill everything in every way,[3] as Adam was called to. This work involves relations not only with believers but with non-believers in two senses: (1) While we are presently working and interacting with non-believers, we should be able to live in peace with them. (2) We will see that the same exhortation given to have peace in the Church is the same exhortation given to have peace with those in the world. We also have dominion in relationships in the hope that God will bring these persons to Himself and to fellowship in Christ with us.

We need the ability to work together and to be a team. We must have a measure of unity, even with those who do not believe, as we learn to work together with them. We have to recognize the limits, and we have to make adjustments without compromising anything moral. More than that, we must learn how to speak appropriately to maintain unity. Perhaps even more so, we must learn how *not* to speak and how to hold our peace. When we do speak, we must speak appropriately in

1. The three-year *Great Books Readings and Discussion Program,* conducted as part of the preparation for congregants to become instructors in Liberal Arts at Logos Preparatory Academy, holds considerable significance. The recorded discussions from this program are anticipated to form the cornerstone for upcoming works focused on interpreting the humanities. These discussions are poised to serve as a valuable resource, laying the foundation for future scholarly endeavors and contributing to the ongoing exploration and understanding of the humanities within the educational framework of The Logos Curriculum and Logos College of Liberal Arts.

2. *Hebrews 10:13.*

3. *Ephesians 1:23.*

a way that would maintain the peace. We will look at Scripture verses explicitly related to this.

The primary concern, however, is for unity among brothers and sisters and unity in the Church. It is for this unity that our Lord Jesus prayed. It is remarkable what concerns are on the Lord's heart as He prepares to go to Gethsemane. As He prepares to suffer, He knows the hour is upon Him. He is in the garden, He is in Gethsemane, and He is going to Golgotha to be crucified. The dominant thing He seems to be praying for is for God to be glorified, for God to be known, for God to be known *in* and *through* and *by* His people, and for the world to come to believe.

He turns to this at the end of his prayer: "I have made you known to them, and will continue to make you known" (Jn. 17:26a). The unity of God's people is to be seen in the context of the larger goal of the glory of God—knowing God and making Him known. This was the burden on the heart of our Lord Jesus as He prepared to go to Golgotha. This is what sustained Him as He hung on the cross: "who for the joy set before him endured the cross, scorning its shame, and sat down at the right hand of the throne of God" (Heb. 12:2b). He is ruling from the right hand of God now, in this age presently, and will continue to rule until all His enemies are subdued to Him.[4]

Jesus, our Lord, prays that they might be one. When He prays that they might be one, He says, "as we are one."[5] The Father, the Son, and the Holy Spirit are one; this is the oneness He is praying for. It is not a oneness of essence; it is a oneness of purpose. Father, Son, and the Holy Spirit are one in *essence* and they are one being, but humans do not have that kind of oneness. As human beings, we do have a oneness of essence; we are all equally human. We will talk about this because it becomes part of the way in which we divide. That they might be one as Father, Son, and Holy Spirit are one.[6] We have the purpose of knowing God and making Him known. It is in knowing God that we are preserved from sin and from turning aside. We are preserved and kept by His name from being torn apart in our trials by discouragement,

4. *Psalm 110:1.*

5. *John 17:22.*

6. Gangadean, *The Westminster Catechisms,* 122–125.

disappointment, resentment, and bitterness in the face of hardship. We are to be protected by the name of God; protect them by thy name.[7]

We know who God is—the God of justice and mercy, the God of love, our Heavenly Father. He cares for us, and He deals with us as His children. When we call upon Him, we find grace to help us in our time of need.[8] We know who God is and what He is doing, and it is understanding who God is and understanding His purpose, in light of who He is, that enables us to persevere. We are to be one as Father, Son, and Holy Spirit are one. We are to be one in knowing Him.

He prays not only for the disciples but for all who would believe in Him. It is almost 2000 years later, and the Church is persevering. It has increased, and it has spread on the earth. Jesus was anticipating this when He prayed that all of us might be one, *again,* "that all of them may be one, Father, just as you are in me and I am in you" (Jn. 17:21a).

The third time, He prays that they might be one in terms of the *functional unity* that we are to have. He says, "I have given them the glory that you gave me, that they may be one as we are one,[9] that the world may believe."[10] As we sang from Psalm 67A, "That so Thy way most holy on earth may soon be known."[11] If we can overcome the divisions that exist among us, if we can overcome sin in these close quarters, in our marriages, in our individual congregations, in the Church, we can overcome elsewhere. Is that true? This is where we need to start.

LET EVERYTHING BE DONE UNTO EDIFICATION

There is a general rule to guide us: Everything we do is to be done unto edification, for the good of others, and to win them to Christ. 1 Corinthians 14:26 says, "Let all things be done unto edifying."[12] Particularly in our words, we have to ask ourselves, 'I feel this strongly, and I want to express it, but if I express it, will it be edifying? Will it

7. *John 17:11.*
8. *Hebrews 4:16.*
9. *John 17:22.*
10. *John 17:21.*
11. *Psalm 67:2, The Book of Psalms for Singing.*
12. KJV.

build others up for their good? Will it draw them closer to the Lord?' This is not a hard rule to think about. We let it slip, but if we think about this, how many of our words will be spoken, and how many will remain unspoken?

We are put to the test when we work together in concrete situations. This is where our faith is made perfect or complete by our deeds. It is not done until after we have a plan, we have a rally, and we say, 'Yes, we can do this!' and we exhort ourselves. We are put to the test when we get into the details of it. You know the expression, "The devil is in the details"? Or, 'the difficulty is in the details'—you might put it that way, but it is also there that we find the grace of God, and it is there that we come into real functional unity. This is one of the things I have been appreciating. I work in philosophy with ideas where I am teaching, and from time to time I have to get involved with some physical activity and service. I appreciate what it takes to get the job done physically, to complete it, and that is where you have to learn to work with others: when it is difficult. There are all kinds of pressures building. Sin from so many sources, in complex ways, weaves itself in, but we should say that "where sin increased, grace increased all the more" (Rom. 5:20b), and we find this reality coming out most when it comes to deeds.

James: Spoken Words

We have been talking about getting a church building, and we have taken the first steps. By the grace of God, we have made progress, and we have to take the first concrete step to put it on the ground before we turn the first shovel. But more things are coming out. James 2:22 speaks about this: "You see that his faith and his actions were working together, and his faith was made complete by what he did." James, in this context, speaks about the word *spoken*. In James 3, in the context of putting things into practice, we speak words, have to make decisions, get things done in a certain way, and move things along. We speak words. At that time, we may say things that are not right. In James 3:9–10 he says, "With the tongue we praise our LORD and Father, and with it we curse men, who have been made in God's likeness. Out of the same mouth come praise and cursing. My brothers, this should not be." Earlier, in James 3:5, he says, "Likewise the tongue is a small part of the body, but it makes great boasts. Consider what a great forest is set on fire by a small spark." We know about the fires we had last year. As

I drive up beyond Payson and drive down, I can see large areas of the forest that have been charred by the Chediski Fire. All it takes is one tiny spark, which can set the whole forest on fire. James says, "Consider what a great forest is set on fire by a small spark. The tongue also is a fire, a world of evil among the parts of the body. It corrupts the whole person, sets the whole course of his life on fire" (Jas. 3:5b–6a).

One word can affect us greatly. If it is spoken in God, it will edify and build up. If it is not spoken in God, it can and will tear down and destroy. It can affect one's whole life. The whole course of a life may be affected. This is exactly what James says, "It corrupts the whole person, sets the whole course of his life on fire, and is itself set on fire by hell" (Jas. 3:6b). What he means is that the principle of hell can be at work in the words that we speak when we say things to express our own self-life and interests rather than to build others up. We are to be concerned about this when we come to our deeds and working together with others in particular matters. Whether husband and wife, whether in the church, whether with unbelievers outside of the church, or anyone outside of the church—we are to take this to heart.

We are to be careful not to judge, as our Lord said, or we too will be judged.[13] This is hard. We want to maintain standards. We want to do what is right, but we may have to do a lot of forbearing with one another, patiently forbearing and trusting God. We have to think about whether what we say would build the other person up, would be edifying, would be profitable, or whether we are expressing our own particular frustration because we have not yet learned to trust in God as we should. When we come to the position of teaching others, there is an attitude that we must have. 2 Timothy 2:25 says, "Those who oppose him he must gently instruct, in the hope that God will grant them repentance leading them to a knowledge of the truth." Words spoken in meekness are more likely to be heard than words spoken in haste when we are upset and angry. We do not have to speak about tone of voice here; we can speak about attitude of heart in terms of our meekness.

---

13. *Matthew 7:1–2.*

PRESERVE THE UNITY OF THE SPIRIT IN THE BOND OF PEACE

> **As a prisoner for the LORD, then, I urge you to live a life worthy of the calling you have received. Be completely humble and gentle; be patient, bearing with one another in love. Make every effort to keep the unity of the Spirit through the bond of peace** (vv. 1–3).

We are to be **"completely humble and gentle"**—I want to go over this because here he is speaking about preserving **"the unity of the Spirit through the bond of peace."** Paul is in prison urging us to live this way; **"to live a life worthy of the calling you have received."** I suppose, as a prisoner, he is being mistreated. It is unfair; it is grossly unfair that he is doing all to honor the Lord, and yet people are treating him in this way. Paul is saying in this state, as a prisoner, to be completely humble and gentle.

Here is a case, on the ground, in a particular circumstance, in a difficult circumstance, and Paul is concerned about the Church. He is a prisoner for the Lord's sake and doing it for the Lord. He wants us all to live this way: be humble, gentle, patient, and bear with one another in love. In love, forbearance occurs. One of the first characteristics of love is that it is patient and long-suffering. In seeking the good of the other, sometimes we cannot always get that good right away, but after a while, if we live in a certain way, we might be heard. We might have to forbear for a while and build up our relationships with others, give assurance, and then be able to speak in that context. If we are going to preserve the unity of the Spirit in the family, in the Church, and with others at work, we have to have this attitude.

Here Paul speaks about fellow believers, but there are those who we hope and pray would become believers, and we must be humble and gentle there also. We are seeking their good. He says, **"Make every effort to keep the unity of the Spirit through the bond of peace"** (v. 3). Is what we are saying consistent with this? Are we making every effort to keep the unity of the Spirit through the bond of peace? Will we maintain this? The wisdom that is from above is first pure and then peaceable.[14] When we do speak and must speak, we must speak with the attitude of being completely humble and gentle, knowing that we

14. *James 3:17.*

come short, not judging lest we be judged.[15] It is a fearful thing because we are so unaware that we might judge others and have faults in our lives—all the more, we should be humble and gentle when we speak.

Will it build the other person up? Will it preserve the bond of peace? We cannot compromise the truth of God, and we cannot compromise on moral matters, but we can speak humbly and gently. These two are not inconsistent. As a matter of fact, we are called to do so. Paul affirms these great truths that are the basis for unity with our fellow believers: **"There is one body and one Spirit—just as you were called to one hope when you were called—one LORD, one faith, one baptism; one God and Father of all, who is over all and through all and in all"** (vv. 4–6). We are called to keep in mind these seven things that are 'one.' On the basis of this, we *preserve;* notice, we do not try to *create,* we preserve it. Because we are one in Christ, we seek to preserve unity.

I have to confess that there are times when I speak philosophically, and it is easy to speak critically and come across in a way I do not intend: presumptuously and arrogantly. This is why it says in James 3:1, "Not many of you should presume to be teachers." I hope it was not a presumption on my part, and perhaps I am stuck there now because I cannot get an outside job and cannot lift heavy things. I am stuck being a teacher. I confess, without even realizing it, I am afraid that I forget when I speak critically. Sometimes, I give my students a hard time when I ask them to do critical thinking. I sometimes just hit them right between the eyes. As I preach on this, I think I should be completely humble and gentle; 'What am I saying here? What am I doing?' I do not want to be namby-pamby. There is a certain amount of give and take when you have a good old intellectual fight in the classroom, but I am afraid that I am not always keeping in mind how critical thinking applied may be perceived.

Sometimes, I speak about believers in popular Christianity and I do some critiquing of it. I hope I do it with a humble and gentle spirit. I suspect I come short in this area much more than I realize. I pray that God will open my eyes to see this and to deal with it appropriately. I do not think there will be a change overnight, but I hope there is some change for the better. Maybe I have set a bad example for many of you in my attitude when applying critical thinking. We can easily

15. *Matthew 7:1–2.*

slip from critical thinking into attitudes about others. So here I am, I suspect—actually, let me put it this way: I know I come short. I am unsure where, when, and how I am coming short. Maybe some of you can help me to see that from time to time. 'You may need to be a little bit gentle there, gently, gently.' Remind me.

DIVERSITY AND UNITY: Parts and Whole

As soon as he speaks about the unity of the Spirit and the oneness that is already there, Paul reminds us of the grace that is given, the various gifts and graces, and our diversity. Several places in Scripture speak about this, and we will mention some of them in passing. The purpose of this diversity is that in Christ we may fill everything in every way.[16] It is in the diversity of the body of Christ, in the many gifts and abilities, that it is true the Lord will fill everything. This is what He means when He says in John 17:22, "I have given them the glory that you gave me, that they may be one as we are one." A glory of one kind is given to one, and another kind of glory to another. He hopes that the body will see its need one for another and be knit together, especially as we keep the goal in mind. Particularly, he mentions the work of those who teach in the Church and those who have taught in the past. He says,

> **It was he who gave some to be apostles, some to be prophets, some to be evangelists, and some to be pastors and teachers, to prepare God's people for works of service, so that the body of Christ may be built up** (vv. 11–12).

The ministry of the Word of God and preaching and teaching in the Church is to build us up in the most holy faith.

In Acts 15, we see this working. Christ promised that the Spirit will be sent and He will lead us into all truth,[17] and it is under the condition of sin we are led into the truth by challenges. There must be divisions among us so that those who are approved may be made manifest.[18] These challenges come. They come again and again, in waves through history,

16. *Ephesians 1:23.*

17. *John 16:13.*

18. *1 Corinthians 11:19* KJV.

and mount up sometimes and become great tidal waves rolling in upon us. We have to meet these challenges. The pastor-teachers and those who from time to time gather together (where we can come together in unity) discuss it, and after much discussion, come to agreement and declare the truth of this for all.[19] We build on this agreement of the truth through the centuries, which is how we come into the unity of the faith. We spoke about the need for the Church to be *one* that the world might believe. We know how scattered we are. We need to be able to *speak* to bring about unity in the Church and to speak in a completely humble and gentle way while we maintain the unity of the Spirit, maintain the bond of peace, and have good speaking relations with others.

There are some persons who, when they differ with you, you know they like you, care about you, and do not have it out for you. There are others who, when they differ, you feel there is an attitude there, and you are unsure. May God give us the grace that when we differ with others, we differ in the context where they know that we care. Sometimes, they may not understand that we care. Sometimes, we have to do 'tough love,' and it may come to that, but as much as possible, we maintain the bond of peace so that we might be able to continue talking and working.

Think about the Muslims and the Jews. We are to be peacemakers. Can we speak in a way that gets us all searching more fully, acknowledging that we all come short, being completely humble and gentle, and speaking as peacemakers? As Christ our Lord said, "Blessed are the peacemakers, for they will be called sons of God" (Matt. 5:9). Can we speak in ways that edify and not condemn and blame? The more we can engage people in terms of looking at the meaning of things they believe most deeply, the less offense will come through, and the greater the concern will be expressed. They will have a sense that we really do care about what they think.

In Logos[20], we are talking about Derrida and Foucault. This week, we are on Postmodernism.[21] We are thinking: How can we speak? Some were talking about the postmodernism that is so rife in classes at ASU,[22]

---

19. Gangadean, *The Westminster Confession,* xvii-xxxii, 349–351; Gangadean, "Paper No. 16: The Historic Christian Faith," in *The Logos Papers,* 103–114.

20. Logos Theological Seminary.

21. Stanley J. Grenz, *A Primer on Postmodernism* (Grand Rapids: William B. Eerdmans Publishing Company, 1996).

22. Arizona State University.

and we were discussing how we can speak to and help students to see, 'Where are you?'—to draw them out at the level of meaning more than truth. First, for your *own* understanding of who God is and what is going on in this person's life, and then to be able to bring it up. We can go genuinely inquiring, 'Where are you?' Take the time to see all the relevant nuances. As I have said, do not kill ourselves with every nuance that there is, but take the time to see the nuances that are relevant. This requires some discernment about what is relevant and what is not. This requires watchfulness.

UNITY OF THE FAITH IN THE CHURCH

We are to come into the unity of the faith within the Church. Can we do this within the Church where there are longstanding divisions? There are different beliefs about the baptism of the Spirit, the baptism of water, and the mode and the subject of baptism. Can we engage with the assumptions so we do not automatically clash on that particular point?[23] Building on the work of the pastors-teachers, can we get to the assumptions and speak? We have to be prepared for this. We have to work for unity. Maintain the unity of the Spirit while we work for the unity of the faith.

Learn to forebear. Not everything has to be said right off. In 1 Corinthians 3, Paul speaks about the diversity there is in the body. Ephesians 4:7 says, **"But to each one of us grace has been given as Christ apportioned it,"** which speaks about unity and diversity. Romans 12 speaks about the diversity that is given in the body. We want to consider and keep in mind the whole question of diversity and unity, the parts and the whole.

By way of Scripture reference regarding the attitudes with which we should engage in this pursuit, in terms of being humble and gentle and being at peace with all men, Ephesians 4:3 says, **"Make every effort to keep the unity of the Spirit through the bond of peace."** I have also been speaking about non-believers, and in Hebrews 12:14, we see this reference: notice the expression, "Make every effort to live in peace with all men." This is not saying all *believers,* but make every effort—the same as it says here, **"Make every effort to keep the unity**

23. Gangadean, *The Westminster Confession,* 291–305.

of the Spirit through the bond of peace," and "make every effort to live in peace with all men." Let us consider whether our words tend toward edification, building up and maintaining peace, or whether our words are inclined to make a strain greater. Remember the idea of teamwork and working together to accomplish the work that God has given us. Sometimes, we have to cooperate with those who do not believe, according to the common grace that is given to them, that we might be able to accomplish our task.

THE ONE AND THE MANY: Diversity without Unity and Unity without Diversity

In terms of diversity and unity, there is a worldly solution and a biblical solution. We might speak about this problem as the problem of *the one and the many,* applied ethically to getting things done. If we have diversity without unity, we have problems. If we have unity without diversity, we have problems. Paul puts it this way in 1 Corinthians 12:14–16:

> Now the body is not made up of one part but of many. If the foot should say, 'Because I am not a hand, I do not belong to the body,' it would not for that reason cease to be part of the body. And if the ear should say, 'Because I am not an eye, I do not belong to the body,' it would not for that reason cease to be part of the body.

This is a denial of diversity, as if one person is saying, 'I must be the eye', or 'If I am not the hand, I am not part of the body.' No, there are diverse members of the body. This is one side of it. The other side of it is in 1 Corinthians 12:21: "The eye cannot say to the hand, 'I don't need you!' And the head cannot say to the feet, 'I don't need you!'" This is taking the eye to be the whole of the body and getting a kind of oneness without the diversity. I want us to think about these two pieces and how they play together, *unity* and *diversity,* and how we can move away from the truth in either direction. If there is diversity without unity, there is no body. If there is unity without diversity, there is no body. If all were the eye, where is the body? If we say, 'If I am not the eye, I am not of the body,' what happens to the body, which is made up of many parts?

Unity of Diversity in Marriage

We have to reckon with diversity, which has many levels. I will name just a few, to begin with. There are divisions that have existed between male and female, going back to husband and wife. The first two persons are where it began, and we are to be one flesh. The two shall be one, diversity and unity, and the work was to be accomplished through this. Apart from unity between husband and wife, it will not be accomplished. Children will not be raised as they should be, will not be given the example, and we will not make progress in that work. We know that there are significant problems regarding the number of divorces and strains in marriage. This is an area that we need to work on.

Body and Soul

Any diversity that the Lord has created can become an occasion for division. We have a body and soul, and there have been those who emphasize the body as a source of knowledge through the senses, summarized in science considering what is based on observation as the whole truth.[24] Some have gone by way of the soul and reason apart from the senses, and these are the rationalists; they have come up with theories, and they have gone aside also.[25] Likewise, in the body and soul diversity, which is intended for unity, we have created a conflict between this life (this-worldliness) and the next life (otherworldliness), where we leave our bodies behind and go on to the next life as disembodied spirits. Or the difference between material and spiritual needs and strains in relationships there. God does not intend this. You are one person, body and soul. You are one person, and male and female are to be one.

Prophet, Priest, and King

Then, there are differences between prophet, priest, and king. We are made to love God with our whole heart. God is one, and we are to love Him wholeheartedly. We know in the history of the Church some have said, "I am of Paul; and I of Apollos; and I of Cephas."[26] We know there was a division between Paul and Barnabas that was quite

---

24. Gangadean, *History of Philosophy*, 93–105, 139–149.

25. Gangadean, *History of Philosophy*, 87–91, 131–137.

26. *1 Corinthians 1:12, 3:4–5* KJV.

acute, and they were such great friends. Barnabas reflected more of the priestly and nurturing, and Paul reflected the prophetic. We know there was a division between Moses and Aaron. Moses went up into the mount and returned with the law, and Aaron let the people go. Being so close to the people, he accommodated them, not knowing how to maintain the line, and they worshiped the golden calf. There are differences between the prophetic, priestly, and kingly among us, and we do not know how to speak with one another because of these different characteristics and the different things we value. Just as men and women have different values according to the peculiar work that they are to do in the kingdom of God, and they naturally gravitate towards and are attuned to those roles: there exists a diversity of tasks within the realms of the prophetic, priestly, and kingly. Often, we may embrace our specific roles without even realizing it.

Why is it that God gave priests? Why not just prophets? The priests have a way of working with people repeatedly over the months and years and being present with them. The prophet is not that kind of person. He does not do that, but there is a *need* to teach the truth this way. There is a *need* for the kings to put these things into practice, hoping that the prophets and the priests have done their work. The kingly people are not going to back up and do that work. They will assume it is there and continue, and they will be very frustrated if it is not there. We need to know there is this kind of diversity in the body of Christ and it is intended for unity. How does Paul put it when he says, "I am of Paul; and I of Apollos; and I of Cephas?" He says, "Is Christ divided?"[27] Christ is Prophet, Priest, and King. Notice that in all of these, there is a *oneness,* a diversity in unity, a unity *through* diversity, a unity *of* diversity, not a unity of sameness. Men have used all of these differences to take things out of proportion.

Ethnic Background

We also have an ethnic background. Where does Scripture speak about this? There is the age, the epoch in which we live, and differences in the progression in the history of the world: before Christ and after Christ, the ancient world, the medieval world, the modern world, and now contemporary. Living in these different epochs, with different

27. *1 Corinthians 1:12–13.*

backgrounds, we do not always appreciate others across backgrounds. As a matter of fact, we have an even shorter time period than epochs, between generations, let us say, the 'X-ers' and the 'Y's.' Have you heard of them? Generation X, Y, and the Boomers are in different stages of life. A generation is a cohort-group,[28] and there are tensions between the generations, real tensions. We have difficulty appreciating and understanding this. There are ethnic differences, which we sang about in Psalm 67A: "That so Thy way most holy On earth may soon be known, And unto every people Thy saving grace be shown" (Ps. 67:2).[29] God intends to bring people from all of these backgrounds. Are we ready for it? Or are we going to impose a Western way upon these other cultures? Can we bring the living water in the cup, the vessel of these nations, without compromising anything moral? I do not know that we know how to do that yet. This is where the study of the humanities would be helpful, to see the humanness of people from age to age.

I was talking to someone last night who is reading *Sailing the Wine-Dark Sea: Why the Greeks Matter*,[30] about the Greek character Hector, Hector's time with his wife, and the tenderness and humanness that is expressed by Hector. We saw the movie Troy,[31] about Helen of Troy, and how they did not display Hector or Achilles rightly. We read this work and see the humanness of these persons and are touched. You feel close to these persons. This is what the humanities should do for us. We should say, 'Yes, I want to see people from every kindred, nation, tribe, and tongue come to the Lord. I want to appreciate the Hamites, the Shemites, and the Japhethites, and all the diversity among them.' God intends this. He wants us to be *one* in Him in the body of Christ. We have work to do, people of God! We have *real* work to do! Let us recognize this work, set our hearts to it, and prepare to work for this unity.

There are ethnic backgrounds, economic backgrounds, battles about rich and poor, and slave and free. There are educational backgrounds.

---

28. Term taken from the framework provided in William Strauss and Neil Howe, *Generations: The History of America's Future, 1584 to 2069* (New York: William Morrow and Company, Inc., 1991). A cohort-group is defined as all persons born in a limited span of consecutive years.

29. *The Book of Psalms for Singing.*

30. Thomas Cahill, *Sailing the Wine-Dark Sea: Why the Greeks Matter* (New York: A Division of Random House Inc. 2003).

31. David Benioff, ed. *Troy*, directed by Wolfgang Petersen, 2004.

Paul speaks about the learned and the unlearned, the wise and the unwise, the Greek and the non-Greek, with respect to the learning that was part of that world. So, there are ethnic backgrounds, but God tells us that all of these differences are to come together, understand, and speak in ways that edify. When we get down to the nitty-gritty, the details, where the difficulties are, we are to learn to work with others and be quick to listen and slow to speak and to speak only for edification.

Uniqueness

Then there is the unique factor in each of us. We may come from the same background, and yet we want to be ourselves. We want to have our autonomy. We want to do what is right in our *own* eyes. We have the question of our self-life versus loving our neighbor as ourselves. We should seek to love our neighbor.

We are to maintain the unity of the Spirit while we work toward the unity of the faith. Clearly, there is a lot of work before us. Most of all, we are to begin this work closest to home, in our families, in this congregation, with brothers and sisters in Christ, and then with those outside. We are to be careful about how we speak and about the words of our mouths.

Now, we are going to close by singing Psalm 139C, which ends by saying, "Search me, O God, and know my heart; test me and know my anxious thoughts" (Ps. 139:23).[32]

32. *The Book of Psalms for Singing.*

3

Maturity, Fruitfulness, Unity, and Fullness

How Do We Attain It, and What Does It Look Like?

2007

Ephesians 4:7–16

[7]But to each one of us grace has been given as Christ apportioned it. [8]This
is why it says:

"When he ascended on high,
he led captives in his train
and gave gifts to men."

[9](What does "he ascended" mean except that he also descended to the
lower, earthly regions? [10]He who descended is the very one who ascended
higher than all the heavens, in order to fill the whole universe.) [11]It was he
who gave some to be apostles, some to be prophets, some to be evangelists,
and some to be pastors and teachers, [12]to prepare God's people for works
of service, so that the body of Christ may be built up [13]until we all reach
unity in the faith and in the knowledge of the Son of God and become
mature, attaining to the whole measure of the fullness of Christ.

[14]Then we will no longer be infants, tossed back and forth by the waves,
and blown here and there by every wind of teaching and by the cunning
and craftiness of men in their deceitful scheming. [15]Instead, speaking the
truth in love, we will in all things grow up into him who is the Head,
that is, Christ. [16]From him the whole body, joined and held together by

every supporting ligament, grows and builds itself up in love, as each part does its work.

WE COME TO A SUBJECT THAT, in terms of our preaching schedule, we will call *occasional,* but there is occasion for it. There seems to always be an occasion for the Word of God and for this Word. I would like us to anticipate and see if we can figure out most of the sermon before it is delivered. This is active listening—active listening in light of all the things that have been said and preached over the months and years. We want to address the question of maturity, fruitfulness, unity, and fullness. You may recall last time we closed with Proverbs 11:30, which speaks about the wise person as one who wins souls: "The fruit of the righteous is a tree of life, and he who wins souls is wise." I spoke about fruit; since then, I have heard that this has stirred up questions in various circles. These questions are one occasion for this message. We are also dealing with the question of diversity and fideism—that is, sources of fideism, which is belief without understanding/proof—in class at Logos Theological Seminary. So, the question of fullness has come up. This has been on our minds and stimulated by circumstances, but we think this is something that is needed. Recall also that at the congregational meeting, we said that this is a young congregation, we are raising families, we need to concern ourselves with raising children, and others are desiring marriage—we need to pray for and with them. We will be talking about maturity—literally and analogically/spiritually. How do we attain maturity, fruit, unity, and fullness? Notice, the question is not *whether* we should attain these; it goes without saying that we should attain them. How do we attain them, and what do they look like when we attain them? We will go through each of these in turn and notice some repeating passages. Each is very intimately connected.

MATURITY:
How Do We Grow and Change?

I would like to draw to our attention a number of Scriptures that speak about maturity so it is explicitly before us. How do we grow and change? In one way, the question leaves us puzzled: 'How do we grow? Well, we just grow; it is a spontaneous thing.' Yes and no. We have to be nourished in order to grow well. Remember we spoke about dwarfs; we have nothing against literal dwarfs, but we do have something against spiritual dwarfs, and we may not be grown up spiritually. Three primary passages address maturity, and there will be a fourth in John 17, which has been quoted in the Focus for the Week on truth, unity, and fruit. These passages are in Ephesians 4, which we have just read. There, it speaks about being built up until we become mature. It says in verse 13 that we "**become mature, attaining to the whole measure of the fullness of Christ,**" and in verse 14: "**Then we will no longer be infants.**" The progression from infancy onward is the process of maturing.

How long does it take? How long does it take for a child, an infant, to become mature? Would we say about five weeks? About five years? Is it about 15 years or 500 years? Do some of them grow up and do not become mature? You sometimes wonder. All of us who have raised kids can relate; some are 30 years old and still at home, that sort of thing; they are 30 going on 13. How do we grow up and change from being infants in Christ—being born again—to maturity? This is a very natural process. Can you anticipate the answer? Just make a note and see whether you can say, 'Oh, yes, this is how you do it.' See if you can anticipate what is coming and what we will be emphasizing.

Hebrews 5:11–6:3

This passage speaks about maturity, and a number of things said in this passage tell us *how* we mature. There are ways that we have interpreted this passage where we have missed a number of things about *how* we become mature, but as we go back, we will see it. Ephesians 4:7–16 is one passage, and the next is Hebrews 5:11–6:2. You should be able to anticipate this. It is from Hebrews chapters 5 and 6. Starting with verse 11:

> We have much to say about this [about Melchizedek], but it is hard to explain because you are slow to learn. In fact, though by this time you ought to be teachers, you need someone to teach you the elementary truths of God's word all over again. You need milk, not solid food! (Heb. 5:11–12).

Is that the theme of maturity? Sure. Growing from infancy up? Yes. Was there interruption? Did it happen automatically? No, it did not.

We would not say it spontaneously happens and we do not have to do anything.

Another question is, did the Apostle give up? Did he say, 'Oh well, you guys are a wasted effort; it is no good.' No, he did not. He says, "You need milk, not solid food" (Heb. 5:12b). He wants to start where they are and continue. "Anyone who lives on milk, being still an *infant,* is not acquainted with the teaching about righteousness. But solid food is for the mature" (Heb. 5:13–14a).[1] Here are the words; they are literally here, comparing infancy to maturity. "Solid food is for the mature," notice, "who by constant use have trained themselves to distinguish good and evil" (Heb. 5:14). This is one of the marks of maturity. You can train yourself in any given situation to distinguish good and evil, under all the disguises that come in.

> Therefore let us leave the elementary teachings about Christ and go on to maturity, not laying again the foundation of repentance from acts that lead to death, and of faith in God, instruction about baptisms, the laying on of hands, the resurrection of the dead, and eternal judgment (Heb. 6:1–2).

Elementary truths, foundational truths, first truths—these are milk, not meat.

Some of you have been inclined to say that some of this content I am teaching is for the mature; no, Paul is saying it is for the immature. The foundation gets in place first for the infants. If you have any questions about this, please do make a note of it and be sure to ask me, and do not let yourself leave here saying, 'Well, this is just for the mature.' No, this foundation is for the immature, for the infants, and it is for everyone, not just for some. I have heard it said often, 'This is a special group; it is selected out in certain ways and these truths are just for some.' Notice that it is the foundation that enables persons to go *from* infancy *to* maturity. Without the foundation, it will not happen. Paul said, "not laying again the foundation" (Heb. 6:1). We need to teach you the elementary truths all over again. "You need milk, not solid food" (Heb. 5:12b).

1. Emphasis added.

1 Corinthians 3:1–3

Hebrews 5:11–6:2 is the second passage. The first was Ephesians 4:7–16, which we will come back to. Then, in 1 Corinthians 3:1–3, Paul speaks of this—growth from infancy to maturity—and he refers to the divisions in the Church and how we are worldly and immature.

> Brothers, I could not address you as spiritual but as worldly—mere infants in Christ. I gave you milk, not solid food, for you were not yet ready for it. Indeed, you are still not ready. You are still worldly.

We are to go from infancy to maturity, but it does not happen automatically. Something happens, and that is the reality of sin that interrupts it. If there were no sin in us and the world, we would make progress naturally, so we have to watch out for how our sin interrupts the process.

He speaks about divisions: "I am of Paul; and I of Apollos; and I of Cephas"(1 Cor. 3:4 KJV), and we will look at this passage in connection with fullness. He says this right here. He goes on to say,

> By the grace God has given me, I laid a foundation as an expert builder, and someone else is building on it. But each one should be careful how he builds. For no one can lay any foundation other than the one already laid, which is Jesus Christ (1 Cor. 3:10–11).

We tend to maintain this in a very narrow, truncated sense, rather than speaking of Christ in all of His fullness. We speak about fullness as one of the central doctrines; Christ in His fullness enables us to come to maturity. The mature is one who has attained **"to the whole measure of the fullness of Christ"** (Eph. 4:13b). What is this? What does this look like? It speaks here about how we will suffer loss if we do not build adequately on this foundation:

> If any man builds on this foundation using gold, silver, costly stones, wood, hay or straw, his work will be shown for what it is, because the Day will bring it to light. It will be revealed with fire, and the fire will test the quality of each man's work (1 Cor. 3:12–13).

Again, the connection between foundation and maturity is being laid out here. This is the work of Paul. What happens then is that we can build without the foundation in place or not build on the foundation, and then our works will be burned. We ask, where is your fruit? Fruit that is lasting. These themes are intertwined.

Ephesians 4:7–16

Let us return to Ephesians 4, as we will continually work through this passage. 1 Peter 2:2 says, "As newborn babes, desire the sincere milk of the word, that ye may grow thereby."[2] How does this work? It involves reading the Scripture with a seeking attitude, with a diligently seeking attitude, not a perfunctory attitude: 'Well, I did my Scripture reading for today.' Well, that is good. 'Phew, I got through that. Now I can go on and have breakfast.' A good way to keep yourself reading is not to have breakfast until you finish reading. Just a little handy tip. "As newborn babes, desire the sincere milk of the word, that ye may grow thereby." This is not all. We are to meditate in the Word as we go out and come in, and there needs to be more than this. We are to use the means.

In Ephesians 4, what are the means by which we are prepared for works of service? The means are—see if you can anticipate it, and I am looking right at it, so you should be able to—the means are the pastor-teachers.[3] Notice, I did not say, "**apostles . . . prophets . . . evangelists**" (v. 11); I just said pastor-teachers. Why did I say this? Because they are building on the work of the apostles, prophets, and evangelists. When you think about the pastor-teachers, you may say, 'that means you should go to church because that is where the pastors are doing their teaching, right?' Yes, that is certainly true, but it is much, much more than this. It is not just the pastor-teachers today but the pastor-teachers *through* Church history. Is that a stretch, or is it that we must affirm this? 'Amen.' You can all say it from time to time. I am okay with it.

We use the pastor-teachers, meaning we use their work as it has accumulated. Where does the work of the pastor-teachers first appear? You should know this by now: Acts 15.[4] What is it connected with? The

2. KJV.

3. Gangadean, *The Westminster Confession*, xvii-xxxii.

4. Gangadean, "Paper No. 16: The Historic Christian Faith," 103–114; "Paper No. 38: The Holy Catholic and Apostolic Faith," 211–216; "Paper No. 60: The Spiritual War (Part II)," in *The Logos Papers*, 329–330.

Holy Spirit leading the Church into all truth.[5] As they come together, through much discussion, they come to a greater understanding of God's truth. If we say, 'It is just me and my Bible,' well, that is true, but we have to make use of these other means as well, which is not bypassing the Scripture. We can always go back to the Scriptures to search them and see that the things that are being said are so.[6] This is part of the ordinary means and the oversight that goes with these means.

Think about the way it is with parents and children. Children are not just left on their own. Parents have to administer the milk. We do not say, 'Hey, kid, there is the milk. Help yourself whenever you want; I am okay with that.' This would be totally absurd. In the analogy of the infant, we have to feed and be sure they do it, and then we have to take care of all kinds of problems with raising kids. Right? There are all kinds of things. They are discomforted, they have to burp, and then they cry, and then they wet their diapers. I do not want to press it too far, but there is an analogy. In caring for spiritual infants, we have to work. This is how we come to maturity. Our father in Christ, or our father and mother in Christ, are the ones who do this work. It happens quite naturally. They call on the phone and say, 'How are you doing today?' You speak together, and they encourage you regularly.

It takes a long time to parent a child, and things are done in stages and seasons. It does take time and effort on the part of others before someone starts to seek diligently. The parents do not just leave it up to the child. The question is: How is that occurring in your life? Are you in a position where that is occurring? Normally, the person who leads you to Christ, whom you have come into contact with, is the person who keeps you and watches over you. They invest labor in prayer, witness, and other ways, and they care about you and want to see you grow up in Christ. It is the most natural way in which this occurs. This part of coming to maturity must be kept in mind.

We speak about different stages. Let us say it takes about 20 years—from 1 to 20—to come into maturity. As Paul puts it, "In fact, though by this time you ought to be teachers" (Heb. 5:12a). Notice you do not start teaching when you are not yet of age. You may witness; anyone can witness about what God has done. You can always witness, but

---

5. *John 16:13.*

6. *Acts 17:11.*

teaching is another matter—it involves a kind of maturity. If you are going to *make* disciples—you have to *be* a disciple. You have to have been discipled; you need to have gone through that process. We should expect, at a certain stage in our life, for this to be happening. You may say, 'Where is the fruit?' But you are just three or five years old in Christ, and you are not very well matured. You have not had much practice; you have not had about 500 instances of practice in witnessing. Notice, we have not asked you to go knocking door to door, but we have asked you to pray. We ask you to continue to witness, to make the most of every opportunity, to know how, not in a contrived way, but most naturally, to give your life as a witness; in a most natural way, to be able to speak a word, and if we are praying about and desiring that, we will find those opportunities. God will open opportunities for us to witness, not in a contrived way that makes the other person feel uncomfortable, but in a way that is quite natural.

God was gracious as I was in for my medical exam. There was a receiving nurse, and we got into a discussion. We began talking pretty soon about reincarnation and Sylvia Browne.[7] My wife was there and she was witnessing against Sylvia Browne, and I was witnessing against reincarnation. It was a different process of witnessing, an interesting contrast. Ask her sometime about it. Then the nurse came in, and we started talking about her life. I suggested that maybe she should look into teaching nursing. Then the anesthesiologist came in and he was trying to set me at ease and talk. He asked, 'What do you do?' I said, 'I teach,' and he said, 'What do you teach?' 'Philosophy.' I did not want to give out too much. Let him inquire if he wants. He said, 'Oh, we are just talking with some others about Plato and *The Allegory of the Cave.*[8] What do you think about that?' We were able to talk about this. I said, 'I do not think Plato was right that very few get it. I think we can all get it. That it is objectively clear, but subjectively difficult. The prisoner who escaped came to see the sun reflected in the water, and that sun was an analogy for ultimate reality. The sun was the source of being and the source of the intelligibility of being.' I knew this got in. You know how you connect at times? It was like he never thought that idea was in Plato's mind. And here I am, wrapped in these clothes,

7. Sylvia Celeste Browne (1936–2013) was an American writer, medium, and psychic who professed belief in reincarnation.

8. The Allegory of the Cave is contained in Plato's *Republic,* Book VII.

on the table, flat on my back, just talking away. It is the most natural thing. Opportunities present themselves, and by God's grace, as we are prepared, we can make use of them and witness.

It has to happen over and over and over again, many times, and if you get stuck in your witnessing, you come back and say, 'Well, I started to witness and I got stuck here,' then we say, 'Let us talk about it,' and in three or four minutes, we clear it up, and you go out again, and you come back. You should expect to do that 500 times before you get it. When one of you asks, 'Where is the fruit?', we say, 'What is the process we have gone through? Is the foundation there? Have we prepared ourselves for doing this work?' We do not just give up and say we cannot have fruit or readjust the standards so we can say, 'Well, maybe we do not have to have that kind of fruit.' Fruit is by the mature, all the way into old age, and that is what we will be ending with when we sing. In old age when others fade, their boughs with fruit shall bend. To show that upright is the Lord, there is no unrighteousness in Him.[9]

All kinds of opportunities for witnessing are happening, such as receiving a letter from an acquaintance who is facing the question: "Once saved, always saved." My mechanic is out there working on my car's engine, and we discuss theology. He has written a work, and I am asking, 'What does he mean by regeneration? What does he mean by the second resurrection?' He has written a paper on this and he is talking about it. And I am wrestling in my mind over uncaused events that someone is writing a paper about, and how Arminianism appeals to freedom and uncaused events in order to explain this world. If certain basic things were in place, my aquaintnace would not be messing around with Arminian theology, and my mechanic would not be out there fighting this battle with Armstrongism and losing time and energy. The Church could be pulled together as one, and the world would believe that God has sent Christ.

We need to know how to witness; there are abundant opportunities, but our heart has to be in it. If our heart is in it, it will come out this way: We will pray to the Lord to prepare us and help us become aware of opportunities to share, and we will be amazed at how this happens. But do not expect to see opportunities if you are not praying about it. Notice, we are not contrary to evangelism; we are teaching a larger

9. *Psalm 92:14–15, 92B The Book of Psalms for Singing.*

view of evangelism because we are not saying you only evangelize by knocking door to door. We do not do that, but there are many other opportunities—much more abundant than the door-to-door approach. We also speak about lifelong evangelism. My wife speaks to her sister and we talk about it often, and we process it. Her sister sees how my wife's response is different from her best friend's response, and we see how over the years that can wear away objections by living a life that reflects Christ. This is what we mean by *ongoing witness.* Some of you say, 'We do not know what that means' in the novitiate.[10] Do not pretend that you do not know or you forgot; let us just say you let it slip.

We have all kinds of witness opportunities in our whole life, in every way. We are preparing people for witness, and it happens in stages, and this is the point of coming to maturity, and there are seasons. We speak about the first five years of the novitiate as just getting the basics in place. Reading the Scriptures through every year. Unless you read the Scriptures through at least three times during the first five years, you do not pass your novitiate. You go to the 6th, 7th, 8th, 9th, 10th year, and you say, 'I have been at this now for ten years, and I still cannot get it.' You can get help, especially in the small group.[11] Then, there are stages beyond this for greater preparation. Discipleship can begin more in earnest after this. How about reading through the Westminster Confession of Faith four times a year? How about setting aside time? You wonder what to do on the Sabbath day? You say, 'I knew it. I knew he was going to mess with our Sabbath day. This is my day.' No, it is not your day. Just plan to read through the Westminster Confession four times a year.

All right, I will give you a break in the first year. Two times a year, but you have to read the Shorter Catechism two times a year also. Make that part of your Sabbath day—incorporate it. I have been through this, teaching it many times over the years; I have read it, but I am continuing to be amazed, struck, and instructed by every reading, every

10. Gangadean, *The Westminster Confession,* 391–395.

11. Small Group is an arrangement to minister to congregants. It is modeled after the pattern set by Moses through Jethro. Small group leaders are placed over ten church members. They are to mentor, encourage, pray, and share a meal together. This is part of the natural process whereby the next generation of leaders in the church is prepared to apply the teaching in their lives and the life of the congregation.

time I reread it.[12] This is the work of the pastor-teachers. Better yet, this is the work of God: the Holy Spirit leading the Church into all truth through the work of the pastor-teachers, that we might be prepared for service, that we might come to maturity, that we might attain to the whole measure of the fullness of Christ.[13] Do not think you can *ever* attain to maturity without this foundation in place, without the work of the pastor-teachers. It is not going to happen. If you say, 'Where is the fruit?' I am going to say, 'Where is the work?' How well in place is this? How is your prayer for fruit? Have you finished your novitiate? Have you been through the next five years of discipleship?

The foundation is to be taught diligently. As we teach it diligently to our children, those in oversight must teach diligently to those under them. As they go out and as they come in—in a life setting, where we interpret the news, and we interpret literature. I know many of you do not like when I comment on movies. You say, 'Oh no, he is going to ruin the movie for all of us.' I watched *Pride and Prejudice* again, the BBC version.[14] There is one phrase that I just had to put on pause. It was when Elizabeth Bennet was speaking about her father and the neglect of her father in relation to his wife and how it has affected the family. I said, 'Wow.' As these movies of sensibility and manners in the British unfold, I have often wondered, 'Where is the father in this?' "Husbands, love your wives, just as Christ loved the church and gave himself up for her" (Eph. 5:25), to bring the Word, to instruct. Mr. Bennet simply let his wife go. I find myself saying, 'Make that woman be quiet.' He was an otherwise quite intelligent man and an attractive man. I would like to hang out with him, but he is not doing the basic work. As you go in, as you come out . . .[15] In this life-like setting where things are natural, as you listen to the news, you read articles on the web—discuss it with others, share it with others, and find some way to connect. This is how the teaching is to occur.

We have to put the teachings into practice to obey God's Word, and to obey His law that sums up all that is required of us. I have recently

12. A significant portion of the insights derived from teaching and studying the Westminster Standards has been published in Gangadean, *The Westminster Confession of Faith;* Gangadean, *The Westminster Shorter and Larger Catechisms.*

13. *Ephesians 4:13.*

14. Andrew Davies, ed. *Pride and Prejudice,* directed by Simon Langton, 1995.

15. *Deuteronomy 6:4–9.*

been reading through the Book of Leviticus and finally discovered why so many people get lost in this book. I think Leviticus is becoming one of my favorite books in all the Bible. Can you imagine that? As soon as I say the word, you are going to get it. Here is the word. You will all agree. It has to do with *holiness,* right? Holiness is set over and against unholiness and uncleanness, or the self-life. Question: Do we have to deal with our self-lives? The Book of Leviticus spells out how the process of sanctification by the priest works. As we start reading it with this piece in the back of our mind, we start looking for things, we start seeing things, and the thing is going to burst open on us; it is going to burst open. Thanks be to God for this. I have known this; I have felt it coming like a fruit ripening, and this time through—and this is one of the reasons why you want to read the Bible through every year, because every time you read it, seeking, you get more out of it—this year the thing just started to break open, as it never had before.

The Levitical priesthood is the principle of oversight in which people are taught holiness and sanctification through the truth. They are taught the truth in a certain way, and they are taught the distinction between clean and unclean, between good and evil, and the curse and the promise. It is all there in the Book of Leviticus, including the mildew in the house. Remember that mildew? You cannot make heads or tails of it. 'I never had mildew in my house. What are we talking about here? Let us just forget that,' and you skip over it quickly.

You know the thing about unclean? We are not supposed to be talking with anyone else or having any interaction when the sin of self-life becomes manifest in our lives. The pastor sees it and those in oversight see it, and they say, 'Guess what, time out.' Instead of natural evil calling us to stop and think, the pastor and those in oversight have to call us to stop and think: Do not talk with anyone else, do not receive others into your house, do not send out cards and invitations as if everything is alright. You are in time-out mode. When it is really deep within us and it has not changed, we go around confessing, 'Unclean, unclean, unclean!' Do not let anyone come near you. Try to put that into practice. See how that works? It is dramatic. We talked about honesty and not going along as if everything is alright when sin is raging in our lives and has gotten the better of us. Leviticus is a book for sanctification, alright? Time out. Do not talk to anyone. Do not receive anyone into your house. Do not make calls out. Stop and think. You are grounded until you get it right. You are grounded until this thing is no longer merely occasional, circumstantial, it is more than skin deep and goes down into the sin in the heart. This is what the priest has to discern. This is why they say, come back in another seven days, and come back in another seven days, and if after so many times it does not show anymore, the priests pronounce you clean. But if it shows up again—'No'—this is sin that comes from within, from the self-life within, and we need to deal with it; we need to stop other things until we deal with this sin. Leviticus has a lot of power in it. This is how the priest taught the people, and we need to go through a process of sanctification *analogous* to this to learn what we need to learn.

Ephesians 4 speaks about the work of the pastor-teachers, and we have said again and again—I am willing to have anyone question me on this—do come questioning as to whether the Westminster Confession of Faith is the high-water mark of Historic Christianity, whether it is the high-water mark of the pastor-teachers. I think we all say there has been nothing greater since. I think we can all say it sums up what has gone before, including Nicea and Chalcedon and the Apostles' Creed.[16] In that sense, it is the high-water mark. Then ask yourself, if this is the work of the pastor-teachers, and it is the work through which we come into maturity and attain to "the whole measure of the fullness of Christ," as spoken of in Ephesians 4:13, then how do we get this into us?

Some have identified the *nerve center* of the Confession of the Westminster Assembly. The nerve center is summed up in the catechism, which begins as no other catechism begins:[17] "Man's chief end is to glorify God, and to enjoy him forever." I think we will all say, 'yes,

16. Gangadean, *The Westminster Confession,* xix-xxxii.

17. Benjamin B. Warfield in his essay "The First Question of the Westminster Shorter Catechism" draws attention to the doxological aim of this question. He states: "No Catechism begins on a higher plane than the Westminster 'Shorter Catechism.' Its opening question . . . sets the learner at once in his right relation to God. Withdrawing his eyes from himself, even from his own salvation, as the chief object of concern, it fixes them on God and His glory, and bids him seek the highest blessedness in Him." He continues: "The Westminster Catechism cuts itself free at once from this entanglement with lower things and begins, as it centers and ends, under the illumination of the vision of God in His glory, to subserve which it finds to be the proper end of human as of all other existence, of salvation as of all other achievements. To it all things exist for God, unto whom as well as from whom all things are; and the great question for each of us accordingly is, How can I glorify God and enjoy Him forever?" Warfield further explains that "The peculiarity of this first question and answer of the Westminster Catechisms, it will be seen, is the felicity with which it brings to concise expression the whole Reformed conception of the significance

amen' to this, but as soon as we say, 'What does it mean?', we begin to stammer, and we begin to lose it. If we ask, 'Glorify God in all that by which He makes Himself known?', when we coordinate it with Shorter Catechism question 101, *Hallowed be thy name,* "to glorify him in all that whereby he makes himself known," it is said, 'Well, I do not know.' And if we ask, 'In all of His works of creation and providence?'—that is how He makes Himself known—then we see how some understandings come short. Remember, sin is coming short of the glory of God. This is what we mean by the *doxological focus* of the Confession.[18] If you think I am making this up and this is a new doctrine, let us distinguish 'new to you' and 'new.' For some people, everything is new; every day, I say it over and over, and it is totally new. But it is not new historically, and if we make connections that are there, even though others do not make them, the question is, 'Ought we to make the connection? Is this building on the Confession?' Or, 'Is this a special work being done by philosophers for the prophet, for the prophetic, and the priestly have no part in this and the kingly have no part in this?' I have heard that kind of question raised. The foundation is for everyone, for everyone to come to maturity, and we need to work on getting this in place.

FULLNESS: The Body of Christ

There are a number of basic Scriptures that we should keep in mind when we start talking about fullness. The first comes in 1 Corinthians 12: the body of Christ. We are one member of the body; we are not the whole body; it is one with many parts. Again, I was amazed as I went through 1 Corinthians, both 12 and 14, how Paul never lets up, and I do not know why I had not seen this as it is so explicit. He never lets up between unity and diversity. Almost in every verse, he speaks about this—he says, different gifts but the same spirit; different administration, but the same Lord; but the same, and it is one—difference in one. He keeps these together. When he reaches 14, he never lets up connecting understanding and edification. This is the chapter often quoted by those who believe in speaking in tongues. What they have

of human life." Benjamin B. Warfield, *The Westminster Assembly and Its Works* (Grand Rapids: Baker books, 2003), 379–400.

18. Gangadean, *The Westminster Confession,* xv-xvi, 345–346.

is ecstatic utterance, not biblical tongues, because it understands no content. A vast portion of Protestants are caught in the charismatic misunderstanding.[19] Paul never lets up on this connection. We are part of the body of Christ; we are one among many, and this connection is made constantly, so please note it.

Earlier, we spoke about other divisions and being worldly. We should put it this way: It does not take a village. It takes a body. A body is one way of speaking organically; it is spoken of in other ways in Scripture. It is a city, and this city is the kingdom of God; it is a kingdom. It is like a whole civilization, a whole alternative way as in the Augustinian sense: the city of God and the city of man. This is what we are talking about when talking about fullness and the body. Explicitly, he says, "And God placed all things under his feet and appointed him to be head over everything for the church, which is his body, the fullness of him who fills everything in every way" (Eph. 1:22–23).

There is a connection between the body of Christ and attaining to the fullness that there is in Christ. This is one passage, and it connects with all the diversity in Corinthians. A second element of fullness is this: love God with all your heart. Your whole heart, fully. Not only with every dimension of your heart but with every intensity. Is that a fair rendition of love God with all your heart? Do not be one-dimensional or two-dimensional persons. Reality is three-dimensional. We are a triune personality, and we are to love God with all of our heart—that is part of the doctrine of fullness.

Another passage that speaks about fullness concerns the division between Paul, Apollos, and Cephas.

> My brothers, some from Chloe's household have informed me that there are quarrels among you. What I mean is this: One of you says, 'I follow Paul'; another, 'I follow Apollos'; another, 'I follow Cephas'; still another, 'I follow Christ.' Is Christ divided? (1 Cor. 1:11–13a).

It is a division between Christ as prophet, priest, and king. What is the answer? Is Christ divided? Does the Church continually divide up over that? According to our personality emphasis, we tend to go one way or the other. We should not speak about these differences unless we

19. Gangadean, *On Natural and Revealed Theology,* 223–228; Gangadean, "Paper No. 122: Contra Charismatic Distinctive," in *The Logos Papers,* 651–653.

are ready to speak about fullness. This is Paul's inseparable connection. As soon as he says this, he asks, "Is Christ divided?" They are one in Christ and we are to be one.

Other passages connected with fullness: "For in him dwelleth all the fullness of the Godhead bodily" (Col. 2:9 KJV). And Ephesians 4:13, **"until we all reach unity in the faith and in the knowledge of the Son of God, and become mature, attaining to the whole measure of the fullness of Christ"** (v. 13). Earlier in this passage, He is to **"fill the whole universe,"** (v. 10b) and even earlier it says, He is to "fill everything in every way" (Eph. 1:23). We are not faithful witnesses to Christ when we give a truncated version of Christ—when we cannot receive from others, in every level, what they have to contribute—when we cannot be knitted together and receive from other members of the body, and give to them. When we are so busy defending our portion because our eyes are off the fullness of Christ, and when we give a distorted, truncated view of Christ, it is not lovely, and the world is not attracted to it. We need to be careful about this.

No one has all, but we are to receive from all others. This is a picture of the body. Sin will continually challenge us, but we are to have dominion over sin. There will be competition among us—because of sin remaining in us—for honor. There will be jealousy, strife, envy, pride, and selfish ambition.[20] Paul warns us against these things. This is the self-life. We should always expect sin to be present. We are not yet fully sanctified. We should expect the neglecting, avoiding, resisting, and denying of what is clear. This remains in us. It comes out in open and hidden ways. It comes out with murmuring and complaining. Instead of crucifying the flesh with the affections and the lusts,[21] we murmur and complain when expectations are put upon us. We should expect sin going into this, including the doctrine of fullness. People will resist it, and I do not mean people in general; I mean each one of you will resist it. Each of us will resist it because sin remains in us, and because of this sin, the narrowness that comes with this sin, and the neglect that comes with it, we will tend to not want to be bothered. We have our favorite areas that we concentrate on, and we do not think we have to be concerned with those who contribute in other areas. Artists

20. Gangadean, *Philosophical Foundation,* 255–265.

21. *Galatians 5:24* KJV.

do not want what business people have to offer, and business people make faces about the artists. And philosophers, 'well, they are a dime a dozen; they are like prophets: a dime a dozen. Who needs them? What are they good for, anyway? This is the real world. Intuition is the real thing; no practice and facts—hard facts; this is the real thing.' Personality, epistemology, and habits of mind overtake us, and we justify ourselves. We do not subject our thinking to critical scrutiny, and we go on in our narrow way. We are called to fullness. We are to attain to **"the whole measure of the fullness of Christ"** (v. 13b). This happens in the context of the body.

Let us look at one other passage connected with fullness, which goes all the way back to Genesis, in the theme, *to fill the earth*. We multiply, replenish, and fill the earth from the fish of the sea, to the animals, to human beings. From the opening words of Genesis: and it was "formless and empty" (Gen. 1:2). We are to form things and fill the earth because Christ, the Logos, is revealed in all things created. God has decreed that the Son will be glorified in this way, including the Incarnation and redemption, and we are to attain to the fullness of Christ.

We are the body of Christ. We, locally, and all the people of God together are the body of Christ. This is the doctrine of fullness, and if we mature, we will attain this fullness. I am laying the groundwork to come to fruit. We come to fruit in the context of maturity, aiming at fullness. Do not expect that if our lives are pretty narrow we can witness adequately. Paul says, "I have become all things to all men so that by all possible means I might save some" (1 Cor. 9:22b).

How do we know what is in a person, to become all things to all men? If we do not know the person, if we have not taken the time and do not have the wherewithal to begin just to know their life journey, where they came from, where they are heading, and know their testimony—at least that; begin with that—how can we become all things to all men?

It takes time to do this. It takes a certain effort in the Church and with nonbelievers. It is all right to let them do a lot of talking in order to learn about them, not in an inquisitive way or a way that will make them feel embarrassed, but to get to know something about their life story. This is one of the most interesting things: minimally to just say, this is brought about by the sovereign will of God and His eternal wisdom who decrees everything. What is this person's life story? It is more interesting to know a life story than a lot of the stuff on TV. You just get to know another person. Even if you never say a word, you are genuinely interested because of God's revelation, because of this person, to know who they are. People find it very easy to talk about themselves. You could always ask questions like, 'How did you come to think that? How did you feel about that?' Just getting into someone's life story, you can ask questions that get them to think. Does that make sense? Fruit is a consequence of this witness. Isaiah speaks of fullness: "The earth shall be full of the knowledge of the LORD as the waters cover the sea" (Is. 11:9). I do not like to repeat that phrase too often because you may just hear, 'Blah, blah, blah.' It goes in one ear . . . Yet this is the doctrine of fullness.

UNITY OF THE SPIRIT AND OF THE FAITH

In connection with unity, what are some of the basic Scriptures that speak of unity? There is the unity of the Spirit spoken of in Ephesians 4: **"Make every effort to keep the unity of the Spirit through the bond of peace"** (v. 3). **"Be completely humble and gentle"** (v. 2a). In connection with this, it says, **"There is one body . . . one Lord, one faith, one baptism,"** (vv. 4a–5) and it is to be kept by being humble and gentle. This is one sense of unity, and we must build on this. If we do not have this in place, we cannot take the next step toward the unity of the faith. The passage goes on: **"It was he who gave some to be apostles, some to be prophets, some to be evangelists, and some to be pastors and teachers, to prepare God's people for works of service"** (vv. 11–12a). The work of the pastor-teachers is to prepare God's people for works of service, **"until we all reach unity in the faith and in the knowledge of the Son of God"** (v. 13a) "who fills everything in every way" (Eph. 1:23b). This is Christ as creator, upholder, redeemer of all things, heir of all things. This is the sense in which "He is the brightness of the Father's glory" (Heb. 1:3 KJV).

There is a unity of the faith we are to attain. What does this look like? If it is building on the work of the pastor-teachers, in all the world, Christians everywhere will hold to the Westminster Confession of Faith. There will be no more divisions within the body of Christ when we come into the unity of the faith. Objectively, apart from how you feel or if you think that is possible, is this true? It is **"until we all reach unity in**

the faith" (v. 13a). How do we attain this as we become mature? How do we deal with others who are Christian? In the whole vast realm of witnessing, start with the unity of the Spirit, maintain humility and gentleness, and take the next step toward the unity of the faith.

There are three sections in John 17. I will mention them briefly. They are from different points of view. They all speak about being one. First is how believers become one—"sanctify them by the truth; your word is truth" (v. 17). Reading on to verse 21, it says, "that all of them may be one, Father . . . that the world may believe." This is *how* they come into unity, and the result of it is that the world might believe. Notice it is speaking about unity and fruit. When we come to unity in the faith, the world will believe. If we cannot deal with problems in the Church, and we are divided, do you think the world is going to be impressed? You ask, 'Where is the fruit?' How are we progressing in dealing with some of these things? We have to find more effective ways to address the issues that create divisions among believers. We need to get back to what is more basic in Romans regarding clarity and inexcusability.

I received something in the mail from a Roman Catholic apologist called *This Rock.*[22] "On this rock I will build my church" (Matt. 16:18). On the outside cover, a woman says, 'You Catholics are all going to hell,' and it said, in just a short moment, she gave this up and became a Catholic. That was a nice, 'come on.' It was more than just a moment, but that was a nice, 'Come on. How did you do that?' In talking with Roman Catholics, why do we bypass the first question about clarity and inexcusability? Why do we give them a free pass? Why do we not ask, why should I believe in God at all, if it is just a matter of faith? Why should I believe in this God rather than Allah? Allah is a good, nice alternative today, right? Why should we give them a free pass on this? We need to back up and learn to witness more effectively so we do not get caught up in all the traditional things about Mary, the Rosary, Purgatory, works, and so on. If they can come back to clarity and inexcusability, we can lay the groundwork for accomplishing so much more. We have to learn to witness. "That all of them may be one, Father, just as you are in me and I am in you. May they also be in us so that the world may believe that you have sent me" (Jn. 17:21). I am not going to get to fruit today, so I will have to pick up on this

22. *This Rock*, was a journal of Catholic apologetics and evangelization. Today it is known as *Catholic Answers Magazine*, www.catholic.com.

topic again. John 17:22 says, "that they may be one as we are one." The kind of unity there is between Father, Son, Holy Spirit; prophet, priest, king—the triune personality—is how we are to be one. This is another dimension of our oneness—our unity. Then John 17:23 says, "May they be brought to complete unity." I think we can remember this: 21, 22, 23. We have numbered them; three times Jesus speaks about unity, that the world might believe.

We go from seeing that a part of maturity is coming into fullness, and part of fullness is to attain unity. The unity of the body is against divisions. It is in this context that the people of God will bear fruit. Much fruit. Fruit that will last. I will speak further about fruit. Let me just say that there are different kinds of fruit. The primary sense of fruit goes back to Genesis. It is clear that it is not numbers. When it says, "make disciples," notice that it does not say "converts." In a sense, there are also numbers of a kind, right? You do not want to minimize numbers. We do not want to neglect that there are other dimensions of fruit, like good deeds, which are not necessarily converts, like giving a glass of water to a disciple, visiting someone in prison, or caring for widows and orphans. These are good deeds, which is fruit, too—in a kingly dimension, in the realm of deeds.

There is also fruit in terms of the fruit of the Spirit, in terms of our character. This is more of a priestly realm of fruit. There is fruit connected with understanding. Our understanding is fruitful, or if we speak in a certain way, it edifies others. There is fruit in all of these dimensions. The Scriptures speak about cooperative work: One plants, another one waters, and God gives the increase.[23] We do not want to fail to recognize these other dimensions of fruit, but all of these will converge, in the end, in bringing fruit. Before we think about maturity and bearing fruit, let us go back to see that prior things are in place. The element of maturity, moving toward fullness, and attaining to unity. Then, we can begin to discuss, understand, and think about fruit. We will have to leave it here for now.

23. *1 Corinthians 3:6* KJV.

4

Unity in the Body of Christ

Fullness Is Attained through Unity

2007

Ephesians 4:7–16

7But to each one of us grace has been given as Christ apportioned it. 8This
is why it says:

"When he ascended on high,
he led captives in his train
and gave gifts to men."

9(What does "he ascended" mean except that he also descended to the
lower, earthly regions? 10He who descended is the very one who ascended
higher than all the heavens, in order to fill the whole universe.) 11It was he
who gave some to be apostles, some to be prophets, some to be evangelists,
and some to be pastors and teachers, 12to prepare God's people for works
of service, so that the body of Christ may be built up 13until we all reach
unity in the faith and in the knowledge of the Son of God and become
mature, attaining to the whole measure of the fullness of Christ.

14Then we will no longer be infants, tossed back and forth by the waves,
and blown here and there by every wind of teaching and by the cunning
and craftiness of men in their deceitful scheming. 15Instead, speaking the
truth in love, we will in all things grow up into him who is the Head,
that is, Christ. 16From him the whole body, joined and held together by
every supporting ligament, grows and builds itself up in love, as each part
does its work.

JESUS' HIGH PRIESTLY PRAYER

JESUS PRAYED FOR HIS PEOPLE. THIS PRAYER, which is called His High Priestly Prayer, is recorded in John 17. Three times in this chapter, He prays that they might be one, that the world might believe,[1] and He prays that He would bring glory to His Father through making His Father known. Let us briefly look at these passages to get unity and making God known into focus. We should note them and remember them so that we can have quick access to them when we want to turn to them and when we want to share them with others.

All of this begins with glorifying God. "Father, the time has come. Glorify your Son, that your Son may glorify you" (Jn. 17:1b). It begins this way. It ends with, "Father, I want those you have given me to be with me where I am, and to see my glory, the glory you have given me because you loved me before the creation of the world" (Jn. 17:24). Then He says, "I have made you known to them, and will continue to make you known in order that the love you have for me may be in them and that I myself may be in them" (Jn. 17:26). This is the love of God coming to us in our having the blessing of eternal life, which is knowing God.[2] It is connected with the Church being one.

In John 17:11, Jesus says, "I will remain in the world no longer, but they are still in the world, and I am coming to you. Holy Father, protect them by the power of your name—the name you gave me—so that they may be one as we are one." There are different senses of the oneness of Christ with the Father, and these work together; they are inseparable, while they may be distinct.[3] There is Christ in His incarnate state as the Son of God, where He submits to the will of the Father even to the point of death. "You are in me, and I am in you."[4] As He puts it in the picture given to us about the vine and the branches: "Abide in me, and

---

1. *John 17:21, 22, 23.* Paraphrased. See the explanation in Sermon 3 in this book: "Maturity, Fruit, Unity, and Fullness" (2007).

2. *John 17:3;* Gangadean, *Philosophical Foundation*, 171–177, 208–211; Gangadean, *The Westminster Catechisms*, 109–111, 321–325; Gangadean, "Paper No. 6: The Good," 29–31; "Paper No. 42: The Moral Law (ML1 Expanded)," 231–235; "Paper No. 106: The Good and Heaven," 547–556; "Paper No. 115: Doxological Christianity," 595–596; "Paper No. 116: The Knowledge of God vs. The Hope of Heaven," 597–598; "Paper No. 117: Knowing and Making God Known," in *The Logos Papers*, 599–601; Gangadean, *On Natural and Revealed Theology*, 33–39.

3. Gangadean, *The Westminster Confession*, 47–60.

4. *John 14:20.*

I in you" (Jn. 15:4 KJV). This is spoken of as God's Word remaining in us, and we obeying that Word. This is the unity between the Son and the Father and between Christ and His people. When He prays "that they may be one as we are one"(Jn. 17:22b), it is the Father, the Son, and the Holy Spirit. The very unity in the Godhead is for us, that we might be one as the Father, the Son, and the Holy Spirit are one.

This oneness comes about, as Jesus says here, "by the power of your name" (Jn. 17:11). The name represents all that God is and the truth of who God is: the truth made known and expressed in the name of God. He is praying that we will be kept through our knowledge of God. It is this knowledge which is transformative and sanctifying. It is this knowledge of God that sets us free, as we will see later on. We are to be kept by the power of His name. We said that the good is powerful, transformative—the most powerful reality there is.[5] Just as knowing the truth sets us free (there is that power), He also says, "Sanctify them by the truth; your word is truth" (Jn. 17:17).

Jesus prays "that they may be one as we are one" (Jn. 17:22b)—"we" meaning Father, Son, and Holy Spirit. Here, He does not say the ultimate purpose, but certainly, He is saying that we are to be one and how we are to be one. In verse 20, He says, "My prayer is not for them alone. I pray also for those who will believe in me through their message." Who are they? This includes everyone since the days of the Apostles—every believer on the face of the earth. Christ is praying that all of us would be one. All of us have come to believe through the word that they have spoken. Notice it is not apart from the word spoken by other believers. Others come in, and we are to be one. "Those who will believe in me through their message, that all of them may be one, Father, just as you are in me and I am in you" (Jn. 17:20b–21a). Again, the unity between the Father and the Son, and the Father and the Son incarnate—this unity is to be among believers and with God. "May they also be in us so that the world may believe that you have sent me" (Jn. 17:21b).

Jesus adds to this, in terms of numbers, that *all* may be one, and He adds—in terms of the purpose—that the world may believe. With the view that not only others will believe, those who hear the word, but *the world* will believe. This belief is connected with the believers

5. Gangadean, *Philosophical Foundation*, 208–211.

being one as the Father, Son, and Holy Spirit are one. He continues in John 17:22, "I have given them the glory that you gave me that they may be one as we are one." We will come back to this point. There is a glory that God gives, and this glory is instrumental and effectual in making us one. The truth is given—the preaching of the Word, the name of God—but there is also, in addition, a glory that is given. We have to look at and specify this glory and understand how it works. "That they may be one as we are one" (Jn. 17:22b). "I in them and you in me," in verse 23, and "May they be brought to complete unity." There is a process going on, moving toward unity. We need to note that the process does not end immediately after we come to Christ; it really begins there. We are to be brought to *complete* unity. "To let the world know that you sent me and have loved them even as you have loved me" (Jn. 17:23).

It would be hard, impossible, to separate the unity of believers from the evangelizing of the world in the mind of Christ. It is stated quite clearly here. Yet, as we look at the condition of things, the Church is not manifesting this unity and it is quite strained. The world is not paying attention and it is disregarding much, if not all, of what we have to say. We need to take seriously this concern of our Lord: that we might be one through the truth, through the name of God, the power of His name, the word that is spoken by others, as well as the glory that is given to us. We can hope and expect the world will believe when we are one. We can hope and expect that the Church will be one. We are not to yield to the view that, 'Well, it has been this way for so long; it will always be this way.' It will *not* be this way forever.

The Word of God will prevail; it will have its way. The Holy Spirit, the Almighty God, is going to work in the body of Christ's members to illumine their minds to bring them to the truth. This truth will set us free. It will sanctify us. We will overcome all those things that divide us, including the lethargy into which our minds have fallen in this kind of hopeless despair: 'What can we say? What can we do?'

We believe that by the preaching of the Word of God—*the* Word of God, without our personal spin on it, but what the Holy Spirit has enabled the Church to see—by preaching the Word, that the bones will be joined to each other, that the bones will come alive. That sinews and flesh will come upon those bones, and the breath of God will enter into these beings, and they will be a great army on the earth. God said to Ezekiel, "Prophesy to these bones and say to them, 'Dry bones, hear the word of the LORD!'" (Ezek. 37:4b). God said to prophesy to these bones, to preach the Word to these bones, and they came alive. We believe the truth of Jesus' prayer will happen, and the world will believe. We say this in the face of many who say it will not happen, or they expect it to happen in the next life, or they expect it to happen when Christ comes and rules in some external display of power and glory rather than the power and glory of the Holy Spirit illuminating our minds to the truth. We affirm this to be true in the teaching of Christ's words: "that all of them may be one, Father, just as you are in me and I am in you. May they also be in us so that the world may believe that you have sent me" (Jn. 17:21).

THE UNITY OF THE SPIRIT AND THE UNITY OF THE FAITH

Let us continue looking at this theme through the passage in Ephesians 4. Here, we need to distinguish between the unity of the *Spirit* and the unity of the *faith*. Ephesians 4:1–3 says,

> As a prisoner for the LORD, then, I urge you to live a life worthy of the calling you have received. Be completely humble and gentle; be patient, bearing with one another in love. Make every effort to keep the unity of the Spirit through the bond of peace.

This is God's call upon all believers worldwide: all who call upon the Lord Jesus Christ in truth. It does not matter what group they belong to; they are brothers and sisters in Christ, and we are to keep the unity of the Spirit. The character that we must have to keep the unity of the Spirit is to be "completely humble and gentle" (Eph. 4:2a). We need to deal with attitudes in our hearts that have been there, where we are not humble, we are not gentle, we are not patient and bearing with one another in love, and we are not making efforts to keep the unity of the Spirit through the bond of peace.

This unity has been established by virtue of the regenerating work of the Holy Spirit and our being grafted into Christ and the body of Christ. He says, "There is one body and one Spirit—just as you were called to one hope when you were called" (Eph. 4:4). Even though we may have different views of this hope in various levels of thinking about it, there is one hope, "one LORD, one faith, one baptism" (Eph. 4:5). We are called to preserve the unity of the Spirit with any other group whose baptism we accept because it aligns with the truth of God's Word. "One God and Father of all, who is over all and through all and in all" (Eph. 4:6)—this includes all believers. Then it says, **"But."** Having spoken about this unity, there is a "but," there is a diversity. Unity is there; the unity of the Spirit is to be kept. We are to speak to our brothers and sisters in Christ *as* brothers and sisters in Christ. We are never to let go of this. If we cannot hold on to this, we cannot go on to the unity of the faith.

Paul says, **"But to each one of us grace has been given as Christ apportioned it"** (v. 7). Remember, we spoke about: "I have given them the glory you gave me, that they may be one" (Jn. 17:22). Now it speaks about grace given to each one distinctly. It says God **"gave gifts to men"** (v. 8b) and specifies some of those gifts and their purpose. First, the one who gives it, the one who descended and ascended, is Christ the Lord. He descended in His incarnation, He ascended in His triumph over sin and death. He ascended, and He said, "All authority in heaven and on earth has been given to me" (Matt. 28:18). Here, it says, **"He who descended is the very one who ascended higher than all the heavens, in order to fill the whole universe"** (v. 10). We have to keep this in mind. This dimension of Christ is why He gave gifts: **"to fill the whole universe"** (v. 10b) and to fill "everything in every way" (Eph. 1:23b). We cannot miss this. Remember, there is a unity between the Father and the Son. The Father has bestowed everything on the Son, given authority over everything in the whole universe to the Son, and we are heirs of this in Christ. The Father desires to bless and to glorify the Son by putting Him in this position and giving Him a people.

The Son's purpose is to glorify the Father and make His name known. He is to fill "everything in every way" (Eph. 1:23b). If our thoughts come short of this, we will not come into the unity of the faith. Is the unity of the Spirit already in place? We have to maintain this, keep it, and continue to the unity of the faith. When Jesus prays that they might be one and be brought into complete unity,[6] He is not referring to the unity of the spirit but to the unity of the faith. That is, we are

6. *John 17:22–23;* Sermon 2: "Maturity, Fruit, Unity, and Fullness" (2007).

to come into it. The same process He specifies in John 17 is the same process elsewhere: through the truth.

He gave gifts to the Church. Among them are the apostles and prophets, and evangelists, and some are pastors and teachers—those two go together. We speak about them as the *pastor-teachers*. The Apostles' work has been done and is contained in the Scriptures. The work of the prophets in laying the foundation for the early Church, along with the contributions of earlier prophets, is documented in the Scriptures. There is the work of the evangelists—they may go out and plant new churches. Then, the regular offices that are established in the Church are the pastor-teachers. We see this happening in the Book of Acts. God did this, Ephesians 4:12–13a says, **"to prepare God's people for works of service, so that the body of Christ may be built up until we all reach unity in the faith and knowledge of the Son of God and become mature"**—comma? There is no comma in what I have read. It all goes together.—**"So that the body of Christ may be built up until we all reach unity in the faith and in the knowledge of the Son of God and become mature"** (vv. 12b–13a). Catch your breath and continue: **"attaining to the whole measure of the fullness of Christ"** (v. 13b)—the One who is to fill "everything in every way" (Eph. 1:23b). We cannot understand the various gifts that Christ has given apart from the goal of filling everything in every way. We must understand the diversity there is in Christ, the richness that is in Christ, and the intention of the diversity, that we be cultivated to develop this, that Christ may fill everything in every way through His body.

Our vision needs to be enlarged. We need to be enlarged, first of all, by believing that we are to be one. We are to be one in this, here and now. Even if 1,800 years have gone by and there has been fragmenting of various amounts in the Church, we are still to be one that the world might believe.[7] There is the unity of the Spirit and the unity of the faith. This passage in Ephesians speaks about four things, and I summarized them in the Focus for the Week. *Preparation:* **"to prepare God's people for works of service"** (v. 12a); the work of the pastor-teachers is to prepare God's people for works of service. It is a preparation, and there is to be service as a result. The members of the body of Christ are to be engaged in a particular kind of service *in* the body of Christ and

7. *John 17:22;* Sermon 2: "Maturity, Fruit, Unity, and Fullness" (2007).

in the world. The ultimate goal is the glory of God and Christ filling everything in every way. There is, first of all, preparation, and we will speak more about this. When this preparation is in place, we will come to maturity. It says, **"until we all reach unity in the faith and in the knowledge of the Son of God and become mature"** (v. 13a).

We begin in an immature state and come to maturity. We cannot make the beginning state of the Christian life—the simplest, lowest common denominator—to be the standard. It is simply wrong. It is unbiblical. It is dishonoring to Christ to think this way. We cannot; we must not allow ourselves to continue this way. We must not confuse the unity of the Spirit—which includes every child of God from the moment they draw their first breath as a believer—with the unity of the faith, which involves maturity in Christ.

We have to note the *means:* the work of the pastor-teachers. Building on the work of the apostles, prophets, and evangelists, the work of the pastor-teachers goes on, and the work of the pastor-teachers is a cumulative work in history.[8] It is not each and every pastor-teacher, separate from others in the past, going directly back to the Apostles. There is a cumulative work going on in history; without this, we will not be prepared for works of service. As the people are prepared for works of service, **"the body of Christ may be built up"** (v. 12b). The body is to be built up both internally and externally. Internally, in terms of what we minister to each other, our sanctification, our strength, and our unity, and externally, in terms of numbers as more members are added to the body of Christ. It is not to stop internally **"until we all reach unity in the faith and in the knowledge of the Son of God and become mature, attaining to the whole measure of the fullness of Jesus Christ"** (v. 13). This is Christ who is to fill "everything in every way" (Eph. 1:23b). Internally, in terms of our knowledge of God and the maturity in our understanding, as well as externally in terms of numbers, it does not stop. The numbers do not stop until all the nations are brought to Christ, until all the nations are discipled. All the nations are not simply to be converted: They are discipled, and they are taught to obey all things whatsoever Christ has commanded.[9] This is the work of the pastor-teachers. As the people of God are prepared,

8. Gangadean, *The Westminster Confession;* Gangadean, *The Westminster Catechisms.*

9. *Matthew 28:18–20.*

the body of Christ is built up, and in that context, we reach unity in the faith. The pastor-teachers doing their work, the people doing their work, the body of Christ being built up, and in that context, we attain to the unity of the faith. Please note the order, and we will specify that more as we go along.

Notice the *extent:* to "**become mature, attaining to the whole measure of the fullness of Christ**" (v. 13b). Can we say that any *one* has? I do not think anyone would even entertain that thought. It is specified here, and it is not just for each one; it is for all of us together because it says, "**until we *all* reach unity in the faith**" (v. 13a).[10] You cannot reach unity in the faith by yourself; it is unity with others. "**Until we all reach unity in the faith and in the knowledge of the Son of God**" (v. 13a). We *all* reach the unity of the faith and in the knowledge of the Son of God. We may have all kinds of different views about who Christ is and what He has done, or how He is going to do His work—the person and work of Christ—but we have to attain unity in this and so become mature. Then, in the mature state, believers continue to serve each other, to become knit together, it makes increase of itself in love, and it should be a kind of crescendoing effect as we grow: It snowballs, and it gets richer, fuller, faster, more magnificent, more powerful, more glorious. It can reach a take-off point; we should expect it to reach a certain take-off point.

There is a *pressing ahead.* It may happen locally in particular bodies, as well as in nations and the world. This is what is expected when we speak about the unity in the body of Christ. It is contrasted with being "**infants, tossed back and forth by the waves, and blown here and there by every wind of teaching and by the cunning and craftiness of men in their deceitful scheming**" (v. 14). There is an Arminian/Calvinist Reformed doctrine that divides people; people quote a verse here and quote a verse there, and you toss back and forth. This is not supposed to happen. In eschatology, they toss a verse here, and they toss a verse there, and they toss back and forth, and they say, 'We do not know,' and they say, humorously supposedly, 'We are pan-mil: it will all pan out in the end.' This is not the biblical teaching. This is being an infant. This is not being mature. This is saying, 'We do not have the foundation in place. We are not established in the goal. We do not

10. Emphasis added.

have the idea of the fullness of Christ and how this will be attained.' It is simply not acceptable. In this, we see **"the cunning and craftiness of men in their deceitful scheming"** (v. 14b). There is a lot of sleight of hand and wordplay with some of these teachings, as people try to make a name and get a following. Ambiguating the word *justification,* as we saw last time by speaking of forensic justification.[11] It has to do with church membership and some boundary laws that we talked about. These are sleight of hand. It needs to come back to the work of the pastor-teachers, where there has been much discussion. We should not listen to any of the cunning and craftiness and we should require them to answer: 'How does that compare with what the Holy Spirit has taught the Church from His Word?' I want to forge a connection with that concept, underscoring the pivotal role of the Holy Spirit in instructing the Church through pastor-teachers. Those whose teachings are contrary to this must feel a sense of obligation to articulate their stance in relation to this teaching, steering clear of any inclination to bypass or neglect it. Is there anything new that you are bringing? Is there something more? Is there something different? Define yourself in relation to *this.* 'Who goes there?' as the night watchman says. Do not give that person a pass. Do not let them avoid the truth. We will not be children tossed back and forth. It is lamentable to witness the state of the Church, where divisions persist and the foundation has not been laid. Basic truths about God, the name of God—who He is and what His purpose is on the earth—are not being seen and understood.

In contrast to the teachings of man and cunning and craftiness is the work of the Holy Spirit through the pastor-teachers in Church history. This is the contrast. **"Speaking the truth in love, we will in all things"**—there it is: fullness—**"we will in all things grow up into him who is the Head, that is, Christ. From him the whole body, joined and held together by every supporting ligament, grows and builds itself up in love"** (vv. 15–16a). These fundamental truths, these foundational teachings, are what hold us together. Based on these truths in us, we minister the Word of God, and the body builds itself up in love. The pastor and the elders do not do that work. It is to be done by each member of the body. The church's leadership equips each member of the body to do the work and calls them to do the work. Each of us here

11. N.T. Wright, *Justification: God's Plan and Paul's Vision* (Downers Grove: InterVarsity Press, 2009).

has to be knit together with the members of the body and what they supply. If you feel you are not knit together, you feel you are standing out there alone, you have to go back and say, 'What has God given me? How can I serve?' If you say, 'Well, there does not seem to be a place for service; it is not recognized,' I do not believe that. I believe that when our gifts are developed, they will perform their function; they will cut a channel to make themselves manifest and useful in the body of Christ. We do not always have to wait for a certain situation to develop.

We have spoken about the unity of the Spirit, the unity of the faith and how we are to come into this, and how this connects with Jesus' prayer that they might be one. Let us notice that it speaks about preparation—preparation, maturity, unity, and fullness. We are to attain to the whole measure of the fullness of Christ; these go together, and they cannot be separated. There is an order in which it unfolds.

FULLNESS AND UNITY

We are being called to fullness. We spoke about this in terms of Christ filling "everything in every way" (Eph. 1:23b), but He starts by filling us, each one, in every way, in every dimension of our being. We should understand there are many dimensions of our being. I want to run through these dimensions briefly. We have stated these before. This is by way of repetition for many, and I am learning very slowly that the main part of teaching is repetition; this has been so hard for me to learn. I do not know why. Someone has to repeat it to me, I guess.

1) Larger Aspect

There is a larger aspect of our person, of our being: we are finite, temporal, and changeable within our being, wisdom, power, holiness, justice, goodness, and truth; this is true of all human beings.[12] We have to understand what the larger aspect is, and the formal content of it. We have to understand how all of those are related, how we are finite, temporal, and changeable, and what each of these words mean. There is a difference between being temporal and being changeable, and how our finitude works in all of this. Even at that point, there is all kinds

12. Gangadean, *The Westminster Confession,* 79–83.

of diversity, as well as unity, in our being human. We want to notice wisdom, power, holiness, justice, goodness, and truth. All of these are distinct and yet united.

2) Narrower Aspect

We can speak about a narrower aspect of our personality, and it makes the difference between being fallen or regenerate, where we are recreated in knowledge, holiness, and righteousness in the core center of our being called *the heart*. This makes the difference between being a believer or not being a believer. We should not have a false unity between believer and non-believer. We should understand how we are recreated in all aspects—our whole heart. To understand what it is to love the Lord our God with our whole being, our whole heart—not only in the practical order of things, not only in the personal-relational-emotional order of things, not only in doctrinal matters but with our whole heart.

3) Triune Personality

This brings us to the third layer of our being—all of this in the context of fullness, and Christ is to fill everything in every way—which is our triune personality. Here, we speak of being created in knowledge, holiness, and righteousness, corresponding with the functions of prophet, priest, and king.[13] We must recognize that there *is* a difference between human beings in terms of differences and emphasis: We have all three in each one of us. Each person has the heart of knowledge, holiness, and righteousness. There is diversity, and there is unity, and this unity is through order. As there is an order within Father, Son, and Holy Spirit, so there is an order between prophet, priest, and king. There is an order between reason, intuition, and sense experience, and we are not to reverse the order and set up one as authoritative, where it should be submitting, receiving, and operating from another. So many of our problems develop here: I am of Paul; and I of Apollos; and I of Cephas. The divisions in the Church that Paul speaks of in Corinthians go back to this diversity. We are not loving God with our whole hearts, we are all going off in different directions, and we are not observing the order. We have to come back and recognize, as Paul said, "Is Christ

13. Gangadean, *The Westminster Catechisms,* 163–168.

divided?" (1 Cor. 1:13a). Christ is prophet, priest, and king, and these are in perfect unity in Him.

4) Body/Soul Unity

We are a body/soul unity. We are not a body. We are not a soul. We are not an angel that happens to be in a body. We are not merely a body. We are a body/soul unity. Here, we have divisions within the Church between being this-worldly and otherworldly. I was thinking today that we have been challenged by Marx, Nietzsche, and Freud, to name just three, on our otherworldliness—a view of disembodied existence in heaven, and receiving the fullness of the blessing in heaven. They were challenging us, and we did not heed that challenge. God raised them up for this, and we still do not pay much attention. We are still continuing in our otherworldly, heavenly view of God's purpose. This view comes out of a misunderstanding of body/soul unity: the soul will go on, and the body will remain behind. We are to recognize the difference between fruit sin in the body, like sexual immorality, and the root sin in the soul, which is a result of emptiness in life, and how we try to fill this emptiness. In sexual immorality, there is an attempt to achieve a certain kind of unity. This desire and drive for unity and fullness is in the sexual union—or it is sought in this—but without the soul, without love, it does not remain. We split body and soul in this way instead of seeing they are a unity and Christ is to fill everything in every way.

5) Male/Female Unity

Then there is the male/female distinction. Male and female are characteristics in God and in man. We are to see them first in God and then in man. This is part of the name of God. "Protect them by the power of your name—the name you gave me—so that they may be one as we are one" (Jn. 17:11b). How badly split are we? How much difficulty is there in men and women not recognizing their position before God, their roles, and not being able to come together very well in marriage? When we marry without this in place, we have so much strain. Consider the feminist agenda and the various reactions it has elicited. These responses, at times escalating to the level of rebellion, are important for us to understand as we strive to honor Christ and fill everything in every way. Remember the covenant of creation and the covenant of marriage from Genesis 2.[14] The name of God is revealed in this, and the name of God is revealed throughout the Scriptures. The covenant of marriage is one of the most basic ways in which the relationship between God and man is spoken of. Christ and the Church: the Church is spoken as the Bride of Christ, Israel, the people of God, and the covenant people. God reveals Himself in the covenant of marriage, and we are to have the truth about this, be established in this truth, and go on to maturity and fullness.

6) Background

Then there are our background factors, including ethnic factors, and we are aware of this more and more now as we become global. We are having to struggle between the core of the gospel and what is of culture. How do we handle it? Do we understand how to deal with people from different backgrounds and affirm what is there?

There is a difference between young and old in the body of Christ, and there is a split: "And he shall turn the heart of the fathers to the children, and the heart of the children to their fathers, lest I come and smite the earth with a curse" (Mal. 4:6 KJV). We are to transmit the wisdom of the previous generation to the next, and we are not to neglect this and run into the pattern that divides the world between the Boomers, and Gen X, and the Millennials. We split off, and are being conformed to the world when we do this, rather than recognizing how we are to be united in Christ. This is all part of our background.

There is a rich/poor division and a Greek/Barbarian division and a slave/free division based on economic factors. How much did Marx consider this? The Greek/Barbarian factor is between the educated and the uneducated. This is the basic point being made in that division: the Greek with their educational development compared to others. Then there is a Jew/Gentile difference between those who are brought up in the Church, covenant people, and those who are not. Relatively speaking, those who come into the Church by way of conversion are like the Gentiles. Those who have been raised in the Church are like the Jews: covenant people. The difference between covenant people and converts has been a source of strain in the Church.

---

14. Gangadean, *The Biblical Worldview,* 147–158.

All of these background factors are to be overcome in Christ through the truth, through understanding the truth, and through having the foundation laid. We are not to have these divisions; we are to be one as Father, Son, and Holy Spirit are one.

7) Uniqueness

Through all the similarities—our background and other similarities—there is a uniqueness in each of us and a particular talent that is given to each in the uniqueness of our being; in a particular way, we are called to show forth the glory of God. Then, we are to relate all of these factors properly. Just as we are to properly relate prophet, priest, and king, we are to relate all of these factors of our personality.

UNITY OF DIVERSITY AND FULLNESS

I began discussing these dimensions of our being in the context of fullness. We are to attain to the full measure of the stature of Jesus Christ,[15] the fullness of Christ is to fill everything in every way,[16] and the fullness is to be in the world: all the nations are to come. There is to be fullness and unity in each person and between persons.

As a reminder, we have spoken about the spiritual war that is age-long and agonizing.[17] I am overcoming my resistance to repetition. The war goes on in a person; think about all the levels and dimensions in a person. It is between persons: husbands and wives, parents and children. In a church, there are differences between us within this group. It is there between churches, in a nation and between nations, and between groups of nations—whole civilizations—and between the kingdom of God and the kingdom of darkness. These are divisions that come to the point of conflict and intense warfare, and as we speak about unity in the body of Christ, all of these are to be overcome. They can be overcome if we understand, not by making male into female—feminizing the culture, as Nietzsche argued against—or female into male, but by recognizing the differences. We are to understand role and gender models and not be confused as we are today. We are not to have a narrow view of what

15. *Ephesians 4:13* KJV.

16. *Ephesians 1:23.*

17. Gangadean, *The Biblical Worldview,* 275–294.

it is to be masculine or a narrow view of what it is to be feminine. These are very close to our personal identity and how we carry ourselves in the world, but we have to go back to the basic truths.

MATURITY AND SERVICE

We are joined and held together as each part does its work. I want to draw attention to 1 Corinthians 12 and go back to the words of Jesus: "I have given them the glory that you gave me, that they may be one as we are one" (Jn. 17:22). 1 Corinthians 12:24–26 says,

> But God has combined the members of the body and has given greater honor to the parts that lacked it, so that there should be no division in the body, but that its parts should have equal concern for each other.

Some parts are more presentable, and some are less presentable. "And the parts that are unpresentable are treated with special modesty, while our presentable parts need no special treatment" (1 Cor. 12:23b–24a). Everything that is covered in clothes is less presentable. If we think of cultures where there are fewer clothes, but there are still some clothes, we are getting to the less and less presentable parts. They cannot be presented publicly, right? Upon the parts that are less presentable, there is more honor bestowed. No one wants to go into your organs and take a look, but try getting along without these organs that are hidden by the skin on your body.

He has given gifts to each. He has given His glory to each of us, and we need each other. There is real difference and real need for each other, and one cannot say, 'I do not need you,' or 'Because I am not like this one, I do not have a part in the body.' "The eye cannot say to the hand, 'I don't need you!' And the head cannot say to the feet, 'I don't need you!'" (1 Cor. 12:21). Everyone is given a particular ability. I hear even the little toe on your foot has a use; I am not sure what it is, but I hear that if it is not there, you feel it, and I am sure that some of you will fill me in quickly about the use of it. I am not saying someone is just to be understood as a little toe in the kingdom of God; maybe like a foot, not a little toe. It is a whole foot; try to get along without anything from your ankle down.

God has made it so, "so that there should be no division in the body, but that its parts should have equal concern for each other. If one part suffers, every part suffers with it; if one part is honored, every part rejoices with it" (1 Cor. 12:25–26). Let us keep the main point: We are members one of another, and every one has a part to play, and notice it says, *equally honored.* It is when we start getting airs about ourselves and think, 'I am more important than you,' the way the disciples ask, 'Who is first in the kingdom of heaven?', and then we start provoking each other and envying and there is rivalry and divisions. Our minds are already off the truth of God when we do this. It is **"as each part does its work"** (v. 16b) and serves in the body that this knitting together occurs, and the concern one for another occurs, and it does not occur apart from that. Each part must *supply* to others and *receive* from others. Without supplying and receiving, there is no knitting together. If one part is just giving and giving and giving and not receiving, it will get exhausted; it just does not work that way in the body. One could have a pretty lame body, and that is, I suppose, the point of so much of the healing of Jesus' ministry: as a sign of our spiritual condition individually, and our spiritual condition together.

We are crippled, we are lame, we are blind, we are deaf, we are dumb. We are unclean with leprosy. Christ wants to heal this body, to have a glorious body, a Church that is without stain or wrinkle—the bride of Christ.[18] We stand as the bride comes in at a wedding, and everyone wants to turn and look at the bride coming in. 'The groom? He is up there.' But the bride: Think about the bride of Christ. All heads in the universe will turn to look at this bride—glorious, shining as the sun; beautiful in splendor, in the holiness of Christ, without spot or stain. He died for this and sent His Spirit to work for this. All these hideous things right now in the Church: they must go; they will go. Christ will have a people, a bride, without spot, stain, wrinkle, or any such thing; glorious as the sun, shining in its strength, **"as each part does its work"** (v. 16b).

There is a connection between coming to maturity and having the foundation laid. In Ephesians 4:13–14, we have already seen that we will become mature, and we will be no more tossed back and forth like children. **"Then we will no longer be infants, tossed back and forth by**

18. *Ephesians 5:25–27.*

the waves, and blown here and there by every wind of teaching and by the cunning and craftiness of men in their deceitful scheming" (v. 14). The contrast is here, as the pastor-teachers do their work: **"It was he who gave some to be apostles, some to be prophets, some to be evangelists, and some to be pastors and teachers, to prepare God's people for works of service, so that the body of Christ may be built up"** (vs. 11–12). In Hebrews 5:11–13, we have the same point made again, and I am building to a point on this matter: foundation and maturity. Hebrews 5 says, concerning Melchizedek, the priesthood of Christ:

> We have much to say about this, but it is hard to explain because you are slow to learn. In fact, though by this time you ought to be teachers, you need someone to teach you the elementary truths of God's word all over again. You need milk, not solid food! Anyone who lives on milk, being still an infant, is not acquainted with the teaching about righteousness.

The Scripture recognizes this condition of being genuinely in Christ, but being an infant, and being an infant even when we should be teachers—this is hideous; this is not comely; it is not right. How many of you parents will fuss over your children if their speech does not develop on time? Now, what if they are 20 years old and acting as if they are one year old? We grieve in the case of Down syndrome, but we also rejoice for what blessing and special conditions the Lord has given. But this is not to be our condition; we are to come to maturity, which is done by having the foundation laid. At the end of chapter 5, it says, "But solid food is for the *mature*"[19]—here is that word again—"who by constant use have trained themselves to distinguish good from evil" (Heb. 5:14). They have trained themselves.

Last week, I spoke about Jesus learning obedience through what He suffered[20] and so He was able to endure the cross.[21] He came to this in true humanity: growing in wisdom and stature, learning obedience by what He suffered. He was able to take on the suffering of the cross in the end by the power of the Holy Spirit enabling Him. Not in His deity, because when He was confronted with the temptation, He said,

19. Emphasis added.

20. *Hebrews 5:8.*

21. *Hebrews 12:2.*

"Man does not live on bread alone." The tempter said, "If you are the Son of God," and He said, "Man does not live on bread alone" (Matt. 4:3–4; Lk. 4:3–4). He faced the temptation as a man; man anointed by the Spirit, enabled by the Spirit—the same is true for all of us—so that He could be a faithful high priest to us.

We are to train ourselves to distinguish—notice—good and evil. How basic can you get? We can talk about fruit sin, but can we talk about root sin? If we cannot see root sin, can we understand the justice of God? Can we learn the fear of the Lord? We have to undergo training to get this, instead of being 20 years old physically and one year old in terms of maturity in the faith. It says in chapter 6, "Therefore let us leave the elementary teachings"—the foundational teachings—"and go on to maturity" (Heb. 6:1a). The word for elementary teachings is the *stoicheia* (*στοιχεῖον*)—the basic elements—and the same word is used for *foundational teachings*. I want to make this point because I am going to connect this with a certain stage that we can measure: Has the foundation been laid?

> Therefore let us leave the elementary teachings about Christ and go on to maturity, not laying again the foundation of repentance from acts that lead to death, and of faith in God, instruction about baptisms, the laying on of hands, the resurrection of the dead, and eternal judgment. And God permitting, we will do so (Heb. 6:1-3).

This passage speaks about the foundational teachings: sin and death and faith in God. What is faith? We need to understand what true faith is, instead of some distortion that we make of faith. Instruction about baptisms is about the work of Christ and the Holy Spirit. The laying on of hands is in connection with the particular calling to which we come. The resurrection of the dead is about eschatology and the rewards that there are in God. These are the fundamental teachings. Is our understanding of heaven consistent with Scripture? How much of this view dominates and blocks us from hearing and leaves us immature? This is the kind of thing that Freud, Marx, and Nietzsche argued against. Their opposition has been raised up by God, in the providence of God, to challenge the Church. We need to hear this specifically, and we have not.

Maturity comes with the foundation. This idea is in the three passages: Ephesians 4:13–14, 1 Corinthians 3, and Hebrews 5:11–6:3.

It is in three Scriptures. The witness of the Scripture in three places should speak to our hearts. Let us look at 1 Corinthians 3. We started in Hebrews 5:11–6:3, and now we come to 1 Corinthians 3. This makes the point again: "Brothers, I could not address you as spiritual but as worldly—mere infants in Christ" (1 Cor. 3:1). Here is the infant-maturity theme again:

> I gave you milk, not solid food, for you were not yet ready for it. Indeed, you are still not ready. You are still worldly. For since there is jealousy and quarreling among you, are you not worldly? Are you not acting like mere men? For when one says, 'I follow Paul,' and another, 'I follow Apollos,' are you not mere men? (1 Cor. 3:2–4).

There is the prophetic-priestly-kingly distinction. We have not overcome this any more than we have overcome male and female tensions in the family between husbands and wives; how a wife is to love her husband, and how a husband is to love his wife, and not make it a sameness principle. There is a certain level in which it is the same love, but it comes out differently. We are not yet getting at this. Husbands and wives are to teach, but they are to teach differently within the marriage. There is teaching with a word, and there is teaching without a word. Trust me, without a word is powerful—much more powerful than we realize. Do not think, 'Unless I can open my mouth and speak, I am not saying anything; I am not doing anything.'

Paul goes on to say,

> By the grace God has given me, I laid a foundation as an expert builder, and someone else is building on it. But each one should be careful how he builds. For no one can lay any foundation other than the one already laid, which is Jesus Christ. If any man builds on this foundation using gold, silver, costly stones, wood, hay or straw, his work will be shown for what it is, because the Day will bring it to light. It will be revealed with fire, and the fire will test the quality of each man's work. If what he has built survives, he will receive his reward. If it is burned up, he will suffer loss; he himself will be saved, but only as one escaping through the flames (1 Cor. 3:10–15).

The foundation is laid by Paul, which connects with the foundation described in Hebrews 6—the need for the foundation to go on to maturity, and the ongoing work of the pastor-teachers in laying this foundation. This foundation consists of doctrine. John 8:32: "the truth will set you free." John 17:17: "Sanctify them by the truth; your word is truth." Romans 12:2: "Do not conform any longer to the pattern of this world, but be transformed by the renewing of your mind." This doctrine has specific content, spoken of in Hebrews 6:1–2, which I just reviewed. The foundation is laid through the work of the pastor-teachers, which is cumulative—especially as summed up in the Westminster Confession (we have talked about that in the past).[22] Within the Confession, we can distinguish between what comes after much discussion and what has or has not been discussed, and there are records of this in church history in terms of what teaching has been discussed. It is not just a matter of notable persons. I have noticed a pattern in many segments of the Church to go back to the Church fathers and not to the Confession. They are not the same thing. The foundation is cumulative, it cannot be bypassed, it cannot be neglected, it must go through much discussion.

This foundation is in place when you put it into practice. Our Lord Jesus, at the end of the Sermon on the Mount, said the one who hears His Word and puts it into practice is like the one who digs down and lays His foundation on the rock.[23] This is the one who puts it into practice. The one who does not is like the one who builds on the sand. Jesus again said, "My mother and brothers are those who hear God's word and put it into practice" (Lk. 8:21). There are some who hear the Word of God and do not do it; they do not conform their lives to it. This is noticed, and it affects fellowship. During holidays, we want to spend time with family, and family are those who hear the Word of God and do it. Not those who hear and it goes in one ear and out the other, or in one ear with some quick response and let it go, or respond with the cares of life that choke the Word, but those who hear the Word of God and do it—with understanding, bearing fruit. If that is where you are, these are the persons you want to hang out with. This is family.

Now, children need care. You do not just say, 'Let it go. They are not doing much.' They need care, but this is different from hearing the

22. Gangadean, *The Westminster Confession,* xvii-xxxii.

23. *Matthew 7:24.*

Word of God and doing it. This is our Lord's Word, and we sometimes feel keenly when we are expected to be with family members of our biological family, but the Word of God is not there.

Then last of all, in the novitiate,[24] we are seeking to establish this in practice in people's lives, and we hope to do more and better. Over the months and years, we have been seeing the need for this. I think most of you have seen the novitiate. Many of you have filled it out a number of times. I think we can say now, at the end of five years, if you are doing the novitiate as you should, you should have completed it: the foundation should have been laid by the end of five years. Foundation should be laid in general revelation, in biblical worldview, in the Confession, and in knowledge of Scripture. It should be laid in terms of personal godliness: putting it into practice in your life, in your home life, as well as your work and your service in the church. The foundation must be in place, in practice, to come to maturity, to come to fullness, to attain to the whole measure of the stature of Jesus Christ, and to have the unity that Christ our Lord prayed for—within the Church, and through this in all the earth, that He might fill everything in every way.

24. Gangadean, *The Westminster Confession*, 389–390.

5

State of the Church: By What Authority?

At the Time of Christ, the Apostles, and the Present

2010

Matthew 21:23–27

[23]Jesus entered the temple courts, and, while he was teaching, the chief priests and the elders of the people came to him. "By what authority are you doing these things?" they asked. "And who gave you this authority?"

[24]Jesus replied, "I will also ask you one question. If you answer me, I will tell
you by what authority I am doing these things. [25]John's baptism—where
did it come from? Was it from heaven, or from men?"

[26]They discussed it among themselves and said, "If we say, 'From heaven,' he will ask, 'Then why didn't you believe him?' But if we say, 'From men'—we are afraid of the people, for they all hold that John was a prophet."

[27]So they answered Jesus, "We don't know."

Then he said, "Neither will I tell you by what authority I am doing these things."

INTRODUCTION

AT THE BEGINNING OF EVERY YEAR, it is appropriate for us to consider where we are, the state of the Church, where we have been, and where we are heading. This is a light-of-nature concern. The

President of the United States presents a State of the Union Address and tells us where we have been, where we are, and where we are going. In the Book of Revelation, our Lord gave a State of the Church message. Chapters 2 and 3 look at the state of the Church from the church at Ephesus to the church at Laodicea, and then He continues on to speak about where it is going.[1] Where it is going is quite clear: It goes from that present state to the state depicted in Revelation 21–22. The City of God completed—beautiful, magnificent, glorious, without spot, stain, wrinkle, or any such thing.[2] Can you believe that? This is where we are going.

When you look at where we are, it does not appear this is where we are going. Especially when you look at where the Church has been for a few centuries, it does not look like this is where we are going. The essence of the State of the Church message is to affirm that despite our current condition, we are committed to progress. We acknowledge our present state but express a determination to learn from trials and mistakes. The primary goal is to enhance our obedience to God with the ultimate aim of reaching our destination. This is a general outline of the message, so you know what to expect.

STATE OF THE CHURCH: Revelation 1–3

The churches in the Book of Revelation were in different states. Ephesus had barely begun to decline. They were still orthodox, but they left their first love.[3] It means, therefore, it is possible to leave our first love. We started quite enthusiastically, and then we get to the place where we are holding on to orthodoxy but not pressing ahead. We do not have

1. After a sevenfold description of the state of the Church in John's age in chapters 2–3, the rule of God through the curse and the promise in an age-long spiritual war is unveiled in a sevenfold vision in chapters 6–20: the seven seals, the seven trumpets, the woman and the dragon, the seven bowls, the woman on the beast, the age-long spiritual war (Armageddon—fought with the sword coming out of the mouth), the thousand-year rule of believers (the millennium, in which all rule, who are raised from the dead spiritually—the first resurrection). Each vision covers the entire period of Christ's rule, from the first to the second coming. Each vision depicts the spiritual war between believers and non-believers under different aspects. Each vision shows the conquest of the kingdom of God over the kingdom of darkness.

2. *Ephesians 5:25–27.*

3. *Revelation 2:4.*

zeal for the work of the kingdom. We are to examine ourselves in light of that. Then in the other messages, we see some churches struggling with sin, a particular kind of recurrent sin: sexual sin.[4]

There is the doctrine of the Nicolaitans and Jezebel and the doctrine of Balaam that had caused the women of Moab to seduce the Israelites.[5] Why is this? Because of what happened in the letter to Ephesus: You have left your first love. We are not diligently seeking, understanding, and enjoying God, so these things begin to take place.

The doctrine of the Nicolaitans came about this way: The deacon, Nicholas, is said to have had a beautiful wife, and all the men wanted to enjoy her company in some way or other, and that was accommodated. It was wrong, but this is how it got off the ground, and then it went further to the teaching of Jezebel in the Church. Some churches were quite weak and were encouraged to hold on. Some were challenged by those who claimed to be Jews and were not.[6] Then we come to Laodicea, a church that had become prosperous and well-established. They had 'their building all paid for, enough building space, a good program, and it was a fun place to be.' They had a reputation for being alive, but the Lord Jesus said, "you do not realize that you are wretched, pitiful, poor, blind and naked" (Rev. 3:17b). We can have a false expression of life in the Church and think we are doing fine. He said, "So, because you are lukewarm—neither hot nor cold—I am about to spit you out of my mouth" (Rev. 3:16). It is kind of disgusting to have this wishy-washy, outward religious form. The state of the Church is in various conditions, but we need to look at this from time to time.

What we are told from the beginning and again in the Book of Revelation, through the seven visions that were given, is essentially the same thing we are told in Genesis. There is going to be a spiritual war. "I will put enmity between you and the woman, and between your offspring and hers"—between believer and non-believer. "He will crush your head, and you will strike his heel"(Gen. 3:15–16).

We find in the Book of Revelation that Christ has ascended; He is seated at the right hand of God because He has shed His blood, and because He is perfectly righteous, He is given the position to rule in the place of Adam. He is subduing all things to Himself through the curse

4. *Revelation 2:14–15.*

5. *Numbers 31:16.*

6. *Revelation 2:9, 3:9.*

and the promise. We find the curse being described in various ways in the different visions. The four horsemen: The first is Christ going out, and then war, famine, and plague. Then, the testimony of the Church and the promise were declared. Then, the shaking of the whole order of things. Then, the vision of the 144,000,[7] the complete number of the redeemed: a multitude so great that no one can number them.[8]

Again, with the trumpets, the curse, and the promise, each vision goes through the spiritual war. It is age-long and agonizing, but they each end with the clear affirmation that the kingdom of God overcomes the kingdom of darkness. In connection with this, it is said at the end of each of these letters to the churches that to him who overcomes, he will be given life.[9] Life is described in many different ways. There is a sevenfold description of life: the same reality in seven descriptions, just as the seven visions describe the same reality.

The Church is badly divided in understanding the Book of Revelation because we are badly divided in understanding the Book of Genesis. If we had understood Genesis 1–3, we would *surely* have understood the Book of Revelation. If we had understood what was clear from general revelation, we would have been able to read Genesis 1–3. We work our way back to what is more basic.

The Church is divided, and sometimes there is conflict within the Church, within a congregation, and sometimes between congregations. We have said this before,[10] but it goes back to conflict within oneself, between belief and unbelief. We are always trying to get back to the more basic, to address it properly, so that we might have hope, overcome, and grow. In every trial we experience, we overcome, and that trial becomes a stepping stone to a greater knowledge of God.

Our Lord says persistently that He will give the promise of life to him who overcomes.[11] In the midst of all of our trials, each and every one, we have this hope to overcome, grow, and make progress toward the goal of the earth being filled with the knowledge of God,[12] which

---

7. *Revelation 14:1.*

8. *Revelation 7:9.*

9. *Revelation 2:7, 11, 17, 26, 3:5, 12, 21.*

10. A reference to the seven levels of the spiritual war. See: Gangadean, "Paper No. 109: The Spiritual War (Dimensions)," in *The Logos Papers,* 573–575.

11. *Revelation 2:7, 11, 17, 26, 3:5, 12, 21.*

12. *Isaiah 11:9.*

is the completed city depicted in Revelation 21 and 22. Those who have gone before, Abraham, Isaac, Jacob, Moses, David, Isaiah, and Daniel, are waiting for this work to be completed. They, without us, will not be made complete.[13] They are that cloud of witnesses watching. The baton of faith has been passed on to us. The faith delivered to the saints is now passed on to us. We must now run with perseverance the race that is set before us.[14]

Current Decay of the Culture

In our day, the culture is more decadent. The culture does decay; the process begins, and the culture goes down. We see this pattern from Ephesus to Laodicea.[15] We are either progressing in God and going upward or progressing downward. Some of you do not have many days to think about. I am here to tell you, since I have had many days (not that many really, but a lot more than you), I remember what the 1960s was like. I remember the 50s. I remember the 30s because the echoes of the 30s come into the 50s and 60s. Just yesterday, I watched a movie from the 30s; it was wonderful just to relax and not have all this gunk thrown at you—very relaxing and refreshing. We have decayed; We are going into greater and greater decay, which means the hostility toward the Word of God is increasing. The decay has crept into the Church, and hostility is increasing there, too. The Lord tells us He is sending us out as sheep among wolves.[16] The world is hostile; they will hate you without a cause, the Lord said.[17] They will cook up all kinds of causes and reasons—there is no shortage, but we must take those thoughts captive as they are brought up.

We have to be careful and we are to watch ourselves continually. It is possible to watch ourselves in the sense of navel-gazing; that is not what I mean by watching ourselves. We are to watch ourselves in terms of our lives, and we are to examine ourselves. One of the ways to examine ourselves is to get involved in discussions with others. We get involved in discussions with others on the basis of a commonly

13. *Hebrews 11:39–40.*

14. *Hebrews 12:1–3.*

15. *Revelation 2–3.*

16. *Matthew 10:16.*

17. *John 15:25.*

accepted standard. The mark of self-examination is a willingness to be open to examination by others in light of our standards; I will always emphasize: *in light of our standards.* If the standard is not in place, we cannot proceed. We will see what this standard is. We have been very, very explicit about our standards.[18] We could not become more explicit. We will specify what these standards are.

The Church has ceased to be salt and light, and we are not the head of the culture. We are the tail compared with 200 years ago. We might ask, is there hope? Can we change? I hope we all agree that we need to change; some may not agree. Some think change is not necessary. Why? Because we will just die and go to heaven and get the fullness of the blessing.[19] We are saying, no, that is not true. Jesus said, go and make disciples of all the nations. Teach them to observe all things that I have commanded you.[20] Take every thought captive raised up against the knowledge of God.[21] Jesus said if we were obedient, we would be the head, not the tail.[22] Clearly, we are the tail. These things are given as clear. We ask, is there hope? Can we change? We do not believe that Jesus is going to come back directly and start to rule in Jerusalem and bring about this change. No, we believe He is seated at the right hand of God now. He sent His Spirit to enable us to hear His Word and to be faithful witnesses. He is ruling now. The kingdom is to grow like the mustard seed, it is to spread like the leaven through the entire lump,[23] and it is like the rock of Daniel's vision, not cut out with human hands, that struck the image, grew, and became a mountain and filled the whole earth.[24]

Sometimes, we might find ourselves so alone when we go about in the culture, and we may ask, 'Am I crazy? Am I the only one?' We go back to the Scripture, which is the rock on which we are established.

---

18. Gangadean, *The Westminster Confession;* Gangadean, *The Westminster Catechisms.*

19. Gangadean, *On Natural and Revealed Theology,* 9–39; Gangadean, "Paper No. 106: The Good and Heaven," 547–556; "Paper No. 116: The Knowledge of God vs. The Hope of Heaven," in *The Logos Papers,* 597–598; Gangadean, *Philosophical Foundation,* 40–41, 71–73

20. *Matthew 28:18–20.*

21. *2 Corinthians 10:4–5.*

22. *Deuteronomy 28:13.*

23. *Matthew 13:31–35.*

24. *Daniel 2.*

As soon as we ask, 'Can we change?' any call for change becomes a challenge to the authorities that exist. We are not speaking about change as a general message of hope and change without substance, as it has been said in politics—"Keep hope alive" and "time for change." No, we are specifying the content of this change. We are very specific, very particular, because our Lord is. Make disciples of all the nations; teach them to observe all things that I have commanded you[25] in the context of eternal life as the knowledge of God[26] and through the work of dominion, the earth is to be filled with the knowledge of God.[27] This content can be challenged, but instead of challenging this standard, many other things are challenged in a very roundabout, indirect way. We want to keep bringing the challenge back to where it belongs.

In the Time of Christ, the Apostles, and to the Present

In the time of Christ and the Apostles through history to the present, this challenge has come to the authorities. When John the Baptist came, he was asked, are you the Christ? Are you the Prophet? Are you Elijah? If not, why are you baptizing?[28] John had to explain this. The authorities sent persons from Jerusalem to question John on this.

From the beginning to the end of His ministry, Jesus' authority was challenged. Early in His ministry, when He cleansed the temple, "the Jews demanded of Him, 'What miraculous sign can you show us to prove your authority to do all this?' Jesus answered them, 'Destroy this temple, and I will raise it again in three days'" (Jn. 2:18–19). He was speaking about the temple of His body. He says, "For as Jonah was three days and three nights in the belly of a huge fish, so the Son of Man will be three days and three nights in the heart of the earth" (Matt. 12:40).

The resurrection shows that the Spirit of God was at work and the Spirit of God is approving. Only God can raise the dead. If God raises Him from the dead, then that is the sign that He has authority. The same sign, that was placed in the ark of the covenant, was Aaron's rod that budded.[29] Resurrection life was showing that God had chosen,

25. *Matthew 28:18–20.*

26. *John 17:3.*

27. Gangadean, *The Westminster Confession,* 353–357.

28. *John 1:25.*

29. *Numbers 17.*

through Aaron, the priesthood. It has always been this way. Toward the end of Jesus' life, the authorities came. He had just cleansed the temple a second time. In connection with this, the chief priests and elders of the people, the authorities—the establishment—came to the temple where He was teaching. They came to Him and said, **"By what authority are you doing these things . . . who gave you this authority?"** (v. 23b). Jesus saw through this. They were not really concerned with authority and legitimacy. They wanted to conserve their own authority, and Jesus, by His very presence and being, was a challenge to this. So Jesus addresses it: **"I will also ask you one question. If you answer me, I will tell you by what authority I am doing these things. John's baptism—where did it come from? Was it from heaven, or from men?"** (vv. 24–25a).

Notice how He made it pointed. He did not leave it: **"Where did it come from?"** He put a choice to them—either yes or no. He made the question explicit. People will dodge through it if you do not make the question explicit. These are the only two alternatives: from God or from man? They discussed it. This is not the discussion they were expecting. They discussed it among themselves to see how they could come up with a response that could keep themselves intact, as against a discussion with the Lord Jesus. Would it be great to have a discussion with the Lord Jesus? Would you expect the Lord to cut out any nonsense in our thinking? If we come humbly, understanding our sin, understanding this is where we are and we need correction, then we are okay and we will be glad when He cuts out the nonsense. But if we do not come with an attitude that we have sin, that we need to be cleansed, and we do not come to be instructed, then we will be resistant. We will have an attitude about it.

They go on to say, **"If we say, 'From heaven,' he will ask, 'Then why didn't you believe him?' But if we say, 'From men'—we are afraid of the people, for they all hold that John was a prophet"** (vv. 25b–26). They are caught in the horns of a dilemma. Typically, what they do, and I have it seen again and again and again, is that they move to silence. This is good in one way: Jesus silenced them, and persons need to be silenced when asking questions with an illegitimate concern. It is also the case they fall into silence and avoid the question. Even if the one happens, the other also happens. **"So they answered Jesus, 'We don't know.' Then he said, 'Neither will I tell you by what authority I am doing these things'"** (v. 27). The implication is that they do not know because they are not really interested in knowing—they are not seeking. If they are not seeking, why should He give them an answer? This question about authority haunted the Lord all the way through His ministry. It is a basic question: **"By what authority?"** (v. 23).

We see this question today in the State of the Church. Paul faced this, again and again, and they attempted to delegitimize his ministry. The Jews who believed and held on to the Mosaic economy did not think it through consistently. Paul, because he was so zealous in drawing out the assumptions and implications of the old system, ended up having Stephen killed.[30] He was going up to Damascus. Now Paul, in that sense, was concerned for consistency in his assumption, which was false, but at least he was concerned for consistency. He pushed it legitimately within that framework. Then the Lord called him, "Saul, Saul, why do you persecute me?" (Acts 9:4b). Paul had a 180-degree turnabout. He went through a process of evaluating the fundamental flaws of his position. But others who had come had not gone through this process of evaluation, and they were trying to mix the two economies, which was a source of a lot of distress to Paul. The Jews who held onto circumcision and the Jews who did not believe in Christ were often opposing him. Paul had to defend the authority by which he was doing these things.

In 2 Corinthians 11:6, Paul says, "I may not be a trained speaker, but I do have knowledge." He is going back to this as his basis. He did not undergo a certain kind of training that may have been expected. In 2 Corinthians 11:23, he talks about work. He says, "I have worked much harder" than they have. These are what you may call the super-apostles. The guys with degrees strung out after their names from the best schools. They supposedly have super-knowledge. He says, "I have worked much harder" than they. Then, he speaks about visions and revelations. He will come to that, and he will speak about it. He said, "I am out of my mind to talk like this" (2 Cor. 11:23), "but you drove me to it" (2 Cor. 12:11). Sometimes, the process of defending one's authority may require something that seems unseemly but necessary under the condition. Paul had said earlier,

> Are we beginning to commend ourselves again? Or do we need, like some people, letters of recommendation to you or from you? You

30. *Acts 7.*

> yourselves are our letter, written on our hearts, known and read by everybody. (2 Cor. 3:1b–2).

This problem of the question of authority came up for Paul.

It came up for the Apostles in Acts 4:9–10. They did a great work, and the work was being spoken of as evil—a typical move. It says, "If we are being called to account today for an act of kindness shown to a cripple . . . It is by the name of Jesus Christ." In His name this is being done, which takes us back to the authority of Jesus, the Word of God incarnate. When they were explicitly told not to preach anymore in His name, they said, "We must obey God rather than men!" (Acts 5:29b).

The problem of the question of authority also occurred in Luther's day. He was in the Church under its authority. However, what he read and struggled with were the implications of purgatory and penance. He pursued this as fully as he could. He saw there was no answer there. He was reading, studying, and teaching the Scriptures; the light dawned on him that not only is this way of salvation by works through penance not acceptable, but salvation is by faith alone in Jesus Christ based on His righteousness. Luther nailed the Ninety-five Theses on the door of Wittenberg, and it spread quickly. Then all hell broke loose. The authorities were incensed that this person would do this. They had all kinds of interactions, and it came to the Diet of Worms, and Luther had to speak. He appealed to the Word of God and the place of reason in understanding the Word. He said,

> Unless I am convinced by the testimony of the Scriptures and by clear reason (for I do not trust in the pope or councils alone, since it is well known that they have often erred and contradicted themselves), I am bound by the Scriptures I have quoted. My conscience is captive to the Word of God. I cannot and I will not retract anything, since it is neither safe nor right to go against conscience. Here I stand. I cannot do otherwise. God help me. Amen.[31]

In the days of the Westminster Assembly, many issues were being addressed, but something essential occurred. Over 100 leaders in the Church came together. They were called by parliament. Each was paid

---

31. Henry Bettenson, *Documents of the Christian Church* (New York: Oxford University Press, 2011), 224.

four shillings a day and excused from their responsibilities for about five years. Later on, the clause 'that sinners may be called by parliament' was stricken from the Confession, yet parliament did call them. They read and discussed. There were differences among them about Church authority. Some favored prelacy or hierarchy, where the Pope was the head of the Church. Some favored the king, Henry VIII, as the head of the Church when he broke from Rome and set himself up as the head of the Church. Some favored a Presbyterian form of Church government and wanted to establish Presbyterianism in the place of episcopacy and the king as the head of the Church, but they wanted to be established. We have now set aside the idea that religion, in that sense, should be established, but this is where they were at that time. There were Congregationalists there, too.

Documents were drawn up: (1) The Westminster Confession of Faith. (2) The Larger Catechism and Shorter Catechism. (3) The Directory of Public Worship because they wanted to cleanse the Church from the remnants of the Mass and the service connected to the Mass. This included the way it was being compromised with a Prayer Book in the Episcopal Church. (4) The Directory for Church Government because there was so much conflict between the rulers and the people, and the ruler's religion was supposed to be the people's religion. They attempted to move in a direction where the ruler would not be involved, but they still affirmed the idea of an established Church. The independents were saying no to this, which was not working out the way it should have.

Today, the conflict regarding authority continues. There is a conflict between science and Scripture, or general and special revelation. The scientists say, 'We have knowledge and you simply believe.' This is used to delegitimize the Church and the voice of the Church. It is a conflict that has gone on for a long time between faith and reason. Some have set these in antithesis, independently of one another, or one above the other rather than seeing the internal connection between the two.[32]

The Church has lost headship in the culture because we have lost connection with the Word of God in its fullness. We are struggling with secularism and pluralism, which say, 'Do not bring any religion into the public square or into public discussions in any shape or form whatsoever, and recognize that there are many religions and one is as

32. Gangadean, *Philosophical Foundation,* 86–100.

good as another.' This is pluralism—pluralism means *many*. These are the dominant forces at work in the culture today. It has come to a point where the Church is ridiculed, the Church is scorned, and people are blaspheming God. Yes, they are blaspheming God because of the failure of the Church. Paul says in Romans 2:24, "As it is written: 'God's name is blasphemed among the Gentiles because of you.'" This is our present state.

BY WHAT AUTHORITY?

The underlying common thread is, "**By what authority?**" (v. 23)—for any difference, for every difference, for every nuance of a difference. I am going to bring out some of this to you. The mere existence of difference is a witness that threatens. You do not have to say anything; the very fact that Westminster Fellowship exists as a distinct work raises the question: Why are you distinct? Why are you a separate work? How do you justify your existence as a separate work? It is felt in the popular churches but most of all by those closest to us. The opposition has come most of all from those who are closest. It is more of a challenge because we are saying we are holding to the Westminster Confession, yet there are these differences.

The Principle of Authority

Let us think about authority and the question, "**By what authority?**" Authority occurs on different levels. First of all, there is a principle of authority. Secondly, there are persons in positions of authority. Thirdly, there are the administrative and procedural elements connected with authority. How does this apply? As far as the principle of authority, what we say is that it is the Word of God. The Word of God has come to us in three different ways. It has come to us in general revelation, it has come to us in Scripture, and it has come to us in the historic creeds. Scripture teaches in John 16:13a, "But when he, the Spirit of truth, comes, he will guide you into all truth." In Acts 15, He leads us into all truth through the work of the pastor-teachers.[33] The pastor-teachers are given "to prepare God's people for works of service, so that the body

33. Gangadean, *The Westminster Confession,* xvii-xxxii, 349–351; Gangadean, "Paper No. 16: The Historic Christian Faith," in *The Logos Papers,* 103–114.

of Christ may be built up until we all reach unity in the faith" (Eph. 4:12–13a). So, there is a place for creeds under the Scripture. Scripture also assumes and teaches the clarity of general revelation.[34] From general revelation, we can see the necessity for special revelation, but it is also true that Scripture teaches the necessity for general revelation. The Word of God comes to us in all these forms, and reason undergirds them all. We need reason as the Word of God, the life of God, which is in all men as light (Jn 1:4). We need reason to understand general revelation. We need reason to understand Scripture, and the creeds, which came after much discussion, which assumes reason. By what authority? By authority of the Word of God, understood as all three: general revelation, Scripture, and historic creeds and confessions. If you wish to narrow it, you may say, 'Wait, that is too broad. Let's just do the Word of God written, as Scripture.' Then we will say, 'Okay, we will do that. Scripture teaches this about Historic Christianity, and Scripture teaches this about general revelation. Let us go by the Scripture.' We cannot get away from it—no way.

When we come to the Scriptures, we use good and necessary consequences. There are differences in understanding the Scriptures. There is a tendency in us to be autonomous and to do our own thing. From the Garden on, we put ourselves in the place of God to determine good and evil and set ourselves as the standard. There is sin of not seeking and idolatry in misconceiving God, who has revealed Himself clearly. There have been divisions connected with this. There is an inability to discuss and unwillingness to discuss. That, perhaps, is a concrete mark. It is one thing to have differences; it is another not to discuss them. There are differences to be sure, but is there a willingness to discuss it? Is there a willingness to discuss it at the basic level and resolve it? Do we simply think we are being faithful witnesses by declaring it and pounding the table? No, the example of Paul is that he entered into the synagogue and he reasoned with them daily.[35] He reasoned with them in Ephesus, in the School of Tyrannus, and so the Word of God spread; this is the example.[36] Our Lord reasoned with them. Our Lord

34. Gangadean, "Paper No. 102: The Clarity of General Revelation," 527–529; "Paper No. 41: What Is Clear About God," 225–229; "Paper No. 112: Why General Revelation Is Basic in the Christian Worldview," in *The Logos Papers,* 583–585.

35. *Acts 17:2, 17:17.*

36. *Acts 19:9.*

used reason in this example concerning authority.[37] Every way you cut it, He is constantly doing this. Why? Because He is the Word of God incarnate, and He is living this out before us. Some people will not like to do this. It raises a question about seeking, understanding, and the reality of sin.

The first level of authority is the principle of authority. It is sometimes experienced in this way, especially by those who are not thinking: 'You are just different. Why are you different? Why can you not be like everybody else?' Has that thought crossed your mind? Yes. We are different from the popular. We are not different from the historical. We are connected with the historical, though we may not be connected with the popular. We will see how this will be applied in our coming to church.

The Person in Authority

It is one thing to have the principle of authority. What about the person in authority? Does this person have insight? Authority is based on insight into the good and the means to the good. Challenges cut both ways. You are invited to challenge and see if there is insight. Should we also say by the same token, *you* will be challenged to see if *you* have insight. Fair? This is exactly fair. Let us start the discussion.

Part of it is seeking and understanding what is clear. Have you seen what is clear? Have you understood what is clear? If you understood what is clear, you would be able to show what is clear. Can you show it? Can the pastor of your church (we are not asking about the person in the pew) show how it is clear that God exists in light of the objections that have been raised? I have been asking this question since before I was a Christian. Before I was a Christian, I would ask: How do you know that God exists? I am still asking it. I am still getting the same answers. The answers are avoiding: 'We do not know; we do not need to know.' You have to ask, 'Is insight, in terms of persons and positions of authority, legitimate?' I feel awkward in saying this because it makes me feel as if I am trying to speak about myself. Hopefully, I am speaking under the Word.

Another question that is raised is, 'What about credentials? Where are your credentials? To what seminary did you go? Have you graduated

37. *Matthew 21:23–27.*

from a seminary and been given a degree from a seminary?' The answer is no. 'Well, there, step down right now. Walk out. Save the people a lot of trouble.' If seminaries were the way to be prepared, then many people have not been prepared throughout history. *Most* have not been prepared who are in positions of leadership. Augustine did not go to seminary. Ambrose did not go to seminary. The Cappadocian fathers did not go to seminary. Going to seminary is not the same thing as being prepared. You can be prepared without going to seminary. Paul did not spend three years with Jesus. They may disqualify him for that. Interestingly, the Lord chose Paul to write the greater portion of the New Testament. People can be prepared by God in a number of ways. Moses probably did not go to seminary. I am not saying I am Moses. That is not the point. The point is the idea that seminary, the usual way, is the best way or the only way to be prepared. The answer is no because most in history have not been prepared in this way. Calvin was a humanist. He was more like a college teacher if anything. The point is that a person needs to be prepared. You definitely need to be prepared. Moses was prepared for 40 years in the backside of the desert. He had training in all the wisdom of the Egyptians.[38] Joshua was prepared for 40 years with Moses. This is not a three-year seminary program.

The seminary can prepare you if it is built on the Word of God: if it accepts the clarity of general revelation, the biblical worldview of creation–fall–redemption,[39] and Historic Christianity.[40] Unfortunately, many seminaries are not. Most seminaries are not; they have turned away from this. To say that preparation is through a seminary credential does not get us far. I hate to mention this, but as far as credentials are concerned, a seminary has examined my work. They gave me a degree from a seminary that says, 'Yes, this degree entitles you to teach.' In the seminary, there were people from the Reformed Presbyterian Church, the Orthodox Presbyterian Church, and the Presbyterian Church in America. They read my work, examined it over a four-year period, from the initial to the final, and said, 'Yes.' They awarded the certificate, if you wish, which says you can teach. I do not think that this certificate is necessary to teach, but if anyone wants to make something of it (and some are trying to), yes, that certificate was awarded.

---

38. *Acts 7:22.*

39. Gangadean, *The Biblical Worldview.*

40. Gangadean, *The Westminster Confession;* Gangadean, *The Westminster Catechisms.*

There is another part of it, and that is fruit. The Scripture says, "By their fruit you will recognize them" (Matt. 7:16). Paul said, "You yourselves are our letter [fruit]" (2 Cor. 3:2a). Anyone can have fruit in one sense. Muhammad has fruit. Baha'u'llah has fruit. Any Tom, Dick, and Harry can go out there and get a following. Having a following is not the point. It must be *in* the Word of God—in the Word of God, especially as it is spelled out in Historic Christianity in the creeds. This is the kind of fruit that we are looking at. It must be connected with Historic Christianity—persons are coming to hear, understand, believe, and put this into practice. If someone challenges us on this point by asking, 'Where's the fruit?' we can say, 'Well, you are the fruit.' Then it works the other way, too: 'Where is your fruit? This church has been here for 22 years, and it has not grown except for people from other churches trickling in?' That does not look good.

Administration and Procedure

Administratively and procedurally, to whom am I accountable? I am accountable to the same person that you are accountable to as far as administration is concerned. Each and every one of us here is always accountable for everything to each other under the Word of God. It is not just me being accountable; it is you being accountable. We are accountable to one another, and the procedure is Matthew 18.[41] If I turn away from this, you can call me to account. If you turn away from this, you can be called to account. Yes, there is a procedure in place, a very explicit, understandable procedure that goes beyond this church. There is an authority beyond this church. If a dispute between us cannot be resolved, we can examine and see whether we are acting according to the Word of God, according to our standards in our constitution. This acts like the higher court, and that court is final. I am telling you a secret that should not have been a secret. Do you know that you can fire me anytime you want? You absolutely can. You can call a meeting anytime you want and fire me.[42] Two-thirds of the elders can say, 'You are out.' It is not that I am not accountable; it is not a Divine Right of Kings show here. We are accountable.

41. Gangadean, *The Westminster Confession,* 391–395.

42. In 2013, Westminster Fellowship changed its by-laws from Congregational to Biblical standards to guard against a take over by congregants on non-biblical grounds.

We should use Matthew 18. Sometimes, we do not use Matthew 18. We try to go to step two before doing step one. Sometimes, we do step one without ever doing step two. Sometimes, we do step one once instead of going back and forth a few times to get the discussion focused and clear it up. I tell you, once we get step one in place, it is in place. Step two has no right to override step one—period. This is what step one is about. You go back and forth until you clarify it. This past year, we were involved in a dispute where step one was overridden and bypassed. It was reconstructed and handled in a new way; therefore, it is not the principle of Matthew 18. Twenty-two years ago, when we used Matthew 18 step one, the presbytery came in and skipped step one. We brought a very specific concern, and they addressed a different concern. Matthew 18 works this way—step one, step two, step three. This is how we are to be accountable. This is in the constitution. You are encouraged to use Matthew 18. Come inquiring and not judging. Consider yourself first and your contribution to the problem. Consider whether the issue is of such a nature that you must do it; you must deal with this. Not every offense must be a Matthew 18 situation. It is not to be in the spirit of, 'Gotcha, I am going to do a Matthew 18 on you, and you will not realize what is coming until I get through with you.' This is *not* the spirit in which one is to go through Matthew 18. Take the beam out of your own eye first to see clearly. Do not come judging. "For in the same way you judge others, you will be judged" (Matt. 7:2). This is the administrative and procedural process of authority.

WHY ARE YOU NOT PART OF A PRESBYTERY?

Some may ask, 'Why aren't you part of a presbytery? After all, do you not say you hold to the Westminster Confession of Faith?' We do not say we hold to the Westminster Standards. We say we hold to the Westminster Confession of Faith. At this time, we cannot put the Book of Church Government into practice. We believe that we can and should, but let me explain why we cannot put it into practice at this time. It is not that we do not want to. We have tried, and we have tried, and we have tried. How have we tried?

Because I am the organizing pastor of this church, I will tell a little bit about my history. After my conversion in 1961, for about 10 years I was in popular Christianity. By this time, I started teaching, wanted more, and discovered Historic Christianity through reading books. In a two to three-year period, I became quite convinced. Notice that it took some time to round it out, become thorough, and go through the process. Then, I became a member of the Reformed Presbyterian Church of North America in 1973, and in 1975, I was an elder in that church, and I was an elder there from 1975 to 1987. In 1987, a question of the moral conduct of the pastor came up, and I appealed this to presbytery. Last night, I was pulling out my old notes on this. I do have those notes available, and we will make them in a form where they can be seen by those who want to see them.[43] I have the date when I wrote those minutes and submitted them to the presbytery to ask the presbytery to come in. What happened is that there was not an application of Matthew 18. It failed, and there was no resolution. The testimony of six witnesses was neglected and avoided, which is still an issue of concern.

Presbytery was brought in, but presbytery did not resolve it. For the next three years, there was an appeal process going on by myself up to a point, and then by David Burton, and it still was not resolved. After this went on, from 1990 to 1993, we tried going to other churches in the Valley that held to the Westminster Confession. Still, we had difficulty because they were not singing the Psalms, and our standing every Sunday and not singing in worship became an increasing burden. They also did not hold to the doxological focus of the Confession.

Between 1994 and 1999, we had organized as a group, not a church—we know the difference between a group and a church. We appealed three times to the presbytery to be formed as a separate work, and that did not come to fruition. In 1999, we returned to the Reformed Presbyterian Church and sat there for nine months seeking membership. Thirty-six or so others went to the RPCNA, and then, in October, I was asked to leave and seek membership elsewhere. Why? Because of my teaching, what we call the Doxological Focus. We have that document, which can be made available.

It is not that we have not tried to be under presbytery. We have tried, and we have tried, and we have tried, and we have tried, and we have tried. Even more recently, when one member was being transferred here, the church would not even recognize our existence as a church.

---

43. The notes are currently archived in the Surrendra Gangadean Memorial Library at The Logos Study Center.

They said that we are not part of the visible Church; we have this in writing, and we will make this available. Why are we not part of the visible Church? The assumption seems to be that only Presbyterian ordination is lawful. The claim that only apostasy is grounds for starting a new work was addressed in 2006. This has been addressed. Those papers will be made available. We do not want to burden the worship service with details, but it is mentioned just to tell you that we have made every attempt. We do believe, all things being equal, that being part of a presbytery is the way to go, but all things are not equal right now. We have made every reasonable effort. If you think we have not made a reasonable effort and we could have done more, please, I ask you, come, and let us know.[44]

Someone said, 'We cannot be Presbyterian in doctrine and not in government.' The Confession has a number of things to say about that. In chapter 1.6, it says there are some things concerning the circumstance of worship and government, "which are to be ordered by the light of nature, and Christian prudence." This is the basic word on this. It does not say anything about committees. It does not say anything about *Robert's Rules of Order*. It does not say anything about small groups. It says the light of nature and Christian prudence are to be used. In WCF 1.10, as far as the doctrine of the Church Council is concerned, they are a subordinate standard to the Word of God. In WCF 31.2, a change has been made in the Westminster Confession, and the change was that magistrates may call synods. This has been eliminated. This is how the Westminster Assembly got started. This is how Nicaea came about, too, and this is how Chalcedon came about. The government and the early Church soon became episcopal. There was a bishop in every city over the other elders, which is the essence of episcopacy. One cannot say this was the history of the Church. It is perhaps more of an issue of light of nature and Christian prudence—what is to be preferred, all things considered equal, if we are in unity. The Church was in unity briefly up to the Council of Jerusalem, so all met at that council. Not long afterward, we started to pull off in different directions. If we can be in unity with the doctrine, yes, that is the way to go. That is how it should be.

---

44. This document is archived in the Surrendra Gangadean Memorial Library at The Logos Study Center. The substance of the charge and the responses will be printed in a book belonging to a series under the category of church government.

It has never been the case that any form of church government, that is, the administrative/procedural, has prevented the Church's decay in terms of the Word of God. Only diligently seeking and self-examination involving discussion can protect us against decay. It never happened, even in the days of Moses. Aaron and Miriam rose up, and many others rose up. The prophet, priest, and king in the Old Testament did not maintain their position. The leaders in Jesus' day did not maintain their position. It was they who opposed Jesus. So, no form of government can prevent decay if there is not an attitude of seeking and understanding. Adam was in the Garden, and guess what? There was no form of church government, and he turned aside. He did not seek and understand. When he was tested, it became clear. This is where decay comes from. "He that cometh to God must believe that he is, and that he is a rewarder of them that diligently seek him" (Heb. 11:6 KJV).

I need to go through some of this quickly. A question has been raised, 'Why do we not have more elders?' Come inquiring. The announcement that was made two weeks ago that we are going to have the congregational meeting but not elect elders has been interpreted as an attempt to perpetuate the "one-person rule." I am the one who is pressing most for electing elders. Others have questions, and we want to give due respect to their questions and let them take the time to resolve them. We also wanted the congregation to see those who are put forward for elder serving in that position more. We would like the congregation to have one year to see up close, but it has been misinterpreted. Even something like honor and respect that is shown is misunderstood as just personal allegiance, rather than seeing that the person may understand the process of thinking and seeing what is clear. They understand the authority of reason and appreciate it, which is why honor is given where it is. No, it is merely taken as personal rather than in principle. We have to be on guard against this. We have to build the walls better. 'Why do we not advertise our presence?' That question has been raised. We certainly advertise our position, which is more basic. We invite people to read the Westminster Confession, and we want to do as much as we can to get persons to read it and make the decision to attend on that basis.[45] This is the basis on which a decision

45. This and many other books to be published is a continuation of the effort begun by Pastor Gangadean to make the position known.

should be made. In all of this, what we see is a need for preparation for persons to come to this church.

NEED FOR PREPARATION

Isaiah 40:3–5 says,

> Prepare ye the way of the LORD, make straight in the desert a highway for our God. Every valley shall be exalted, and every mountain and hill shall be made low: and the crooked shall be made straight, and the rough places plain: And the glory of the LORD shall be revealed.[46]

This is what needs to be done in our witness. The way has to be prepared. John the Baptist was preparing the way. This was predicted at the end of the last book of the Old Testament, Malachi.

> Behold, I will send you Elijah the prophet before the coming of the great and dreadful day of the LORD: And he shall turn the heart of the fathers to the children, and the heart of the children to their fathers, lest I come and smite the earth with a curse (Mal. 4:5–6 KJV).

The ending word of the Old Testament: "curse."

The way must be smooth. Certain things must be in place. People must understand that for everyone here seeking to bring others to the church, a witness must ask, God is the "rewarder of them that diligently seek him" (Heb. 11:6b KJV), do you agree? Do you understand sin is not seeking and not understanding and not doing what is right? Or are we just talking about fruit sin? This needs to be in place. It is not seeking and not understanding that leads to not doing what is right. There is an internal development. These are not just three phrases scattered here. There is an internal connection. Adultery is due to not diligently seeking God. Physical adultery is due to spiritual adultery. Sexual uncleanness is due to not being devoted to God. This is the primary way sin manifests itself, according to Romans 1. People who come to church need to know this, and not only this, but sin and death,

46. KJV.

and the curse and promise—both the curse and the promise. Do we even understand the curse and the purpose of the curse? Its purpose for cleansing; its purpose to restrain, recall, and remove sin from persons. The sin is not just not seeking, but self-deception and self-justification about not seeking. Have you repented of this sin? Persons need to be asked this question *before* they come. People need to be reading the Confession *before* they come.

We are seeing the need for people to understand what Scripture says about marriage and divorce so they can accept the biblical sanctions for divorce. This is something that has been in place in history. Much of our time was spent this week, about 40-plus hours or more of intense time, because this piece was not accepted. We have gone so far so quickly. If you are the guilty party, you lose your rights; as if you were dead. You do not have rights to your kids anymore. You forfeited those rights. You forfeited your property rights. Those who come to be married should know and understand that if you sleep with someone, you are *prima facie* obligated to marry that person unless the father overrules. Only by putting these concrete precepts in place can we begin to discipline ourselves for godliness. If you do not go through the courtship process, the Church will not be involved in your marriage. You should all know this. We have been saying this, and I will make it more explicit. These are some of the things that need to be spelled out before persons come—prepare the way.

We need to see evidence of seeking and understanding. Someone said they wanted to come to church, but they have not been reading the Scripture. Yesterday, I said to them, "Read the Scripture." I asked them, "Can you say why Jesus came?" They floundered on this. If I had said the words, they would have said, 'Oh, yes, that is what I mean.' I did not want to put any words in their mouths. They are going to read the Scriptures and tell me their understanding. I remember doing this with Kelly 15 years ago. I would not budge with Kelly. Not that she asked me to budge, not that I did not want to budge, but Kelly went through the process of reading the Scriptures and answering: Who is Jesus Christ? There is a process to understanding sin and forgiveness of sin through Christ and to understanding cleansing. When you come to the Church, you are coming to be cleansed. That cleansing is going to get down to the deepest level in you. All your personality and background is going to come to the fore. All your history is going to come to the fore. This is what we are finding. People's personal history stretches far back and still needs to be dealt with in the process of sanctification—prepare the way.

The way has to be prepared for each person before they come. The basics need to be there. We are not saying they have to be mature in faith, but in principle, there must be commitment and understanding. There must be some credibility to ensure commitment and understanding. If this is not in place, and people are not reading the Scriptures, what we will end up with is persons coming and then leaving. When they leave, they will have to justify their leaving. The way they justify their leaving is often by accusing and blaming us. Then we have to clean up the mess by talking to everyone who has been spoken to in that way. The church does not want to do this. It does not have time for this—prepare the way; get the basics in place before coming. When someone comes, they should continue to grow and not have to back out and create problems.

We are operating by the authority of the Word of God, by the standards. We have made this clear to everyone. We invite people to consider the standards before coming.[47] We invite them not to consider us but to consider the standards. After one has considered the standards, then consider us in light of the standards. This is the purpose of the three-month period when one first comes. You are holding to the standards. You are seeing if we are living according to the standards. Examine us. Please do. We want to see whether you come and you have enough discipline to come regularly. If you do not, then you cannot take the vow; you cannot be a member. We believe that we can have hope to grow more securely, faithfully, and in greater unity, if we apply the standards that we profess. "The law of the Lord is perfect, converting the soul: the testimony of the Lord is sure" (Ps. 19:7a KJV). The testimonies of the Lord delight the believer. They are clean. They are the rejoicing of our hearts. We, by the grace of God, need to put this law in our hearts.

John gave the vision of the state of the churches at the beginning of Revelation, and then he went through the seven visions: the age-long,

47. Gangadean, *The Westminster Confession of Faith: A Doxological Understanding* and *The Westminster Shorter and Larger Catechisms: A Doxological Understanding* were both written with the purpose of preparing current and future congregants at Westminster Fellowship. A thoughtful engagement with the material contained in these books will anticipate and prevent questions regarding church membership.

agonizing spiritual war, and good overcomes evil. Then he spoke about that glorious City of God, the New Jerusalem; we are still to seek this city with all of our hearts. We are to learn from all of our challenges, trials, and mistakes to put the Word of God into place more faithfully. It is a city with foundations and high walls; it is protected. These walls are to protect and defend against attacks from outside. By the grace of God, we will do this.

6

Prepare the Way of the Lord

The Ministry of the Church in Taking Thoughts Captive

2012

Isaiah 40:1–5

1Comfort, comfort my people,
says your God.

2Speak tenderly to Jerusalem,
and proclaim to her
that her hard service has been completed,
that her sin has been paid for,
that she has received from the LORD's hand
double for all her sins.

3A voice of one calling:
"In the desert prepare
the way for the LORD;
make straight in the wilderness
a highway for our God.

4Every valley shall be raised up,
every mountain and hill made low;
the rough ground shall become level,
the rugged places a plain.

5And the glory of the LORD will be revealed,
and all mankind together will see it.
For the mouth of the LORD has spoken."

RETURN FROM CAPTIVITY

ISAIAH SPEAKS COMFORT TO THE PEOPLE OF GOD. At the end of chapter 39, he sees their captivity in Babylon, and in chapter 40, he is considering their return from captivity. At the beginning of Isaiah, we see the condition of the people—the outward form of religion, going through the motions, their hearts are far from God—and the wickedness that has grown in the culture. We see the judgment of God on Judah through Assyria, and now, judgment will be by Babylon. Even amid this, Isaiah is speaking the Word of God, speaking of the promise being fulfilled, that the child who is to be born of a virgin will rule on the throne of David and will establish righteousness in all the earth. We are called in the context of coming out of captivity to **"prepare the way for the Lord"** (v. 3). We have had double revelation—general revelation and Scripture—so when we turn away from the Word of God, we go into hard service in captivity. This comes to an end, the Prophet foresees, and we have received from the Lord's hand double for all our sins.[1] In this case, 70 years, because for 70 years, we did not observe the sabbatical year in the land and the renewal that is to be ours if we are devoted to God.[2] We had, in effect, turned aside to the world to become like the world, and now we are being called back and brought out of the world.

Isaiah 40:3 Connected with John 1:23

This passage in Isaiah 40:3, which says a voice of one calling in the desert place, **"prepare the way for the Lord,"** is spoken of in the Gospel of John by John the Baptist. In John 1:22–23, the priests and Levites ask him, "Who are you? Give us an answer to take back to those who sent us. What do you say about yourself?" John answers them in the words of Isaiah the Prophet, "I am the voice of one calling in the desert, 'Make straight the way for the Lord.'" We make a definite connection between the words spoken by Isaiah and the words spoken by John. Isaiah says, **"A voice of one calling: In the desert prepare the way for the Lord; make straight in the wilderness a highway for our God"** (v. 3). In John, it seems to come out, "I am the voice of one calling in the

1. *Isaiah 40:2.*

2. *Jeremiah 25:12–14; 2 Chronicles 36:20–21.*

desert" (Jn. 1:23). As John is in the wilderness, he does not say to make a straight path in the wilderness. There is sufficient reason to say he is in the wilderness after captivity in our apostasy, having received double from the Lord's hand. This could be a very discouraging condition, but the prophets are sent to speak the Word of God and give us hope that God will accomplish His purpose. For it says here, **"For the mouth of the LORD has spoken"** (v. 40:5b). In verse 8, "The grass withers and the flowers fall, but the word of our God stands forever." It was that Word from which we have turned away. There is a ministry of preparing the way of the Lord, and in a condition of apostasy, it is the voice of the prophet, one like Elijah who is crying in the wilderness, calling men to prepare the way of the Lord. We will see what that preparation involves.

Luke 1:17 and 1:76 Connected with Malachi 4:15

In the passage in Luke 1:17 and 1:76, the angel speaks to Zacharias about one who is to be born. He says explicitly that he will go before Him in the spirit and power of Elijah, and he will prepare the way of the Lord. In verse 17, "he will go on before the LORD, in the spirit and power of Elijah," and notice what this preparation of the way of the Lord involves: "to turn the hearts of the fathers to their children and the disobedient to the wisdom of the righteous—to make ready a people prepared for the LORD." We have further confirmation that this word of Isaiah spoken under these conditions refers to John the Baptist, who is to prepare the way of the Lord. What is happening here, we believe, will happen whenever the people of God are backslidden and in a state of captivity; we come out of captivity after the Lord's hand has been upon us, and we come out of it as the way of the Lord is prepared. The way is prepared by turning the hearts of the fathers to their children and the disobedient to the wisdom of the righteous. This connects expressly with Malachi 4:5–6 at the end of the Old Testament. It says,

> See, I will send you the prophet Elijah before that great and dreadful day of the LORD comes. He will turn the hearts of the fathers to their children, and the hearts of the children to their fathers; or else I will come and strike the land with a curse.

The curse will come if there is no repentance or obedience. In Luke 1:17 and 76, the angel speaks about this One who prepares the way of the Lord, and Malachi 4:15 brings together the ministry of Elijah. The prophetic ministry prepares the way of the Lord in the condition of coming out of captivity. The teaching that turns the hearts of the fathers unto the children, and the children to the fathers, is something that we are called to do according to the law of God. In Deuteronomy 6:4–9, we are told to teach God's law diligently to our children. As we rise up, sit down, go out, and come in, we are to have this law and be reminded of the law by tying it to our hands, our foreheads, the fringes of our garments, and our doorposts. We are to be meditating in the law of God day and night. We are to teach them diligently to our children. The hearts of the fathers are to be turned to the children to teach them, and the children are to be turned to hear and obey the wisdom of the just so the way of the Lord will be prepared. There will be a highway in the desert, **"make straight in the wilderness a highway for our God"** (v. 3b). This highway is straight. It is through the desert place. It is the shortest distance between two points. It is the fastest, wisest way, and to accomplish this highway, **"Every valley shall be raised up, every mountain and hill made low; the rough ground shall become level, the rugged places a plain"** (v. 4). As a result, **"the glory of the LORD will be revealed, and all mankind together will see it"** (v. 5a). This is the ministry that prepares the way of the Lord. This is how it is done, how it is to be accomplished.

Deuteronomy 6:7 Connected with Moral Law 5

Deuteronomy 6:7 reminds us of the call to teach our children diligently in keeping with the Word, turn the hearts of the fathers to the children, and the children are to be instructed in this. This has been said before in the giving of the law itself in the fifth commandment, which says, "Honor your father and your mother, so that you may live long in the land the LORD your God is giving you" (Ex. 20:12). This commandment is concerning what true authority and wisdom is.[3] Your father and mother represent the historically accumulated insight; we should not neglect it but heed it. It is to be communicated to our children so the way of the Lord will be prepared, a straight path will be made, and the glory of the Lord will be revealed. This is also a reminder of our baptismal vows. We take vows to diligently teach our children to

3. Gangadean, *Philosophical Foundation,* 221–229, 247–254.

provide them with a God-centered education.[4] Not a God-centered education in word only but in reality, in truth, and in detail. Diligently teaching our children is also spoken of in connection with circumcision. In Genesis 17, when Abraham was 99 years old, he received the sign of circumcision. Genesis 18, when God was going to bring judgment on Sodom, says:

> Then the LORD said, "Shall I hide from Abraham what I am about to do? Abraham will surely become a great and powerful nation, and all nations on earth will be blessed through him. For I have chosen him, so that he will direct his children and his household after him to keep the way of the LORD by doing what is right and just, so that the LORD will bring about for Abraham what he has promised him" (Gen. 18:17–19).

The sign of circumcision was to come to Abraham and his house, and with it, the teaching regarding regeneration and keeping the law of God, just as it is in baptism.[5] There is a contextual warning: If we do not diligently teach our children, we go the way the world has gone, into sin more and more to the point of Sodom and Gomorrah, then judgment will come: "or else I will come and strike the land with a curse" (Mal. 4:6b).

THE MINISTRY OF ELIJAH

This ministry that is called to prepare the way is and has become focused on the ministry of Elijah. A number of times, Scripture says that John is Elijah, the one to come. The angel says it, Malachi says it,[6] Isaiah says it, and the Lord Himself says it:[7] he is Elijah, who is to come. There are manyfold witnesses to how this preparation comes about. Let us take some time to look at the ministry of Elijah and consider it, as it says he is the one, or this is the way in which we are prepared.

---

4. Gangadean, *The Westminster Confession,* 388.

5. Gangadean, *The Westminster Confession,* 143–148, 291–305; Gangadean, *The Westminster Catechisms,* 191–192, 281–286.

6. *Malachi 3:1.*

7. *Matthew 11:1–19.*

First of the Prophets: Call to Repentance

Of all the prophets, we might say that Elijah is the first of the prophets in a new order from Moses. Moses gave a revelation, but Elijah did not give any new revelation. He calls us back to Moses' revelation; it is a ministry of calling back. He is the first in that order, even though there were some prophets before him; his position takes prominence when the people have gone into apostasy. Elijah appears on the scene in 875 B.C., about 58 years after the kingdom is divided—probably in 933 B.C. After ruling for about 20 or 22 years, Jeroboam, the king of northern Israel, died. This account is given to us in 1 Kings 17 and elsewhere in Scripture. Isaiah ministers during the time of Ahab. So, he is the first of the prophets in a prominent sense during the time of apostasy. Some of the others were not so much, but by the time we come to Ahab, there is widespread apostasy in the northern kingdom in a relatively short time. We will see how widespread it is. We will anticipate and see, so much so that Elijah thinks he is the only prophet of the Lord left[8]—that is widespread. Because as far as he knew, all the prophets of the Lord were killed by the prophets of Baal under Jezebel's direction. He appears in a time of widespread apostasy and calls the people back.

During Widespread Apostasy

This apostasy is not new; it is actually ancient. We certainly see it in the days of the golden calf when Moses brought the law—Baal worship. And again, during the time of the judges, the people repeatedly turned back. In the case of Saul, his own heart turned away. It came to expression in Solomon through Jeroboam down to Ahab, and the Sidonian princess, Jezebel. This is not something new. It is so widespread that Elijah thinks he is the only prophet of the Lord left. If there are other prophets, as we learned there are, they have gone into hiding. Obadiah has taken 100 prophets of the Lord and hidden them in two caves, and has been feeding them because Jezebel is seeking to wipe them out and is killing them wherever she can find them.[9] Elijah is not hiding, so he

8. *1 Kings 19:10.*

9. *1 Kings 18:4.*

is crying out in the wilderness. He is not hidden in the wilderness or cave with the other prophets, but he is crying out.

Elijah Calls Down the Curse

Elijah explicitly told Ahab and the court that "there will be neither dew nor rain in the next few years except at my word" (1 Kgs. 17:1b). There has been neither rain nor dew for three years. During that time, the word had gotten through to Ahab as he was hunting Elijah to kill him because he struck at the root of Baal worship, that is, prosperity and ways in which we seek to attain prosperity in a worldly way. When famine comes on the land, everything starts to wither and blow away. Those who promise abundance and fertility are left merely speaking the words. He understands that the situation is ripe for the curse, and calls on the curse by the Word of the Lord: "there will be neither dew nor rain in the next few years except at my word" (1 Kgs. 17:1b). Here is a case where the earth is being struck with a curse, as it says in Malachi: "or else I will come and strike the land with a curse" (Mal. 4:6). Elijah, as Moses before him, had the power to strike the earth with a curse. Ten times with Moses, it came down; it also came down with Elijah. This is one reason why both Moses and Elijah are found on the Mount of Transfiguration with our Lord Jesus.[10] They have a particular prominence in connection with the two aspects of the prophetic ministry. Moses was not in the wilderness; he was with the people. The people had not gone into apostasy; they were being brought out of captivity. In that case, captivity was not so much one of disobedience, but in the providence of God, they were being oppressed by the world.

Elijah is a voice crying in the wilderness. The specifics of this can be seen in contrast to others. It is a spiritual wilderness, a desolate place, because the Word of God is not being honored. He is lifting up his voice; he has pronounced a judgment; he has done so publicly and calls on a curse. There is no rain, and he is told to go to the Brook Cherith and stay there, and the ravens will feed him. Elijah is from Tishbi, about 30 to 40 miles south of the southern part of the Sea of Galilee, and Tishbi is about five miles from the Brook Cherith. He was born and raised in Tishbi and is now told to go to Cherith and wait there to be fed; it is familiar territory. He stays there, and the ravens feed

10. *Matthew 17:1–9; Mark 9:2–9; Luke 9:28–36.*

him, which itself is a sign to him. He is seeing the water dry up in the creek—springs are running out and not being fed by new rains. As the water dries up, he sees that the Word of the Lord is standing according to how he has spoken it: "there will be neither dew nor rain" (1 Kgs. 17:1b). He is being fed by a raven, an unclean bird, bringing food and delivering it to him—special express. Out of the mouth of the raven into his mouth—an unclean bird.

This becomes a sign to Elijah of what God tells him next: Leave Cherith and go to a widow in Sidon. Interestingly, this is where Jezebel is from. Now, he is going to be fed by an unclean widow just as the raven was unclean, but God is working through this. Zarephath is on the coast of Palestine, about 100 miles north of the Brook Cherith. It is south of the capital city of Sidon but north of Tyre. There he is with a widow, and there he is fed. He is waiting on the Word of God. He is showing God's grace. There were many widows, Jesus said, in Elijah's day, but it was the widow of Zarephath to whom he went.[11] This is a rebuke to the people for the uncleanness of heart because of their unbelief.

On Mount Carmel

The Word of God comes to Elijah again, and he goes and shows himself to Obadiah, a servant of Ahab, and tells him that he will appear. Obadiah is concerned because Elijah may disappear, and then he will be stuck and he will lose his head. He reminds Elijah that he is serving the Lord by protecting the prophets. Elijah says, "As the LORD Almighty lives, whom I serve, I will surely present myself to Ahab today" (1 Kgs. 18:15). Both Ahab and Obadiah are out trying to scrounge all through the hills and the valleys for some little bit of water and for some green grass to feed the horses and the cattle. They are dying from lack of food and water. It is a dire situation. Ahab is told that Elijah will meet him. Elijah comes to meet Ahab, and Ahab tries to blame Elijah.

> 'Is that you, you troubler of Israel?' 'I have not made trouble for Israel,' Elijah replied. 'But you and your father's family have. You have abandoned the LORD's commands and have followed the Baals' (1 Kgs. 18:17b–18).

11. *Luke 4:25–27.*

Elijah confronts Ahab with his sin of turning away from the Lord and turning to Baal. He calls the king to repentance boldly and clearly.

Elijah tells Ahab to gather all the prophets of Baal, go to Mount Carmel, and the Lord will show Himself. So all the prophets of Baal and the prophets of Ashtoreth, over 800, are gathered at Mount Carmel, which is also on the coast. As they are gathering, Elijah speaks to the people. He says, "How long will you waver between two opinions?" (1 Kgs. 18:21a). There is a double-mindedness on their part. Double-mindedness regarding what? Whether Jehovah is Lord or whether Baal is Lord. It has to do with their idolatrous conception of God, which is an endemic view. It is certainly here, in the Christian Church and in our hearts, as we think about connecting godliness with gain as if that is how we know God's favor is with us. The people are halting between these two, and Elijah reproves and calls them back. He tells them what he will do regarding the sacrifice, and the God that answers by fire is the Lord. In other words, Elijah will give them proof of a certain kind—a proof that is a visible sign. A proof that will cause the people to reject the authority of the false prophets and turn to the Lord. Elijah prays that at the time of the sacrifice, the people might see the Lord turning their hearts back again. Here is the ministry of Elijah, turning the hearts of the people back again by giving them proof of who God is, and it is done so clearly that they will reject the prophets of Baal—they will reject their authority.

The prophets of Baal made their offering, called upon Baal, cut themselves, and shouted. Elijah taunted them some. Then he presented the offering, soaked with water, drenched with water, and called upon God. God answers by fire, and the people shout, "The LORD—he is God!" (1 Kgs. 18:39). We are going to see this is not really the way that it should happen, but it happened that way because the people were in unbelief. Jesus said, "Unless you people see miraculous signs and wonders . . . you will never believe" (Jn. 4:48). He said to Thomas, "Because you have seen me, you have believed; blessed are those who have not seen and yet have believed" (Jn. 20:29). So it is really a rebuke to the people that they would require this kind of visible manifestation to believe. We know they had all the visibility they wanted at Sinai,[12] yet they turned

12. *Exodus 19.*

away.[13] Something more is happening here. The Lord is turning the hearts of the people back to Him. Between God and Baal, there is the concept of the good. Is the good the prosperity of this world? Or is the good knowing God, the one who gives prosperity? We are not slipping off the knowledge of God for prosperity as the good. The hearts of the people are being turned back in their understanding, not to the way of Baal and that view of good and evil, but to the Lord God—enough to speak to their hearts. This turning back to the Lord has two phases. After this proof, the people are called upon to execute judgment, and they do so by killing the prophets of Baal and Ashteroth—over 800 prophets. The people reject false authority in affirming that the Lord is God. This is an essential part of what is needed to prepare the way, that is, to no longer have this double-mindedness and to wholly give oneself to the Lord.

Elijah Flees from Jezebel

Word got back to Jezebel, and she sends word to Elijah, "May the gods deal with me, be it ever so severely, if by this time tomorrow I do not make your life like that of one of them" (1 Kgs. 19:2b). Elijah fears; he thinks and believes he is the only one left. He has seen what has happened to the prophets of the Lord; they have been killed. As far as he knows, he was the only one left until Obadiah said otherwise, and the others are hidden. Now, it is like he stirred up a hornet's nest, and they are coming after him. She is really incensed, and she sends word that she is going to kill him. It is a little bit telling of the relationship between Ahab and Jezebel, who rules in that house. It is not according to the Word of God. In the end, she is the one who is thrown down and trampled underfoot, and the dogs ate what remained of her. She is the one who fell.[14]

Elijah, fearing for his life under these conditions, flees. He flees over 100 miles south to Beersheba. Reaching that place, he becomes exhausted. Raised by the angel, he is given food, goes again, receives more food, and continues the journey to Horeb for 40 days and 40 nights. It is at Horeb, where God appeared to the people of Israel, that he entered a cave. Elijah is operating with the view that he is the only

13. *Numbers 10:11–14:45.*

14. *2 Kings 9:30–37.*

prophet left. He is certainly the only one left who is speaking out. Where are the others? Hidden in a cave. It does not seem quite the way it should be.

God in the Gentle Whisper

There at Horeb, God speaks to him: What are you doing here? Elijah explains, they have killed all your prophets. I am the only one left, and they are trying to kill me, too. God is going to speak to him, so he is told to go out. Then comes a mighty wind that breaks the rocks, and God is not in the wind. Then, an earthquake shakes the mountains, and God is not in the earthquake. There is a fire, and God is not in the fire. Then there is a gentle whisper, and Elijah covers his face, and goes out, and the Lord says, "What are you doing here, Elijah?" (1 Kgs. 19:13b). Again, he repeats, "I have been very zealous for the LORD God Almighty. The Israelites have rejected your covenant, broken down your altars, and put your prophets to death with the sword. I am the only one left, and now they are trying to kill me too" (1 Kgs. 19:14). A voice of one crying in the wilderness. God says, "I reserve seven thousand in Israel—all whose knees have not bowed down to Baal and all whose mouths have not kissed him" (1 Kgs. 19:18). This is a remnant; they are not prophets. They are believers, but they are not prophets. I suppose among them are 100 prophets who are hiding in caves. There is a measure of truth in what Elijah is saying, but God is sovereign and ruling. He reserved 7,000 who had not bowed their knees to Baal. A remnant is preserved, as is true at all times. God provides for continuity: Go now, anoint Hazael, king of Damascus, anoint Jehu, king of Israel, and anoint Elisha.[15]

Elisha's Double Portion

The next passages in 1 Kings and 2 Kings do not yet speak about Hazael and Jehu, but they speak of Elisha. Elisha is called, and he leaves and follows Elijah. When the time comes near for Elijah to leave, he asks, "'Tell me, what can I do for you before I am taken from you?' 'Let me inherit a double portion of your spirit,' Elisha replied" (2 Kgs. 2:9). Elijah replied, "if you see me when I am taken from you, it will be

15. *1 Kings 19:15–16.*

yours—otherwise not" (2 Kgs. 2:10b). Three times, Elijah says, wait here, I am going on to Bethel, then Jericho, and then the Jordan. Elisha shows his determination to have this double portion, and he will not be parted from Elijah—three times. He knows that the time of his departure has come; the other prophets, the school of prophets that have gathered, speak of his departure. Then comes the chariot and horses of fire. They divide Elijah from Elisha. Elijah is taken up in a whirlwind into heaven. As he goes, Elisha sees what is happening, and he cries out, "My father! My father! The chariots and horsemen of Israel!" (2 Kgs 2:12a). The cloak of Elijah falls, then Elisha takes up the cloak of Elijah, and he returns. As he returns, he does what Elijah did to the Jordan; he strikes it with the cloak, the waters part, and the other prophets there see it. This is not a double portion—to merely strike it as Elijah would do and have the waters part. In an important respect, he does receive a double portion in that he ministered twice as long as Elijah, for 50 years, while Elijah ministered for 25.

We know that when Elisha died, his bones were in his tomb, and as others were burying their dead, their lives were threatened by invaders. The person who was to be buried was thrown on Elisha's tomb, and the person came alive. Others were brought to life by Elisha and by Elijah. The widow's son of Zarephath is brought back to life. God provides for continuity through Elijah and an increase: a double portion. This is God's sovereignty, upholding His will on the earth and providing when it seems you are the only one left. God reserves some for Himself, providing for continuity and a double portion in the case of the prophetic ministry. This is the ministry of Elijah, and we have to see how this applies.

TWO PHASES IN TURNING THE HEARTS

The First Phase: From Baal to God

The turning of the hearts of the fathers to the children and the hearts of the children to the fathers have two phases. The first phase, spoken by Elijah, is to turn the hearts of the people back to the Lord. This is how Elijah puts the word, "that you are turning their hearts back again" (1 Kgs. 18:37b). What is the first phase of turning back the hearts of the fathers? There is double-mindedness; there is a halting between two opinions—between Baal and God. Proof was given; falsehood loses authority and is destroyed. The people are being turned from one way to another, from worldliness to godliness, from a worldly view of the good to the good in God, from wealth and honor to the view that their reward is in God, in connection with doing His work.

What is it that men are seeking in this world? It is spoken of as wealth and honor and perhaps honor instrumentally to gain wealth. We have a concern for the praise of men more than the praise of God. In John 5:44, Jesus says, "How can you believe if you accept praise from one another, yet make no effort to obtain the praise that comes from the only God?" They want to have an earthly reward—material benefit. They want to be served rather than serve others, rather than seeing that their reward is in the Lord, in knowing God.[16] They have this view of the good because they have been living under false principles of authority, which was what gave authority to the prophets of Baal. Baal worship has a tangible, visible reward here on the earth. That tangible, visible nature is something they could see, rather than the reward connected with their faith or understanding the glory that has been revealed. We see the connection between the people's weakness in understanding what is clear and their view of the good. They have to see the sign answered by fire from heaven. Remember, Nadab and Abihu saw God answering in the sacrifice by fire coming down from the presence of the Lord, but they did not understand and were consumed.[17] It was a reproof, a rebuke, to the people, and there is a connection between their lack of faith and their view of the good. Instead of seeking to have faith as understanding, they turn to sight, and they seek a good that is visible—tangible, here, now, in this world, in worldly terms.

This is not just in unbelievers; this is in believers, too. The disciples, to the very end, to the very night of Gethsemane, were arguing who is the greatest.[18] They were talking about sitting at the right hand of Jesus and His kingdom. They were asking, "are you at this time going to restore the kingdom of Israel?" (Acts 1:6b). They were seeking a visible, tangible kind of kingdom. They wanted to rule. We see it also

16. Gangadean, *Philosophical Foundation,* 171–177, 208–211; Gangadean, *The Westminster Catechisms,* 109–111, 321–325; Gangadean, *On Natural and Revealed Theology,* 33–39, 127–139; Gangadean, *History of Philosophy,* 61–64; Gangadean, "Paper No. 117: Knowing and Making God Known," in *The Logos Papers,* 599–601.

17. *Leviticus 10.*

18. *Matthew 18:1–4; Mark 9:33–36; Luke 9:46–47.*

in the church, "For when one says, 'I follow Paul,' and another, 'I follow Apollos,' are you not mere men?" (1 Cor. 3:4). Christ is not divided. Their eyes are not on the good, which is a source of unity, so they divide and say that one is better than another. "The eye cannot say to the hand, 'I don't need you!' And the head cannot say to the feet, 'I don't need you!'" (1 Cor. 12:21). 'I am greater than you.' If that is true of the disciples, who were with Jesus for three years, can we say it is true of us? Can we say it is true of those who give themselves most to follow the Lord? Can we say it is true of those who are in Logos?[19] There are various subtle, surreptitious ways of comparing ourselves with one another in terms of who is the greatest.

Pride—'I know more than you do; I should rule. You shouldn't have that position. Look at your life.' We think we know, and we make judgments rather than come inquiring. We think more highly of ourselves than we ought, rather than operating according to the measure of our faith and understanding. 'See, I know as much as or more than the other person and should be honored at least as much.' We want praise and the position of rule. Jesus said, "I am among you as one who serves" (Lk. 22:27b). He washed the disciples' feet. There is an open rebuke to them. He says, "wash one another's feet" (Jn. 13:14b). Instead of judging one another, if you see someone overtaken by a fault, then by the Word of God, the truth that sanctifies, bring the Word to the other person to wash their feet. We have pride in ourselves, which comes out in many ways. It is hidden under our self-deception and self-justification, and it has to come to be manifest. We are not to judge anything before the time.[20] Wait until the Lord brings it to light. Wait until the fruit is born. Do not think we know so as to make judgments of others in a premature way. Also, be careful when you judge, for you will be scrutinized in the same way. The details of your life will be examined, too. Rather than judging one another, we are to wash one another's feet using the Word of God. Particularly, this is true of the oversight, which is to bring the Word of God to bear. Think about it not in psychological terms but in terms of the Word of God. We have this satanic principle of self-life within us. We want to be worshiped as he wanted to be worshiped. We want to be honored by men more than

19. Logos Theological Seminary.

20. *1 Corinthians 4:5.*

the praise of God. We have sin remaining, and Satan said, "All this I will give you . . . if you will bow down and worship me" (Matt. 4:9).

We have to recognize pride under the cover of sin, self-deception, and self-justification, and repent of it. We have to humble ourselves in order to repent, and we have to look at our lives and what the Lord has brought to pass. We have to look at our lives and our marriages and the details of what has come to light in our marriages before we judge another person's marriage—our children, our work, and our fruit. Are we still hankering after Baal and worldly ways, or are we seeking the Lord? Are our hearts being turned back to God, turned away from worldly ways?

The Second Phase: From the Good to the Means to the Good

The second phase is the hearts being turned away from Baal to the good, and then in turn, to the means to the good, and that has to do with children. The good is by children and for children. The Lord tells us, "Be fruitful, and multiply, and replenish the earth, and subdue it: and have dominion" (Gen. 1:28 KJV). Without the good in place as a source of unity, life falls apart in every way. Marriage falls apart in all the intimate, delicate features of a closeup relationship day after day after day. Instead of looking at the other person as a helper suitable in pursuit of the good, we have our own view of self-life and all its limitations, as well as the lack of satisfaction. We do not give ourselves to educating our children. We have given ourselves over to a welfare state. We have social security that will take care of us in our old age, and we do not need children as much anymore. They were cheap labor on the farm, and now most of us are not on the farm. Society has, more and more, given itself over to abortion, a disregard of children in education, and a disregard of history and accumulated insight. The culture is going into decay, increasingly rapid decay, as we see the effects of the worldview of people manifesting itself in the vote in politics, manifesting itself in the school system, and manifesting itself in the kind of discourse that is going on. It is a worldview that is being manifest—not individual, isolated truths, which is a distortion; this is a falsehood of what is really happening. All aspects of culture always occur in the context of a worldview.

When the hearts of the fathers turn to the children, the man, as the head of the household, will teach his wife to be faithful in bringing the Word of God by example and by deeds. He is to engage in family devotions—in instructing his family as he rises up and sits down. He is to encourage and uphold the wife in doing her part, in nurturing the children, not as the good, not with healthy bodies and a lean, meager, shriveled soul, but as whole beings. We can be very careful for the physical well-being of our children and not think about their spiritual and moral well-being, and not carefully guard them and teach them well. He will teach his wife and his children and join with others in doing this because the good that he is turned to is: **"the glory of the LORD will be revealed, and all mankind together will see it"** (Is. 40:5a). This is another way of speaking about Isaiah 11:9: "the earth will be full of the knowledge of the LORD as the waters cover the sea." This is the reward man has, knowing God and the satisfaction that comes with knowing God. Anything else that he takes and drinks will leave him thirsty. "Everyone who drinks this water will be thirsty again, but whoever drinks the water I give him will never thirst" (Jn. 4:13–14). It is a meaningful life—a life that is increasingly full of meaning as against a meaningless life that is increasingly lacking in meaning. A meaningless life is being emptied in every realm: what love means, what a commandment means, what baptism means; everything is being emptied of meaning to the bare external form without any substance or meaning in it.

This is a result of the sin of not seeking the Lord diligently and understanding. When we teach, we are to turn the hearts of the children to the wisdom of the just. It is not only diligently teaching; it is teaching the wisdom of the just, which is a historically accumulated insight. We are not free to do without this insight. Evangelicals who ignore the historically accumulated insight summed up in the creeds may be zealous but without knowledge. They may have truths and be able to speak these truths, but the truths are isolated, and in isolation, they do not stand. When these truths are together and reinforced in the proper order in the system as a worldview, these truths stand. If you want the glory of the Lord to be revealed, it starts with teaching our families. This is how the way of the Lord is prepared. This is how a highway in the desert is made, and the rough places plain. When this happens, when this preparation comes, then the glory of the Lord is revealed. It is revealed in a way that all flesh shall see together. This seems to include having the good not just for me and myself, but for the church, and not just the church locally but the Church at large, so that the world may see and believe.

This can be done, and we are learning, as we struggle with sin year after year and day after day, what is needed. In the instruction of our children, we are to prepare the way for hearing, which means the basics must be in place. This starts with Common Ground about what the Word of the Lord is as reason in all of us, made in His image and capable of thinking, and with integrity, and in the nature of argument—less basic and more basic. Truths are to be supported, not just affirmed fideistically, but supported. It has to do with the most basic things—clarity of general revelation, understanding the sin and death that God calls us to repent of, and a view of what the good is and how we are to achieve it. Common Ground with clarity regarding sin and death and the good, eternal life—not this false view of heaven, which is really a form of Baal worship. The view of 72 virgins in heaven is gross Baal worship. They are looking for a sexual paradise. That is what the good is. How blatant can you get? The Christians may not be that gross, but they are still looking for the good as something of the absence of the curse and not the knowledge of God. They are looking for Eden instead of the City of God.

These are the basic things that we begin with. We have to speak not just about clarity and inexcusability but about the clarity of general revelation—all that is clear about God and man, and good and evil from general revelation. This needs to be taught to the children and this means in the grammar stage up to the dialectic stage—and notice it does not stop at the dialectic; it goes on to rhetoric.[21] So, by the time you are 16, you are pretty well grounded in rhetoric, knowing how to express yourself suitably in so many situations. If you think you just grab it in grammar, throw it out, and then you have it, you are wrong. You are missing it; you are merely professing it. If you cannot show what is clear, then you do not know what is clear; you have not really repented and you need to be brought back to that. Grammar is not enough, and dialectic is not enough; it needs to go on to rhetoric. By the time they are 16 and ready to go out and witness, they have a good sense of what is suitably said under what circumstances. They know how to think on their feet. They would know how to read a situation

21. The Logos Foundation Editorial Board, *Grammar Catechisms: Philosophical, Theological, and Historical Foundations* (Phoenix: Logos Papers Press, 2023).

and communicate effectively. They would not have to have someone hold their hand. This is what it is to prepare the way of the Lord.

We teach them general revelation. In the grammar stage, we teach them all the worldviews that exist. In the dialectic stage, we teach them how those worldviews manifest themselves in the histories of the various civilizations in the world and we teach them how to take these thoughts captive. In the rhetoric stage, we teach them how to communicate this knowledge to others. We also teach them Scripture—redemptive revelation. Starting with the foundation, the biblical worldview in Genesis 1–3, where there is a system of truth.[22] This is a system within special revelation. Added to special revelation are general revelation and Historic Christianity.[23] A rope is made of many strands. Similarly, truth is woven together, and then we have something strong. This is what a system provides. It is not a bunch of truths rolled up in a ball, but each of the truths are woven together in their place appropriately so that we have something very strong. This is the preparation that is needed.

We also teach Historic Christianity, the justification for it, and the focus of it. It is not soteriological or traditional reformed, or worldview reformed, but doxologically reformed.[24] All of this is being woven together as we understand the Scripture and general revelation; we come back to the Scripture and Historic Christianity and continue weaving these truths together. This is how we make a highway in the desert. When this is made, when hearts are prepared, then the glory of the Lord is revealed. The prophetic ministry is called for this—**"prepare the way of the LORD"** (v. 3a).

Our education should be worldview-centered, with critical thinking, and the Great Books are—broadly speaking—the content of great events, or we may say great revelations. It is not just college preparatory; it is life preparatory. Our education is preparing us for life. This is what the Logos class in the spring is going to do. We have been saying for 10 years and more that Logos is committed to this.[25] We have been doing

22. Gangadean, *The Biblical Worldview.*

23. Gangadean, *The Westminster Confession,* xv-xxxii, 349–351.

24. Gangadean, *The Westminster Confession,* xxix-xxxii; Gangadean, "Paper No. 115: Doxological Christianity," in *The Logos Papers,* 595–596.

25. Pastor Gangadean taught at Logos Theological Seminary for more than 25 years. The content of his courses will be available in forthcoming publications. Logos Theological Seminary is the ordinary means for training the members of Westminster Fellowship to teach in the home, the church, and the academy.

the Great Books studies.[26] We want to continue this, increase it, and enlarge it. In the worldview, we see a system, we see unity and fullness in a system, and we see fruit coming out of this system: the culture is the fruit of this worldview. Many are saying today that we have lost the culture. Many are saying that recently we have crossed the tipping point, and that may be so. It has the appearance of it. It is so because the way has not been prepared.

Our worldliness may continue to hold us in double-mindedness. We are halting between the two opinions. We are not quite ready yet to destroy the authority of the priests of Baal in our lives. It still comes in subtle ways, by what is said as well as what is not said, in every movie you watch, every life story you see, and every interpretation that is put out there before us. Unless we are careful, we just take it in, and we do not even know it. We are in captivity and do not even recognize it. We justify it one way or another by the idea of heaven or by the idea that the Lord is coming soon. We will not give ourselves to this.

The Word of the Lord comes not in the mighty wind, not in the earthquake, not in the fire, not with great outward display, but as a quiet whisper: This is the way; this is the truth; walk in it. As we benefit from this prophetic ministry, we will be able to pass on what we have learned to the next generation so that they have a double portion of the Spirit that God has put upon us because we have participated faithfully in the prophetic ministry of the Lord. Teach them diligently to your children, to the next generation, or the Lord will strike the earth with a curse. Elijah's ministry began striking the earth with a curse—"there will be neither dew nor rain" (1 Kgs 17:1b). There is need for that voice in this generation, not prophets hiding in caves, but the voice crying in the wilderness, **"prepare ye the way of the LORD"** (v. 3). Let us pray.

We pray, Lord, that as a result of your Word coming to us, we will lift up our voices and declare glad tidings of great joy of this One who has come full of grace and truth, who suffered and died for our sins, who has been raised for our justification, and who is seated at the right hand of God, that we will honor you in the Word of the Lord that is forever. That all flesh shall see your glory and come and bow before you.

Grant, Oh Lord, that we be a people whose hearts are turned to you to prepare the way of the Lord. Grant your blessing, Lord, to be upon

26. Three years of discussions on the Great Books will be made available in future publications. These discussions demonstrate how to apply the basics to interpreting literary works.

your people, we pray. Now may the grace of our Lord Jesus Christ, the love of God the Father, and the fellowship of the Holy Spirit, be and abide with you now and forever. Amen.

7

UNITY IN THE GOOD

That They May Be One: Unity of Diversity

2013

John 17:13–23

13"I am coming to you now, but I say these things while I am still in the
world, so that they may have the full measure of my joy within them. 14I
have given them your word and the world has hated them, for they are
not of the world any more than I am of the world. 15My prayer is not that
you take them out of the world but that you protect them from the evil
one. 16They are not of the world, even as I am not of it. 17Sanctify them
by the truth; your word is truth. 18As you sent me into the world, I have
sent them into the world. 19For them I sanctify myself, that they too may
be truly sanctified.

20"My prayer is not for them alone. I pray also for those who will believe
in me through their message, 21that all of them may be one, Father, just
as you are in me and I am in you. May they also be in us so that the world
may believe that you have sent me. 22I have given them the glory that you
gave me, that they may be one as we are one: 23I in them and you in me.
May they be brought to complete unity to let the world know that you
sent me and have loved them even as you have loved me.

"THAT ALL OF THEM MAY BE ONE . . . **that the world may believe"** (v. 21). I believe that God has sent Christ and that we are sent into the world even as He is sent into the world. In Christ's prayer, three times, He prays that they may be one. Christ is praying for the unity of the Church. We have other Scriptures that speak about this. We are to come into the unity of the faith.[1] There is a reality of our diversity. This diversity is the basis of all that is to come into unity. The basis of this unity is the one, most basic reality, the truth of Scripture as it is seen in Christ and accomplished by Christ; that is, we have unity in the good.[2]

The term *the good* is not used in Scripture, but the word *good* is used. It is used very early in Scripture—good and evil.[3] Even before that, it is structured into our being. The concept of the good is spoken of as a goal of life, which is implicit in the way we are made and in the Sabbath as a goal that will be accomplished.[4] The term *the good* is another term for *the goal.*

I want to bring this concept into focus in a greater way. Terms that are connected with this should be connected and always connected, such as love. Hence, The Focus for the Week is on love: "By this all men will know that you are my disciples, if you love one another" (Jn. 13:35). This verse again speaks about the world and the witness to the world. Love is to seek the good for the other and, by the grace of God, with the other.[5] "Man's chief end" is how the Westminster Shorter Catechism begins. It begins with the idea of the end in itself, the end of all ends, the goal, the good: "Man's chief end is to glorify God and to enjoy Him forever."[6] This is how the Gospel of John begins. The Word of God makes God known.[7] In John 17, Jesus says, "I have brought you glory on earth" (Jn. 17:4a). He wants His disciples to glorify God: "Herein is my Father glorified, that ye bear much fruit" (Jn. 15:8a KJV), even as it was in the beginning, "Be fruitful and increase in number; fill the earth and subdue it" (Gen. 1:28a). This unity is to be nothing less than the unity that there is in God. Jesus prays in John 17:18, "**As you sent me into the world, I have sent them into the world,**" and John 17:22–23, "**may they be one as we are one: I in them and you in**

---

1. *Ephesians 4:11–13;* See sermon 2: "Unity of the Spirit and Unity of the Faith."
2. Gangadean, *On Natural and Revealed Theology,* 33–39.
3. *Genesis 1:4, 10, 12, 18, 21, 25, 31.*
4. Gangadean, *The Biblical Worldview,* 125–146.
5. Gangadean, *Philosophical Foundation,* 245–254.
6. Gangadean, *The Westminster Catechisms,* 3–4, 171–183, 208–211; Gangadean, "Paper No. 6: The Good," 29–31; "Paper No. 106: The Good and Heaven," in *The Logos Papers,* 547–556.
7. *John 1:18.*

me." The outcome of this is **"that the world may believe"** (v. 21b). The importance of the idea of unity and the world believing is made clear by the Lord, and this is sometimes said to be the High Priestly Prayer.

What we need now is to understand what it means to pray **"that they may be one"** (v. 22a). What is this unity? We need to understand what unity is and to be able, therefore, to work for it. There are several levels by which we may begin to understand this. We can speak of it from Scripture, from general revelation, and from Historic Christianity. The Catechism says: "Man's chief end is to glorify God"[8] and "The first commandment requireth us to know and acknowledge God to be the only true God, and our God; and to worship and glorify him accordingly."[9] In the first petition of the Lord's Prayer, "we pray that God would enable us, and others, to glorify him in all that whereby he maketh himself known."[10] Scripture says: "For although they knew God, they neither glorified him as God nor gave thanks to him" (Rom. 1:21a) and "for all have sinned and fall short of the glory of God" (Rom. 3:23). We can see this in the case of Adam.[11] He turned away from the good and turned to evil. This was the choice. Turning away from the good is evil, and we are turning to evil.

Adam was to seek the knowledge of God as his chief end and was to do the work of dominion.[12] The work of dominion was to be accomplished through increasing and filling the earth:

> Be fruitful, and multiply, and replenish the earth, and subdue it: and have dominion over the fish of the sea, and over the fowl of the air, and over every living thing that moveth upon the earth (Gen. 1:28b KJV).

This should tell us that the work of dominion is vast. How vast? One idea of vast is "as the waters cover the sea" (Is. 11:9b)—full. "The LORD is exalted over all the nations, his glory above the heavens" (Ps. 113:4). We not only have the vastness of the waters but also the vastness of

8. *SCQ. 1.*

9. Gangadean, *The Westminster Catechisms,* 57–59.

10. Gangadean, *The Westminster Catechisms,* 100.

11. Gangadean, *The Biblical Worldview,* 37–54, 159–176.

12. Gangadean, *The Westminster Confession,* 353–357; Gangadean, *Philosophical Foundation,* 207–219.

the heavens above the earth and skies. You can see why it will take the earth being filled to accomplish this work, which involves naming the creation, understanding its purpose, what it is good for, and ultimately showing forth the glory of God in particular ways. We are to fill the earth with the knowledge of God, and the Sabbath day was for this purpose.

We have often spoken about the foundation, and I want to focus on one aspect. We can refer to this aspect as the good; it is the cornerstone[13] of the foundation. I am quite aware of Christ saying, "I am the way and the truth and the life" (Jn. 14:6a). We understand Him as the Word of God who makes God known, that brings this truth into focus, and this is how John speaks of Him.[14] The doxological focus is embodied fully in Christ, and we are to have the same purpose as He has: to glorify God.[15] It is spoken of Jesus, "who for the joy set before him endured the cross" (Heb. 12:2b), "In bringing many sons to glory" (Heb. 2:10a), in bringing redemption to the whole earth—restoring man, to fulfill the covenant promise, to *undo* what Adam did, and to *do* what Adam failed to do. This is where the focus of our Lord is. In focusing on our Lord, we also focus on what He focuses on. If we simply focus on the Lord and not see what He is focused on, we distort Him—we are conjuring up in our minds our own imagination of Him. The good, eternal life, the knowledge of God, and the glory of God are what Christ is focusing on.[16] The good is the cornerstone and evil must be understood in relation to the good. There are not two things, good and evil, as if they were a dualism, but there is good and the turning away from the good, which is evil. We have to define evil in relation to the good; we do not define good in relation to evil. Good is the original concept and all the more why we can understand this is the cornerstone.

---

13. Gangadean, "Paper No. 4: The Cornerstone," in *The Logos Papers,* 21–25.

14. In reference to the seven senses of the Word of God in the Gospel of John. See: Gangadean, *The Westminster Catechisms,* 113–114.

15. Gangadean, *The Westminster Confession,* xxix-xxxii, 85–87, 99–102, 353–357, 377–382.

16. Gangadean, *Philosophical Foundation,* 171–177, 208–211; Gangadean, *The Westminster Catechisms,* 109–111, 321–325; Gangadean, *On Natural and Revealed Theology,* 33–39, 127–139; Gangadean, *History of Philosophy,* 61–64; Gangadean, "Paper No. 115: Doxological Christianity," 595–596; "Paper No. 116: The Knowledge of God vs. The Hope of Heaven," 597–598; "Paper No. 117: Knowing and Making God Known," in *The Logos Papers,* 599–601.

Evil can be spoken of in two ways: as a *source* and as a *view*. As a source, evil is what we call autonomy, where we put ourselves in the place of God to determine good and evil as it was in the Garden: "you will be like God, knowing good and evil" (Gen. 3:5b), that is, determining good and evil. As a view, evil is distorting what truly is the good. We have to keep both of these in mind. There is a sense in which we may refer to the principle or the source of autonomy as a formal principle, and the particular thing that we turn away to is the content. "We all, like sheep, have gone astray, each of us has turned to his own way" (Is. 53:6a). Every one of us has put ourselves in the place of God.

As the good brings unity and life, sin brings death and disunity—breakup, breakdown, division, and disunity. We sometimes break the connection that God has spoken of and made between sin and death. God said, "for when you eat of it you will surely die" (Gen. 2:17b). Spiritually, we died.[17] In keeping with the way God has created things, things become increasingly manifest. Who we are becomes more and more manifest. You can look around, and we see little children; we do not know what will be in their future, but they grow, and what is in them becomes more and more manifest. This is pretty clear. A seed that is put in the ground cannot be distinguished much from other seeds, but it is all there, in the DNA, and it comes out and becomes manifest. Under various circumstances, it becomes manifested in various ways. So, too, with death, it grows and becomes manifest. As life grows and becomes manifest—the whole earth is to be filled with the knowledge of God.[18] So death can grow and increase and fill the earth: "See, darkness covers the earth and thick darkness is over the peoples" (Is. 60:2a).

I want to bring into focus that there are certain characteristic places and ways in which disunity comes about. When we look at the human body, we see that it is made up of many parts. These parts differ, and the differences can be a source of disunity. How do you know what a part is? From my wrist to my elbow, there is one part. While there may be a break in the forearm, there may be more characteristically distinguishing points between joints. The breaks or disunity comes in wherever there is a difference that God has made.

---

17. Gangadean, *The Biblical Worldview,* 37–54, 177–217.

18. *Isaiah 11:9; Habakkuk 2:14.*

One thing is characteristic of creation: No matter how we cut it or where we look at it, it is both complex and a unity. This unity involves an intricate, delicately balanced, very finely-tuned process. As we deal with health concerns in the body and the visible as a sign of the invisible, we see how fearfully and wonderfully we are made.[19] Last night, I was reading about balance. I was researching what goes on in the ear and all the intricacies there. Everything is so intricate, even the atom and the subatomic particles—intricate, ordered, balanced, finely-tuned, and so is our body. He made our natures, not just our visible body, but our visible body is a sign of the invisible. Paul speaks about unity throughout 1 Corinthians 12–14. Just as we are very fearfully made, delicate, wonderfully balanced, ordered, and finely-tuned, so is this matter of sin and evil. This means the good is like that, too. It will take the whole human race all of history to name the parts and the relations among them. We experienced a major breakthrough in the early 1950s. I believe it was Watson and Crick who discovered the DNA. So much that was sought after for so long just came together. It is marvelous to read about how that came about.[20]

I want to talk about the parts and where divisions and disunity come in. We want to look at the way we are made and begin to look at how, characteristically, divisions occur and how those divisions arise because we are not focused on the good. The good is what enables us to care for one another, appreciate one another, and honor one another as each part, made in the image of God, is able to do a particular work and become united and contributes. There is not an idle part. Some say the tonsil is idle, we do not need that anymore, or the appendix is a vestigial organ, or maybe the little toe we can do without, but the big toe, I do not know, I do not think so. I do not want to lose any part. Keep it all together very finely-tuned. What are these parts that we need to keep in mind? Let us just say this is the beginning. You have heard some of these things before. Keep in mind the analogy of the body of Christ. We together are the body of Christ, which is analogous to our body. The visible reveals the invisible, and disease involves various kinds of imbalance. If one part suffers, all parts suffer. We are knit together as

19. *Psalm 139:14.*

20. James D. Watson, *The Double Helix: A Personal Account of the Discovery of the Structure of DNA* (New York: Scribner Classics, 2011).

each part does its work. The body makes increase of itself in love. We have to name the parts and understand how divisions come in.

DIVISIONS WITHIN THE BODY

There is, first of all, division within ourselves and each person; there is a double-mindedness. Why? We are created finite, temporal, and changeable, and we change from good to evil. Even in our restoration (redemption), sin remains, and we go back and forth. The flesh wars against the spirit, which is the old nature against the new.[21] There are different aspects of our being: in our thinking, our presupposition, our personality, and our whole history—not only individually, but our history corporately. The particular condition we are in at any given moment, existentially, which may be dominating whether we are left to ourselves or not, is our mood. All these come into the picture when we speak about divisions within ourselves. It is not just division with others; it is first within ourselves.

Against this double-mindedness, we are to have integrity versus hypocrisy.[22] We are to come to maturity with the foundation in place. We are to be submitting ourselves to the Word of God so that we are not just saying and not doing and thereby deceiving ourselves. Division within ourselves can be summed up as acting contrary to our own nature—a division within ourselves. It is a form of spiritual suicide when we deny our nature. Spiritual suicide goes on to spiritual murder and goes on to deicide: killing God, first by destroying His Word that comes—killing the prophets—and then when Christ Himself comes, we kill Him. This is what sin does and it begins with the division within ourselves and unbelief dominating. Think about Israel in the desert. When they came out of Egypt, they murmured and complained. Were they seeking after the good with strong desire? Or were they lusting after eating and drinking, flesh and comfort, and sexual immorality? They ate and drank and rose up to play, engaged in pagan revelry, and worshiped the golden calf. The mind is not on the good; therefore, we turn aside to the things of the flesh and the lusts of life. There is a discernible pattern by which turning aside and apostasy comes about.

21. *Galatians 5:17.*

22. Gangadean, *Philosophical Foundation,* 199–205.

First: Larger Aspect

When the good is not present, every difference in our being becomes a source of division. We speak about the larger aspect of human nature that we all share equally. Formally, we all are finite, temporal, and changeable in truth, and have the capacity to understand. This capacity remains even when our minds are darkened; it is redirected. We understand falsely, or we understand in light of a false principle. We develop huge schemes and ways to justify ourselves.[23] At this level, division comes in where we act contrary to our nature as made in the image of God. All other sources of division spring from the most basic aspect of our being; division comes from within us, so when we start dealing with evil, we are not to look at the evil in the other person; we should look at the evil in us. We are already losing the war when we look at the evil in the other person first, e.g., our spouse. We have to look at it first in ourselves.

Second: Narrower Aspect

We can speak about our narrow aspect, having fallen away in Adam. God restores us to faith. Where the larger aspect pertains to form, in which we deny reason itself—neglect, avoid, resist, and deny reason—the narrower aspect is the specific content of our belief. We are fallen. We were created in knowledge, holiness, and righteousness but fell away from this. We are restored, recreated, in Christ's knowledge, holiness, and righteousness, but in seed form, and it grows over time. Unbelief is within a person, and we confront unbelief in ourselves and others—both. There are all kinds of degrees of understanding, misunderstanding, and ignorance. We can speak of these degrees in several ways, including our personality, background, and mood.

Third: Triune Personality

We come to the third level of human nature, our triune personality. As we said, we are created with knowledge, holiness, and righteousness. "Love the LORD your God with all your heart and with all your soul and with all your mind and with all your strength" (Mk. 12:30). These

23. Surrendra Gangadean, *The Contradictoriness of Sin: A Reading of Paradise Lost* (Phoenix: Logos Papers Press, 2024).

differences are areas in which we serve as prophet, priest, and king. We see these divisions within ourselves. 'Our head says one thing, and our heart says another' because of a split going in a certain way—a split at the first level of our understanding. In 1 Corinthians, we see this particularly: "One of you says, 'I follow Paul'; another, 'I follow Apollos'; another, 'I follow Cephas'" (1 Cor. 1:12). And the answer is, "Is Christ divided?" (1 Cor. 1:13a). No, He is not. His focus is on the glory of God. These things are perfectly united, and God has given each part of the body a particular glory so that we may have care for one another, the same care. We are not honoring some above others. The uncomely parts—upon these we bestow more abundant honor, in terms of our needs.

There is a diversity of gifts, both in terms of the characteristic calling—prophetic, priestly, and kingly—and in terms of the particular ways in which they are played out, as spoken of in 1 Corinthians 12. I was thinking about some of these divisions and how they have occurred between Paul and Barnabas. They were friends, and the dispute was so great that they separated. Barnabas wanted to take John Mark, and Paul said, no, let us take Silas—a keen division—and they departed.[24] They were close friends. Why? Because while the good may be in place, the order by which the good is to be achieved is not seen. We are a triune personality; there is an order within us, as there is within the Triune God, and that has to be observed: **"that they may be one as we are one"** (v. 22b). Think about Moses and Aaron. Moses goes up the mountain, Aaron is left, and Aaron accommodates the people. Moses comes down, breaks the tablets, and breaks up the golden calf. Aaron gives a lame excuse, accommodating the people.[25] There are strengths and weaknesses, and there are virtues connected with each personality. When they are separated because we are not focused on the good, we become divided and fall and break.

Christ embodies the distinctions in the human heart, within the offices of prophet, priest, and king, and within the principles of knowledge, holiness, and righteousness. It is hard to deny that this is a place where we divide. "'I follow Paul'; another, 'I follow Apollos'; another, 'I follow Cephas'" (1 Cor. 1:12a). Divisions within the Church go back

24. *Acts 15:37–39.*

25. *Exodus 32:22–24.*

to this. What is going on here? Our virtues will be elevated improperly because the good is not in place. We are not seeing virtues as a means to the good. Nurturing is elevated by Barnabas, who wants to nurture John Mark instead of thinking about the exigencies of the situation, what had happened, and the degree of opposition that occurred. Paul said he was not ready. Later, Paul will say, "Get Mark and bring him with you, because he is helpful to me in my ministry" (2 Tim. 4:11b). The existential particulars need to be observed in connection with the good and how to achieve it. So, the good is a source of unity.

Fourth: Body/Soul

We are created a body/soul unity; the visible body reveals something about the invisible soul (the eyes and ears of our visible body reflect our spiritual understanding). God reveals the distinction between matters concerning the soul and those concerning the body, granting the ability to discern between them and perceive their respective order. This understanding also extends to recognizing what serves as a sign of the reality versus what is more basic—these all come into the picture here. If we are given to feeling and do not distinguish between feelings of the body (appetites) and feelings of the soul (need for meaning), we may go after pleasure as the good. About 45% of the world's population is priestly.[26] They exalt their virtue, and when it is combined with priestly feminine or priestly masculine, it could intensify in various ways. All of these have to be connected. We may end up being a Christian hedonist. It may come out very innocently: 'It's not fun anymore.' Well, what about joy connected with the good? We do not hear that talk. It is not a joy anymore because the good is not in place; we are just drudging our way through. The kingly orientation is to take action and get things done, and they may speak about duty. 'This is your duty, just do your duty, it is right.' Then, we speak about the right rather than the good.

The Church has a major split between those who consider duty and the virtues as the good. Suppose a kingly woman upholds the virtues of the feminine as the good without observing the order of male and female, and we run into a certain problem. Or suppose a priestly man

26. In a clarifying remark, Pastor Gangadean said: "I am giving you a rough estimate; if you want to know where I am getting my figures from, I can discuss it with you. It is just a rough estimate."

upholds the feelings and devotions and the virtues connected with those and holds up pleasure as the good. We have heard the statement, 'You are not my type.' Well, there are body types and personality types, and usually, the body type tells you something about the personality. Certain persons are naturally attracted, but then their eyes are not on the good; that natural attraction becomes a 'natural attacking.' Instead of attracting, it is an 'attacking,' because you had expectations of the other. Because the good is not in place, it gets distorted, and all the more because you had those expectations, and it becomes difficult. There is no single husband-wife relationship that does not get embroiled in this. In our epistemology—how we know—in all the natural dividing parts where the differences are, one part and another part without the good, is where the conflict comes in.

Many people struggle with understanding what is of the body and what is of the soul. Many struggle with understanding the soul ruling, and the soul being in proper order in knowledge, holiness, and righteousness. Some people are led by their feelings of pleasure and others are led by duty. The latter can easily become legalists; they want everything spelled out, 'Tell me what to do in order, and detail it out.' This is often because the principle is not understood or the work to apply the principle is not there. We sometimes begin to make rules and impose them on others, which becomes another source of conflict. Dressing rules, drinking rules, eating rules, recreational rules—oh, you name it, we can come up with a rule. Those in the bureaucracy come up with many rules, and since the good is not in place, the thing creaks along, cracks, and eventually breaks down. Some of you have older vehicles and know what it is like when vehicles break down. Strains develop in the characteristic places in which it breaks down.

There is a body/soul unity. We were reading about Maimonides and Aristotle and Greek dualism, where they say 'taste not, touch not, handle not,' coming out of Greek dualism and making the body a source of evil rather than the soul.[27] All of these are characteristic breaking points, and there are not only dualists among the Greeks; there are also dualists among the Persians, Indians, etc. Many civilizations developed this line of thought. In some places it dominated, and history was hindered. The work of God is hindered because the good is not in place. We fall

27. Gangadean, *Philosophical Foundation,* 129–131.

into the antinomies of duty and pleasure, and some people do duty in order to get pleasure. Some say, 'If I do not get pleasure from doing my duty, I do not want to do it.' It is not just the duty; it is not just the virtue. Virtue is a means to the good, but it is not the good. God has given virtues to the members of the body, and if we have the good in mind, it will work the way it should, and pleasure will come with it. Growth will occur, and the pleasure that comes with growth.

Fifth: Male/Female

I hardly need to speak about the distinction between male and female, which is the next aspect. We have larger, narrower, triune, body/soul, and now male/female. God made us in His image; He made us male and female. There is, in God, both the work of creation and the work of providence; from the very first utterance when God created the vast body of material of the universe in the form of water, the Spirit of God hovered over the waters.[28] The Spirit was imbuing it with certain conditions, preparing it for the next work, hovering like a hen over her chicks, covering this work having brought it into existence, sustaining it, and preparing it to go on. Man is in a feminine role toward God. God created, and then He commanded man to develop, nurture, and bring it to its fullness so that it may show forth the glory: two distinct works, creation and providence—in order.

The masculine and feminine in God are revealed in the visible male and female differences. Our very visible anatomical differences are a sign of this difference. Female is to nurture life. Male is to initiate life. However, we do not understand their complementarity, and the masculine and feminine virtues are held up by themselves, and we miss it. We should say that the virtues of the priest are connected with devotion and feeling, and the ministry of the king is connected with will, action, and deed; each accomplishing a goal in a certain way, but without the good, both of these can be exalted in a way that fragments.

Male and female are a unity; they are one in God. He made us in His image: "male and female he created them" (Gen. 1:27b). Creation and providence are united in God: initiating, preserving, nurturing, and bringing to fullness—this is all one in God. Is Christ divided? This is where divisions come in because the good is not adequately

---

28. *Genesis 1:1–2.*

in place. There is a temporality of our being; we are finite, temporal, and changeable; in addition to this, the larger aspect, the narrower, the triune personality, the body/soul, and the male/female. We grow, not only change as in the narrower aspect from good to evil, but we grow. We grow not just individually but over time and place, and we grow in a community context; we have a background factor that we need to deal with.

Sixth: Background

Let us think about some dividing points. First, there is education. I watched an episode where the French aristocracies were saying of the servants that they were not capable of thinking; they were just servants. The servant objected, 'I do not want to be considered an animal.' Some make distinctions on the basis of education, and some make distinctions on the basis of economics. Karl Marx made a distinction between rich and poor. Sometimes, it is ethnicity. 'I came from this tradition, this time and place.' We can think about going back further to the three sons of Noah, and the differences and virtues that developed and transmitted themselves over time.[29] Some were dead-ended because they went out so far and fast from the center that they lost connection with the center. They lost connection with the historically accumulated insight, and they are out there in the wilderness trying to make it on their own without understanding all that has been done and accomplished in history. Their virtue enabled them to go out fast, but their virtue became a vice when disconnected from the good. It is just, 'I want new territory, a new change of scenery, more fertile soil, and I go on out.' Things get passed on from parents; there is a historically accumulated "insight" in traditions. We get locked into our traditions, and this becomes a source of division. The Scripture says, "from every nation, tribe, people and language" (Rev. 7:9). These will be redeemed, and the kings of all the earth will bring their glory into the house of God.[30] God can redeem these differences by bringing into focus the glory of God.

29. Arthur C. Constance, *Noah's Three Sons: Human History in Three Dimensions* (Grand Rapids: The Zondervan Publishing House, 1975).

30. *Revelation 21:24.*

Seventh: Uniqueness

Lastly, there is a unique element. Brothers, think about James and John and their differences. Brothers, think about Peter and Andrew. Think about Jacob and Esau. Think about the twelve sons of Jacob. Think about the diversity in your own children, with your own siblings: how different you are, yet you have the same background. What happened? There is a unique element in each of us, in which we uniquely reflect the glory of God. We do not try to imitate the uniqueness in another person. It is not cool; it does not work. Let Socrates be Socrates. Let others be what they are.

We cannot exalt the uniqueness of our being at the expense of others. Scripture says, "Love your neighbor as yourself" (Mk. 12:31b). It also says, "But I say unto you, Love your enemies, bless them that curse you, do good to them that hate you" (Matt. 5:44 KJV). To love someone involves a commitment to seek the good for them and to do it in ways that will most facilitate them coming into the good, taking into account their particular background and personality, and bringing this about. In the process of education, we must lay the foundation well in the prophetic, priestly, and kingly because if one gets past a certain age, it is a lot more difficult to have that person back up, given their disposition and orientation. Regarding our background and personality, we might say: because there is an order in our triune personality, and there is an order within the gifts—prophetic, priestly, kingly—and because the priestly depends on the prophetic and the kingly depends on the priestly and the prophetic, as a person gets older, they are not inclined, if they are priestly, to do prophetic work. The kingly are not going to do the priestly work; they are going to assume that is in place, and they are going to go from there. So, there are things to be gotten in the first stage of education, for all, and in the dialectic, and in the rhetoric. If the prior pieces are there, they flow one from another. There is an order. There is a time order. There is a developmental sequence that is natural for us as human beings.[31] "There is a time for everything, and a season for every activity under heaven" (Eccl. 3:1). We are to connect with the times and seasons.

31. The Logos Foundation, *Grammar Catechisms,* xiv-xvi; Dorothy L. Sayers, *The Lost Tools of Learning* (Louisville: Glh Publishing, 2017).

Because of their personalities, combined with their uniqueness, some may tend to emphasize different ways of knowing. Some emphasize tradition. Conservatives and liberals are different on this point. Conservatives tend to be deontologists. Liberals tend to be hedonists; pleasure is the good. This is a major difference. Pleasure is not the good; it is the effect of possessing what really is the good—lasting pleasure.[32] The virtues are not the good, and the rules of tradition are not the good; they are a means to the good. If it is separated from the good, you lose it. Think about Aristotle trying to get the virtues balanced to the golden mean without the good and trying to overcome the antinomy of going to the left and right. The Bible speaks about this. In addition to these dividing points, there is a tendency to go to the left and to the right. Scripture says no; it commands us to meditate on the law day and night.[33]

We are to understand the way God has made the world. No one is to think more highly of themselves than they ought.[34] We are to understand our limits according to the measure of faith God has given us. We are to act properly and connect with the means to maturity. There is an order assumed, and if it is not in place earlier when it is the time and season to get it in place, it will be all the more difficult later. This is what we are speaking about in regard to preparing the way. Do not exasperate your children. Do not expect obedience without preparing them. We need to prepare them according to their gifts and their abilities. We need to be discerning. There is something for all of them as they develop over the years. When we discipline our children, we have to know how they are going to process it. With some, we can use corporal discipline, others a word, and some a look. We need to be discerning in terms of the personality of the child.

Everyone needs some things in common, such as discipline, and we are to prepare the way of the Lord by raising children appropriately. We are to have a view of the whole and the complexity of things, and we need to know how we need to order these things, and how they work together. Instead of pulling apart at every conceivable level, we are to be pulling together at every conceivable level. Why? Because the

32. Gangadean, *Philosophical Foundation,* 171–183.

33. *Joshua 1:8; Psalm 1:2.*

34. *Romans 12:3.*

good is in place, the goal is in place. Man's chief end is to glorify God.[35] We can say this in word and not understand what it means. We need to recognize that we may begin to use words without understanding or wisdom to put them into practice. We may just say the words at a grammar level stage, a level of knowledge, which is not the same as a level of understanding, which is not the same as a level of wisdom—*in that order*. We need to know what we need to progress on.

The formal definition of knowledge used is that some subject/person (*S*) knows a proposition (*P*) if and only if *P* is true, *S* believes *P*, and *S* is justified in believing *P*. This has been drilled into us in the educational system—*not*. Unfortunately, this is not the case.[36] Possessing knowledge is much more than *S* knows *P* if he gets it at the grammar level and gets arguments at a grammar level. You can get arguments at a grammar level and just repeat them without understanding their assumptions and implications. Many congregants have complained to me, saying, 'Look, these guys are just using words. They do not have it in their lives.'[37] I would respond, 'Yes, I know that. I know that. We have to keep working on deepening understanding from grammar to dialectic to rhetoric.' We have never said that profession and repetition without understanding are what knowledge is. Defining propositional knowledge in regards to life should be stated as: *S* has knowledge if *S* knows how to apply *P*. First, he applies it to himself, then his own household, then to society round about him, and lastly, to understand all of history. Then it can be said that *S* knows *P*. True understanding (discipleship) is not finished until the rhetoric comes in. The rhetoric is really never finished. We are growing in this. We can speak about the stages of an apprentice, a journeyman, and a craftsman. Progress in this is part of our temporality. There is a spiritual war that is going on at every level within a person, between two persons, husband and wife, parent and child, siblings, family, church, workplace, and in the state. Divisions occur because the good is not in place.

35. *SCQ. 1.*

36. Gangadean, "Paper No. 72: What Is Knowledge? (Concise Version)," 381–383; "Paper No. 73: What Is Knowledge? (Expanded Version)," in *The Logos Papers,* 385–390; Gangadean, *Philosophical Foundation,* 49–59.

37. This statement is in reference to those in the church undergoing practicum. Younger men who are being prepared for the ministry. The discrepancy between the doctrine and the life of those who profess belief needs to be bridged through the process of discipleship. See: Gangadean, *The Westminster Confession,* 385–386.

Beyond a person, there can be groups within a church. There can be conflicts between churches and in a nation. We are culturally divided about 50/50 now. There may be a certain percentage that does not vote. A lot of the elections are almost 50/50. It is generally the deontologists who are more conservative against the liberals who are more consequentialists/hedonists. There is about 45% of each. That constitutes 90% of the population. The other 10% just shake their heads and say, 'I am not voting.' We can see where these breaks are, and it is because the good is not in place. Jesus prayed, **"that all of them may be one . . . that the world may believe"** (v. 21). We are not to be like the world without the good. We are to try and discern what good and evil are in relation to the good and to seek it.

The spiritual war is also between nations within the world—World War I and World War II. The last time we spoke about this, we said we were to prepare for war. We talk about 'the war to end all wars.' The only war that will end all wars is the spiritual war. We do not war as the world does.

> For though we live in the world, we do not wage war as the world does. The weapons we fight with are not the weapons of the world. On the contrary, they have divine power to demolish strongholds. We demolish arguments and every pretension that sets itself up against the knowledge of God, and we take captive every thought to make it obedient to Christ (2 Cor. 10:3–5).

This is the war that will end all wars, at which point the nations "shall beat their swords into plowshares, and their spears into pruninghooks: nation shall not lift up sword against nation, neither shall they learn war any more" (Is. 2:4 KJV). And "the earth will be full of the knowledge of the LORD as the waters cover the sea" (Is. 11:9).

We, the body of Christ, are to be focused as Christ is focused on the end and the means to it. We are to engage in this work. This is the redemption that He is bringing into the world. May God grant us grace to hear and to put this Word into practice.

8

A House Divided

Witness and the Need to Overcome Divisions

2015

Mark 3:20–35

20Then Jesus entered a house, and again a crowd gathered, so that he and
his disciples were not even able to eat. 21When his family heard about this,
they went to take charge of him, for they said, "He is out of his mind."

22And the teachers of the law who came down from Jerusalem said, "He is
possessed by Beelzebub! By the prince of demons he is driving out demons."

23So Jesus called them and spoke to them in parables: "How can Satan
drive out Satan? 24If a kingdom is divided against itself, that kingdom
cannot stand. 25If a house is divided against itself, that house cannot
stand. 26And if Satan opposes himself and is divided, he cannot stand; his
end has come. 27In fact, no one can enter a strong man's house and carry
off his possessions unless he first ties up the strong man. Then he can rob
his house. 28I tell you the truth, all the sins and blasphemies of men will
be forgiven them. 29But whoever blasphemes against the Holy Spirit will
never be forgiven; he is guilty of an eternal sin."

30He said this because they were saying, "He has an evil spirit."

31Then Jesus' mother and brothers arrived. Standing outside, they sent
someone in to call him. 32A crowd was sitting around him, and they told
him, "Your mother and brothers are outside looking for you."

33"Who are my mother and my brothers?" he asked.

34Then he looked at those seated in a circle around him and said, "Here are my mother and my brothers! 35Whoever does God's will is my brother and sister and mother."

A HOUSE DIVIDED CANNOT STAND

A HOUSE DIVIDED CANNOT STAND. This is a basic truth. It is clear. It applies widely, broadly, everywhere, and in every way. Denying this truth as it is manifested in miracle by attributing the work of God to Satan, when this truth is so clear, shows a degree of intellectual depravity, a degree of unbelief that is so great, that it has gone beyond the bounds of redemption. It is an eternal sin; it will never be forgiven in this life or in the life to come. When we go so far in denying the truth, then we are let go by God, to go our way.

Matthew 12:43–50 says when an evil spirit goes out of a man, it moves around in arid places, seeks to find a resting place, returns, and finds the house swept and clean—mere outward appearance—not filled by the Spirit who was denied. Then that spirit takes with it seven other evil spirits, and the end of that man is worse than before. We are never left where we were before the truth came. Either we are transformed by it—in repentance, the renewal of our mind—or we are hardened and go further down. When we speak about truth and mercy, we often speak about truth and grace. Grace and truth come by Jesus Christ,[1] and were it not for the grace of God, the truth that comes would cause us to harden and to perish.

The basic point is that a divided house cannot stand, which is a necessary truth. It is not that we can never be divided. We can be for a time, but it cannot remain so; it will not stand. Satan's kingdom will not stand. Is that because it is divided? I would say, ultimately, 'Yes.' But then Jesus says, **"How can Satan drive out Satan? If a kingdom is divided against itself, that kingdom cannot stand"** (vv. 23b–24). It is divided in a way that differs from what is spoken of in Matthew 12. Here, we have the manifestation of the work of the Holy Spirit being attributed to Satan and the idea that Satan will cast out Satan. No, he does not, and the Lord explicitly addresses this when He says,

1. *John 1:17.*

> When an evil spirit comes out of a man, it goes through arid places seeking rest and does not find it. Then it says, "I will return to the house I left." When it arrives, it finds the house unoccupied, swept clean and put in order. Then it goes and takes with it seven other spirits more wicked than itself, and they go in and live there. And the final condition of that man is worse than the first (Matt. 12:43–45a).

It is not that Satan is casting out Satan. On the latter end, that man is worse than before. If the change is not truly done in the Lord, replaced by the truth of God, this is how God works—the final condition is worse. When God works to destroy the works of the devil—he is a liar and the father of it, and the destroyer—the latter end of that man is *not* worse than before, because the Spirit comes in and does His redemptive work. But there is a kind of change where the Spirit of God does not come in, the house is empty, and the end of that man is worse than before. We have to make these comparisons when we try to work our way through this.

Christ's Family Is Divided

Interestingly, the event in Mark is set in this context:

> **Then Jesus entered a house, and again a crowd gathered, so that he and his disciples were not even able to eat. When his family heard about this, they went to take charge of him, for they said, 'He is out of his mind'** (vv. 20–21).

Jesus' family implies that Jesus is out of His mind. Our family might say this of us, and it could be true, but not of Jesus, right? With us, it is probably not true, but we always have a question mark hanging there. With Jesus, there is no question mark. This is remarkable, is it not? All these crowds are coming to Jesus. What is it about the crowds coming to Jesus? Here is what is going on. Jesus said,

> Do not suppose that I have come to bring peace to the earth. I did not come to bring peace, but a sword. For I have come to turn "a man against his father, a daughter against her mother, a daughter-in-law against her mother-in-law—a man's enemies will be the members of his own household" (Matt. 10:34–36).

When it gets to the mother-in-law and daughter-in-law, you know it has gone to the ends of the earth; it is done; it is finished. This is not merely natural. There are mother-in-law and daughter-in-law relations that are spiritual and beautiful. Think of Naomi and Ruth: "Where you die I will die, and there I will be buried" (Ruth 1:17a). In the Lord, family is a blessing. Outside of the Lord, what was intended for a blessing becomes a curse. His own family heard about Him and came to Him to—notice this—**"take charge of him"** (v. 21b). It was like having some child, perhaps one who is not developed the way he should be, and the child is out there and, 'Oh boy, let us go get Billy.' Billy is four years old, intellectually, when he should be 20, and you go to take charge of Billy and bring Billy back. His own house did not believe in Him. They had the truth. They did not believe it. What divided them in this house divided, was belief and unbelief. Of course, unbelief does not see itself as unbelief; it is only *unbelief* from the point of view of *belief*. So, they think, 'We believe what is true, and you have gone off the deep end,' and they came to take charge of Jesus.

They tried this once before when Jesus was 12 years old, when He stayed back in Jerusalem at the temple, in His Father's house, and was talking about the law of God: asking and answering questions. Jesus apparently loved dialogue on the subject. This was the thing to do and the place to be. His parents came back and chided him: "Son, why have you treated us like this? Your father and I have been anxiously searching for you" (Lk. 2:48b). He says, "Didn't you know I had to be in my Father's house?" (Lk. 2:49b). They had the Word spoken to them: they had the testimony of the wise men from the east, the testimony of the shepherds, and had all of these visions, but they still did not quite get it. I am sure this says something about the extent of our unbelief. In this event in Mark, they came to get Him, and I suppose His mother was among them. Maybe we can ease this—maybe the brothers were, would you say, embarrassed by Jesus? Perhaps they think He is giving the family the appearance of being weird, and they have someone who is half a bubble off plumb.

The family said, **"He is out of his mind"** (vs. 21b), and they went to take charge of Him. At the end of this account concerning the teachers of Jerusalem, Jesus' mother and brothers arrived. They were on their way—they were part of this one event. As they are on their way, the house divided is brought in. They send someone in to call Him on behalf of his family, and because of the crowd, Jesus replies,

> **'Who are my mother and my brothers?' he asked. Then he looked at those seated in a circle around him and said, 'Here are my mother and my brothers! Whoever does God's will is my brother and sister and mother'** (vv. 33–35).

The spiritual reality is the reality. The physical reality is a sign of the spiritual. We can have the sign and not have the reality, and we could try to take the sign *for* the reality; this false understanding—misunderstanding—is common.

Two Levels of a House Divided

In this passage, we have at least two levels of a house divided. One is Satan's house: Is it divided? Of course, Satan may want to give appearances. He wants to appear as an angel of light who brings enlightenment of knowing the truth and speaking the truth, but this is an appearance. What Jesus did, and was doing, could not be attributed to Satan. There is another level in which Satan, as a sinful creature, is divided against himself. My master's thesis in English was on *Paradise Lost.*[2] The subject was the contradictoriness of sin through Milton's handling of Satan. Some were saying, 'Satan is the real hero of Paradise Lost; he comes off looking better,' and 'Milton could not quite contain his character, and maybe Milton was just expressing thoughts that he himself had not really wrestled through.' Stanley Fish, who was one of the early guys in postmodern theory, was one person taking this sort of position.[3] I had written, and I tried to show from the text, how it was otherwise. Satan is always caught in his own contradiction, including when he says, "Better to reign in Hell, than serve in Heaven" (I.263)[4]—the egoist. The outward circumstance was that he had been turned into a serpent, and he was writhing on the floors of hell. That is not ruling; writhing is not ruling. There is a line on Satan that says:

---

2. Surrendra Gangadean, *The Contradictoriness of Sin: A Reading of Paradise Lost* (Phoenix: Logos Papers Press, 2024).

3. Stanley Eugene Fish, *Surprised by Sin: The Reader in Paradise Lost* (New York: Palgrave MacMillan, 1997).

4. John Milton, *Paradise Lost* (New York: Oxford University Press, 2004).

Him the Almighty Power
Hurled headlong flaming from the ethereal sky
With hideous ruin and combustion down
To bottomless perdition, there to dwell
In adamantine chains and penal fire,
Who durst defy the Omnipotent to arms (I.44–49).

There is a contradiction. You cannot defy the Omnipotent. There is contradictoriness in Satan; therefore, he will fall, and with him, his own kingdom; it cannot be sustained. The light shines in the darkness, and the darkness cannot overcome it,[5] no matter how far we go.

I was imagining a scenario where someone is trying to object to clarity—Common Ground—and still talk. He would have to say, 'I am not committed to reason,' and then we ask, 'And why are you here?' 'Well, I am here to simply disrupt what is going on.' And the response is to ask, 'And why should we allow that?' What would he or she say? 'Why should we listen to you?' What would he say? What can he say? Some things are self-evident and clear; we cannot get around it, just as a house divided against itself cannot stand.

SEVENFOLD LEVELS OF THE SPIRITUAL WAR

What I would like to do in this message is to bring into focus the pattern and system in which the spiritual war expresses itself in divisions. Two patterns are operating simultaneously and interacting. In terms of persons, divisions are at every level. In terms of spheres or aspects of life, divisions are at every level. In each person, there are several aspects, and this truth applies in all of those aspects: if there is division, it will not stand. At the level of persons, that is, in each person and between persons: if there is division, it will not stand.

Division is not a bad thing, in and of itself. In our original condition at creation, it was a bad thing. In our fallen condition, it is not a bad thing. As a matter of fact, division is a good thing in our fallen condition. It is a good thing to have belief opposing sin in us. This is why God said in the Garden, "I will put enmity between you and the woman" (Gen. 3:15a). This is a good thing. Of course, in their fallen condition, they had left the truth of God, been seduced by Satan, and

5. *John 1:5.*

now came under his sphere of influence—his rule—because of their unbelief, because they bought into the lie of Satan: the ethical egoism, the self-centered existence. They bought into that and put themselves in the place of God to determine good and evil for themselves, as if they were God—it cannot be.[6] It cannot possibly be. Good is according to the nature of a being, and we do not create our nature as we find ourselves with this nature. We cannot create. We cannot determine the nature of anything. We do not have the power. We cannot even create a speck of dust or an atom. We cannot create an electron or give it its charge. We cannot create anything. We are not creators. Only God is the Creator, and God determines the nature of things in creation. Good is according to the nature of things, so we cannot determine good and evil.

We bought into Satan's lie, and God said, "I will put enmity" (Gen. 3:15a). Since it was a matter of believing the lie, "I will put enmity" means God is restoring us to the truth. By bringing us to the truth, He is putting us at enmity with Satan, and He is putting enmity between those who believe Satan and those who believe the truth. "Between your seed and her seed" (Gen. 3:15a). He, *the* seed of the woman, will crush your head: destroy. "And you will strike his heel": inflict harm upon, but not in the same measure as "crush your head" (Gen. 3:15b).

"I will put enmity," God said. Jesus said, "Do not suppose that I have come to bring peace to the earth. I did not come to bring peace, but a sword . . . a man's enemies will be the members of his own household" (Matt. 10:34, 36). There is a familiarity that breeds contempt in that we take it for granted, and we explain things away improperly. We try to find natural causes in the circumstances of this present event, as against saying, 'This is from God.' We are not paying attention; we are writing it off. A prophet is not without honor except in his own house and in his own country. Jesus was a prophet; not simply a priest, but a prophet. He does not say, 'A priest is not without honor.' He says, "A prophet is not without honour" (Matt. 13:57 KJV). The prophet comes challenging us to repent in the realm of truth. More often than not, a priest comes focusing on the growth process, and hopefully, when repentance is called for, the priest will be faithful and call for it, but there is a different process. Jesus said, "I did not come to bring peace, but a sword" (Matt. 10:34).

---

6. Gangadean, *The Biblical Worldview*, 37–54, 177–195.

Let us review these various levels quickly. I want us to get a sense of the comprehensiveness of this conflict, war, and division—all of these go together.

First: In Each Person

Division is in each person, and it is in each person in every sphere of life. Just because the Scripture does not say it, and we are unaware of it, does not mean it is not there. It is in each sphere of life; that means it is also in the thinking sphere. It is not just between thinking and doing, as if the conflict is there. The conflict is right down the middle, throughout the entire heart. This is what is called *total depravity*.[7] The whole heart is affected. Aquinas and others thought that the intellect was exempt.[8] 'Aristotle was a brilliant philosopher. He will take us so far, and grace will complete it.' He made a nature-grace schema, complete-incomplete. This still goes on today in the way the Roman Catholic Church thinks about the world. 'They have gone far; we just need to complete it by grace,' so the call to repentance is not there, and grace is said to be administered immediately, directly, through the sacrament—as against saying, no, Aristotle failed to see what is clear.[9] He was a dualist, and even a dependent dualist is not the same as a theist who affirms that the universe was created. Just to make matters a little more interesting, al-Ghazali saw that Aristotle did not get it. Aristotle could not really account for the existence of the soul over and against the body, and personal immortality. Aristotle thought that matter was eternal, not created. Al-Ghazali rejected Aristotle, and with Aristotle, rejected reason and philosophy, and he turned to mysticism.[10] Al-Ghazali is second in influence in Islam only to Muhammad, and his move accounted for the turn away from reason. When we turn away from reason, we naturally turn to violence.[11] What is happening with

7. Gangadean, *The Westminster Confession*, xxvii, 99–110, 369–376.

8. Gangadean, *History of Philosophy*, 93–105

9. Gangadean, *Philosophical Foundation*, 132–134.

10. Al-Ghazali, *Al-Ghazali's Path to Sufism: His Deliverance from Error* (Louisville: Fons Vitae, 2000), 51–64.

11. Robert R. Reilley, *The Closing of the Muslim Mind: How Intellectual Suicide Created the Modern Islamist Crisis* (Wilmington:ISI Books, 2010).

Islamic terrorism has direct roots in the failure to see what is clear. A house divided. Intellectually, division as unbelief is in our thinking.

We may not be aware of unbelief *as* unbelief. Peter certainly was not when he confessed that Jesus is the Christ—"You are the Christ, the Son of the living God" (Matt. 16:16b)—but was there unbelief? Yes. "'Never, LORD!' he said. 'This shall never happen to you!'" (Matt. 16:22b). There was unbelief in his understanding of what Christ should do. Jesus would labor with His disciples, and after He was raised, He said, "How foolish you are, and how slow of heart to believe all that the prophets have spoken! Did not the Christ have to suffer these things and then enter his glory?" (Lk. 24:25–26). What do you think the coats of skin were about?[12] What do you think the sacrifices were about? What do you think the Day of Atonement is about? What do you think Passover is about? Are these just outward rituals, or do they signify Christ to come? "How foolish you are, and how slow of heart to believe all that the prophets have spoken! Did not the Christ have to suffer these things and then enter his glory?" Just because we are unaware of our unbelief does not mean it is not there. Just because it is not *said* to be there in this passage does not mean it is not there. This is a form of literalism, not contextualism.[13]

The division is within the person, that is why the Scripture says, "Sanctify them by the truth; your word is truth" (Jn. 17:17). "Be transformed by the renewing of your mind" (Rom. 12:2). "Then you will know the truth, and the truth will set you free" (Jn. 8:32). "Father, forgive them; for they know not what they do" (Lk. 23:34 KJV). It starts in the mind; this is why Christ began His ministry with the call to repentance: "Repent: for the kingdom of heaven is at hand" (Matt. 4:17). This is why there are trials of faith, to compel a change of mind and in our thinking.

The conflict is within each person, at the most basic level: in the thinking, in the understanding, in the use of reason to see what is clear. This is where the conflict begins; it is between belief and unbelief. I was thinking about this coming into church and thought, actually, it is more like a relationship between the self and God. In terms of the way it comes through the mind, it comes through the human being; it is

12. *Genesis 3:21.*

13. Gangadean, *On Natural and Revealed Theology,* 18–22; Gangadean, *The Westminster Confession,* 41–44.

between self-life and God, between belief and unbelief. In the Garden, this is how it is manifest. They did not believe what God said. They believed the lie. "You will not surely die" (Gen. 3:4a). It is cognitive, having to do with true and false; it is not just dispositional. This is why Scripture says, "Sanctify them by the truth" (Jn. 17:17a).

The conflict is between belief and unbelief in each person. The solution is: "If anyone would come after me, he must deny himself and take up his cross and follow me" (Matt. 16:24b). The solution is synonymous, parallel, to the trials of faith. Through suffering, we enter into glory;[14] through suffering, we come to understand and see the glory of God. Trials of faith are throughout our lives. We may have big trials, but they are throughout our lives because if God were to deal with us and try to cleanse us all at once through trials, it would be too much to take—it is called gradualism. We are transformed by renewing our minds, seeing the truth more and more, and growing in faith. Sanctification is being *transformed* by the renewing of our mind. There is a conflict in each person. We are divided against ourselves in our thinking. Scripture says, "A double minded man is unstable in all his ways" (Jas. 1:8 KJV), and it says, the trials of faith are so that you might be holy: "without holiness no one will see the LORD" (Heb. 12:14b). We are wholly devoted to the Lord. *Purity of Heart Is to Will One Thing* is a work by Kierkegaard on holiness.[15] It is certainly consistent with holiness, with not being double-minded.

There is a conflict, and all of the conflicts begin at the level of one's thinking, and there is a way to deal with it—a way to get the truth into us. The Church is for discipleship, so we bind ourselves by our vow.[16] No one required a vow of us. We could have not taken the vow and not been a member. Church attendance is approached casually by those seeking the benefits of church membership without taking the vow. This is like saying: 'I want to have the benefits of married life without taking a marriage vow.' Why should anyone accept that way of approaching things? Vows, or commitments, are natural, and discipline is on the basis of the vow,[17] and the Church is to make disciples—not converts, *per se*. The process is not to be done in two stages. 'You first

14. *Acts 14:22.*

15. Søren Kierkegaard, *Purity of Heart Is to Will One Thing* (New York: Rough Draft, 2013).

16. Gangadean, *The Westminster Confession*, 385–388.

17. Gangadean, *The Westminster Confession*, 245–252.

make converts, get them in the church, and then work on them.' That is an interesting strategy, is it not? But what happens is usually this: first, you get them in the church, and then you have to accommodate many things in the process. Instead, we could bring them in and have them be adherents. Before we bring them in, we evangelize them, and they come in. We bring to them Historic Christianity before they come in, and after they come in, we go through a period before they commit to becoming members. After three months, if it is going along seriously, they can say, 'Okay, I commit,' and maybe after some time, then they commit.

There are reasonable ways, ways that are peaceful and pleasant. After this, we continue to work on it when trials come our way, and the sins of youth—longstanding, deep-seated patterns of life—surface, and we talk to oversight, those in the priestly ministry, and they say, 'Yes, this looks like it is heart deep. It is not merely circumstantial. We need to deal with this.' This process is symbolized to us in all the rituals of cleansing, when the Israelites had a skin infection become manifest.[18] Leviticus teaches us about the process of sanctification. Sometimes, you have to come back a few times over a long time, and you may be unclean for a while, but then you recognize the uncleanliness and come back into the congregation. Is self-life ruling, raging, in you? Do you understand some of the basics? Have you really understood this? Is it manifest in your reading the Word of God, praying, teaching your children, and being submitted to the Word? If it is not, then it is not in keeping with our vows, the nature of the church, and sanctification. The Church is for discipleship in order to deal with the war that is in us.[19]

Second: In Each Household

Divisions are in each household, within our closest relations, including parents and children. It is first between Adam and Eve. Then it is between Adam and Eve, and Cain and Abel: between parents and children. Then it is between Cain and Abel: between siblings. Three relations in the household—divided. There is a connection between

---

18. *Leviticus 13.*

19. Gangadean, "Paper No. 40: The Church (Expanded)," 221–223; "Paper No. 56: The Gospel (Summary)," 303–313; "Paper No. 134: Worship, the Sabbath, and the Church," in *The Logos Papers,* 679–682.

division in oneself and division with others. We have self-life and sins of youth that are longstanding and deep-seated. And by sins of youth, we do not just mean events that happened in youth, but a way of life that is manifest. Parents were not there to discipline; they were *there,* but they were not *there*. You were in the same room and ate about 15,000 meals together—multiply three meals, times the number of days, for so many years, and you get the figure.

Parents were *there* but were not *there*. They went through the motions but missed the meaning. Parents had all that time to instruct, and they were not as focused as they should have been. They were divided. They did not see the goal, and so the kid got away. And the parents excuse themselves by saying, 'What happened to the kid? Kids nowadays, you know? Kids nowadays have iPhones and smartphones. Kids nowadays do not have to work on the farm and hoe potatoes; when you have to hoe potatoes, you have to prepare and process the potatoes because you cannot go down to the local store and buy them. They had to stamp out the potatoes, dry them, store them, and freeze them. There are all kinds of problems with kids nowadays. They do not learn work ethic.' We are to adjust and find other ways to connect with and discipline the children. We do not just throw up our hands.

A house divided cannot stand. The most explosive manifestation of this is divorce. Unbelief is dominant in one to such a point that he or she says, 'I am out of here; forget the vow. The vow means nothing; it is just words.' At least, we think of it that way. How often does divorce happen? This is a house divided, and it did not stand—it broke. This is because of unbelief in both, and the particular chemistry, and the accumulated effect of this: from generations past, sins of youth, and our own attitude. A vow is taken and there is discipline according to it, which just gets tossed by the wayside. We do not listen to the Word—even our own words, even our own vows.

Third: In Each Church

People come into the church and leave. "They went out from us, but they were not of us" (1 Jn. 2:19 KJV).[20] Put it this way: Those who

20. Gangadean, "Paper No. 64: Aaron's Rod," 341–352; "Paper No. 65: Aaron's Rod (Outlined)," in *The Logos Papers,* 353–358.

left were never here. Their heart was not with the distinctives.[21] But instead of saying, 'Our heart was not with the distinctives,' which would be the fair, honest, truthful thing to say, they said, 'We thought our hearts were with the distinctives, but I guess our hearts weren't with the distinctives. Over time, it became manifest and did not make sense to us. We are much more interested in happiness as the good than the knowledge of God as the good. Is fun so wrong?' It is why many of us are still Edenic hedonists. You want to have the pleasures of Eden. You want to get back into the Garden of Eden, run around the back way, and try to sneak through the oleanders, but there was a Cherubim. There was a Cherubim and a flaming sword that said, 'No, not going to happen. It is not prudent.' Let's face it: We are Edenic hedonists, are we not? Whether it is 72 virgins, or whatever you want these days—it is *à la carte*. If someone is pursuing that line consistently, the logic of it is, 'at least they are consistent,' but only in a narrow way. It is in each church. I am looking at 14-year experiences and seeing the break that occurred. I am looking at 35-year experiences and seeing the break that occurred. In the end, it was the same thing: there was not an interest in the good as the knowledge of God, but the good is something else.

Fourth: Between Churches

Historically, the divisions have been here, and they persist, and they extend their rule. It is not *thine* is the kingdom and the power and the glory but *mine* is the kingdom and the power and the glory, forever, amen. Can you imagine Nebuchadnezzar saying that? "Is not this the great Babylon I have built as the royal residence, by my mighty power and for the glory of my majesty?" (Dan. 4:30). Can you imagine Pharaoh saying that? Can you imagine some Roman emperor saying that? Yes. Can you imagine Hitler saying that? Yes. Can you imagine Stalin or the Middle Kingdom in China? Some emperor saying that? The one who buried the Terracotta Army in the tomb with him, thousands and thousands. It is the same sort of thing that Pharaoh did in Egypt. 'I am the divine Son. I maintain order in the world—Ma'at.' It is the same thing Hindus say; the Brahmins say by chanting these mantras, 'I make you, the sun, what you are. I maintain the cosmic order by

21. Gangadean, *The Westminster Confession*, 345–395.

my ritual act.'[22] We put ourselves in the place of God, and it does not last. None of these empires lasted. They were intended for thousands of years, and they never lasted. They crumbled soon after. This quest to be forever and ever; Achilles: glory, immortality through that; *The Epic of Gilgamesh*: immortality; the Third Reich would be 1,000 years.[23] No. We pray, "For thine is the kingdom, and the power, and the glory, for ever. Amen" (Matt. 6:13b KJV).

Fifth: In Every Nation

Do we get power to get glory and kingdom? The British Empire did not last, it fell apart. The nations in Europe vied with each other for a kingdom. A house divided; division is in each nation. I am thinking about the Church of England and its effects, and the empire that followed it. The church has departed from the historical achievements of the Reformation. The wars of religion have left a bad taste in people's mouths. The Church was divided, division is between the churches.

It is in every nation. The War of Independence was perhaps against the British Empire and its pretensions, but we had a Civil War: "A house divided against itself cannot stand."[24] Lincoln made reference to that principle. In the *Gettysburg Address,* he also asked if a nation can still conceive and endure to the last. Today, the way we understand *Life, Liberty, and the pursuit of Happiness;*[25] we have emptied it of its meaning. The voice of clarity, to speak up against that misconception, has not been raised by the Church, and we are slipping into a culture polarized more and more between the left and the right.

---

22. An explanation of why chanting the mantras is necessary for the well-being of all mankind: Duty of Brahmins from the Chapter "The Vedas," in Hindu Dharma (kamakoti.org).

23. Hitler said, "I intend to set up a thousand-year Reich and anyone who supports me in this battle is a fellow-fighter for a unique spiritual—I would say divine—creation . . . Rudolf Hess, my assistant of many years standing, would tell you: If we have such a leader, God is with us." Quoted by Richard Breiting in Adolf Hitler, and H. R. Treveor-Roper. *Secret Conversations with Hitler: The Two Newly-Discovered 1931 Interviews.* (New York: Farrar, Strass, and Young, 1953).

24. Abraham Lincoln, "'A House Divided': Speech at Springfield, Illinois," June 16, 1858.

25. From the Preamble to the Declaration of Independence.

Sixth: Between Nations

It is in every nation, and it is between nations, as in World War I and II, and between civilizations. We speak about *The Clash of Civilizations,*[26] and ultimately, it is between the kingdom of God and the kingdom of darkness, and that is how it comes to expression in the Book of Revelation.

A house divided cannot stand. We should not be divided, starting within ourselves, within our households, within our churches, in our nation, and in the world. Division occurs in every aspect of our being—not only in our thoughts but in our hearts, in the sense of knowledge, holiness, and righteousness: loving God with all of our hearts, and the heart is split right down the middle.

The division occurs between the soul and the body. Think about what Jesus said, when He had fasted 40 days: "Man does not live on bread alone" (Matt. 4:4). Think of Jesus in the Garden of Gethsemane: "nevertheless not my will, but thine, be done" (Lk. 22:42b KJV). The body was suffering, but the soul ruled. Jesus said, "Man does not live on bread alone" (Matt. 4:4). There is an order within the body and soul, and if that order is observed, unity is maintained. Remember, after He fasted, His Father could give Him legions of angels to minister to Him, and they did—there is explicit reference to this—His Father could deliver Him. Jesus said to Peter, "'Put your sword back in its place,' Jesus said to him, 'for all who draw the sword will die by the sword. Do you think I cannot call on my Father, and he will at once put at my disposal more than twelve legions of angels?'" (Matt. 26:52–53).

Division is also between male and female. In the values and virtues in a culture. Division is in our background: out of every nation, kindred, tribe, and tongue.[27] It is in the uniqueness of our being, in our ego, our pride, our self-life, and our wanting to exalt ourselves.

Jesus said, **"If a house is divided against itself, that house cannot stand"** (v. 25). A person, a nation, a church divided cannot stand. What is at root in all of these things—in all of them—is a matter of truth, particularly the truth about what is eternal life, what is the good,[28] not

26. Samuel P. Huntington, *The Clash of Civilizations and the Remaking of World Order* (New York: Simon & Schuster, 1996).

27. *Revelation 7:9, 14:6.*

28. Gangadean, *Philosophical Foundation,* 171–183, 208–211; Gangadean, *The Westminster Catechisms,* 109–111, 321–325; Gangadean, *On Natural and Revealed Theology,* 33–39.

being mistaken about it, and not just coming to profess it with our lips. "These people come near to me with their mouth and honor me with their lips, but their hearts are far from me" (Is. 29:13a). He says, "My mother and brothers are those who hear God's word and put it into practice" (Lk. 8:21).

Seventh: The Kingdom of God versus the Kingdom of Darkness

The war that we are facing is what we call a *spiritual war*. Spiritual war is total war. It is initiated by God. It affects every relation and group of relations. It is through every aspect of our being. Starting within each person and working out from there, it goes to others. It does not have to be that way. Christ has brought salvation. He is the One who brings us to know God. "Grace and truth came through Jesus Christ" (Jn. 1:17). He brings us, by His Word and His Spirit, to know, that we might enter into the glorious liberty of the sons of God. While it is sobering—how deep and wide this truth of a house divided is—it is not without hope. As a matter of fact, to recognize how deep and wide it is is to acknowledge the reality of sin and embrace the need for salvation, which comes through Christ Jesus our Lord. In Him, all the fullness dwells, and we are complete in Him.[29] He is the Word of God by whom all things are made and upheld, He is heir of all things,[30] and He is calling us to fill everything in every way.[31] The way this happens is by having the foundation in place—the basic truths—then we can go onto maturity, fruitfulness, unity, and fullness. "I have come that they may have life, and have it to the full" (Jn. 10:10b). Jesus is more perfectly aware of this than we are. He has died to forgive sin, and He rules by His Word and Spirit to deliver us from the power of sin. He teaches us by His Word that this will come about so that we can have hope, persevere, and go from strength to strength daily. It all comes down to this: By His grace, we know His truth, and we are strengthened by His grace. We know His truth, and we grow like the tree planted by the waterside that brings forth its fruit in season.[32] Let us press on daily in seeking Him, daily with our eyes on the goal of salvation—being set

29. *Colossians 2:9.*

30. *Hebrews 1:2–3.*

31. *Ephesians 1:23.*

32. *Psalm 1.*

free from sin, to know Him. Knowing Him, in itself, is such a blessing, such a reward, that it takes on its own life and keeps us going, keeps us sacrificing, so that, as Paul said, "I consider everything a loss compared to the surpassing greatness of knowing Christ Jesus my Lord" (Phil. 3:8a). This is our hope. Amen.

9

Little Foxes and Dead Flies

The Good Is the Source of Unity

2004

John 17:20–25

[20]"My prayer is not for them alone. I pray also for those who will believe in me through their message, [21]that all of them may be one, Father, just as you are in me and I am in you. May they also be in us so that the world may believe that you have sent me. [22]I have given them the glory that you gave me, that they may be one as we are one: [23]I in them and you in me. May they be brought to complete unity to let the world know that you sent me and have loved them even as you have loved me. [24]"Father, I want those you have given me to be with me where I am, and to see my glory, the glory you have given me because you loved me before the creation of the world. [25]"Righteous Father, though the world does not know you, I know you, and they know that you have sent me.

THE UNITY OF THE CHURCH:
Progress and Greater Unity

There is certainly talk about unity in the prayer of our Lord, is there not? Connect this with the little foxes; this is in the Song of Solomon: "Take us the foxes, the little foxes, that spoil the vines: for our vines have tender grapes" (Song of Sol. 2:15 KJV). The context is about love flourishing in the relation between the man and the woman, and the call is to deal with the little foxes that spoil the vine. You can see the theme of unity. As love flourishes, their vine is growing, and little foxes can destroy it. Little foxes come and gnaw at the vine, and the gnawing kills the outer layer through which the vital sap goes up to the rest of the vine. The vine needs the outer layer to flourish and produce fruit.

In Ecclesiastes 10:1, we have a reference to dead flies. "As dead flies give perfume a bad smell, so a little folly outweighs wisdom and honor." Again, our lives and the witness of our lives could be a hindrance in terms of our folly, and may hinder the work that we are called to do. You might wonder—this is part of active listening—why is it that we are talking about this? We talked about this in the prayer, for all seasons, that we might flourish and our love may grow in knowledge and depth of insight. Previously, we spoke about the fear of the Lord, that it is the beginning of wisdom, and what wisdom is, but what does that have to do with unity and dead flies and little foxes? As we understand this, we can see. And why now?

We have been praying for months concerning the building,[1] and this is not the cause of the message; this is, at best, the occasion. It is always the case that we should be in unity, be mindful of unity, and have one heart and mind. We have also been speaking about our distinctives[2] centered on the knowledge of God, which is the good.[3] All of this is going to be wrapped together in the message and it is going to come out with particular applications at this time. Whenever we attempt to go forward, it requires a greater unity of purpose, and anything that would hinder this unity will be felt. Approaching important decisions regarding the building and going forward has been the occasion for allowing our needs and concerns, how we understand them, and the worldview that goes with this to become manifested. Decisions allow understanding to surface.

---

1. Westminster Fellowship purchased land and was in the process of building a church building. This message is given in the context of seeking increased agreement to secure further progress in establishing the church.

2. Gangadean, *The Westminster Confession,* 345–395.

3. Gangadean, *Philosophical Foundation,* 171–177, 208–211; Gangadean, *The Westminster Catechisms,* 109–111, 321–325; Gangadean, *On Natural and Revealed Theology,* 33–39, 127–139; Gangadean, *History of Philosophy,* 61–64; Gangadean, "Paper No. 115: Doxological Christianity," 595–596; "Paper No. 116: The Knowledge of God vs. The Hope of Heaven," 597–598; "Paper No. 117: Knowing and Making God Known," in *The Logos Papers,* 599–601.

In the past weeks, I have been hearing things that tell me that our measure of unity is wanting, and it is being manifest, and this is the way it is often enough. Attempting to move forward brings out the best and sometimes the worst in us, and we have to deal with it. The division was there. These sources, stress points, and divisions—they were there. The little foxes were there. The dead flies were there, but as we come together to move forward, they manifest more.

THE OFFICE OF THE PASTOR: Protect and Feed

The pastor's office carries twofold purposes: In the name of the Lord Jesus Christ, I must *protect* the flock. Jesus prayed that they might be one that the world might believe.[4] He prayed that the Father would protect them and keep them through the Lord's name. I must protect the flock. A special charge is given to those in oversight. Secondly, I must *feed* the flock: bring the Word, nurture, and encourage. This is what husbands do in their relationship with their wives—they are husbandmen. They protect, and they provide. In the name of Jesus Christ, who is the bridegroom, and under His oversight and authority, I must do what I can to watch and protect the flock.

First of all, *I must protect* against divisions and the worldviews and assumptions that contribute to our judgments that may divide us. I must bring the Word of God before the congregation, week by week, and through the week as we meet in council with others. I am particularly tuned into this. So when I hear what congregants say, I make three, four, or five implications as to where this will go down the road. I must be anticipating, and this anticipation is not always valid, but I, in a sense, have to think worst case: If this is the case, where will this go? This is part of being watchful, and I have to watch myself not to misinterpret and take things out of context improperly. Nevertheless, it is a reality, and there are virtues that we speak about, such as integrity: If someone were to live consistently with what they are saying here, what would that be? As Paul said, "a little leaven, leavens the whole lump" (Gal. 5:9).

4. *John 17:21–23.*

Second, I have to be concerned about the question of integrity and love, and being open and honest as I hear things said to me. I have to ask, What if the person being spoken of knows this is being said? Can we be open and honest? Can we have integrity? Do these comments tend to build up the body of Christ, or does this tend not to build up or hinder it? Does what we do build others up? Does it spur us on to good work?[5] Or is it a source of discouragement? I have to be particularly concerned about this whether I like it or not. This church is a new work getting off the ground and getting started. I am particularly concerned about getting it established, stabilized, and strengthened, so all the more, I am concerned about the matter of unity and stability for a new work. Maybe five years down the line, ten years down the line, these things can happen. Perhaps they will be more easily absorbed, but currently, I have to be watchful against anything jeopardizing the work and unity, which can cause people to turn aside and become discouraged. I am concerned about this.

EXAMPLES OF LITTLE FOXES AND DEAD FLIES

We are going to look at some of the little foxes that spoil the vine and the dead flies that cause the ointment of the apothecary to send forth a stinking savor. We will do it in the context of love, over and against division, and the prayer of our Lord Jesus Christ that we may be one that the world may believe. A primary reason for the world not believing is due to our division. When we talk about unity with the larger Church, we, by implication, talk about unity here, in this church. It comes down to unity between one person and another person, and certainly, unity within a household.

Unwholesome Talk

I am looking at things that divide. What are some of these things? What are some of these little foxes? Ephesians 4:29 says, "Do not let any unwholesome talk come out of your mouths, but *only* what is helpful for building others up according to their needs, that it may benefit those who listen."[6] The words of our mouth can build up or tear

5. *Hebrews 10:24.*

6. Emphasis added.

down. We should evaluate: Are our words inclined to build up? Is it helpful, is it edifying? When we get together and talk, what do we talk about? Is it edifying? Or are we concerned about things in our hearts and our interests without necessarily thinking about others? We want to unburden ourselves; there is a need to express ourselves.

There are times and places for discussion about areas of our interest. I thank God for my wife because she, more than anyone else, is someone to whom I can unburden myself and share. What has been built up over the years is a trust that makes it possible for me to do so. I can go to her and groan before her. There are places where we can unburden ourselves. Patricia takes it into context, and we pray. This is the context of prayer day by day, the context of life lived together through many trials. This makes it possible to speak, and I thank God for that. We do need to speak. Can we speak to others who will hear and understand, and can we deal with the things that may come out in our lives in a way that does not divide and discourage the body? Do we have persons like this in our lives, or smaller groups, where we can speak in a way that is connected with always coming back to the Word of God and living in this mode? Do we have someone who will encourage us this way—not just share with us in our folly? Do we have someone who will not just go along with us in our weakness? Let us watch out for unwholesome talk. Paul makes it about all forms of unwholesome talk, including the casual: Let *no* unwholesome talk . . .[7] He specifies later on coarse jesting and foolish talk.[8]

Gossip

More often than not, there are things that we are concerned about, and we find others are not concerned about this. We do not understand why they are not concerned about this, and we think there is something off with these persons—'they are not spiritual,' and we say things about them that are not right. We say things about them to others (third parties) because we cannot go to them. At this point, it becomes gossip. I have been hearing about and am concerned with gossip, and I know that people are offended and separated—walls have gone up. We will see how this is. It is natural for this to happen

7. *Ephesians 4:29.* Emphasis added.

8. *Ephesians 5:4.*

because we think that gossip is unreasonable. It is a natural alienation according to the moral law known from general revelation. Human society is a society of rational beings. We exclude and include on the basis of the *perception* of rationality.[9] When we think others are not being reasonable, distance comes, walls go up, and love cools—there are divisions. We can make some specific rules about this. We have had the rules in Scripture, and perhaps we could specify them again. This is under the heading of unwholesome talk, which is not helpful. The Psalm that we are memorizing this month says, he "casts no slur on his fellowman" (Ps. 15:3b). He casts no slur, no slighting remark. Notice how delicate this is: a slur or a slighting remark. The exhortation is that *no* unwholesome talk come out of our mouth, nothing negative, but rather positive. Only that which is "helpful for building others up," notice this qualifier, "according to their needs" (Eph. 4:29). This means we are to have a sensitivity about others, what their needs are, and what will build them up. This means negatively, we are not to say things to others that are good otherwise, but in this case, would discourage or hinder others; this is part of communicating. We have to anticipate our *interpreted* meaning and not simply our *intended* meaning. "Do not let any unwholesome talk come out of your mouths" (Eph. 4:29).

Gossip can be identified as: (1) a statement about another person. We are not talking about the attitude behind the statement. That is already a problem, but we are talking about when it becomes manifest. (2) It is a statement about another person to a third person. The person about whom the statement is made is not there, has not heard, and is not hearing what you are saying. (3) You have not said it to them, you would not say it to them, and you would not want it repeated to them. If you cannot be open about what you say about another person, and you would not want it to get back to them, it is gossip. It is a slur. It is slander. It is ruinous and divides the body of Christ. Scripture warns us. The little foxes: they are the little things that destroy the vine. There are bigger things, like the boars that come into the field and destroy the vine.[10] This sermon discusses little foxes—small things that can destroy vines. You have to watch the unwholesome talk. Some of us are inclined to be easygoing in the way we talk. We like to talk about

9. Gangadean, *Philosophical Foundation,* 231–243.

10. *Psalm 80:13.*

details. We have to watch the details. It is like uncovering someone's nakedness when we speak about their fault. Remember Shem and Japheth, who walked backward and covered their father's nakedness;[11] that was a physical nakedness. When we talk about people's faults, it is uncovering their nakedness. It is a humiliating and shameful thing to do. We do not want to do this. We do not want to be part of it. We do not want to look at it. We do not want to hear it. Some of us may not realize that we are doing this, but the precepts call us to stop and think. Can I say this to others? Do I need to go into all these details? Is this edifying to the other person? Does the other person really want to hear this? Are we sensitive in this way?

Sometimes, we have to have a sensitivity that bears with one another—a sensitivity that forbears. If gossip continues—it is a habit—it becomes a real problem. You should not even have acts that qualify as gossip. So gossip is:

1. About another person who is not present.
2. To a second person, about a third person who is not present.
3. We would not want it repeated.

You have not said it to the person, you are not going to say it, and you do not want it said by others. If you listen to gossip, you are participating in it. To participate in it is sin and divides. This is one of the little foxes that come out. We know how easy and frequent it is for this to come out.

Special Interest Groups (Cliques)

Here is another area: in times of our fellowship, there is a problem with cliques. We should call them *special interest groups.* "'I follow Paul'; another, 'I follow Apollos'; another, 'I follow Cephas'" (1 Cor. 1:12). 'That other person is not my personality type. They do not appreciate some of the things that I talk about.' When we get together, we talk about things we are interested in, and others who do not share that interest feel left out and alienated, so we pull back and say, 'I am going to let it go. I do not want to go here and just talk about this thing all the time. I hear this over and over, and there is no talk about any other subject.'

---

11. *Genesis 9:23.*

How are we to deal with this? We have said from general revelation that the good is the source of unity.[12] We should mind the same thing: be on the same goal. We might say with our mouths what that goal is, but we do not have the same goal in our hearts, in our thinking, and in its application. It manifests in this way: what do we talk about when we come together? How is it connected with that which is common and familiar? There is a special interest, but the special interest is not the good. At best, our interest is a means to the good. Do we relate our special interest to the good, to the goal? For example, there are special needs and concerns regarding mothers with children. When we come together, do we relate our thinking about our children and our talk about our children to the good, the goal? It is at this point that you have unity. It is at this point that others can participate. If it is not related to the good, it becomes a problem.

Antinomy of Virtue and Happiness

Remember, we can easily go off into virtue ethics. Certain virtues are connected with our special interest, and if we treat these things as *ends in themselves* rather than *means to an end,* we have virtue ethics, and the virtues will be distorted. Or, we can have its antinomy in happiness ethics (consequentialism).[13] Virtue ethics tends toward legalism, and when we get together, we talk and expect others to follow certain practices rather than see the goal and the many ways we are all heading toward the goal. We have expectations; we put burdens on others. I know of someone who has had difficulty being in the congregation because it was thought that a woman with a career is out of place. Some books that teach this have been read and circulated in the congregation, which has percolated up to my attention. Other books have been written about how to be feminine, and there are books on diet. These things are interesting; if we have concerns in these areas, then we should educate ourselves, but sometimes we reinforce our thinking with material from outside that does not share our worldview, spirituality, or the goal.

---

12. Gangadean, *Philosophical Foundation,* 171–183; Gangadean, *On Natural and Revealed Theology,* 33–39; Gangadean, "Paper No. 6: The Good," in *The Logos Papers,* 29–31.

13. Gangadean, *Philosophical Foundation,* 172–174, 181–182; Gangadean, *On Natural and Revealed Theology,* 129–130.

Because we ourselves do not have the goal closely in place, our virtues are not heading toward the goal, and it becomes a source of disunity.

Marriage or Children as the Good

The other person is not the good in marriage; marriage is not the good. We could talk about marriage as if it were the good, but it is not. We can talk about children as if children were the good, but they are not. The good is *by* and *for* children, as all things were created *by* God and *for* God. Children are not the good. We have to make decisions about children in relationship to the good. Our talk must connect these particulars with the good. The education of our children must be connected with the good.[14] Otherwise, our education becomes deficient, it becomes virtue ethics, and virtues separated from the good become distorted, deficient, and not that helpful. Many are deontologists and many are hedonists. Deontologists tend toward law and legalism. The hedonists tend toward freedom and enjoying freedom. Both of those can divide.

Do We Really Have the Good in Common?

When we come together, do we really have the good in common? Is that part of our thinking? Can we relate what we are saying to the good—the knowledge of God, the earth to be filled with the knowledge of God?[15] Are our virtues and concerns here? If we had the good in place, we would not have cliques forming. We would not feel uncomfortable in this or that other clique, and be in and out. The good is the source of unity. Christ wants us to have this unity. He prayed that we might be one, that we will not be divided.[16] Notice, in this context, how He makes the knowledge of God the focus: "this is eternal life: that they may know you" (Jn. 17:3a), and "I have made you known to them, and will continue to make you known" (Jn. 17:26a). We can give lip service to the knowledge of God. It is very easy to give lip service. I

14. The Logos Foundation, *Grammar Catechisms,* xi-xxvi.

15. Gangadean, *Philosophical Foundation,* 171–177, 208–211; Gangadean, *The Westminster Catechisms,* 109–111, 321–325; Gangadean, *On Natural and Revealed Theology,* 33–39, 127–139; Gangadean, *History of Philosophy,* 61–64; Gangadean, "Paper No. 115: Doxological Christianity," 595–596; "Paper No. 116: The Knowledge of God vs. The Hope of Heaven," 597–598; "Paper No. 117: Knowing and Making God Known," in *The Logos Papers,* 599–601.

16. *John 17:21–23.*

have been in places where we talked the lingo for years, and then push came to shove, and the whole thing fell apart because the good was not in place. I was being patient, I thought. Not pressing it but going gradually, but it was not there in the end. Let us not take what is being said for granted.

We have different interests, which should be brought back to common interests. Catch for us the foxes, the little foxes, that ruin the vineyards, our vineyards that are in bloom.[17] Let us capture the foxes. Let us capture our thoughts that seem good otherwise, but they are virtues apart from an active, vital, connection with the good and the goal. How much wisdom can there be in this?

How should we think about children? Some questions have come up and are coming up about birth control and the number of children we should have. How do we connect that with the Scripture and the good? It is easy, it really, really is easy, once the good is in place. There is a connection between having children and dominion, and there is responsibility involved for the good. If we have the good in mind, we can clearly know and answer questions of that sort in detail. There may be some areas that require a certain amount of wisdom, depending on where a person is in their own particular area of life. We do not suggest one thing for everybody in the same way, and we are not to set rules and expectations that bring division.

The source of unity is the good, not the law understood apart from the good. There is unbelief that is manifest, and words that we speak come from unbelief. Let us put it this way: there is a lack of understanding. If we understood certain things, we would not indulge in certain thoughts; those would have been settled. Understanding comes out of seeking diligently, and the doctrine that informs, and the extent to which we see the knowledge of God as the good, and how much this is really on our hearts. If this is our desire, if this is really our delight, then many, many, many questions can be settled. Our doctrinal awareness and seeking reflect our maturity. This is where our trustworthiness and our dependability become manifest. It is revealed whether we are on the same page on this matter, whether when we should be teachers, but we have need for someone to teach us the first principles again.[18]

---

17. *Song of Solomon 2:15.*

18. *Hebrews 5:12.*

Unity requires seeking diligently, maturity, understanding, and being on the same page concerning the good, eternal life.

WE ARE TO BE KNIT TOGETHER BY WHAT EVERY JOINT SUPPLIES[19]

Jesus said, "**I have given them the glory that you gave me, that they may be one**" (v. 22), and that glory unfolds differently, and we can be knit together. If we see the fullness of the good and the breadth of the eternal life Christ has for us—the fullness that there is—we will have an appreciation of one another, be knit together, and honor one another. What would our view of service be if we had the good in place? Earlier, we mentioned the Psalms being for all seasons and for the whole dimension of life. The unity we are to have can only come in the fullness of Christ. It must be fullness to encompass *all* diversity, not leaving any out, but it must also be that diversity is related to the goal. Otherwise, it will simply be quirky and eccentric. If this is what we are meditating on and if this is our heart's desire, we will always be thinking in this way; our words will be pleasant, encouraging, and building others up. We will not have acts of folly, and words of folly, that are sent forth as stinking savor. There is a factor here about reputation. Others notice how we conduct ourselves and what we say and do. There is a certain subliminal level of trust, understanding, and dependability that is operating. There may not be anything positive, but a lack of anything positive is something that is noticed. When the positive is there, it is noticed, and it is appreciated. Like a sweet savor, it just has an effect. It is noticed when things are negative: foolishness and things that are not edifying.

We have to become, by the grace of God, consistent in this. We recognize that we are struggling, but there can be consistency even when we are struggling. We all confess that we have sin. We need the Word and correction, but is there a sense that we are persisting in pushing on, like the race that Paul speaks of? "I have fought the good fight, I have finished the race, I have kept the faith" (2 Tim. 4:7).

Our lives should be consistent in our supply; this becomes a source of unity. We sometimes want to supply to others what they do not need

19. *Ephesians 4:16.*

because we have a narrow view of the goal and do not see the richness of the good. We may expect others to supply to us in a certain way. Scripture says that everyone is to bear his own burden, and we are to bear one another's burdens. The context of this—"Bear ye one another's burdens" (Gal. 6:2 KJV)—is bringing the Word of God, restoring people who are overtaken in a fault; it is like foot washing. This is the context in which Paul speaks in Galatians 6:1–5. In that short section, both of these points are being made:

> Brothers, if someone is caught in a sin, you who are spiritual should restore him gently. But watch yourself, or you also may be tempted. Carry each other's burdens, and in this way you will fulfill the law of Christ. If anyone thinks he is something when he is nothing, he deceives himself. Each one should test his own actions. Then he can take pride in himself, without comparing himself to somebody else, for each one should carry his own load.

We may think, 'Yes, we can affirm the truth and bear one another's burden,' but is this affirmed in the context of the good? Everyone should bear their own burden. Is this in the context of the good? If we are not pursuing the good, it becomes overly burdensome. We are to see it in light of the good—the goal—as the source of unity. This is the sense in which we would be one, as our Lord Jesus prayed.

Those in leadership positions are especially called upon to be above reproach and respectable. Deacons, likewise, are to be respectable. That is, for me, scary. It is a special burden on me to even say this because as I say this, I know I am going to be more responsible and, having said it, it is very easy for one to say, 'Well, look at that. That is off, and this is off.' I do not like to talk about or preach about this, but those in leadership positions have to be respectable, above reproach, and worthy of respect. If we are going to be heard, if what we say is going to be heard, we must have a life that is consistent with what we say; otherwise, people will just blow us off. 'That person is just talking, and we do not want to just merely listen to talk.' Maybe just merely listening to it would be what you call 'enabling what is not right.'

The atmosphere that should come from this message is not, everyone is walking on eggshells now. The atmosphere should certainly be watchful, but we have cause to think about the extent to which what we profess in common—the goal of the knowledge of God—is, in fact, in place. When the goal is in place, there is a broad and easy way in the Lord. I am aware of the Scripture that says, "For wide is the gate and broad is the road that leads to destruction" (Matt. 7:13), but what I am saying is that there is a path in the Lord where there is no stumbling; it is not up and down, it is not going uphill, as you sometimes have to do in hikes where the route is running up the hill and running down again. It is like making a highway in the desert for the Lord.[20] This is the way the Christian faith should be. We should not be walking on eggshells about this. We should take it to heart. The goal is the one big thing that we are talking about. When this one big thing is in place, everything else will fall into place. Insofar as the other things are not falling into place, it is because the one big thing—the goal—is not in place. We do not have to be on pins and needles. It is not walking on eggshells when we come to the big thing, the goal, because if we realize we come short in this, we say, 'Lord, this is what I long for; this is what I want. Lead me to go in this way.'

Some words are not edifying and do not spur one another on to good works. Some words are discouraging. Some words show a lack of understanding: words of folly. Those are the *dead flies*.[21] They contribute to divisions in the body, and we are to be watchful against this.

We are coming, now, to the Lord's Table, and the Lord's Table particularly speaks to us about this unity that we are to have. Let us think about this Word of the Lord as we come to the Lord's Table. In preparing our hearts for this, let us sing from Psalm 116A.[22]

20. *Isaiah 40:3.*

21. *Ecclesiastes 10:1.*

22. *The Book of Psalms for Singing.*

10

UNITY AND EDIFICATION

Working from the Unity of the Spirit to the Unity of the Faith

2014

Ephesians 4:1–16

1As a prisoner for the Lord, then, I urge you to live a life worthy of the
calling you have received. 2Be completely humble and gentle; be patient,
bearing with one another in love. 3Make every effort to keep the unity
of the Spirit through the bond of peace. 4There is one body and one
Spirit—just as you were called to one hope when you were called—5one
Lord, one faith, one baptism; 6one God and Father of all, who is over all
and through all and in all.

7But to each one of us grace has been given as Christ apportioned it. 8This
is why it says:

"When he ascended on high,
he led captives in his train
and gave gifts to men."

9(What does "he ascended" mean except that he also descended to the
lower, earthly regions? 10He who descended is the very one who ascended
higher than all the heavens, in order to fill the whole universe.) 11It was he
who gave some to be apostles, some to be prophets, some to be evangelists,
and some to be pastors and teachers, 12to prepare God's people for works
of service, so that the body of Christ may be built up 13until we all reach
unity in the faith and in the knowledge of the Son of God and become
mature, attaining to the whole measure of the fullness of Christ.

> [14]Then we will no longer be infants, tossed back and forth by the waves, and blown here and there by every wind of teaching and by the cunning and craftiness of men in their deceitful scheming. [15]Instead, speaking the truth in love, we will in all things grow up into him who is the Head, that is, Christ. [16]From him the whole body, joined and held together by every supporting ligament, grows and builds itself up in love, as each part does its work.

THE SERMON TOPIC IS UNITY AND EDIFICATION. Twice, this chapter speaks about how the body might build itself up in love: **"For the perfecting of the saints, for the work of the ministry, for the *edifying* of the body of Christ"** (v. 12).[1] Then,

> **From whom the whole body fitly joined together and compacted by that which every joint supplieth, according to the effectual working in the measure of every part, maketh increase of the body unto the *edifying* of itself in love"** (v. 16).[2]

Unity and edification—these are connected. We want to bring this out and apply it.

THE THEME OF EPHESIANS:
Unity and Fullness

The theme of fullness is throughout the Book of Ephesians. Jews and Gentiles are brought together in one body as part of fullness. The application is that believers and non-believers are to be brought in and to be one body—Jews and Gentiles. Jews were the body of believers; Gentiles were outside of the faith; the Gentiles are to be brought in. When that unity occurs, we achieve a greater fullness. There is a natural connection between unity and fullness expressed all the way through the book. This chapter speaks about **"the whole measure of the fullness of Christ"** (v. 13b). Jesus ascended **"higher than all the heavens, in order to fill the whole universe"** (v. 10b). He is seated "in the heavenly realms, far above all rule and authority, power and dominion" (Eph. 1:20b–21a).

---

1. KJV. Emphasis added.
2. KJV. Emphasis added.

The Book of Ephesians goes back to Genesis 1–3: the biblical worldview. As the covenant head, Christ stands in the place of Adam to *undo* the sin of Adam by removing sin as the Lamb of God and to *do* what Adam failed to do. Jesus does so by sending the Spirit, who initiates, sustains, and completes the work. The work given to Adam is basic; it is from the beginning and includes all of mankind in the work of dominion.

We are talking at Logos[3] about the work involved in the humanities. The humanities study the question, 'What is man?' We want to get to the universals in man: all men, everywhere, all times. The first and most basic universal truth in man is this: man is in the image of God,[4] and this is further defined by the work given originally, "Let them have dominion" (Gen. 1:26 KJV). Dominion includes all subjects. God gives grace to different members, and we use this to say, 'Thank God I do not have the grace for math,' or, 'I do not have a math gene.' Instead, we should recognize that math is a preparation for philosophy; it clarifies the mind and focuses it. The mind distills the problem through an equation, and it has to balance out to the last number. Is that not marvelous and beautiful? You cannot say, 'Good enough, close enough' in math. This is not government work. This is the government of the universe work, which measures the stars and balances everything out[5]—$(10^{10})^{123}$ It totally blows your mind and should comfort you because that is where $(10^{10})^{123}$ applies to the details of your life. God has us dialed in. He has us in His crosshairs. He will bring trials of faith to our lives to cause us to grow. These are bullets of grace that enable us to grow and become mature in the faith—God's beautiful bullets.

---

3. Logos Theological Seminary.

4. *Genesis 1:27;* Gangadean, "Paper No. 144: *The Biblical Worldview* (Part IV)," in *The Logos Papers,* 725–732; Gangadean, *The Westminster Confession,* 79–83.

5. This number is taken from Roger Penrose's calculation regarding what initial entropy conditions had to have existed in order for the universe to have been created according to the Big Bang Theory. And for the universe to then ultimately be supportive of life coming into existence randomly? What are the odds that these exact conditions could have existed at the time of the Big Bang? The explanation for this claim can be found in Roger Penrose, *The Emperor's New Mind: Concerning Computers, Minds, and the Laws of Physics* (Oxford: Oxford University Press, 1999).

Perfection, Unity, and Fullness

Perfection is connected with unity and fullness. Perfection expressed practically is completeness; it is synonymous with the term *maturity*. God requires us to observe perfection. Every Lord's Day, we notice perfection and completeness. Completeness of the work of creation in anticipation of the completion of the work of dominion, and this work will be completed when there is fullness: when the earth is *full* of the knowledge of God as the waters cover the sea.[6]

When combined in Scripture, the numbers seven and ten stand for completion, perfection, maturity, and fullness. These numbers go together. There is an interconnection between perfection (seven) and fullness (ten). Paul develops the theme of unity and fullness in Ephesians 4. He moves *from* the unity of the Spirit *to* the unity of the faith. We often notice the unity of the Spirit—**"one Lord, one faith, one baptism"** (v. 5)—we are all one, and we affirm this. But verse 13 states, **"until we all reach unity in the faith."** This is distinct from the unity of the Spirit. One is to be *maintained*—**"Make every effort to keep the unity of the Spirit through the bond of peace"** (v. 3)—and the other is to be *attained*: **"until we all reach unity in the faith"** (v. 13a). The unity of the Spirit entails going from the condition of immaturity to maturity, and the key to this is every part doing its work,[7] starting with the unity of the Spirit, maintaining and keeping this, until we come to the unity of the faith. We will not get to the unity of the faith if we do not keep the unity of the Spirit. We probably will not keep the unity of the Spirit unless we are directed toward the unity of the faith. These are connected. It affects our attitude towards others—in other words, 'Why do I need you?' Given our inclination toward self-centered existence—self-life, autonomy, the essence of sin, coming short of the glory of God—the question naturally arises: 'Why do I need to deal with other people?' Unless we have an idea of the fullness to be attained, we do not see our need for others, and we generally think, 'If I do not need you, I do not really have to forbear.' But if you think you do not need another, you have a false view of self

6. *Isaiah 11:9;* Gangadean, "Paper No. 104: Eschatology (Twelve Points)," in *The Logos Papers,* 539–544.

7. *Ephesians 4:16.*

and God's purpose and plan. These two—the unity of the Spirit and the unity of the faith—are greatly tied together.

Paul goes into applications after speaking about doctrine, which is a typical pattern in the Epistles. The remainder of the book, from chapters 4–6, regard applications. Notice the application includes the spiritual war;[8] it is part of the work of Christ as the second Adam. Christ is doing what Adam failed to do by completing the work. He is going to crush the head of the serpent.[9] He will accomplish this through His body, the Church, brought into existence by the Spirit. The Spirit begins this work by regeneration.[10] We must be born of the Spirit if we are to enter the kingdom of God.[11] We enter by birth, we grow to maturity, and the completion of this work is the City of God—vast, magnificent, beautiful, strong, complete, rich; from the Garden of Eden to the City of God. It was there from the beginning, however much we may have noticed or failed to notice it, depending on how diligently we sought the Lord and our degree of consciousness and consistency.

Paul calls attention to the change needed: **"I urge you to live a life worthy of the calling you have received"** (v. 1b). This is where we are going. To use a metaphor to make it a little cleaner: we are at the bottom and going to the top. We are at the bottom of the Grand Canyon, the Colorado River, at bridge level, walking across the water. I will give us that much. We are not going down another 20 yards. We have got to go to the top. We look up and think, 'Oh, Lord, send a helicopter. Oh, Lord, I wish I had mules.' We are going to take one step after another, and we will make it out. Many have done it before. If we come with some preparation, we will make it. We may get halfway and say, 'I think I will camp here the rest of my life.' No. As we go up, the air gets rarer, and the steps are painful. We will feel our muscles burning. If we made it through Devil's Corkscrew we know that is where mind and body split. You guys do not know what I am talking about, do you? Some of you do. You are going to have to go through it and experience it directly. It is a journey, going from the bottom to the top; we are going to maturity. We are walking, worthy of the calling; this is where we are

8. *Ephesians 6:10–20.*

9. *Genesis 3:15.*

10. Gangadean, *The Westminster Confession,* 143–206; Gangadean, *The Westminster Catechisms,* 191–207.

11. *John 3:1–21.*

going. We are going to the heavenly city: the City of God. That does not mean you bail out at death and get there. No, you are going to be waiting for others. "God had planned something better for us so that only together with us would they be made perfect" (Heb. 11:40); they are not complete without us.

We have to pass the work on in such a way that those who are after us will move it forward. It is something like a relay race. We are passing the baton; we run as fast as we can, giving the next person a head start to go ahead. This is a metaphor that we could use to clarify. We are going to pass the doctrine on to the next generation. Unless, of course, the Lord does a work that we had not imagined where in the next 20 years, the work will be complete. It is very unlikely. When I was about 20 years younger, I thought, 'In my lifetime. In my lifetime.' Time goes on and I think, 'No. I wish, I hope. Lord, will you not do it, please?' Alright. Get prepared. Alright. Pass it on. I am at the, 'Alright, get ready, pass it on' stage. You guys are going to be doing it. The X-ers and Ys are going to take over from the boomers—the old boomers and the young boomers. The boomers still have some life in them. They still have some kick in them. They go out like Winston Churchill did; he is an example of an old boomer. Reagan and Kennedy were the Ys. Truman: he was the X-er. God does a consolation of the generations to work together in such a way that we get the work done.[12] There is work to be done to establish the City of God.

APPLICATION IN ATTITUDE: Be Completely Humble and Gentle

Paul goes into application after speaking about doctrine. He begins with, **"I urge you to live a life worthy of the calling you have received"** (v. 1b), and he speaks of attitude: **"completely *humble* and *gentle*"** (v. 2a).[13] They go together. *Humble:* "Blessed are the poor in spirit" (Matt. 5:3a). We must understand ourselves in our creatureliness, in our dependence; we have no good in ourselves; we should have a proper attitude of ourselves and what we are to do—a humility of mind. *Gentle:*

12. This statement is in reference to generational patterns in William Strauss and Neil Howe, *Generations: The History of America's Future, 1584 to 2069* (New York: Harper Perennial, 1991).

13. Emphasis added.

We are not into our self-life, we are not defending ourselves, we are trusting and depending on God to bring things about. "Blessed are the meek, for they will inherit the earth." (Matt. 5:5). The message given here is repeated time and time again. What is said in the Sermon on the Mount[14] is also said in the fruit of the Spirit.[15] And it is said in the law—"Love the LORD your God with all your heart" (Deut. 6:5), and is summarized in 1 Corinthians 13.

Think of it this way: the Lord uses repetition. You slow down the mind. You repeat it, and you get the message through. We see this pattern of repetition in Scripture. The same thing is said a number of times. It may be three times, or it may be seven times. In the Book of Revelation, the message is given seven times. There are seven visions of the same reality: spiritual war, age-long and agonizing, and good will overcome evil.[16] By the time we get this message—the same message seven times, not different messages, but the same message seven times, we begin to say, 'Oh yeah, I guess that is true. That is right. Yeah, I got it.' The Lord knows that we are slow learners. The Spirit is a masterful teacher. He says the same thing in different ways seven times, and then we say, 'We get it.' Is not the Lord gracious? Is He not patient? Is He not kind? Is He not wise in teaching us in this way?

These truths about humility and gentleness are stated elsewhere in Scripture. It is good to have repetition. The importance of repetition in teaching others is very hard for me to learn. You say it once; that is it. Actually, I used to follow the Confucian model: I give 1/10, and you get the rest, instead of saying the whole thing seven times. That should do it. Scripture repeats often and sufficiently. We are to be long-suffering and forbearing with one another in love. The first rule of love is that it suffers long. "Love is patient, love is kind" (1 Cor. 13:4a). This is how we keep the unity of the Spirit, in love. "**Make every effort to keep the unity of the Spirit through the bond of peace**" (v. 3). Long-suffering and forbearing one another in love. "Peter came to Jesus and asked, 'LORD, how many times shall I forgive my brother when he sins against me? Up to seven times?'" (Matt. 18:21). Jesus threw fullness at them:

---

14. *Matthew 5–7.*

15. *Galatians 5:22–23; Ephesians 5:9.*

16. Surrendra Gangadean, *The Book of Revelation: What Must Soon Take Place. Doxological Postmillennialism* (Phoenix: Logos Papers Press, forthcoming, 2025).

seventy-seven times.[17] Notice there is a ten added in there. Do you want to challenge the wisdom of our Lord? No, you do not want to do that. The disciples thought they were smart and gracious and knew things. Jesus took their thoughts captive. The disciples were out fishing all night, overwhelmed, and He said, "Throw your net on the right side" (Jn. 21:6a). Jesus has a real sense of humor. He has; He laughs often. He probably had a humorous intent in the back of His mind when He said, "You give them something to eat" (Mk. 6:37a). He sees them scrambling. He probably gave an eye roll. It comes out in the Word, "'O unbelieving and perverse generation,' Jesus replied, 'how long shall I stay with you? How long shall I put up with you?'" (Matt. 17:17a) We can speculate that there is humor involved in this instance. We got it from Him. Did you know that? Humor. This is perhaps the most redeeming aspect of human personality. When a person gets the joke, it shows intelligent life, it shows that they understood and made the connection. Humor is only humorous when you get it.

We are to forbear with one another in love. "Love is patient" (1 Cor. 13:4a). In the little things, we do not run off and use Matthew 18[18] the first time offense is taken. We have to raise consciousness and consistency by writing emails and going back and forth, then take step two (step 2 of Matthew 18). You do not even have to write the email the first time. You wait on it; you forbear, but you do not want to overdo it. Long-suffering is not everlasting suffering. God is not everlastingly suffering; He is long-suffering, and this can be abused. We know this; and God knows this. If we abuse it, we just heap up more wrath on ourselves, and when the fall comes, it is harder. This is how we keep the unity of the Spirit. We have an attitude of mind, not self-centered, lowliness of mind, meekness manifesting, long-suffering, forbearing with one another. **"Make every effort to keep the unity of the Spirit through the bond of peace"** (v. 3).

Everyone has self-life; everyone is tuned into it. There is nothing we know more thoroughly than self-life. You cannot fake it with one another. People can smell it. We often do it cynically. We may joke about it, but it is there. Instead, we are to be an aroma of Christ. Aromas and odors are very powerful. We sometimes use the expression, 'That stinks,'

17. *Matthew 18:21–22.*

18. Gangadean, *The Westminster Confession,* 391–395.

and then it is questionable, and you have to sniff it two or three times. Then you bring your sniffer in—the one with hyper-sniffing abilities, just in case your sniffing is not right. 'Does it seem odd to you?' I ask my wife, 'Is this food still good?' She says, 'Ooooh!' Her expressions are ten times mine. That is the beauty of it. There is no question about it when she communicates. That is a blessing, to have that degree of sensitivity and help. We keep the unity of the Spirit. It is based on the fact, **"There is one body and one Spirit—just as you were called to one hope when you were called—one LORD, one faith, one baptism; one God and Father of all"** (vv. 4–6a).

MAINTAIN THE UNITY OF THE SPIRIT

I am going to be seeing someone whom I knew 52 years ago; I have known him since 1962. Shortly after my conversion, I lived with this person, and he has now gone into Eastern Orthodoxy. He is bringing the book by Peter Gillquist,[19] who left Campus Crusade to go into the Orthodox Church. I have always wanted, and I am being required now, to deal with this topic.

In any case, there is **"one body and one Spirit . . . one hope"** (v. 4), **"one LORD, one faith . . . one baptism"** (v. 5). I have to maintain the unity of the Spirit with others who are in the body. Where it is uncertain, we may reckon with it, but where it is more definitely certain—and we may never be fully certain, but as certain as best we can tell, with the use of the means—we are to maintain unity until we come into the unity of the faith. I am hoping that may happen even though it is difficult to see people come into the church and then leave. It is like people who have left Protestantism to go into Catholicism. It is almost as if the errors are compounded. Those are the people and situations that we need to work with. Maintain a unity by the attitude of being completely humble and gentle; affirm it.

Is the Eastern Orthodox priest that I knew back in the early 60s a believer? Are certain persons in the Roman Catholic faith believers? Are certain Presbyterians believers? Certain persons who were in our congregation, and are not here now, are they believers? Certain persons

19. Peter E. Gillquist, *Becoming Orthodox: A Journey to the Ancient Christian Faith* (Chesterton: Ancient Faith Publishing, 1992).

who are in our congregation and are still here, are they believers? Sometimes, you do not know; you have to say, 'They are making a credible profession of faith, and they are walking accordingly.' Leave it in the Lord's hands until He makes it clearer. Maintain the unity of the Spirit with them.

ORDER OF HUMAN PERSONALITY

We can understand with whom to maintain the unity of the Spirit, and we also understand how to maintain the unity of the Spirit. Maintaining the unity of the Spirit is by lowliness, meekness, long-suffering, forbearing with one another, and with those who make a credible profession of faith and whose lives are consistent with this. It goes on, **"But to each one of us grace has been given as Christ apportioned it"** (v. 7). God gives diversity in the body. In Romans 12, Paul discusses diversity. In 1 Corinthians 12 and 14, he explains diversity—*one body, many parts*[20]—and it is where diversity enters that we have trouble. It is not just diversity at the level of gifts, abilities, and talents but diversity at the level of personality. "'I follow Paul'; another, 'I follow Apollos'; another, 'I follow Cephas'" (1 Cor. 1:12a). We have to work through this, and understand the dynamics and the order in which it must be worked through.

Prophetic persons change in certain ways, priestly persons change in certain ways at certain times, and kingly persons expect the prophetic and the priestly to be in place. When the kingly are 21 years old, do not expect them to go back and do priestly work or prophetic work. They expect it is in place in their lives, and it is going to be a distraction for them to go back and get it in place. It is not that they cannot, but you just have to prepare the way a little bit more and say, 'Look, this was not in place when you were growing up. What was your background? What did they teach you? Where were they in terms of Historic Christianity? How conscious and consistent were they in that?'

We are getting into the diversity factor and the many levels of diversity. You should know the seven aspects of human nature:[21] (1) Larger aspect (2) Narrower aspect (3) Triune personality (4) Body/soul

20. *1 Corinthians 12:4–31.*

21. See Sermon 4: "Unity In the Body of Christ"; Gangadean, *The Westminster Confession,* 79–83; Gangadean, *The Westminster Catechisms,* 133–135.

(5) Male/female (6) Background (which is manifold) (7) The unique element of human personality.

As part of our biblical view of man, anthropology/psychology, we should have this as a standard piece. Much of this is in Genesis. God made them body and soul; we are a body/soul unity, not just a soul stuck in a body. We are male and female. There is a difference between male and female. Understand the difference, and learn how to bring them together, like a dance. Characteristically, I hear guys say, 'I do not dance.' You see in movies often, where the guys do not dance, and the girls want to dance. They seem to be more into that. Then the guys have to go out, and they may be stepping on their toes, and they have to lead in dancing, and the girl sometimes has to nudge and help them to know how to lead in dancing. It is all part of a very special relation between male and female, but they are both in God. We are made in the image of God. Masculine and feminine are in God. We have to understand this. He is the one who called all things into being, but He is also working through the Spirit to nurture this being. "And the Spirit of God was hovering over the waters" (Gen. 1:2b), preparing it for the next step, "Let there be light" (Gen. 1:3a). All of these things are there in the creation account.

THE RULE OF CHRIST

In Ephesians 4:8, Paul quotes from Psalm 68. It begins, "May God arise, may his enemies be scattered" (Ps. 68:1a). It speaks about how the Word goes out to the ends of the world, and all the nations come in. This is the context of Psalm 68. You should go back today and read through all of this Psalm; go back and go over all of it, see it, and catch it. This Ephesians quote is coming out of that, and we should be reminded. **"This is why it says: 'When he ascended on high, he led captives in his train and gave gifts to men'"** (v. 8). Christ is raised, seated at the right hand of God, given all power and authority, and He sends the Spirit to give that power and authority to His Church. "I am going to send you what my Father has promised; but stay in the city until you have been clothed with power from on high" (Lk. 24:49). He is going to give power and authority, through the Spirit, to His people.

Paul draws out the implication:

> **(What does 'he ascended' mean except that he also descended to the lower, earthly regions? He who descended is the very one who ascended higher than all the heavens, in order to fill the whole universe)** (vv. 9–10).

He ascended, and by implication, He descended, and He ascended back up, far above all the heavens, that He might fill all things, that He might fill the universe.

The Son declares the Father. The Son is the One in the innermost being of God, the Word of God, who is in the innermost being of God, the only begotten. This is how it is said in the Greek: *monogenes* (*μονογενὴς*), *theos* (*Θεὸς*), the only begotten God, "has made him known" (Jn. 1:18b). "No one has ever seen God, but God the One and Only, who is at the Father's side, has made him known" (Jn. 1:18). "No one has ever seen God" (Jn. 1:18a), ever. "Whom no one has seen or can see" (1 Tim. 6:16). This includes Moses.[22] The Son makes Him known; the Son who is present in man as reason,[23] in the world as general revelation,[24] in history as Scripture,[25] incarnate,[26] sending the Spirit to lead us into all truth[27]—He has made Him known. He is "full of grace and truth" (Jn. 1:14b). He, "who is at the Father's side, has made him known" (Jn. 1:18b).

This is the context of the gifts of Christ. What are these gifts? "**It was he who gave some to be apostles, some to be prophets, some to be evangelists, and some to be pastors and teachers**" (v. 11). There are four categories: apostles, prophets, evangelists, and pastor-teachers. We know who the Apostles are. We know what the pastor-teachers are.[28] This office is *pastor-teacher*. It is assisted by others who stand here and bring the Word. They may be teachers, not pastors, but they

22. *Exodus 33:11–16.*

23. *John 1:4.*

24. *John 1:10.*

25. *John 1:11.*

26. *John 1:14.*

27. *John 16:13.*

28. Gangadean, *The Westminster Confession*, xv-xxxii, 349–351; Gangadean, "Paper No. 16: The Historic Christian Faith," in *The Logos Papers*, 103–114.

are under the office of the pastor-teacher. It is the regular teaching of the Word, and it is built on the work of the evangelist, and sometimes someone has to be an evangelist and pastor-teacher. Founding pastors are a kind of evangelist. Sometimes, you must also be like a prophet and function in the prophetic ministry, and build on the Apostles. The prophetic ministry is particularly responding to challenges that are raised against the truth, that the work may go on. Sometimes, one person may combine all of these. Paul was an apostle, doing prophetic work, evangelist work, planting churches, and for some time, in one place, doing regular teaching. Evangelists plant new churches; they go out and get persons together and get churches organized, and then the pastor-teachers take over. These gifts are connected and united. The idea and purpose of these gifts is that with specialization, coordination, and cooperation, we can do the work better.

LET ALL THINGS BE DONE UNTO EDIFICATION

"For the perfecting of the saints" (v. 12a KJV). Here is this word: "***perfecting* of the saints,"**[29] bringing them to maturity. It is not for believers themselves, but **"to prepare God's people for works of service, so that the body of Christ may be built up"** (v. 12). The body is built up by keeping the unity of the Spirit, forbearing with one another in love, with an attitude of lowliness. This means there is not to be a whiff of the self-life, but we are to have lowliness of mind, be forbearing, and affirm unity. We maintain the unity of the Spirit, and then we benefit from the work of the gifts that God has given to the Church for bringing us to maturity, perfecting the saints, for the sake of ministry, and not just in and of ourselves, but that we might bear fruit. "This is to my Father's glory, that you bear much fruit" (Jn. 15:8a)—fruit that will remain, and for the building up of the body of Christ.

We take a membership vow and affirm it in the novitiate,[30] that in our works of service in the home and in the church, we seek first the kingdom of God and His righteousness for the edifying of the body of Christ. In 1 Corinthians 14, we see that all things are to be done for the building up of the Church, orderly, unto edification, and for the

29. Emphasis added.

30. Gangadean, *The Westminster Confession,* 387–390.

glory of God: "So it is with you. Since you are eager to have spiritual gifts, try to excel in gifts that build up the church" (1 Cor. 14:12). "You may be giving thanks well enough, but the other man is not edified" (1 Cor. 14:17). "When you come together, everyone has a hymn, or a word of instruction, a revelation, a tongue or an interpretation. All of these must be done for the strengthening of the church" (1 Cor. 14:26b). "But everything should be done in a fitting and orderly way" (1 Cor. 14:40). "So whether you eat or drink or whatever you do, do it all for the glory of God" (1 Cor. 10:31). These are general rules for how to conduct affairs in the Church.

We must be mindful of glorifying God and the edification of the Church.

> 'Love the LORD your God with all your heart and with all your soul and with all your mind and with all your strength.' The second is this: 'Love your neighbor as yourself.' There is no commandment greater than these' (Mk. 12:30–31).

We should be mindful of this. We come short in many ways that are distracting others from paying attention. It has been brought to my attention that during Logos, some people are talking with each other, making noises, and hindering others from being edified by the content. Do all things unto edification. If you greet someone early in the morning loudly, it could be counted as a curse.[31] You are expressing *your* feelings more than a concern for the other person. We do not want to do anything that distracts from attention to God. "All of these must be done for the strengthening of the church" (1 Cor. 14:26b), unto the edification of the body.

TRIALS OF FAITH AND OVERCOMING

This is where the self-life oozes out of us. This is why the way to grow is through trials, and we should bless the Lord for trials. "These have come so that your faith—of greater worth than gold, which perishes even though refined by fire—may be proved genuine and may result in praise, glory and honor when Jesus Christ is revealed" (1 Pet. 1:7). Through trials our understanding increases, which is joyful. Through

31. *Proverbs 27:14.*

trials, we come to understand the law of God. *The truth,* in connection with a system of beliefs, or worldview, is the truth that sanctifies. It is truth by connecting the dots, by putting together, the Greek word is *suniémi* (*συνίημι*).[32] This is the truth that sanctifies. This is "of greater worth than gold, which perishes" (1 Pet. 1:7). We have to come to it through the curse, through trials, through the promise.

"Give us today our daily bread" (Matt. 6:11)—healing and health are one aspect, strife and protection, and famine and provision are other components (war, famine, and plague). We are going to face the curse and trials in this way, and it is going to be every day, for hours, sometimes multiple hours, and sometimes you get inundated: 'This is a big wave. The last one was just 4 feet high. This one is about 40 feet high and is going to take you down.' All we can do is duck and go under and just stay under. The Lord wants us to overcome in all situations. He wants us to grow. To overcome, we have to understand it as a trial of faith. We pray, "And lead us not into temptation, but deliver us from evil" (Matt. 6:13a KJV). Evil remains in us; it is brought out by the trials. When Jesus was in the wilderness, it was called a *temptation,* but it could have just as well been called a *trial of faith.* If faith is being tested, if it goes toward sin, it is a temptation to sin, as against moving toward God. Temptations and trials of faith are going to come daily.

In this life, we will have trials, many trials, and with much suffering comes much learning. The trial of faith is intended. This is *the* central part of every trial of faith: it is so that our faith may grow. We groan, we think it is over, and it just seems overwhelming. "The rest were to get there on planks or on pieces of the ship. In this way everyone reached land in safety" (Acts 27:44); on broken pieces of ship, my brothers and sisters, we make it to the shore. While you are making it to the shore on broken pieces of ship, there may be a coral reef out there. They are sharp like razor wire, and when you get cut on them, they leave a kind of poison in your body; it does not heal well. On broken pieces of ship, my friends, my brothers, we will make it.

> Therefore, my brothers, be all the more eager to make your calling and election sure. For if you do these things, you will never fall, and you will receive a rich welcome into the eternal kingdom of our LORD and Savior Jesus Christ (2 Pet. 1:10–11).

32. Definition: to set together, to understand.

You might respond, 'What? That is not abundant. I am making it just by the skin of my teeth.' Yes, the skin of *your* teeth, but underneath were the everlasting arms. Our Lord said that He "will never leave you nor forsake you."[33] You are overcoming trials, and even if you perish, "in all these things we are more than conquerors through him who loved us" (Rom. 8:37). We are like sheep for the slaughter, and if we perish, we do so not whining, not terrified, but trusting in God.[34] This is why we pray, "your will be done" (Matt. 6:10)—to know what to do and to submit to His will in all things.

We do not know His hidden will, but we know His decreed will. God sometimes wants us to glorify Him by suffering. John the Baptist, the Prophets, Paul, and the early Church had a good sense of this. The early Church elevated martyrs, and the word for witness became one who sealed their witness with their blood. It generally means the *witness*—faithful witness. We are more than conquerors through Him who loved us, so we prepare the saints for works of service, "**until we all reach unity in the faith and in the knowledge of the Son of God and become mature, attaining to the whole measure of the fullness of Christ**" (v. 13), who is to fill "everything in every way" (Eph. 1:23b).

We have to grow in our understanding of the completeness of Christ. The widespread rejection of Christ in the modern world is in large measure due to the incomplete picture that believers have painted of Christ. We are to build on the historically cumulative insight so as to attain "**unity in the faith and in the knowledge of the Son of God and become mature, attaining to the whole measure of the fullness of Christ**" (v. 13b). Negatively, it says, "**Then we will no longer be infants, tossed back and forth by the waves, and blown here and there by every wind of teaching and by the cunning and craftiness of men in their deceitful scheming**" (v. 14). All kinds of waves come against us and we are called to wait upon the Lord, submit, persevere, and learn through trials of faith.

---

33. *Deuteronomy 31:6* ("Be strong and courageous. Do not be afraid or terrified because of them, for the LORD your God goes with you; he will never leave you nor forsake you"), *Deuteronomy 31:8* ("The LORD himself goes before you and will be with you; he will never leave you nor forsake you. Do not be afraid; do not be discouraged"), and *Hebrews 13:5* ("Let your conversation be without covetousness; and be content with such things as ye have: for he hath said, I will never leave thee, nor forsake thee").

34. *Isaiah 53:7.*

'The holy catholic and apostolic faith.' I am going to have to deal with this claim. The claim is being made that *this church,* and *this church* more than any other church, holds to the holy catholic and apostolic faith. The Anglicans can make a claim, but they do not get there. Roman Catholics tend to look down on them: 'You guys are wannabes. You are really new, and you try to make your buildings look old and classical as if you always had it. No, we are not buying that.' Eastern Orthodox says, '*We* are the ancient church.' And here we are, Presbyterians. Johnny-come-lately saying, 'No, we hold to Historic Christianity.' How do you do that? What is the sleight of men? Cunning and craftiness? Is it tradition, or is it the apostolic faith? Is the apostolic faith coming through the apostolic teaching, doctrine, and holding to the doctrine? This is the one who continues it.[35] Yes, starting with Acts 15. To what extent has the Roman Catholic Church departed from the biblical view of the sacraments? They hold to sacramental theology, which is contrary to Acts 15. This is not Historic Christianity. We have to cut it off at the knees. Remember the Black Knight in Monty Python: "Come back here . . . I'll bite your legs off!"[36] He ended up crying. The guy is down that far. They do not give up. Some people will not give up, but we just leave them after a while. What do you think happened to him? He bled to death? That is what I am thinking, but that did not happen in the movie.

We have to deal with **"the cunning and craftiness of men in their deceitful scheming"** (v. 14b), in shifting from doctrine to appeal to papal succession and taking what is a sign—the laying on of hands—as the reality. No, the sign is not the reality. We have to respond with humility and gentleness. **"Be completely humble and gentle; be patient, bearing with one another in love"** (v. 2), affirming the unity of the Spirit, and not declaring, 'This person is not a believer.' **"Until we all reach unity in the faith"** (v. 13a).

"Instead, speaking the truth in love, we will in all things grow up into him who is the Head, that is, Christ" (v. 15). We are not to respond in exasperation. When we get exasperated, it shows that we are really reaching the limits of our understanding. It does not mean we

35. Gangadean, *The Westminster Confession,* xv-xxxii, 349–351; Gangadean, "Paper No. 16: The Historic Christian Faith," 103–114; "Paper No. 60: The Spiritual War (Part II)," in *The Logos Papers,* 329–330.

36. Graham Chapman, ed. *Monty Python and the Holy Grain,* Directed by Terry Gilliam, 1975.

do not draw the line somewhere, but it means we draw the line where it needs to be drawn: when we have done the work, in our witness. We are being forced, through challenges and witness, to grow up:

> **We will in all things grow up into him who is the Head, that is, Christ. From him the whole body, joined and held together by every supporting ligament, grows and builds itself up in love, as each part does its work**" (vv. 15b–16).

We are members of the body, and the God of wisdom has given grace to everyone. "**But to each one of us grace has been given as Christ apportioned it**" (v. 7). Each one of us is given grace. He is "full of grace and truth" (Jn. 1:14b), and each member has a part to play, and each member *must* play that part if we are going to come into the unity of the faith.

We are compacted, knit together, and held together by that which every joint supplies. If you are not supplying anything, if you are just receiving, it will not happen. You have to be giving. Notice: "**joined**"—connected—"**held together by every supporting ligament**" (v. 16a). Every joint, not one missing; what every member supplies.

We do not have exams in Logos, as such, at this time, but we do have an examination process that is going on that is very real: You know them by their fruit,[37] by the words spoken, and the deeds done. It is a very appropriate, subtle, insightful evaluation that is going on by watching your manner of life and attitude and every word that comes out of your mouth—or does not come out. You know them by their fruit. Oversight sees where persons are supplying, connected, and where persons are connected appropriately. Some are making a lot of noise about their service, and others are doing silent service that is effective, and it is bearing fruit. We ask you to evaluate yourself in the novitiate, and we check whether your evaluation is close to the evaluation that we know in other ways. It is for your benefit to evaluate yourself and, if there is a big disparity, to get feedback. "**From him the whole body, joined and held together by every supporting ligament, grows and builds itself up in love, as each part does its work**" (v. 16b).

Someone, another pastor in another church, years ago, said, 'There are two kinds of people in every church. There are carriers, and there

37. *Matthew 7:16.*

are riders.' Think about a big tree being carried; some are carrying that tree, and some are sitting on the branches of the tree being carried. This is not Christian; this is not lowliness and love in serving. We are all to supply what God has given us. You cannot say, 'I do not have any grace.' This is like saying, 'I am not part of the body of Christ.' Repent, believe the gospel, and submit yourself to the discipline to prepare. This is how the body increases: **"joined and held together by every supporting ligament, grows and builds itself up in love"** (v. 16).

We are to make use of the means to come into the unity of the faith and maintain the unity of the Spirit as we come. Everyone has something to contribute and is to be doing so or making definite steps, noticeable steps, in progress. Everyone is to make use of the work of the pastor-teachers built on the apostles, prophets, and evangelists. God has ordered things this way. Do you see the wisdom of this? Do you admire the wisdom of God in this? Do you bless the Lord for this?

We can have an increase. I learned an imprecatory prayer against the creatures of the land that devour plants. Someone so tender that their feet would not touch the ground was communicating to me the imprecation that she felt toward creatures that devour the fruit. I would not quite urge that upon us, but we should have fruit, and fruit that remains—not fruit that is gobbled up before it gets where it should be. May the Lord bless us so that we bear fruit to His glory.

11

INTEGRITY AND UNITY

The Gap Theory: From Hearing to Doing

2015

1 Corinthians 3:1–15

1Brothers, I could not address you as spiritual but as worldly—mere infants in Christ. 2I gave you milk, not solid food, for you were not yet ready for it. Indeed, you are still not ready. 3You are still worldly. For since there is jealousy and quarreling among you, are you not worldly? Are you not acting like mere men? 4For when one says, "I follow Paul," and another, "I follow Apollos," are you not mere men?

5What, after all, is Apollos? And what is Paul? Only servants, through whom you came to believe—as the Lord has assigned to each his task. 6I planted the seed, Apollos watered it, but God made it grow. 7So neither he who plants nor he who waters is anything, but only God, who makes things grow. 8The man who plants and the man who waters have one purpose, and each will be rewarded according to his own labor. 9For we are God's fellow workers; you are God's field, God's building.

10By the grace God has given me, I laid a foundation as an expert builder, and someone else is building on it. But each one should be careful how he builds. 11For no one can lay any foundation other than the one already laid, which is Jesus Christ. 12If any man builds on this foundation using gold, silver, costly stones, wood, hay or straw, 13his work will be shown for what it is, because the Day will bring it to light. It will be revealed with fire, and the fire will test the quality of each man's work. 14If what he has built survives, he will receive his reward. 15If it is burned up, he will suffer loss; he himself will be saved, but only as one escaping through the flames.

CONTEXT FOR THE MESSAGE:
Can We Overcome Divisions?

RECENTLY, I SPOKE ABOUT *THE SIN OF THE FATHERS* and how that is passed on to the third and fourth generations. Presently, we speak about integrity and unity, summed up in the third commandment, which says He will not hold us guiltless,[1] which ties into the Word of God to Moses when He revealed Himself; the sin of the fathers affects the third and fourth generations.

Previously, we heard preaching on Acts 15, and there were two major events concerning unity. One was doctrinal: "Unless you are circumcised, according to the custom taught by Moses, you cannot be saved" (Acts 15:1b), and all the assumptions and implications. There were epistemological assumptions in the way people were thinking about circumcision; they were taking the sign for the reality. The other was the conflict between Barnabas and Paul over how best to proceed with the work in wisdom.[2]

The Scripture reading is from 1 Corinthians 3, where the division between Paul and Barnabas is mentioned. We are concerned with unity. **"I am of Paul; and I am of Apollos"** (v. 4 KJV), and you might add from the first chapter, "and I of Cephas" (1 Cor. 1:12 KJV). There are divisions in the body along personality lines.

We have recently tried to talk to others about a conference on the unity of the faith,[3] so this theme is of ongoing concern. It is also part of the context of Jesus' High Priestly Prayer: that they may be one that the world may believe.[4] In terms of our witness and counting our days aright, we are to be faithful witnesses in our daily worship—Word, worship, witness. The concern is with unity and what is necessary for unity.

A question was raised to me about discipleship, "Teaching them to observe all things whatsoever I have commanded you" (Matt. 28:20a KJV), and how to put that into practice. Someone asked, 'How do we do that?' The question has remained with me because it raises the concern

1. *Exodus 20:7.*

2. *Acts 15:36–41.*

3. The Unity of the Faith Conference took place at Arizona Christian University on April 18, 2015. The transcription of Pastor Gangadean's lecture can be found in: Gangadean, *On Natural and Revealed Theology*, 107–118.

4. *John 17:20–23.*

about a split between hearing about what we should do and putting it into practice. The need for unity is not just among believers but within the believer. There are discussions in the women's biblical foundation class concerning the question, 'How do you put this into practice?'

A friend of years ago recently shared a book connected with his longstanding concern of trying to close the gap between knowing and doing. He has quoted me as saying, 'Our beliefs affect our actions.' This is ambiguous. 'Our beliefs *can* affect our actions,' 'Our beliefs *should* affect our actions,' or, 'Our beliefs *do* affect our actions.' Which of those is it? I would say that our beliefs do affect our actions, and if this is the case, then there is no gap between our beliefs and our actions. Devoting one's life to closing a gap that does not exist is not going to be fruitful. How do we understand unity?

I have been reading Nehemiah and Malachi in my personal devotions. It seems that within 40 years of having made a covenant renewal commitment, promising to do certain things and making sacrifices to live in Jerusalem, Malachi is reproving the priests for not maintaining the honor of God by allowing lame sacrifices to be brought, showing that they do not reverence His great name.[5] A concern I have is, are we doomed to see this go on again and again and again? Will the walls of Jerusalem—the foundation, walls, and gates of the City of God—be established? Will it come about, or will we go through the cycle perpetually? This is the context in which we are speaking about unity; it is an ongoing context. We have said in times past that if the Church does not repent, the culture will decay, and it will bring judgment, and we struggle with this reality. We struggle in the face of so much that is not being given heed or paid attention to. The question is, can we maintain faith, hope, and love? Can we go from strength to strength? Will we make it? Will we make it just barely, or will we make it with an abundant entry so that the earth is filled with the knowledge of God?[6] At the Congregational Meeting, I quoted from Psalm 89E: God's hand will cause the hand of His king to be upon the farthest seas, and the nations will come:

> I also will impose his hand upon the rolling sea;
> And on the mighty rivers all I'll make his right hand be.

5. *Malachi 1:8.*
6. *Isaiah 11:9; Habakkuk 2:14.*

'Thou art my Father and my God,' He unto me shall cry;
'The rock of my salvation sure, on whom I will rely.'
I'll make him My firstborn, above all kings of every land;
My love for him I'll ever keep; My covenant firm shall stand.
And I will also make his seed, forever to endure;
And as the days of heaven are, His throne shall stand secure.[7]

CHRIST:
I Will Build My Church

I quoted from the statement made by Jesus in connection with Peter's confession: "*I* will build my church" (Matt. 16:18a).[8] This is not about *us* succeeding. This is about *Christ* succeeding. The question can be put this way: He said, "I will build my church." Will Jesus Christ succeed, or will His death be overcome by human sin rather than His death overcoming human sin? When we put the question in that stark way, we have to back off and say, 'Of course, Christ will succeed.' But when and how becomes a source of confusion for many: What success means, whether it is the Second Coming, premillennial, pre-rapture, mid-tribulation—are a few versions of 'Christ will succeed.' 'He will rapture us out of this place.' Or, the amillennial view is where 'the Church and the world will grow side by side to the end, and Christ will succeed; He will get His elect, which may be a small number, but He does say few would be saved. Right, did He not say that?' Yes, He did say that, so why am I speaking about all the nations coming? Because it also says that all the nations will come. How do you put those two together? They are contradictory, are they not? It is easily put together: One is at a certain time, and the other is at another time. Are there a few that are being saved *now*? Since the disciples were asking about what they saw *then* and they were expecting many to be saved *then and there*—rather than what Jesus had told them: the kingdom starts like a mustard seed, and it grows[9]—there is no conflict between these two. Few were saved at one time, but the number will increase in history until it encompasses the whole earth.

7. *Psalm 89:25–29, The Book of Psalms for Singing.*

8. Emphasis added.

9. *Matthew 13:31–32; Mark 4:30–32; Luke 13:18–19.*

I am continually exercised by this day in and day out, morning, noon, and evening. I am thinking, reflecting, eating, and sleeping on this idea: Can we get through? Can we come to unity? Will the world come to believe? "That they all may be one . . . that the world may believe" (Jn. 17:21 KJV). I want to go further this morning in addressing this concern. I believe the answer is yes. I have not given up. I am almost dead, but I am not quite dead—not altogether. As long as I have some breath, I am going to lift up my voice and cry out. You are going to have to kill me before you silence me. This is the context. Do not think I am picking on you. I am coming from a particular context. If it does feel like I am picking on you, that is not me; that is the Holy Spirit working conviction.

SOURCES OF UNITY: Beginning with Epistemology

There are five sources of unity I would like to mention. There is Common Ground,[10] which includes reason, integrity[11] (the subject today), Rational Presuppositionalism,[12] and the Principle of Clarity.[13] You may say, 'I have heard that a number of times. We are not going to go over that again, are we?' We are going over it in part.

Can you tell me what it means when the Scriptures speak of man as created in the image of God? Can you tell me if it is necessary to begin with what is clear? Can you cite one of the best examples, easily accessible to all of us, of beginning with what is clear in epistemology, metaphysics, and ethics? Is this just something played around with here

10. Gangadean, "Paper No. 2: Common Ground," 9–13; "Paper No. 50: Common Ground (Part I)," 275–276; "Paper No. 51: Common Ground (Part II)," 277–279; "Paper No. 52: Common Ground (Part III)," 281–282; "Paper No. 53: Common Ground (Part IV)," in *The Logos Papers,* 283–286.

11. Gangadean, *Philosophical Foundation,* 199–205; Gangadean, *History of Philosophy,* 3–12; Gangadean, *The Westminster Catechisms,* 237–240; Gangadean, "Paper No. 51: Common Ground (Part II)," 277–279; "Paper No. 64: Aaron's Rod," in *The Logos Papers,* 341–352.

12. Gangadean, *Philosophical Foundation,* 19–23; Gangadean, "Paper No. 101: Rational Presuppositionalism," 521–526; "Paper No. 52: Common Ground (Part III)," in *The Logos Papers,* 281–282; Gangadean, *On Natural and Revealed Theology,* 59–66.

13. Gangadean, *Philosophical Foundation,* 3–5, 287–292; Gangadean, *The Westminster Confession,* 1–13; Gangadean, "Paper No. 53: Common Ground (Part IV)," in *The Logos Papers,* 283–286.

by a retired philosophy teacher still thinking about the glory days? Is that what this is about? Or is this the real substance of life?

Have you heard of the *Declaration of Independence*? Yes, you have. I have given you that much of a clue. I have given you at least 70%. Can you get the rest of the 30%? If you cannot get the rest of the 30%, you are not thinking; you are not alive. You need to repent. Where does Thomas Jefferson speak about clarity? Where does he speak about epistemology? "We hold these truths to be self-evident." Is that about clarity? Yes. Is it an epistemological claim? Yes. In what sense is it self-evident? Do all men hold it as self-evident? No, that may have been held by common sense at the time, but as time has passed, it has come under increased challenges. What about metaphysics? "That all men are created equal." Do all men say that we are created equal? Does this say something about God, the Creator, and man, the creature? Does this say something about the central themes of metaphysics? Yes. What about ethics? "They are endowed by their Creator with certain unalienable Rights, that among these are Life, Liberty and the pursuit of Happiness."[14] He got it right in all three and has it wrong on all three. He is right formally in starting with the self-evident—epistemology, but he is wrong in *what* is self-evident, and *how* it is self-evident.

Common Ground and Application

Common Ground says that we start with reason.[15] Is it self-evident that we are thinking? Is that more basic than saying that God exists? It seems to me that it is self-evident, if you are thinking at all. Yes; if you are not thinking, as I said, you are dead, and if you are dead, then you need to repent. How do you repent of being dead? Say to the Lord, 'I am dead.' You confess with your mouth,[16] 'Yes, I am dead. I am dead in trespasses and sins.[17] I have acted contrary to my nature, as made in

14. The Preamble of the *Declaration of Independence.*

15. Gangadean, *Philosophical Foundation,* 10–15; Gangadean, *History of Philosophy,* 25–35; Gangadean, *On Natural and Revealed Theology,* 41–57; Gangadean, "Paper No. 5: Reason (The Handout)," 27–28; "Paper No. 44: Reason in Itself," 255–256; "Paper No. 48: Reason and the Word of God," 267–269; "Paper No. 57: Reason (Applied)," 315–316; "Paper No. 92: The Relevance of Reason," 485–491; "Paper No. 111: Common Christian Misconceptions About Reason," in *The Logos Papers,* 579–582.

16. *Romans 10:9.*

17. *Ephesians 2:1.*

your image. I have not diligently sought you; I have not understood; I do not have faith based on understanding. I have fideism but no faith.[18] I have pietism but not biblical piety.' You get the picture. Where does the Scripture speak about this? Where does the Confession speak about this? What are the opening words of the Confession? I want to call on you by name, but I cannot do that because this is not a class. This is preaching. Are you not glad? 'Oh, thank God for preaching.'

These are the opening words of the Westminster Confession regarding the basic truth of epistemology (the light of nature and the use of good and necessary consequence) and metaphysics (what is clear about God and man, and good and evil):

> Although the light of nature, and the works of creation and providence do so far manifest the goodness, wisdom, and power of God, as to leave men unexcusable; yet are they not sufficient to give that knowledge of God, and of his will, which is necessary unto salvation (WCF. 1.1).[19]
>
> The whole counsel of God concerning all things necessary for His own glory, man's salvation, faith and life, is either expressly set down in Scripture, or by good and necessary consequence may be deduced from Scripture (WCF. 1.6).

Do you know what good and necessary consequences are? They are inferences—an inference goes backward to assumptions and forward to implications. This is how the Scripture is sufficient: through the use of good and necessary consequences. This is reason. This is Historic Christianity. We are going to be ending with good and necessary consequences when we come to Malachi at the end of the sermon. We can recite points about Common Ground and we have a grammar-level knowledge of it,[20] but we do not have dialectical-level knowledge. We cannot explain it and show it from sources, and we cannot apply it.

---

18. Gangadean, *Philosophical Foundation,* 32–45, 121–127; Gangadean, *History of Philosophy,* 3–12, 163–167; Gangadean, "Paper No. 21: Faith and Reason in Christianity," 135–138; "Paper No. 28: Prepare the Way of the Lord," 171–173; "Paper No. 98: Faith and the Word of God," 511–514; "Paper No. 128: Abraham's Faith," 665–666; "Paper No. 129: Faith and Reason in the Life of Abraham" in *The Logos Papers,* 667–669.

19. Gangadean, *The Westminster Confession,* 1–46.

20. The Logos Foundation, *Grammar Catechisms,* xvi-xvi.

MAN, THE IMAGE OF GOD: Seeking and Understanding

Our job as oversight is to lay this foundation. If the foundation is not laid, do we get upset and angry and start screaming? No. Do we pull out our beard the way Ezra did?[21] No. Do we pull out other people's beards as Nehemiah did?[22] No. What do we do? What would Jesus do? How many times has He done it? He did it many times. He said, "He who has ears, let him hear" (Matt. 11:15). There are many times and circumstances in which He says this. He comes back to integrity and hypocrisy: hearing lightly and thoughtlessly and not understanding. If you notice, in the announced Focus of the Week, *hearing and understanding,* "the one who received seed that fell on the good soil is the man who hears the word and understands it" (Matt. 13:23a). We have a tendency to go toward the outward, toward the minimal, toward the literal; the same kind of tendency was there in Acts 15: "Unless you are circumcised, according to the custom taught by Moses, you cannot be saved" (Acts 15:1b). They became very zealous for circumcision as the outward act, in a ritual way, without thinking, without understanding, and without faith. This gets back to the sin, which is not seeking and not understanding.[23] This gets back to sin from general revelation, as an act contrary to our nature as human beings, made in the image of God.

If We Know It, We Can Show It

The first aspect of our being made in the image of God is that we are thinking beings. It is self-evident that we think. It follows by inference that reason is the laws of thought: identity, non-contradiction, and excluded middle. Does it then follow, by good necessary consequences, that reason is the test for meaning? Does it then follow that reason is self-attesting? Does it then follow that nothing else is self-attesting? Does it then follow that reason is the most basic authority? Does it follow from the Scripture, Historic Christianity, and general revelation, that

21. *Ezra 9:3.*

22. *Nehemiah 13:25.*

23. *Romans 3:10–11; Psalm 14:2–3, 53:1–3;* Gangadean, *The Biblical Worldview,* 33–54, 177–196; Gangadean, "Paper No. 146: *The Biblical Worldview* (Part VI)," in *The Logos Papers,* 741–745; Gangadean, *The Westminster Catechisms,* 144–15; Gangadean, *The Westminster Confession,* 99–110, 369–376.

reason is the Word of God in all men, by virtue of our being made in the image of God? We are to use reason to seek and understand—we understand by making connections. It is not a small thing and we need to be able to go through this and understand it at more than a grammatical level. So yes, you can say, 'I have heard this. I have heard this. I have heard this. Not again.' If you have heard it but have not understood it, so that it is not coming out in practice, there is a lack.

If we say we are interested in understanding but we are not diligently seeking, there is a lack of integrity; there is no consistency between the two. There is a lack of integrity and a conflict within my being—there is no unity. I am acting contrary to my being, as rational, made in the image of God.

Incidentally, angels are also rational. How are we different from angels? It is self-evident that we think, and it is also self-evident that we are sentient. We do not just have feelings but also sense impressions: sight, sound, smell, taste, touch, et cetera. Those are from our senses, which we have in common with the animals. We are rational animals. Have you ever heard that before? Man is the image of God. If you think about it at all, you see that we are rational animals, and reason rules over the body. Understanding that reason rules over the body is how we preserve the unity between those two aspects of our being, body and soul, and we are concerned about unity.

"Man does not live on bread alone, but on every word that comes from the mouth of God" (Matt. 4:4). If we had integrity, we would not say one thing and do another. Our principal concern should be to examine ourselves to see whether we have consistency in what we think, say, and do. If you profess clarity yet are not able to see and show clarity, what should we say? We should recognize that our hypocrisy (claiming to know when we do not) is rooted in idolatry and autonomy. There is an axis in our being, between the first three commandments. There is a tight connection between *autonomy:* determining good and evil for myself, going my own way, putting myself in the place of God; *idolatry:* conceiving of God after my own image rather than myself in the image of God; and *hypocrisy*. When we end with hypocrisy—failing to do what we say—it is like saying it is manifest in the outward act of unrighteousness. The outward act is grounded in autonomy, idolatry, and hypocrisy.

Build on Historically Cumulative Insight

The law *can* search us, but the only way the law *will* search us is if we meditate on it by using good necessary consequences, looking at assumptions and implications, and applying it to ourselves and the world around us. It is the Word of God. It is sharp, it is powerful, and it is beautiful. It convicts. The law of God is written in the hearts of all humans, but we have to benefit from our parents and the historically cumulative insight. When the command says, "Honor your father and your mother" (Ex. 20:12), we understand this as saying, 'Your father and mother should have honored their father and mother.' Right? They should have honored those who have gone before. We are talking about honoring the historically cumulative insight. If we do not, what will happen? We will not "live long in the land the LORD your God is giving [us]" (Ex. 20:12b). As the Israelites were taken out, we will be taken out. The culture decays. We have to connect living in the land with the historically accumulated insight—through the cornerstone, the moral law, the foundation[24] and redemptive history unfolded in Historic Christianity through historically cumulative insight.[25]

Did historically cumulative insight not happen in Acts 15? Did it not manifest itself there in a notable beginning? Yes, and it goes on to the next: the Apostles' Creed and what it teaches against Greek dualism. The historically cumulative insight continues in the councils and creeds on: the Triune God, Christ is God and man, predestination, free will, and grace.[26] Does not the Westminster Confession build on all of these? Is the Westminster Confession the latest and fullest confession? Did not the London Confession of the Baptists depart from this? The London Baptist Confession did not build further. The Westminster Confession goes beyond the Church of England and the Thirty-nine Articles. It builds on them, and it goes beyond. This is what historically cumulative insight is. This is what it is to honor your father and your mother, and if they do not honor their father and mother, and if the sin (singular) of the fathers (plural) comes down to us, then we are to give honor to whom honor is due. We are not to feel bound by our father and

24. Gangadean, *On Natural and Revealed Theology*, 93–106.

25. Gangadean, *On Natural and Revealed Theology*, 71–92.

26. Gangadean, "Paper No. 16: The Historic Christian Faith," in *The Logos Papers*, 103–114; Gangadean, *The Westminster Confession*, xix-xxix, 349–351; Gangadean, *On Natural and Revealed Theology*, 107–118.

mother simply because they are in that position but because they have maintained the connection in the historically cumulative insight. This is the law; it is right here. This is why we are commanded to meditate on the law of God day and night.[27] The law is the source of unity.

The law is teleological, not deontological. Kingly personalities tend to take the law as deontological. Priestly persons tend to take the law as consequential—happiness, fun, and joy. Prophetic people can distort everything by denying the law. There are false prophets. We are to watch ourselves. He who has ears to hear, let him hear.

Can we make it? Remember this is the context: Can we make it? Yes. God has given us everything we need. It is here. When we hit the wall, we need not despair and bang our heads against the wall but we start digging to get under the wall, figure out a way to rock climb and get over the wall, or drill a hole through the wall. We are not going to let it stop us. Jesus said, "I will build my church" (Matt. 16:18a), and, "do this in remembrance of me" (1 Cor. 11:24b). In remembrance of Him till He comes—"For whenever you eat this bread and drink this cup, you proclaim the LORD's death until he comes" (1 Cor. 11:26).

Bridging the Gap Between Hearing and Understanding

I was going to title the subject of the message: "God of the Gaps" or "The Gap Theory." I figured that was a little bit too esoteric. "Integrity and Unity" is closer; we may feel more comfortable with it. There is no gap between our thinking and our feeling. I will say that once more for everyone's benefit. There is no gap—I did not stop there, period. I said, there is no gap between our thinking and our feeling. The third time is the charm. There is no gap between our thinking and our feeling. This is not to say there is no gap; it is just that it is not between our thinking and feeling. There may be a gap between our hearing and our hearing. They have ears to hear, but they do not hear. He who has ears, let him hear what the Spirit says to the Church.[28] We hear *outwardly* without hearing *inwardly* with understanding, that is, with faith. This is where the gap is. We keep concentrating on the gap between thinking and feeling, and we miss that the gap is within the thinking. The gap

27. *Joshua 1:8.*

28. *Revelation 2:17.*

in the thinking is more basic, is it not? We see a perfect example in Peter's thinking:

> "But what about you?" he asked. "Who do you say I am?" Simon Peter answered, "You are the Christ, the Son of the living God." Jesus replied, "Blessed are you, Simon son of Jonah, for this was not revealed to you by man, but by my Father in heaven. And I tell you that you are Peter, and on this rock I will build my church, and the gates of Hades will not overcome it. I will give you the keys of the kingdom of heaven; whatever you bind on earth will be bound in heaven, and whatever you loose on earth will be loosed in heaven" (Matt. 16:15–19).

After this, Jesus told the disciples He was going to go up to Jerusalem and die. Peter said, "Never, LORD! This shall never happen to you!" (Matt. 16:22b) 'Far be it from you, Lord. Do not have those negative thoughts. You ought to be positive, Lord. I know it is looking bad, but just hang in there.' Jesus looked at Peter. "Get behind me, Satan! You are a stumbling block to me; you do not have in mind the things of God, but the things of men" (Matt. 16:23). How can this be? In one moment, Peter confesses, "You are the Christ"—God had revealed this to him. Apparently, the Lord did not reveal the other part to him, but Jesus—God incarnate—was telling Peter what was to happen and Peter was correcting God. We are to be "quick to listen, slow to speak and slow to become angry" (Jas. 1:19b). The Lord rebuked Peter. Was there a gap in Peter's understanding?

On the road to Emmaus, "he opened their minds so they could understand the Scriptures" (Lk. 24:45). This is what faith is. Faith is understanding.[29] At least one side of it. The other side is trusting in God in terms of His character, where we do not know the outcome of a circumstance, but we know God's character, which is the basis of our trust. This is believing *in* (trusting), not believing *that*. The belief *that* God is just, holy, merciful, infinite, eternal, and unchangeable, precedes believing *in*. This was the thesis of my master's degree in philosophy—an account of religious belief, and distinguishing between believing *in* and believing *that*. It was also the point at which I hit a wall with my doctoral degree. I was seeing the distinction between meaning

29. Gangadean, *The Biblical Worldview*, 3–20.

and truth, and the problem lay in meaning. I made this distinction and passed it on to you, but I had to wrestle with it a great deal.[30] What I am talking about now is understanding the meaning of what is said. That comes by diligently seeking.

SPIRITUALLY DISCERNED: Having Ears to Hear

We can distort every source of unity and, through sin, it becomes a source of disunity. The reading of Scripture was from 1 Corinthians 3, and I noticed that just before Paul got to that portion of the letter, he said, "The man without the Spirit does not accept the things that come from the Spirit of God, for they are foolishness to him, and he cannot understand them, because they are spiritually discerned" (1 Cor. 2:14). Is Paul saying 'spiritually intuited,' apart from inference and connection? He just said 'understand,' so we cannot say spiritually discerned is apart from understanding as in a direct, immediate impression. It must be an insight of understanding, and we must remember all the Scripture says about understanding. Because the worldview is not in place, they cannot understand it. When Paul spoke to the Greeks in Athens about Jesus as resurrected from the dead, it was foolishness to them.[31] In dualism, the whole point of life was for the soul to be separate from the body. The soul being in the body was a punishment, a degradation, and to speak about the resurrection was foolishness to them; they could not understand it.[32] It was spiritually discerned. That is, it is discerned in the context of the biblical worldview and biblical assumptions.

Paul in Hebrews 5:12 speaks about the immaturity of believers that hinders them from understanding: "In fact, though by this time you ought to be teachers, you need someone to teach you the elementary truths of God's word all over again. You need milk, not solid food!" Because the foundation is not in place, you cannot grasp it. You are operating from the basic principles of the world, not the basic principles

30. Gangadean, *Philosophical Foundation,* 19–23; Gangadean, "Paper No. 101: Rational Presuppositionalism," 521–526; "Paper No. 52: Common Ground (Part III)," in *The Logos Papers,* 281–282; Gangadean, *On Natural and Revealed Theology,* 59–66.

31. *Acts 17:16–34.*

32. Gangadean, *Philosophical Foundation,* 129–137; Gangadean, *History of Philosophy,* 87–105, 111–114.

of the Triune God. Let me ask: Is there any distinction between knowledge and holiness? Here are the three parts: knowledge, holiness, and righteousness. We may also distinguish prophet, priest, and king. Is there any conflict between knowledge and holiness in Scripture? Is there the smallest distinction between knowledge and holiness? Does it not say, "Sanctify them by the truth; your word"—your Logos, truth with a capital "T," which means the whole of the Logos, the worldview—"is truth" (Jn. 17:17). Does it speak of a gap between knowledge and holiness? No, it does not. Does it not say, "Then you will know the truth, and the truth will set you free" (Jn. 8:32)? Do we have to add something to the truth to get from truth to freedom? "Be transformed by the renewing of your mind" (Rom. 12:2). Is there not an automatic flow from the one to the other? In the unity within the Father, Son, and the Holy Spirit, the Son, the Word of God, comes from God naturally, automatically, eternally, and necessarily.[33] It is an eternal relation. Do you have to add something? No.

Hearing at the Grammatical Level

If knowledge and holiness are in place, would there not be a devotion, seeking, growing, and putting it into practice: righteousness? Then how is it that I hear people say, 'I know this, but what do I do? How am I supposed to put it into practice?' Why is there a gap? I am saying the gap originates first in understanding. We hear it at a certain level but do not understand it as we should. We think we understand it because we know the words, and we think, 'I have heard this before.' Yes, you have heard it at a *grammar level,* mere words, ritual hearing, outwardly like others heard: "Unless you are circumcised, according to the custom taught by Moses, you cannot be saved" (Acts 15:1b).[34] You see the outward reality, "Man looks at the outward appearance, but the LORD looks at the heart" (1 Sam. 16:7b). It is the same with empiricism. "A wicked and adulterous generation asks for a miraculous sign!" (Matt. 12:39a)—an outward, visible sign, without understanding what the sign signifies. It is not seeking diligently and not understanding. This is what we are after: seeking diligently and understanding. As long as

33. Gangadean, *Philosophical Foundation,* 144.

34. Gangadean, "Paper No. 60: The Spiritual War (Part II)," in *The Logos Papers,* 329–330.

I have breath and I am in this body, I will remind you of these things, for your faith, for the edification of the body, to get understanding.

Do you understand, or are you at the grammar level? Your words, interpretations, and deeds reveal how far along you are. It is very easy to say. How far along are you in seeing what is clear? Can you show what is clear? You may not roll your eyes outwardly at me, but I can see them with the eye of faith rolling inwardly. The spiritual man discerns all things, right?[35] You are looking at me, and you are smiling, and you say, 'Why does he not get lost?' 'Get lost now.' I can feel it, you know? No, I cannot feel it. I am just playing with you on that one.

Integrity: Taking Baby Steps

I remind you, the way Paul did. 'You need milk? Okay, let us go over it again.' It is called baby steps. Take more baby steps. This is integrity, from the moral law analysis and application. If you do not understand—there is a good reason why you do not understand, but it is not excusable—you take baby steps, little steps. This is what we are encouraging you to do. We may say to someone, 'Have you talked to your friends? Are they praying for you? We will work with you with baby steps.' In other words, "For when for the time ye ought to be teachers, ye have need" to take baby steps (Heb. 5:12 KJV). You need milk[36]—these basic things of the truths of God: the foundation. Paul said,

> **By the grace God has given me, I laid a foundation as an expert builder, and someone else is building on it. But each one should be careful how he builds. For no one can lay any foundation other than the one already laid, which is Jesus Christ. If any man builds on this foundation using gold, silver, costly stones, wood, hay or straw, his work will be shown for what it is, because the Day will bring it to light. It will be revealed with fire, and the fire will test the quality of each man's work. If what he has built survives, he will receive his reward. If it is burned up, he will suffer loss; he himself will be saved, but only as one escaping through the flames** (vv. 10–15).

---

35. *1 Corinthians 2:15.*

36. *Hebrews 5:12.*

He said, "not laying again the foundation of repentance from acts that lead to death, and of faith in God" (Heb. 6:1b).

Everything in our nature, made in the image of God, is intended for unity, and we have made it for disunity. Male and female are in the image of God. They are intended for unity. There is a real difference. Are there conflicts between male and female? How do you deal with it? The difference between prophetic, priestly, and kingly is like that between male and female. There are real differences; they are there and are intended for unity. There is an order. Just as there is an order between prophet-priest-king, there is an order between male and female, and we may not observe it. God recognizes sin in both. If the man does not believe, how is the woman to respond in a way consistent with the feminine? Men have failed, and they failed badly, but women have also failed. Parents have failed, but children have also failed. Scripture says, "Honor your father and your mother, so that you may live long in the land the LORD your God is giving you" (Ex. 20:12), and "fathers, provoke not your children to wrath" (Eph. 6:4a KJV). "Wives, submit to your husbands as to the LORD" (Eph. 5:22). "Husbands, love your wives, just as Christ loved the church" (Eph. 5:25a).

Every place where there is diversity, in our sin—our autonomy, our idolatry—it becomes a source of disunity, whereas it should be for unity. That includes the uniqueness of our personality and our talent. As Paul says, "We have different gifts, according to the grace given us" (Rom. 12:6a), and talent is in the uniqueness of your being. Everyone has talent; get to know the other person and find out.

Everyone has a uniqueness. It is intended for unity, like we are all members of the same body, intended for unity. But we turn around and undermine other members.

> If the foot should say, 'Because I am not a hand, I do not belong to the body,' it would not for that reason cease to be part of the body. And if the ear should say, 'Because I am not an eye, I do not belong to the body,' it would not for that reason cease to be part of the body (1 Cor. 12:15–16).

We do not have concern for the unity of the Church. If we have the goal of the knowledge of God in place, realize that it is corporate, cumulative, and communal, and understand all that it takes to accomplish the goal, we will have unity.[37] It just shows that we do not have the cornerstone[38] in place. We probably do not have the cornerstone in place because we do not have Common Ground in place. We cannot get to the Principle of Clarity[39] because we cannot get to integrity, and behind it is our commitment to the use of reason.

What is amazing is that in the humanities, as in the sciences, God has created an orderly world. By the grace of God, we can understand that world, or certainly make progress in understanding it, and we can understand where we are having difficulty. This is encouraging. We can say, 'This is what we need to do. Let us see if we can take baby steps to move.'

I believe the foundation *can* be laid, in the way Paul said, "laying again the foundation" (Heb. 6:1). We have to say, 'Look, the foundation isn't laid.' What needs to be laid is the foundation. This is how we lay the foundation: This is the first part—foundation is always laid in the ground. You never have an ethereal foundation floating in the air. It is in the ground. That is why we spoke about ground first, and we call it *Common Ground:* what is necessary for thought and discourse.

Diversity becomes a source of disunity in our unique talent and integration, and that is also true in our background. "From every nation, tribe, people and language" (Rev. 7:9). "There is neither Jew nor Greek, slave nor free, male nor female, for you are all one in Christ Jesus" (Gal. 3:28). All of our background factors are intended for our unity, and we use them to fight against each other. At any level of human nature and the diversity that there is, the challenges of non-believers are intended for us to grow. These are challenges intended for our good and for our growth in understanding. Prophetic, priestly, kingly, the body/soul, male/female, our background, our uniqueness; diversity is intended for our unity. If we are concerned with consistency, starting out with what is more basic, we will have unity.

God has made the world. God is one. God is not divided. God has expressed Himself in everything that is made originally. Therefore, all these things that are made are in fundamental unity. There is no

37. Gangadean, *Philosophical Foundation,* 207–219.

38. Gangadean, "Paper No. 4: The Cornerstone," in *The Logos Papers,* 21–25.

39. Gangadean, *Philosophical Foundation,* 3–5, 287–292; Gangadean, *The Westminster Confession,* 1–13; Gangadean, "Paper No. 53: Common Ground (Part IV)," in *The Logos Papers,* 283–286.

conflict—by good and necessary consequences. If there is a conflict, it is because of sin that has come in, and we are coming short.

The appropriate time to take baby steps is when you are a baby. It is consistent with Paul saying, "though by this time you ought to be teachers, you need someone to teach you the elementary truths of God's word all over again" (Heb. 5:12a). We have situations here where people have not had instruction when they were young. This connects with the sin of the fathers, which comes down to the children of the third and fourth generations.[40] Consider how you were brought up, particularly regarding your father—his role, presence, involvement with discipline, and the principle of objectivity (paternal discipline), not sympathetically feeling with you (maternal nurturing). The sympathetic feeling is needed, but that is not the bone on which the sinew rests. How was it for you? Were you disciplined to gain self-control when you were young? From when you were six months old? When that has not been in place, the lack of self-control is present, and we are wrestling with it and dealing with it. For one reason or another, it was not in place.

THE NECESSITY FOR LAYING FOUNDATION

We said that the Church is the pillar and the ground of the truth.[41] At the end of Malachi, which is where we want to end, the truth comes out quite clearly. Jesus continually concludes, "He who has ears to hear, let him hear." Seven times in the Book of Revelation to the seven churches, this is expressed.[42] This means it is important. Jesus also said a number of other times: "Blessed rather are those who hear the word of God and obey it" (Lk. 11:28). Those who hear and put it into practice have the foundation. "My mother and brothers are those who hear God's word and put it into practice" (Lk. 8:21). Hear and do. I am not talking about the outward hearing, but inward hearing, with the understanding, and doing. The one who hears and understands, that is the one who bears fruit. The gap is between hearing and hearing: hearing outwardly but not hearing inwardly.

"'Surely the day is coming; it will burn like a furnace. All the arrogant and every evildoer will be stubble, and that day that is coming will set

40. *Exodus 20:5.*

41. *1 Timothy 3:15.*

42. *Revelation 2:2, 11, 17, 29; 3:6, 13, 22.*

them on fire,' says the LORD Almighty. 'Not a root or a branch will be left to them'" (Mal. 4:1). Jesus ended His public ministry by the charge of hypocrisy against the leaders who appeared righteous outwardly. This is called *wickedness*. It is a special use of the term *wickedness*. Malachi calls the people to remember the law of Moses. Then Scripture says:

> See, I will send you the prophet Elijah before that great and dreadful day of the LORD comes. He will turn the hearts of the fathers to their children, and the hearts of the children to their fathers; or else I will come and strike the land with a curse (Mal. 4:5–6).

The same Word of God is found throughout Scripture. Family life is broken down. Men may be concerned about giving their kids a financial inheritance at the end of their lives rather than giving them a legacy and a heritage by disciplining them in the early stages, which is where the true heritage and legacy come in.

This is what it takes to stop and think, take baby steps, and put it into practice. Notice: it is not over; there is a way forward. The Church is the pillar and the ground of truth, and it starts with the ministry of the prophet:

> See, I will send you the prophet Elijah before that great and dreadful day of the LORD comes. He will turn the hearts of the fathers to their children, and the hearts of the children to their fathers; or else I will come and strike the land with a curse (Mal. 4:5–6).

"Honor your father and your mother, so that you may live long in the land the LORD your God is giving you" (Ex. 20:12). He will restore us, but notice how it is restored. It begins with the prophetic ministry, but it is in the family and by parents, particularly fathers. He is the covenant head. He is responsible to see that the children are instructed. This is how the Scripture ends in the Old Testament.

Can we do it? Can we make it? Are we seeing what is necessary to lay the foundation and, if necessary, take baby steps? Can we come into unity at every level of our being which God has made? Every level. "That they may be one as we are one" (Jn. 17:22b). By the grace of God, I believe we will. God will accompany the preaching of the Word by His Spirit and grace and cause His Word to have its effect.

12

The Unity of the Body of Christ

Unity Applied to the Church

2020

Ephesians 4:11–16; 1 Corinthians 12:27–31

Ephesians 4:11–16

[11]It was he who gave some to be apostles, some to be prophets, some to be evangelists, and some to be pastors and teachers, [12]to prepare God's people for works of service, so that the body of Christ may be built up [13]until we all reach unity in the faith and in the knowledge of the Son of God and become mature, attaining to the whole measure of the fullness of Christ.

[14]Then we will no longer be infants, tossed back and forth by the waves, and blown here and there by every wind of teaching and by the cunning and craftiness of men in their deceitful scheming. [15]Instead, speaking the truth in love, we will in all things grow up into him who is the Head, that is, Christ. [16]From him the whole body, joined and held together by every supporting ligament, grows and builds itself up in love, as each part does its work.

1 Corinthians 12:27–31

[27]Now you are the body of Christ, and each one of you is a part of it. [28]And in the church God has appointed first of all apostles, second prophets, third teachers, then workers of miracles, also those having gifts of healing, those able to help others, those with gifts of administration, and those speaking in different kinds of tongues. [29]Are all apostles? Are all prophets? Are all teachers? Do all work miracles? [30]Do all have gifts of healing? Do all speak

in tongues? Do all interpret? 31But eagerly desire the greater gifts. And now I will show you the most excellent way.

WE WANT TO FOCUS ON THE UNITY of the body of Christ as derived from the unity of the law of God,[1] its assumptions, and its implications. This is a distinct dimension of unity, different from what is spoken of in Ephesians 4 regarding the unity of the Spirit, unity of the faith, and functional unity.

What struck me recently since last preaching is the division that there is in the body of Christ, and it became clearer as we reflected how the divisions in the body are particularly addressed in the second commandment. We want to look at the second commandment in light of Genesis 2–3 and in light of the first commandment, tracing how each subsequent commandment builds upon the preceding ones.[2] This is what we mean by understanding the unity of the body of Christ in terms of its *assumptions* and *implications* derived from the moral law in human nature.

The unity of the body of Christ is spoken of in the second commandment; this unity assumes the concept of *the good,* which is the source of unity.[3] As we think further, the good is the source of unity in every way, at every level, and in every dimension of life. For simplicity's sake, we can say that if we had the good in place, we would have full unity. This requires us to pay attention to the first commandment and the first sin, for it was there that unity was first broken. Original sin is not only first historically, but it is first in that all sin originates from the first sin.[4]

The second commandment says, "You shall have no other gods before me" (Ex. 20:3). The first sin, the temptation, was in light of the command of God: "but of the tree of the knowledge of good and evil you *shall not* eat" (Gen. 2:17a NKJV).[5] Notice how strong the words

1. Gangadean, *Philosophical Foundation,* 171–284; Gangadean, *History of Philosophy,* 61–69; Gangadean, *The Westminster Catechisms,* 215–267; Gangadean, *The Westminster Confession,* 207–221; Gangadean, *On Natural and Revealed Theology,* 127–139, 166–178.

2. Pastor Gangadean stopped at the fifth commandment in this sermon, but the principle still holds regarding the unity of the body as rooted in the moral law.

3. Gangadean, *Philosophical Foundation,* 171–177, 208–211.

4. Gangadean, *The Biblical Worldview,* 37–54, 177–217.

5. Emphasis added.

are: "shall not." It says, "Of every tree of the garden you may freely eat; but of the tree of the knowledge of good and evil you *shall not* eat, for in the day that you eat of it you shall surely die" (Gen. 2:16–17 NKJV). The word "shall" carries a strong connotation, historically and grammatically.

UNITY AND THE FIRST COMMANDMENT: Assumptions and Implications

We have the first command in the moral law from general revelation, and we have the first commandment historically in special revelation: "you shall not eat, for in the day that you eat of it you shall surely die" (Gen. 2:17b NKJV). The details of the temptation and sin reveal our sin is that of autonomy where we put ourselves in the place of God to know, that is, to determine good and evil, which is strictly and strongly forbidden in the first commandment. "You shall have no other gods before me" (Ex. 20:3). There is a warning connected with the first command in the Garden: "for in the day that you eat of it you shall surely die" (Gen. 2:17b NKJV). There is a double connection. In the day, in the very day that you eat, you shall surely die. Notice the word "surely." This is speaking of spiritual death, although many of us do not pay much attention to the distinction between spiritual death and physical death. We are a body/soul unity, and our souls die (spiritually) because of the sin of not regarding God.

What happened when Adam and Eve broke the first command in the very first sin, and what happens when we break it? The breaking of the command showed that they did not understand what the good was, and they mistook the cause of sin for sin itself. 'What do we mean by that?' If we obeyed God, we would have life and the enjoyment of God, and if we disobeyed, we would have death. There is a certain pleasure and enjoyment that comes from glorifying God. In the temptation in the Garden, three aspects are specified as having appeal: "When the woman saw that the fruit of the tree was *good for food* and *pleasing to the eye,* and also *desirable for gaining wisdom,* she took some and ate it" (Gen. 3:6a).[6] It was "good for food"—it had power to benefit them by eating of it. There is an element of power as a natural virtue in eating it.

6. Emphasis added.

It was "pleasing to the eye." There is a pleasure connected with its beauty, which can be spoken of as sensual happiness. It was also "desirable for gaining wisdom." There exists a form of praise intertwined with wisdom, a glory that accompanies it, fostering a sense of pride in oneself and one's accomplishments, both individually and in comparison to others—a renown that is earned. *Power, pleasure,* and *pride* are involved in the first sin, and all of this is rooted in our self-life. Having broken the first commandment, we put ourselves in the place of God, and as a result, we put ourselves at enmity with God. The first most basic disunity, between God and man, began by their first sin. If they had preserved the good, there would have been unity between God and man.[7]

Secondly, there came a disunity between those who believed in God as God—Creator and determiner of good and evil—and those who turned away from this. There is a second disunity between man and man, between believer and non-believer, between theists, who believe in God the Creator and ruler, and atheists, who deny God the Creator and ruler. The first major division comes in disobeying the first command by putting ourselves in God's place (autonomy).

THE SECOND COMMANDMENT

In the second commandment, "Thou shalt not make unto thee any graven image, or any likeness of any thing that is in heaven above, or that is in the earth beneath, or that is in the water under the earth" (Ex. 20:4 KJV), we are called not to liken God—who is spirit, infinite, eternal, and unchangeable—to anything in creation, particularly the material order of creation and the visible, which is finite, temporal, and changeable. Denying God as Creator (by putting ourselves in the place of God) naturally leads to the breaking of the second commandment where we liken God to ourselves, not just in general ("you shall be like God")[8] but in particular: to liken God to "myself," to "me." This is where idolatry begins because only in God is there fullness. After the first disunity between God and man (the Fall), and between believer and non-believer (spiritual war), there is disunity among those who

7. Gangadean, *The Biblical Worldview,* 147–176; Gangadean, *The Westminster Confession,* 111–120.

8. *Genesis 3:5.*

profess to believe in God but who liken God to themselves in the area of personality distinction.

We are made in the image of God: triune. We are to love God with our whole heart: our mind, our soul, and our strength.[9] We are to worship Him in knowledge, holiness, and righteousness. We have diverse gifts and abilities—though we have all elements in us, we are stronger in one area than another—and that is where we have the beginning of idolatry, where we liken God to ourselves in the area of our particular strength. This may be in the area of knowledge, where we profess ourselves to be wise and become fools,[10] or in the area of feelings and pleasure with regard to relationships. We may speak about relationships as love and we see love as a feeling that is emphasized. Sometimes, it is a particular kind of feeling, not just affection, but it often comes to be identified with the lowest common denominator: the physical expression of that feeling in the sexual act, and we confuse love (the reality) and feeling (the sign) because it feels right. The sexual act is said to be accompanied by feelings of beauty, attractiveness, pleasure, and happiness. Love is made into an agent of power. 'Love is what makes the world go round.' The romantic poet Keats said, "Beauty is truth, truth beauty,—that is all Ye know on earth, and all ye need to know."[11] So we may elevate love as the good, or we may elevate power or outward deeds. We may make action primary and judge ourselves and others in light of this. We may reduce the good to a minimum in terms of outward righteousness, such as happened with the Pharisees in misunderstanding the law of God. This problem is not just in the Pharisees, we have it in our lives. We have seen this occurring again and again in the Church as well as outside the Church.

In the Church, divisions among personalities come up in this way: "I am of Paul" and the element of the prophetic gift; "I am of Apollos" and the eloquence and beauty of his rhetoric; and "I am of Cephas" and actional leadership.[12] These are the major sources of distinction, which is also expressed in the polytheistic gods. We can cluster them under these categories: Apollo and Athena for *knowledge,* Aphrodite for *love,*

---

9. *Mark 12:30.*

10. *Romans 1:22.*

11. John Keats, "Ode on a Grecian Urn," Poetry Foundation, 2019, https://www.poetryfoundation.org/poems/44477/ode-on-a-grecian-urn.

12. *1 Corinthians 1:12.*

and Zeus for strength and *power.* Notice Zeus is the king of the gods and ruler. We might say that there are 1,000 other manifestations connected with these three divisions, and maybe even millions of manifestations; as a matter of fact, there might be billions of manifestations of gods. There are over 300 million gods in India—this is conservative. This is an example of every man does what is right in his own eyes by breaking the first commandment: determining good and evil by what pleases *him.*

The divisions are not just in terms of our personality difference. They are there in our body-soul distinction, our male-female distinction, and all the myriad aspects of our background. We elevate our background, in its particularity, to be the saving power. We rely on our own strength and give ourselves a place of importance in our own minds. We think our particularity is the determining factor, what will bring about change, what we have to contribute, and what will save us. We worship the works of our own hands and our own strength and virtue, and this is where the idols and idolatry come from. It is like looking at different parts of the elephant and saying, 'It is like this, it is like this, it is like this,' and it is none of those, and it is, rather, all of those and more, seen in its fullness.[13] Regarding the division, "I am of Paul; and I of Apollos; and I of Cephas" (1 Cor. 1:12 KJV), the answer is, "Is Christ divided?" (1 Cor. 1:13a). To put it in terms of the parable of the blind men and the elephant, is the elephant divided? No, it is one. It is the body of Christ. It is not just the body: it is the body of *Christ,* who is living His life through the body.

There is a source of disunity when we put ourselves in the place of God, not just in general, but specifically 'myself' with all the particularities of 'my' being, including 'my' uniqueness. It is out of this uniqueness, every man doing what is right in his own eyes,[14] differing in background from those closest to us, that comes the idol factory. John Calvin said that "the human heart is a perpetual idol factory."[15] It is an idol because we liken God to ourselves, and we may go down beyond ourselves to the creatures, to birds and four-footed beasts and creeping

13. James Baldwin, "The Blind Men and the Elephant," 2019, https://americanliterature.com/author/james-baldwin/short-story/the-blind-men-and-the-elephant.

14. *Judges 21:25; Proverbs 21:2.*

15. John Calvin, *Institutes of the Christian Religion* (Peabody: Hendrickson Publishers, 2009), 54–55.

things and particular kinds of creeping things, which symbolically get associated with idols.[16]

Think about the Native American Indians who connect with a creature: the hawk, the wolf, or some element or activity in nature such as running water. It could be the worm as my brother, as my alter ego with which I identify, in contrast to other creatures. We liken God the Creator to the finite, temporal, changeable creature and integrate downward into all the diversity in nature. You shall not commit idolatry, and you shall not liken God to the creation—this has application to the divisions that exist in the body of Christ, which hinder the unity of the body.

The good is the source of the unity of the body of Christ. This goes back to Moral Law 1 and Moral Law 2 where we misunderstand who God is and who we are, and this brings about disunity. In Moral Law 2, we have the second level of disunity—distinctions among those who worship God. Think of Cain and Abel. A number of the founding fathers were deists, but they mixed in a certain amount of Christianity. Deism mixed with some Christianity was very much the spirit of the age that was coming out of rationalism and the Enlightenment of the previous century.

THE THIRD COMMANDMENT

The third moral law is an implication and an assumption. The third commandment has to do with division within oneself, which is twofold: *logically* in our thinking and *existentially* in our lives. The third commandment says, "Thou shalt not take the name of the LORD thy God in vain" (Ex. 20:7 KJV). Do not empty the revelation, the Word of God, of its meaning. We can do so objectively in Moral Law 2 through idolatry and autonomy and subjectively within ourselves in Moral Law 3 through divisions within oneself. This is where hypocrisy comes in.

The good is a source of unity in every way: in each law and among *all* the laws of God. We are not to be unconcerned about understanding; rather, we are to examine ourselves to see whether what we profess makes sense, whether it is largely emptied of meaning or contradictory.

16. *Romans 1:23.*

We are to be concerned for consistency. If we diligently seek and are concerned for consistency, we will have knowledge.[17]

There are three aspects, or areas, of unity. We want to focus on the unity in Christ's body. This is spoken of in Ephesians 4:11–16. Christ is risen, He has ascended on high, and He sent the Spirit, and through the working of the Spirit, He **"gave some to be apostles, some to be prophets, some to be evangelists, and some to be pastors and teachers"** (v. 11). These are what we call gifts of persons in the Church and the function of those gifts. While apostles and prophets, in the original sense, are not continuing, others continue, such as evangelists, pastors, and teachers. These are mentioned again in 1 Corinthians 12:29: **"Are all apostles? Are all prophets?"** Divisions are being addressed in 1 Corinthians 12, and these are given together for the perfecting of the saints—making the saints perfect, not in an absolute sense of perfection where it is no longer developing and changing, but mature, in the sense of *full.* It says, **"For the perfecting of the saints"** (v. 12 KJV), to bring us to a certain level of maturity sufficient for our function, **"for the work of the ministry"** (v. 12 KJV). The perfecting of the saints is to bring them to maturity—if we have the foundation in place, we can go on to maturity and be fruitful.

Unity of the Spirit

"For the perfecting of the saints, for the work of the ministry, for the edifying of the body of Christ." (v.12 KJV) This is to continue until we all come into the unity of the faith. This is a second sense of unity, specifically within the body. If we go back to the first part of this chapter, it speaks about how we must "Make every effort to keep the unity of the Spirit through the bond of peace" (Eph. 4:3). Unless we think someone is not a believer, and we have good objective grounds for thinking so, including the church's oversight, we are to receive others as believers. We may differ with other believers on doctrine, we may differ with them on life, and it may be painful to us, but we cannot treat that believer as a non-believer if we have reason to think that they are a believer. We are to greet them when we see them. We are not to turn our backs. We are to recognize that they are brothers and sisters, and it does not mean that we will have a certain level of fellowship, but we

17. Gangadean, *Philosophical Foundation,* 199–205.

can maintain a connection so it is clear to them that we affirm them, as far as we can tell, as believers. This is the first sense of unity—the unity of the Spirit.

Unity of the Faith

The work of the pastor-teachers, through teaching doctrine, is to bring us to the unity of the faith, which involves all that has gone on in Historic Christianity.[18]

Scripture says, **"Till we all come in the unity of the faith, and of the knowledge of the Son of God"**—who makes God known—**"unto a perfect man, unto the measure of the stature of the fullness of Christ"** (v. 13 KJV). Remember the fullness of Christ. We are to ask, "Is Christ divided?" We are not to think, 'I am of Paul or of Apollos or of Cephas.'[19] **"That we henceforth be no more children"**—Notice, if we do not have the basics in place, we will be—**"tossed to and fro, and carried about with every wind of doctrine, by the sleight of men, and cunning craftiness, whereby they lie in wait to deceive"** (v.14 KJV). Falsehoods have divided Christians into hundreds and hundreds of different denominations. Each one has its own little twist. Even sects have several divisions among themselves. Every man separates and does what is right in his own eyes and tries to justify it by sleight of hand and cunning craftiness. **"But speaking the truth in love"**—*the* truth, *the* whole truth (not *a* truth, but *the* truth: the Logos)—**"may grow up into him in all things."** Notice it says *all* things. He is the head: **"which is the head, even Christ"** (v. 15 KJV). He is the head and **"From whom"**—Christ—**"the whole body fitly joined together and compacted by that which every joint supplieth"** (v. 16 KJV). This is the second sense of unity—the unity of the faith.

Functional Unity

Each part of the body has a role to play, and everyone is to supply to the others nearest to it and far from it. We are knit together, fitly joined together, compacted, and connected strongly by that which every joint

18. Gangadean, "Paper No. 16: The Historic Christian Faith," in *The Logos Papers,* 103–114; Gangadean, *The Westminster Confession,* xix-xxix, 349–351.

19. *1 Corinthians 1:12–13.*

supplies. If we are not supplying our part, and we are not being knitted together, then we will not be compacted. Remember, "Jerusalem is built like a city that is closely compacted together" (Ps. 122:3). Jerusalem is like a city compact and strong in unity. This is accomplished by the effectual working in the measure of every part, and different parts have different measures and assignments. When we do this, we make increase of the body. This is how the body is built up, both in numbers and to maturity. We edify ourselves in love as each part does its work in obeying the commandments of God.

Let us look at 1 Corinthians 1:10–11:

> Now I beseech you, brethren, by the name of our LORD Jesus Christ, that ye all speak the same thing, and that there be no divisions among you; but that ye be perfectly joined together in the same mind and in the same judgment. For it hath been declared unto me of you, my brethren, by them which are of the house of Chloe, that there are *contentions* among you.[20]

Divisions manifest at the level of contentions; we are contending. We should be contending for the faith, but we are just contending for our limited part. "Now this I say, that every one of you saith, I am of Paul; and I of Apollos; and I of Cephas; and I of Christ'" (1 Cor. 1:12 KJV). The last group are the ones that are particularly pious and did the others one up by saying, 'Well, I am of Christ.' Paul's reply is simply this: "Is Christ divided? Was Paul crucified for you? Were you baptized into the name of Paul?" (1 Cor. 1:13). There is a threefold division manifesting here, and these are not all of the divisions—there are many subdivisions within the larger divisions.

I will read 1 Corinthians 3:1–9 and keep the context in mind. "Brothers, I could not address you as spiritual but as worldly—mere infants in Christ" (1 Cor. 3:1). When we do not have the first principles, we are like babies. His language is stronger here: "I gave you milk, not solid food," (1 Cor. 3:2a). The same idea as in Hebrews 5:11–6:2. "For you were not yet ready for it" (1 Cor. 3:2b). As in Hebrews, "We have much to say about this, but it is hard to explain because you are slow to learn" (Heb. 5:11), "Indeed, you are still not ready. You are still worldly" (1 Cor. 3:2b–3a). Some may use the term *worldly Christian* in

20. Emphasis added.

the sense that one could be a believer—forgiven—but yet to be cleansed, and especially cleansed at the first level of the first principles, the most basic truths, where we do not yet have this in place. "For since there is jealousy and quarreling among you"—notice the tenth commandment; going all the way to that—"are you not worldly? Are you not acting like mere men?" (1 Cor. 3:3b). Think of, 'I am of Athena,' 'I am of Aphrodite,' 'I am of Zeus'; the same thing that they are doing, we are doing among ourselves.

When we do not have the first principles in place, we are like the world. "For when one says, 'I follow Paul,' and another, 'I follow Apollos,' are you not mere men?" (1 Cor. 3:4). The good is a source of unity. If you understand the good—how great it is, how grand it is—we will see that we cannot achieve it by ourselves. We have to work with others. This is only if the good is in place. The good is the knowledge of God through the work of dominion, given to mankind in the beginning: "Be fruitful, and multiply, and replenish the earth, and subdue it: and have dominion over the fish of the sea, and over the fowl of the air, and over every living thing that moveth upon the earth" (Gen. 1:28 KJV). It is corporate, cumulative, and communal, culminating in the Sabbath. All of this is in the Scripture, from the very beginning, and we do not pay attention, which is a violation of Moral Law 3, "You shall not misuse the name of the LORD your God" (Ex. 20:7a).

> What, after all, is Apollos? And what is Paul? Only servants, through whom you came to believe—as the LORD has assigned to each his task. I planted the seed, Apollos watered it, but God made it grow. So neither he who plants nor he who waters is anything, but only God, who makes things grow. The man who plants and the man who waters have one purpose, and each will be rewarded according to his own labor (1 Cor. 3:5–8).

We may absolutize particular gifts and think this gift is what the fullness of Christ is. We are to be on our guard against this way of thinking. Scripture says, "For we are God's fellow workers; you are God's field, God's building" (1 Cor. 3:9). Paul speaks about the grace of God and how to deal with it, about his work as laying foundation, and that no one is to boast in men.

Psalm 97:7 says, "All who worship images are put to shame, those who boast in idols—worship him, all you gods!" We boast in our strength, we boast in our achievements, we boast in the work of our hands, we think that our gifts are necessary and sufficient to save us, and we do not see the need for others in the body of Christ.

We read 1 Corinthians 12:27–31 for the Scripture reading to emphasize that if we have the good in mind—the knowledge of God through the work of dominion—we will avoid these divisions and will be in unity.

We have gone through commandments 1–3 to come to the unity of the body of Christ in functional unity. We are to maintain the unity of the Spirit. We are to strive for the unity of the faith by building on Historic Christianity through cumulative insight. In functional unity, we live according to the Historic Christian Faith, according to the measure of our faith, recognizing our diversity and our need for one another in the body of Christ. We cannot say, "Because I am not an eye, I do not belong to the body" (1 Cor. 12:16a); if the whole body were the eye, where would hearing be? What a distortion this would be. Try to draw a person as one big eye—that is it. No ear, nothing else—and then say, 'This is the real power.' Would this not be a caricature? Would this not be a distortion? Would this not be an idol? It most certainly would be. On the other hand, someone might say, 'I have no need of you.' Can you imagine the hand saying of the foot, 'I have no need of you?' Okay, just stay there and move your hands, but you have no foot to move your body. Where would that get you? It will get you nowhere.

The metaphor of the body helps us to see visibly what should be clear spiritually if we had the good in place. Only if we have the good in place will this come into focus. In connection with the third commandment, we want to say that the good is clear and it is because we are not seeking that we do not understand what is clear. The good is clear from three sources. We have said this a number of times.

THE GOOD IS CLEAR: Three Sources

The Good Is Clear from General Revelation

The good for a being is according to the nature of that being. The good for man as a rational being is the use of reason to the fullest. We know this because reason in man is self-evident; it is self-evident that we think, and that there are laws of thought—and these are reason, that is, reason in itself, reason as a test for meaning, it applies to being as well as thought, and it is natural—the same in all, we are made in the image of God—believer and non-believer have reason. "The true light that gives light to every man was coming into the world" (Jn. 1:9). It cannot be resisted; it cannot be overcome. "The light shines in the darkness, but the darkness has not understood it" (Jn. 1:5). It is fundamental to every aspect of human personality. Can you imagine man without thought? If we say, 'reason is fundamental,' we say, 'thought is fundamental,' and therefore, 'reason as the laws of thought is fundamental.' We cannot avoid it. We cannot set it aside. There is no substitute for it. It is the very first form of the Word of God, coming into all men as life; the life of the Logos is coming into all men as light: that by which we see and understand, by which we understand all revelation (general revelation, Scripture, and Historic Christianity). It comes to man as made in the image of God, with the ability and responsibility to think. This gets us to the sixth commandment, but we will come back to that another time.

The good is clear. If it is clear that good for a being is according to the nature of the being, that we think, and that thought is fundamental, then it is clear that the good for man is the use of reason to the fullest, to grasp the nature of things in a concept, expressed in words. The nature of things as created, finite, temporal, and changeable, reveal the infinite, eternal, and unchangeable. So the good for man, from general revelation, *is* and *must be*, and *can only be,* the knowledge of God. How do we know this from creation? By the work of dominion. As we develop the powers latent in the creation, we can come to see the nature of things. Without developing these powers, we will not see it; we will not understand it, and we cannot name it. It is clear from general revelation.

The Good Is Clear from Special Revelation

The doctrine of creation has five subpoints,[21] including man as the image of God and being given the work of dominion, which is corporate, cumulative, and communal. The work of dominion will be completed. The Sabbath is given as a reminder of our origin and hope of the completion of the work.[22] Yet, we have many men—the vast majority of the Church historically—saying that the good is heaven,

21. Gangadean, *The Biblical Worldview,* 91–108.

22. Gangadean, *The Biblical Worldview,* 125–146.

and we receive it by a direct vision.[23] This does not involve reason and understanding; we receive it completely in the next life, so by implication, the good in heaven destroys the need for working together with others in unity now. If I can receive the fullness of the blessing when I die and go to heaven, as opposed to waiting for the work on earth to be completed, then why do I need others? The first commandment is broken in the very first sin of man in failing to understand the good. Anything that comes short of what is said in Genesis 1—to have dominion understood for the purpose of knowing God and glorifying God. The whole earth is full of His glory, and we are to fill the earth with the knowledge of His glory[24]—anything less than this, or other than this, is breaking the first commandment by putting ourselves in the place of God (autonomy). In unbelief, we come up with all kinds of distortions to the point of being hideous, particularly when we stop to think about it and understand it, it just does not make sense. Every Wednesday night in Logos[25], we dedicate considerable time to preparing for the publication of the good and the beatific vision.[26] Recently, we examined Jonathan Edwards' position and observed distortions that came by putting the feelings and pleasure of enjoying God as the goal over the pursuit of the knowledge of God by seeking and understanding through the work of dominion. We need to recognize this shortcoming in ourselves and in the Church and work to correct this hindrance to the knowledge of God and take it captive.

All that I am saying here is encompassed under the general heading of *preaching the gospel.* Repent. Repent of root sin, for the kingdom of heaven is at hand[27] and the goal of the kingdom of heaven is God's rule over all on earth, to make His glory known. Repent. Repent through

23. Gangadean, *On Natural and Revealed Theology,* 9–39; Gangadean, "Paper No. 106: The Good and Heaven," 547–556; "Paper No. 116: The Knowledge of God vs. The Hope of Heaven," in *The Logos Papers,* 597–598; Gangadean, *Philosophical Foundation,* 40–41, 71–73.

24. Gangadean, *Philosophical Foundation,* 171–177, 208–211; Gangadean, *The Westminster Catechisms,* 109–111, 321–325; Gangadean, *On Natural and Revealed Theology,* 33–39, 127–139; Gangadean, "Paper No. 115: Doxological Christianity," 595–596; "Paper No. 116: The Knowledge of God vs. The Hope of Heaven," 597–598; "Paper No. 117: Knowing and Making God Known," in *The Logos Papers,* 599–601.

25. Logos Theological Seminary.

26. Gangadean, *On Natural and Revealed Theology,* 9–32.

27. *Matthew 4:17;* Gangadean, "Paper No. 56: The Gospel (Summary)," in *The Logos Papers,* 303–313.

the call of the curse upon us in every way. The curse is calling us to repentance.[28] The kingdom of heaven is at hand; this is the good. The curse comes with a promise; the promise of the kingdom of God. This is all-encompassed under *preaching the gospel*, as Christ and the prophets have preached it.

The Good Is Clear from Historic Christianity

The good is clear from general revelation, it is clear from the Scripture (Gen. 1–3), and it is also clear from Historic Christianity in what we call the doxological focus,[29] in the very opening words of the Confession: "Although the light of nature, and the works of creation and providence, do so far manifest the goodness, wisdom, and power of God, as to leave men inexcusable . . ." (WCF. 1.1). The curse and the promise are connected with sin and death; sin and death are connected with clarity and inexcusibility. These are foundational truths from Scripture, but they are in the Confession. And it goes on:

> God hath all life, glory, goodness, blessedness, in and of himself; and is alone in and unto himself all-sufficient, not standing in need of any creatures which he hath made, nor deriving any glory from them, but only manifesting his own glory in, by, unto, and upon them (WCF. 2.2).

God decrees all things for the praise of His glory: "By the decree of God, for the manifestation of his glory, some men and angels are predestinated unto everlasting life [to the praise of His glorious mercy]; and others foreordained to everlasting death [to the praise of His glorious justice]" (WCF. 3.3). God has all glory in Himself. He creates only to manifest His glory in, by, unto, and upon men, and His decrees are for His glory. His decrees are carried out in the works of creation:

> It pleased God the Father, Son, and Holy Ghost, for the manifestation of the glory of His eternal power, wisdom, and goodness, in the beginning, to create or make of nothing the world, and all things therein, whether visible or invisible, in the space of six days, and all very good (WCF. 4.1).

28. Gangadean, *The Biblical Worldview,* 55–68, 275–294.

29. Gangadean, *The Westminster Confession,* xvi-xxxii, 345–351.

He created it to the praise of His glory. In providence, He rules "to the praise of the glory of his wisdom, power, justice, goodness, and mercy" (WCF. 5.1). He rules to make His glory known, even through the Fall; God was pleased to permit the Fall, "having purposed to order it to his own glory" (WCF. 6.1).

This is the doxological focus. Though it is in the Confession, few have I heard who make these connections. We manifest a lack of seeking and lack of understanding. We come to the Confession, we read it with a lack of seeking and lack of understanding, and we empty it of meaning to the bare minimum and sometimes fill it with all kinds of things that are erroneous (in ignorance). Here we are: we are sitting in the darkness, waiting, hopefully, for the light to dawn upon us, and that light comes through the preaching.

THE FOURTH COMMANDMENT

The good is clear. The fourth commandment in particular underscores this: "Remember the sabbath day, to keep it holy" (Ex. 20:8 KJV). The first, most basic, and lasting eschatological declaration: as God completed his work of creation and rested, man, the image of God, will complete his work of dominion and rest. As creation is revelation, so dominion brings knowledge of this revelation. As a result of the corporate work of mankind through the ages in naming and ruling over the creation, the earth will be filled with the knowledge of the LORD as the waters cover the sea.[30] One day in seven is set aside for worship and as a reminder. Yet again, we reduce the Sabbath to the minimum of its meaning; we distort it, and then we discard it. The Sabbath is given in connection with the work of dominion, given to mankind, which is corporate, cumulative, and communal, and in the earth filled with the knowledge of God, not in some beatific vision in heaven. We have broken commandments 1–4.

THE FIFTH COMMANDMENT

If we listen to historically accumulated insight, pay attention to it, do not depart from it, and do not limit it to the five points of Calvinism

30. *Isaiah 11:9.*

of Reformed soteriology, we will get the doxological focus, and we will get the focus on the knowledge of God. We must glorify God "in all that whereby he maketh himself known" (SCQ. 101), in all His works of creation and providence.[31] That is, we know His glory is revealed therein, and we make it known, and the outcome is naturally and necessarily the earth filled with the knowledge of God. The good is clear. It is the source of unity, and we do not now have this source of unity. Therefore, the body of Christ is divided, individual believers are divided within themselves, families are divided, and everyone is going off and doing what is right in his own eyes rather than seeking the good, which is clear in every way.

OVERSIGHT GIVEN TO PREPARE GOD'S PEOPLE FOR WORKS OF SERVICE

We see where we are. Here we are. What are we to do? Christ has given to the Church offices to prepare God's people for works of service so that we come to maturity. The way we do this in the Church is by our worship: we worship in spirit and in truth. It is by discipleship, and discipleship involves the process of, when needed, calling to stop and think. The elders are to watch for this need. Where we see the basic first principles are not in place, we are to bring it to your attention: 'It is not in place, you need to stop and think. If you persist in it, we may *require* you to stop and think.' We watch that people are coming into the Church through baptism (regeneration), and coming into the Church through the door of repentance, in principle. We need to put the principles into practice and learn to *see* what is clear, starting with the clarity of general revelation, starting with His eternal power and divine nature. We have said this many times, and it is all right if we say it many times; it just means every time you hear it, if you are not objecting to it, even if you hear it lightly and thoughtlessly, you are responsible for it and you can and will be held responsible for it. You are not to take the name of God in vain. The elders can come to you and say, 'Well, do you remember when we said this? Do you agree with this? How far have you gotten in your ability to show what is clear? Can you show the eternal power of God? Can you show why God must

31. *WCF 4.1, 5.1.*

be eternal? Can you show that there must be something eternal? Can you show that God is the only eternal being? That the physical world exists, and the physical world is not eternal? That the soul exists? That the mind is not the brain? Can you show the soul is not eternal, in contrast to other worldviews like dualism, Hinduism, and others? That the soul does exist, in contrast to Buddhism (*anatman*); can you show that it is not momentary consciousness, momentary contact of the *skandhas*—the sense impressions from the sense organs and the sense object? Can you show that it is not the case that *all is dukkha*,[32]—that nothing is eternal—there must be something eternal, and what it is that is eternal? Can you show special creation—that each is created after its own kind? That mankind is different from animal kind? Can you show that evolution is false thinking?' You need to be able to show all of these; the Church is to call you to do this, and you are to teach your children diligently. We may especially try to ask you to teach your children diligently, and you must know it before you can bring your children for communicant membership. We are putting these things into practice more and more, so expect this. It is coming. You agree to it in principle; now let us put it into practice.

Can you answer the problem of evil that has troubled many people in many ways? Can you show that natural evil is due to more evil, that original creation was very good, that physical death is imposed, and that it is not imposed as a punishment, but as a call back? Can you show it in detail from Scripture, as well as from reason? Can you show the necessity for Scripture? Can you show that only Genesis qualifies as Scripture because only Genesis speaks of creation–fall–redemption?[33]

Can you show that Christ has come in fulfillment of the Scriptures? Can you show that the Spirit has come through the origin of the Church and its growth into all the earth through the pastors and teachers in the creeds and confessions? Can you see our failure to answer questions for the last 400 years in the modernist period, in the postmodern condition? Can you take those thoughts captive?[34]

Can you engage in the current culture war of secularism and relativism, postmodernism, and ethical relativism that is confronting us and is capturing all the institutions, including the Supreme Court? Can you

32. "All is *dukkha*" is the first of the Four Noble Truths in Buddhism.

33. Gangadean, *The Biblical Worldview*, xvii-xlvi.

34. Gangadean, *Philosophical Foundation*; Gangadean, *History of Philosophy*.

do this? Can you seek first the kingdom of God in all the relationships of life? Are you called to do this? Have you acknowledged this? Have you repented of your sin of failing to see what is clear, and are you able to see what is clear? To all the elders and small group leaders: are you able to continually urge this upon the people and help them to self-evaluate, and help them to restrict themselves according to the extent to which they have faith, that we may understand what the good is, and our need one for another, because the good is corporate, cumulative, and communal?

Do we show our appreciation for the work of God through Church history? All of this has come upon us, and it has come upon us very urgently in our day, coming back to the curse being intensified through the plague that is widespread, and with the plague,[35] the famine that can come, and with the plague and famine, it may also come as warfare. God is abundantly able to intensify the curse, but we are to proclaim the promise with the curse. Are we able to proclaim the promise faithfully in our day? If not, then let us humble ourselves in repentance and prayer.

Let us pray. Father in heaven, we thank you, and we love you. We say that your Word is holy, it is true, it is full in every way, and we have come short, in every way, in our response. Forgive us, and uphold us, and help us as a Church, as the body of Christ, to give ourselves faithfully to be the body of Christ, to not hold to anything that would divide us—that we may not go our own way in our idolatries, but hold the good clearly in mind, see all the blessings in the fullness of Christ, to govern ourselves wholly to this, that your name may be hallowed in all the earth. Oh Lord, you know us, you know our hearts, you know our prayers: how fragile and weak they are. Bind us together as your body, make us whole, that the name of our Lord Jesus may be magnified in all the earth: that there is no one like Him, the king of righteousness. We ask and pray in His name. Amen.

35. In reference to COVID–19.

13

That They May Be One, That the World May Believe

Sanctification and Repentance for Unity

2020

John 17:1–3, 11, 17, 20–23

1After Jesus said this, he looked toward heaven and prayed: "Father, the
time has come. Glorify your Son, that your Son may glorify you. 2For you
granted him authority over all people that he might give eternal life to all
those you have given him. 3Now this is eternal life: that they may know
you, the only true God, and Jesus Christ, whom you have sent.

11I will remain in the world no longer, but they are still in the world, and
I am coming to you. Holy Father, protect them by the power of your
name—the name you gave me—so that they may be one as we are one.

17Sanctify them by the truth; your word is truth.

20"My prayer is not for them alone. I pray also for those who will believe
in me through their message, 21that all of them may be one, Father, just
as you are in me and I am in you. May they also be in us so that the world
may believe that you have sent me. 22I have given them the glory that you
gave me, that they may be one as we are one: 23I in them and you in me.
May they be brought to complete unity to let the world know that you
sent me and have loved them even as you have loved me.

INTRODUCTION

THE LORD PRAYS FOR THE GLORY OF GOD. The glory of God comes through the unity of the Church, then the world believing, all of which is how God is glorified.

There are five main points related, in order, in this message. The first is the prayer for unity in the summary verse: **"that all of them may be one . . . that the world may believe"** (v. 21). The concern of our Lord here is the glory of God; this is connected with the knowledge of God, which is eternal life.[1] The second main point is that the good is the source of unity—first in each person and then among all. Third, there are divisions among us, "among you" as Paul says in Corinthians (1:10–12), among believers. I will give a partial list of those divisions with several main points, and then bring this into focus. The fourth point is that we are to be sanctified through the truth to overcome these divisions: **"Sanctify them by the truth; your word** [your Logos] **is truth"** (v. 17). Fifth is application—how this is to work out in particular detail as we come to unity.

THAT THEY MAY BE ONE THAT THE WORLD MAY BELIEVE: The Glory of God, the Knowledge of God, Eternal Life

Glorifying God

In John 17, Jesus prays about the glory of God. This is true from the beginning to the end of His entire prayer, which tells us this is the focus of His prayer. In many places throughout the prayer, we cannot doubt this is the focus of the prayer. **"Father, the time has come. Glorify your Son, that your Son may glorify you"** (v. 1a).

Definition of Eternal Life

Glorifying God consists in knowing God, knowing His glory, and making His glory known. This knowledge of God is declared in the Spirit to be eternal life. **"Now this is eternal life: that they may know**

1. Gangadean, *Philosophical Foundation,* 171–177, 208–211; Gangadean, *The Westminster Catechisms,* 109–111, 321–325; Gangadean, *On Natural and Revealed Theology,* 33–39, 127–139.

you, the only true God, and Jesus Christ, whom you have sent" (v. 3). Glorifying God is in the knowledge of God, which is eternal life.

Keep Them by Your Name So That They May Be One as We Are One

In John 17:20, Christ prays that believers may be kept through His name, that they may be one as he and the Father are one. The Father is glorified in the Son, and the Son is glorified in those whom God has given to Him: Those present with Christ, those who will believe,[2] and all men in the future as the kingdom grows and all are brought to believe. So He prays, **"that the world may believe . . ."** (v. 21b).

Sanctify Them Through Your Truth

Sanctification through the truth is necessary to overcome divisions. Believers are not one; they are divided, there are divisions, and sin remains in them, so He prays, **"Sanctify them by the truth,"** and then he adds, **"your word** [your Logos] **is truth"** (v. 17). We will look at the term, "the word," and how it is translated from *Logos*. "In the beginning was the Word [the Logos]" (Jn. 1:1a). We see in John from chapters 1 to 16, and now in 17,[3] a sevenfold source of what is called *the truth:* the truth of the Word, of the Logos.[4] In John 1:4, the life of the Logos is in all men as light: "In him was life, and that life was the light of men." We see it in the creation, in John 1:10: "He was in the world, and though the world was made through him, the world did not recognize him." We see it in redemptive history: "He came to that which was his own, but his own did not receive him" (Jn. 1:11). We see it in the Incarnation in John 1:14: "The Word became flesh and made his dwelling among us." Then we see it in sending the Spirit to lead the Church into all truth in John 16:13. We see it personally/subjectively in the word to Nicodemus: "You must be born again." We are born of the Word of truth,[5] and in John 17:17: **"Sanctify them by the truth; your word is truth."**

---

2. *John 17:20.*

3. *John 8:32, 14:6, 16:13, 17:17.*

4. Gangadean, *The Westminster Catechisms,* 113–114.

5. *John 3:3, 5–8; Ephesians 2:8–9; 1 Peter 1:23.*

We need to understand the term *truth* as *the Logos* in its fullness. A mistake that we make, where there is a lack in our thinking, is that we confuse *truth,* which is the sum total of the Word, with *truths.* Jesus said of Himself that He is "the way and the truth and the life" (Jn. 14:6), and those who remain in Him will come to know the truth, and the truth will set them free.[6] This is truth in its fullness, not truth in its minimum. **"Sanctify them by the truth; your word is truth"** (v. 17).

That They All May Be One in Us That the World May Believe

In 17:21, He again prays that they all may be one: **"that all of them may be one, Father, just as you are in me and I am in you. May they also be in us so that the world may believe that you have sent me."** At this point, He prays for those who will believe in Him through the teaching of His disciples. This includes us, we have come to believe because of the Apostles' ministry. He prays, **"that all of them may be one . . . that the world may believe"** (v. 21). He calls on all believers to be one, in all ages: past, in His day, present (in our day), and then future, **"that the world may believe."** All of whom He prays, **"that all of them may be one,"** include all who believe. We see that Jesus shows a keen awareness that the world is to be brought to believe. He commissioned His disciples to go and make disciples of all nations, all peoples.[7] Through carrying out the Great Commission He is doing what Adam failed to do. That is, through His offspring, having dominion in the earth, so that the earth may be filled with the knowledge of God.[8] Jesus is concerned to glorify God and He reflects this understanding explicitly and implicitly in all that He says. This is the context of our concern in this sermon, **"that all of them may be one"**—all believers—**"that the world may believe"** (v. 21); that all the world may glorify God as was intended from the beginning in the Garden of Eden.[9] This is our focus. How do we come to this unity? We will speak about it generally, in summary form, first. This is main point number two: the good is the source of unity, first in each and then among all, and we define evil in contrast to the good.

---

6. "If you hold to my teaching, you are really my disciples. Then you will know the truth, and the truth will set you free." *John 8:31b-32.*

7. *Matthew 28:18–20.*

8. *Isaiah 11:9.*

9. Gangadean, *The Biblical Worldview,* 21–36, 109–146.

THE GOOD IS THE SOURCE OF UNITY: In Each, Then among All

Definition of the Good

The good is not something that is imported from philosophy and is being imposed on Scripture. We see the concept of the good in the Historic Christian Faith,[10] in the Westminster Standards, the high-water mark of the Reformation. Shorter Catechism Question 1 is a summary statement of the chief end of man. Notice these words: *chief end*. There may be many secondary ends, but the chief end, the end of everything, the ultimate goal of everything, "is to glorify God, and to enjoy him forever." *The chief end*, or the end of all, is understood as *the good*.

The Good Is Not Virtue: Virtue Without the Good Becomes a Vice

Having said that the good is the chief end, we have to say immediately that the good is not the means to the good. The means to the good are of various kinds: moral, natural, and instrumental; the means to the good are virtues.[11] Often, human beings, including believers, raise up virtues, especially their particular virtue given to achieve the good, as *the* good. What happens when we put the means in place of the end (the virtues, which are the means, without the good), is that the virtues turn against themselves and against others. Virtue without the good, with something else in the place of the good, becomes a vice. We may feel sincerely that this is what we should be doing, but sincerity is not integrity.[12] Often, with the approach of focusing on the law and the virtues as an end in itself rather than a means to the good (to eternal life, to the knowledge of God), both become distorted and reduced to the minimum, and we lapse into legalism, where we are trying to spell out the law in terms of a few particulars. This was a major problem in the Jewish community in Jesus' day. We end up straining at gnats in legalism and swallowing camels.[13] The good is the source of unity, and virtue as a substitute for the good is a mistake.

---

10. Gangadean, "Paper No. 16: The Historic Christian Faith," in *The Logos Papers*, 103–114; Gangadean, *The Westminster Confession*, xix-xxix, 349–351.
11. Gangadean, *Philosophical Foundation*, 172–174.
12. Gangadean, *Philosophical Foundation*, 199–205.
13. *Matthew 23:24*.

The Good Is Not Happiness

The good is not happiness; we are to glorify God *and* to enjoy Him forever. The enjoyment, pleasure, and happiness come from glorifying God. Happiness is the effect of possessing the good, and when we try to go for happiness apart from the good, not as an effect of the good—when we go for it directly—we end up with all kinds of problems. When we take to be good that which is not the good, we work counter to the unity for which our Lord prayed. The good is not happiness.[14] The Israelites in the wilderness worshiped the golden calf, and later on they continued in idolatry. The golden calf symbolized prosperity, fruitfulness, health, and wealth, as some people say today: the health and wealth gospel.[15] It was a religion taught by Jeroboam, the son of Nebat, who caused Israel to sin. It draws upon our deceitful lusts. We are not to be presumptuous and think that we cannot slip into this. As a matter of fact, many have already slipped into it in terms of having their desires fulfilled, and gaining a certain amount of pleasure/fulfillment, but it does not last. Remember, David fell into temptation with Bathsheba in this way, and the Lord brought him out of it.[16]

In our culture today, the focus on happiness as the good is hedonism; it is individual happiness, sometimes called ethical egoism, and sometimes called narcissism. This is in contrast to a group identity and a group fulfillment in utilitarianism: the greatest happiness for the greatest number, which comes out in collectivism. We see prominent representatives of these positions in the history of philosophy in the 19th century between Nietzsche, emphasizing the individual focus, and John Stuart Mill, emphasizing a communal focus; but both of these are errors. One comes out of taking happiness (the effect) for the good, and the other comes out of taking virtue (the means) for the good, and this is a big division. Ninety percent of us lose sight of the good; without the good, we do not have unity; instead, we have disunity and discord. When we understand the end in itself, the means to the end, and the effect of possessing the end, we can get the good clearly in mind.

---

14. Gangadean, *Philosophical Foundation,* 174.

15. Bruce Wilkinson, *The Prayer of Jabez: Breaking Through to the Blessed Life* (Colorado Springs: Multnomah Books, 2005).

16. *Psalm 51.*

The Good Is Clear from General Revelation: Human Nature and the Moral Law

We can understand that human nature is rational, that the good for man as a rational being is knowledge, and that this knowledge is the highest knowledge, which is the knowledge of God.[17] The good for man as a rational being is the use of reason to the fullest; reason is used to understand the nature of things; the nature of things created reveals the nature of God; therefore, the good for man as a rational being is the knowledge of God.

The Good Is Clear from Special Revelation: Man, the Image of God

From Genesis 1, man is created in the image of God:

> And God said, Let us make man in our image, after our likeness: and let them have dominion over the fish of the sea, and over the fowl of the air, and over the cattle, and over all the earth, and over every creeping thing that creepeth upon the earth (v. 26 KJV).

The outcome of dominion is not an end in itself; the outcome of dominion is the glory of God. The earth is to be filled with the knowledge of God, and the Scriptures emphasize this by giving to man the Sabbath in Genesis 2:1–3. As God completed His work, man will complete his work. Again, all of these things will be missing when we do not have the good in place, and then we will not even notice these Scriptures.

The Good Is Clear from Historic Christianity: SCQ. 1, 46, 101; WCF. 4.1, 5.1

We spoke about Shorter Catechism Question 1 and other questions such as Question 46: "What is required in the first commandment? The first commandment requireth us to know and acknowledge God to be the only true God, and our God; and to worship and glorify him accordingly." And Question 101: "What do we pray for in the first petition? In the first petition, which is, 'Hallowed be thy name,' we pray that God would enable us, and others, to glorify him in all

---

17. Gangadean, *Philosophical Foundation,* 208–211.

that whereby he maketh himself known; and that he would dispose all things to his own glory." We put these questions together, and we see that we are to glorify God in all that by which He makes Himself known, in all of His works of creation and providence, the result of which is the earth filled with the knowledge of God as the waters cover the sea.[18] As a result of the rule of the Messiah, the earth will be filled with the knowledge of God. Remember, connect this with Jesus' prayer and His understanding of His ministry: to *undo* what Adam did and *do* what Adam failed to do, to glorify God, and to fill the earth with the knowledge of God.[19] Remember also Isaiah 6:3: "Holy, holy, holy is the LORD Almighty; the whole earth is full of his glory." We are to come to this. Then John 17:3: **"Now this is eternal life: that they may know you, the only true God, and Jesus Christ, whom you have sent."** The major contrast to this is the view that the wider church has come to hold: a literal, non-contextual reading of Scripture, which says, 'The good is heaven'—a kind of outward, physical enjoyment. Those who do not make it outward and physical move to a beatific vision[20]—a mystical view of knowledge. The Lord said that it is the knowledge of God through His name, the revelation He has given, and His Word.

The Good Is Clear from the Fall: Original Sin

Last of all, the good is clear from the account of the temptation in the Garden. The focus is on the tree of the knowledge of good and evil; this is central. The temptation has to do with knowing good and evil.[21] We can know good and evil from general revelation, from Scripture, and from Historic Christianity. In the temptation, man lost the knowledge of God; he believed the lie: "You will not surely die . . . For God knows that when you eat of it your eyes will be opened, and you will be like God, knowing good and evil" (Gen. 3:4–5). The focus is on good and evil, and we need to keep it there. We will come back to this and see how we are to overcome disunity by coming back to the proper

18. *Isaiah 11:9; Habakkuk 2:14.*

19. Gangadean, *The Westminster Confession,* 121–135.

20. Gangadean, *On Natural and Revealed Theology,* 9–39; Gangadean, "Paper No. 106: The Good and Heaven," 547–556; "Paper No. 116: The Knowledge of God vs. The Hope of Heaven," in *The Logos Papers,* 597–598; Gangadean, *Philosophical Foundation,* 40–41, 71–73.

21. Gangadean, *The Biblical Worldview,* 159–176.

understanding of good and evil, and by watching the heart condition where we, in autonomy, put ourselves in the place of God to determine good and evil. Considering our autonomous disposition, it is necessary to address it as a posture, a disposition of our hearts, in terms of whether we will apply ourselves to know good and evil.

The good is a source of unity; we can know the good in many ways, which is clear. One would think that because it is clear, we would know it, but they did not know it in the Garden. Human beings have it spelled out in Historic Christianity, but the Church has not paid attention to it, so we have to ask: What is going on here?

THERE ARE DIVISIONS AMONG YOU (BELIEVERS): List of Disputes

This brings us to point number three: there are divisions in the Church. Paul speaks about them in 1 Corinthians 1. There are not just divisions between the Church and the world; there are divisions within the Church. I would like to open this up a bit by listing some of the disputes that I have encountered recently, and perhaps you might have, too.

First of all, how do we understand the current crisis of COVID–19? There are divisions among us as to whether it is to be feared greatly or not at all. People have strong convictions on both sides. We have discussed it quite a bit, and we have not yet come to a resolution, but we can and we should. I would like to address that later.

A second source of division is about technology and the effects of 5G, and radiation from cellphones, towers, and satellites. There are those who say 'it is nothing,' and those who say 'it is very significant and it can bring about great harm.' We could go through the details, but I am just noting here that there are divisions among us.

Thirdly, there is a division about what is often referred to as the deep state. How high up in the world does evil go, and how is it manifested in decisions? These things get even more complicated by saying, 'Yes, the deep state is controlling technology and using 5G in connection with COVID–19 to wipe out the human population, and we might have 90% of the human population that will be destroyed by sterilization.' We have differences on this, and the question is, can these differences be settled? I hope this is not getting on your nerves and I hope you are not saying, 'Wow, this is too close to home. Can we talk about something a little bit further away?' Well, not really. Jesus said **"that all of them may be one"** (v. 21a), and the good is a source of unity, and there are divisions among us, so the question is raised: How well do we know the good? How well do we know what the good is? I do not mean that we profess it and have some intuition or grammatical acquaintance of it, but how well do we know it in terms of understanding, so as to be able to respond to all of the objections that there have been historically and presently about the good? We all have some view of the good. We may have a mixture of views, leading to a split between profession and deed: what we say in word in contrast to what we actually do.

I have listed three; here is a fourth one, if you think those are not bad enough. Education; educating our children. Where will we send them to school? What schools? On what basis do we make our decisions? We have said in our baptismal vows: "Do you promise to provide . . . him/her with a God-centered education?"[22] How do we understand a God-centered education? From tradition? From our background, our upbringing? Or is it from what is being taught in Scripture, what is being taught in this church from the doxological focus?[23] Among the things that we are to teach our children and prepare them for is understanding the need for a relationship with Christ.[24] Could your children answer faithfully if they were asked, 'Why do you need Christ?' Could they answer follow-up questions? In the fourth point of our baptismal vows, we ask,

> To the end that he/she may grow in the Christian life, do you promise to pray for him/her, and to train him/her to read the Bible, to pray, to keep the LORD's Day, and to understand the nature of the Church, the value of its worship and fellowship, and his/her need to seek communicant Scriptural Membership in the Church?[25]

Is your child ready at 13 years old to answer the questions called for in the baptismal vow? Do you lead by example, with husband and wife together in unity and parental discipline, to seek first the kingdom of

22. Gangadean, *The Westminster Confession,* 388.

23. Gangadean, *The Westminster Confession,* xxix-xxxii.

24. Baptismal Vow Point Three: "Do you promise to teach him/her of his/her sinful nature, of the plan of salvation which centers in Jesus Christ, and his/her own personal need of a relationship with Christ?"

25. Gangadean, *The Westminster Confession,* 388.

God and His righteousness in all relationships of life? These are the questions that will come up, which will reveal where divisions are in our understanding.

Divisions Come from Within: Misunderstanding

Divisions come from within each person. It is not just within the other person that there are divisions, but within ourselves, our understanding, our faith, or our misconception. Remember Peter and Jesus; Peter confessed the truth that "You are the Christ, the Son of the living God" (Matt. 16:16), but then "Peter took him aside and began to rebuke him. 'Never, LORD!' he said. 'This shall never happen to you!'" (Matt. 16:22). There are admixtures of belief with unbelief in each person and this is where divisions arise. We may profess, 'This is the good,' and then turn around and mix it with unbelief because sin remains. Remember, Jesus prayed, "**Sanctify them by the truth; your word is truth**" (v. 17), and the Lord brings trials of faith into our lives to this end.

Divisions Come from Within: Triune Personality

Divisions arise from our triune personality—in prophet, priest, and king. Jesus said, "**I have given them the glory that you gave me**" (v. 22a). His glory comes out in terms of what Christ was given as prophet, priest, and king,[26] and we are given abilities to fulfill these offices of Christ under Him. It is the good that brings this diversity into unity. Throughout the greater part of 1 Corinthians, Paul deals with divisions in the body.

> If the foot should say, 'Because I am not a hand, I do not belong to the body,' it would not for that reason cease to be part of the body. And if the ear should say, 'Because I am not an eye, I do not belong to the body,' it would not for that reason cease to be part of the body (1 Cor. 12:15–16).

I am not the eye, so I am not of the body, or you are not the hand, so you are not of the body. We divide along these things because we do not keep Christ and the good in mind. Christ is not divided, and He is unified in this one thing: to glorify God and bring all the nations of the world so that we can attain to the fullness of His glory. Our

26. Gangadean, *The Westminster Catechisms,* 163–168.

personalities are a source of disunity, but they are a source of unity if they are ordered as they should be in terms of prophet, priest, and king. In our self-life, we distort them. We take our virtues as the good, and divisions become manifest. The prayer of our Lord Jesus is, "**That all of them may be one . . . that the world may believe**" (v. 21), and "**Sanctify them by the truth; your word is truth**" (v. 17), that we would come to know the good we failed to know in the Garden of Eden.

Divisions Come from Within: Background/Tradition

We have been brought up—almost every one of us—without the teaching we now have: the doxological focus. In families, churches, and culture, there has been a lack of the foundation and historically cumulative insight. In our background, there is a lack of this truth, and in its place was a world of falsehood. Our worldview was built on a false view of the good in all dimensions. We are held captive by the world through our upbringing or tradition. It is our default position. We are not to think that we can get out of this degree of worldliness apart from the use of ordinary means, which are what God ordained—as if we can get over our tradition, and false tradition, by a miracle. We can disregard the use of means. Rather, Paul says in Romans 12:1–2: "offer your bodies as living sacrifices, holy and pleasing to God—this is your spiritual act of worship." Our background and tradition are spoken of in the exhortation: "Do not conform any longer to the pattern of this world," instead we are to overcome it: "but be transformed by the renewing of your mind." Here it is again, "**Sanctify them by the truth; your word is truth**" (v. 17). This is how we deal with the lack of truth in our background and the presence of falsehood in its place. We are to be transformed by the renewing of our minds.

Divisions Come from Within: False Assumptions and Intuitions

We take truth to be comfort because we rely on our tradition as the basis for truth. We default to our upbringing, what we are comfortable with, what we are familiar with. We go back to tradition. Unless we are watching and praying, we think and talk from this perspective. We are to remember that Christ warned us about pursuing the faith in our own way, with false assurance.

> Many will say to me on that day, 'LORD, LORD, did we not prophesy in your name, and in your name drive out demons and perform many miracles?' Then I will tell them plainly, 'I never knew you. Away from me, you evildoers!' (Matt. 7:22–23).

False assurance is thinking we are okay when we are not, and continuing in error. This has to be changed.

Divisions Come from Within: Male and Female Differences

We know today that there is a great deal of conflict between men and women. Marriages have broken down. Bitterness has come in. Everything has been poisoned. Men have not done what they should, and women have not done what they should, either. According to Ephesians 5:25–33, men are to love their wives by bringing the Word of God to them; this Word is to cleanse and sanctify. Men do not do this faithfully. They may be unable to acknowledge that they come short, or they may be intimidated because their wives will react negatively because the Word interferes with their feelings, and the men 'are not giving enough attention to their feelings.' Yet, the Scripture says that wives are to submit to the biblical teaching of their husbands. Often, the lack of submission is occasioned by the failure on the part of the man. 'Why should I believe him or trust him?' Things are strained. There is quarreling, some end in divorce and the painful hell of that, and the kids see it, and they turn aside. There is a tearing down of one's house[27] in not understanding and abiding by this. If a husband does not believe, what is the wife to do? She is to win him without a word: "Wives, in the same way be submissive to your husbands so that, if any of them do not believe the word, they may be won over without words by the behavior of their wives" (1 Pet. 3:1). The wife is to have a meek and quiet spirit and not give way to fear.

Divisions Come from Within: Body/Soul Relationship

There are divisions among us going back to the body and soul, and their relationship: knowing by sense experience from our bodies rather than knowing by reason from our souls or minds. We put the practical

---

27. *Proverbs 14:1.*

and the psychological first, not truth, and reverse the order of things. It often comes out as based on sense experience; it leads to literalism—not observing context and going by the outward and physical, the sign versus the reality. This is a major source of division among us. The epistemological question of how we come to truth naturally arises: 'Is it through sense experience or reason?'

Divisions Come from Without: Culturally

Galatians 3:28 says, "There is neither Jew nor Greek, slave nor free, male nor female, for you are all one in Christ Jesus." All of these differences become sources of divisions as our traditions kick in. Colossians 3:11 says, "Here there is no Greek or Jew, circumcised or uncircumcised, barbarian, Scythian, slave or free, but Christ is all, and is in all." The Scythians and different tribal views are brought into play, but it says, "Christ is all, and is in all." We are not to identify ourselves apart from Christ and God. In Galatians, Paul says, "for you are all one in Christ" (Gal. 3:28b). And Paul asks, "Is Christ divided?" (1 Cor. 1:13). There are divisions among us that have been persisting since Paul's day. The same divisions seem to recur.

Jesus prayed, **"That all of them may be one . . . that the world may believe"** (v. 21), that God may be glorified, and the earth may be filled with the knowledge of God. The way to come to this unity is through the truth. **"Sanctify them by the truth; your word"**—your *Logos*—**"is truth"** (v. 17). Divisions mean that sin remains: root sin, and not just root sin but root sin complicated to the third degree by self-deception and self-justification, and the curse remains. The curse is God's way of calling us back. When Jesus prays, **"Sanctify them by the truth; your word is truth"** (v. 17), this is what He has in mind: the reality of sin and the need for cleansing from sin by the truth, with a capital T, in terms of the fullness of the truth.

Sanctification begins with the first principles—the elementary truths, the *stoicheia* (*στοιχεῖον*)—the milk of the Word. There are layers in these first principles, or foundational truths, as is spoken of in Hebrews 5–6.[28] The Book of Revelation says there are 12 layers. We can see that there is a process going from one to the other, step by step. There are stairs, so

28. Gangadean, "Paper No. 36: The Pillar and Ground of the Truth," 201–206; "Paper No. 37: The Seven Pillars," in *The Logos Papers*, 207–210.

to speak. Scripture refers to it as a ladder; think about Jacob's ladder.[29] We are to think of the less basic in light of the more basic. We think of the finite in light of the infinite, as in the second commandment; do not liken the infinite to the finite (the infinite God to the finite creature).[30] If we have the more basic in place, we will have the less basic. If we do not have the less basic, this is a sign that we do not have the more basic. In terms of these disputes that we talked about before, this is the way truth applies, this is the way truth comes in, with the basic truths first, and if we have the more basic, we will have the less basic.

We might say that it goes back to our view of the good—to good and evil—as it did in the Garden. It goes back to our knowing what is clear about God and not yielding to the temptation: "you will be like God, knowing good and evil" (Gen. 3:5b). What is good and evil is clear from general revelation, determined by God's act of creation, each after its kind, after its nature. Good for a being is according to the nature of the being. These are the first truths and principles that need to be in place if we are going to be sanctified. If we have the foundation in place, we will go on to maturity, fruitfulness, unity, and fullness. These things are spoken of in Hebrews 5 and 6. "Let us . . . go on to maturity, not laying again the foundation of repentance from acts that lead to death, and of faith in God, instruction about baptisms, the laying on of hands"(Heb. 6:1–2a). With that, it says, "though by this time you ought to be teachers, you need someone to teach you the elementary truths of God's word all over again" (Heb. 5:12a). We would be fruitful if we had the foundation in place. If we are mature (having the foundation), we will be fruitful, we will come to unity, and through this unity, we will come to fullness. The fullness is the earth filled with the knowledge of God, as Jesus is seeking in John 17. When we do not have the foundation in place—from general revelation, from Scripture, from Historic Christianity, and personally, subjectively, by regeneration and sanctification—we will have divisions, apostasy (further departure), decay in the culture, and collapse. If you are concerned about what is going on in the culture today, you should think about the Church's failure to be salt and light and how that has affected the culture. Has

29. *Genesis 28:10–17.*

30. Gangadean, *Philosophical Foundation,* 185–198.

the Church been able to take the world's thoughts captive, or has the Church been taken captive by them?

SANCTIFY THEM THROUGH THE TRUTH, THY WORD (LOGOS) IS TRUTH

"**Sanctify them by the truth**" (v. 17a). We are to examine ourselves to see if we are in the faith. I am going to list several points connected with self-examination. We will close the service with Psalm 139C, which says, "Search me, O God, and know my heart; test me and know my anxious thoughts" (Ps. 139:23). We are to remember sin, the reality of sin—root sin—and the complication of this with self-deception plus self-justification, the curse in connection with this third level of sin, and the promise. 1 John 1:9 says, "If we confess our sins, he is faithful and just and will forgive us our sins and purify us from all unrighteousness." Forgiveness and cleansing. The concern about sin comes out in the preaching of the gospel. The Focus for the Week is titled simply, "The Gospel," and it is taken from Matthew 4:17, which says, "From that time on Jesus began to preach, 'Repent, for the kingdom of heaven is near.'" In these words, is summed up the whole teaching about good and evil. We are to repent of sin, evil, and seek first the kingdom and the goal of the kingdom: the knowledge of God. We are going to focus on the gospel in the remainder of the preaching.

Self-Examination and Repentance of Root Sin

"Repent: for the kingdom of heaven is at hand" (Mt. 4:17b KJV). Repent, the kingdom of heaven is at hand. What are we to repent of? We are to repent of root sin. What is the root sin? No one seeks, no one understands, no one does what is right.[31] "But without faith it is impossible to please him: for he that cometh to God must believe that he is, and that he is a rewarder of them that diligently seek him" (Heb. 11:6 KJV). Because we have not diligently sought the Lord, we do not understand; we do not understand the meaning of things, and there is death that is due to sin. Because we do not seek, we do not understand the meaning of things. We use the words, but we do not understand. If we ask, 'Repent of what?' The response is, 'Sin.' We ask, 'Well, what

31. *Romans 3:10–11.*

is sin?' We may rattle off the answer to the Shorter Catechism question,[32] but if we do not get back to the clarity of general revelation, we cannot have a saving understanding. It is because we did not seek and understand what is clear from general revelation that we are in sin and we need Christ. This is often confused in many ways, and we will try to spell out some of those ways. Then we will apply it. How are we to live if we have not seen the fruit of repentance of root sin?

The first area for sanctification is through self-examination. Have we repented of root sin? Have we heard the gospel? Have we thought about what it means when we say, 'Repent.' I talked with a number of people this week, and I asked them what they have heard and about their backgrounds, and they have not heard this word, and if they have heard this word, they have not heard it connected with root sin. Root sin remains unrepented of.

Self-Examination Through the Lord's Table

We are to come to the Lord's Table, discern the Lord's Body, and not divide it. If we do not hold to the Historic Christian Faith—what the Holy Spirit has done in leading the Church into all truth—if we neglect this teaching, if we have not seen what glorifying God and enjoying Him forever is, in connection with the goal of the earth filled with the knowledge of God, we will divide the body of Christ.[33] Misunderstandings at the basic levels will affect everything else, including how we think of our kids' education. This is the second place we are to examine ourselves.

Self-Examination Through Church Vows, Worship, and Discipleship

We are to examine ourselves through church vows: membership vows, marriage vows, and baptism vows.[34] We have already spoken of vows when we read from the baptismal vow. In the baptismal vow, we are to teach our children the purpose of the Church and their need to seek communicant membership. "To understand the nature of the

32. *SCQ. 14.* "What is sin? Sin is any want of conformity unto, or transgression of, the law of God."

33. *1 Corinthians 11:17–34.*

34. Gangadean, *The Westminster Confession,* 245–252.

Church, the value of its worship and fellowship, and his/her need to seek communicant Scriptural Membership in the Church?"[35] What is their understanding of the Church? What is worship, and what does it mean to worship in spirit and in truth?[36] How does this work out? How is this different from other positions? This is what parents are to teach their children according to the vows. They examine themselves in these doctrinal areas, but not just in teaching the children; they have to put it into practice in their marriage and exemplify what marriage is supposed to be.[37] They are also to exemplify what membership is supposed to be. What are the standards of the Church? Understanding that the Church is for worship and discipleship;[38] we are to make disciples, first in the Church, and discipline is needed to teach—to observe all I have commanded you.[39]

Self-Examination Through the Novitiate

We might remember, in terms of self-examination, that we have the novitiate.[40] We can go on to maturity only if the foundation is laid in our lives. The purpose of the novitiate is to establish the foundation in our lives. The purpose of the self-evaluation of the novitiate is to help those in oversight know of your progress in having the foundation laid.

Self Examination Through Fiery Trials

We are to examine ourselves through the trials of faith that the Lord sends—fiery trials. Through suffering, we are to learn holiness, devotion to the Lord, to the good, and we are to bear up under it and come to understand. There is a foolish complacency in the human heart that makes a person resistant to correction or instruction. In either case, there is no love of wisdom and no diligent seeking to understand. While some in complacency do not seek, no one, apart from suffering, is diligent

35. Gangadean, *The Westminster Confession,* 388.
36. Gangadean, "Paper No. 134: Worship, the Sabbath, and the Church," 679–682; "Paper No. 135: On Worship," in *The Logos Papers,* 683–684.
37. Gangadean, *Philosophical Foundation,* 245–254; Gangadean, "Paper No. 138: Concerning Marriage," in *The Logos Papers,* 695–700.
38. Gangadean, *The Westminster Confession,* 385–386.
39. *Matthew 28:18–20.*
40. Gangadean, *The Westminster Confession,* 389–390.

in seeking. While the beginning of wisdom is to avoid suffering, only through much suffering do we enter more fully into wisdom.

Self Examination Through Oversight

Last, there is the church oversight—the discipline for discipleship—where you are not judging yourselves; you are presenting yourselves to see how you are doing in your understanding, in your repentance of sin, and in seeking first the kingdom of God. It is in this way that the truth comes into us by which we are sanctified. Christ prays, "**That all of them may be one**" (v. 21a). The good is the source of unity. There are divisions among us because we do not understand good and evil properly. It is summed up in the gospel: repent of root sin and seek first the kingdom of God.[41] We have to learn good and evil, which is the root of sin—our failure to know good and evil as it occurred in the original sin in the Garden of Eden.

APPLICATION: Repent, the Kingdom of Heaven Is at Hand

What are the applications of this? In general, we put it this way: We are to "Repent, for the kingdom of heaven has come near" (Matt. 4:17), and we are to repent of root sin and seek the good with understanding. If we do not understand, it is proof that we are not seeking; this is spiritual death—it is a lack of understanding of the meaning of things. We use words without meaning; we empty words of their meaning. In doing so, we take the name of God in vain, which affects us and goes down to our children to the third and fourth generations.

If You Have Not Heard the Call to Repent of Root Sin, Then You Have Not and Cannot Call Others to Repentance

If you have not heard the call to repent—and here I am speaking about the repentance of root sin and death, that is, the conviction of sin and death—if you have not heard this call and responded to this in repentance, then you cannot, and have not been able to call others to repent. If you are not making the call to others, it raises the question whether

41. *Matthew 4:17; 6:33.*

you have heard the call, whether you have repented, and whether you have been convicted of sin and death. We are speaking about root sin, as against using the Word in some secondary or tertiary sense. This is the first application. If you have not heard the call—been convicted of, and repented—you are not going to call others to it, and there will not be fruit.

If You Have No Fruit of Repentance, Then You Have No Ground to Believe That You Have Repented

You may end up in the place of saying, "LORD, LORD,"[42] not doing what He says and not doing all that He has commanded, and dividing the body, in contrast to what our Lord is saying. If we do not have the good clearly in place, and we do not have the seed of repentance and the fruit of it, we have no grounds to believe that we are indeed regenerate. Unless we see the fruit, we have no grounds for the assurance of faith.

If You Have Not Taught Diligently in the Household, Then You Should Expect No Fruit

If you have not taught your household, beginning with teaching your wife, and if parents are not teaching the children, then you will not have fruit. You will have people who are traditional believers, and perhaps have a belief in God so that when they die, they will go to heaven—but this is not the good—and many, many, many things will be set aside, not paid attention to, and not listened to, because the goal is heaven and none of these things are relevant for heaven. This is what we find mostly in the Church, so we are not to be presumptuous and think, 'Well, others do that, but we do not do it.' We see whether your child is being taught, and whether they are understanding, and whether *you* understood and were teaching them. We believe that if you understand, you will teach them. You teach according to what you understand. This is another dimension of fruit: not just in your own life (you only are able to show what is clear), but in the lives of your children.

---

42. *Matthew 7:21.*

Be Transparent: Confess to God and Others—I Cannot Show What Is Clear

If knowledge of the basics is lacking, confess it to God and to others. You can say, 'I cannot show what is clear. I believe it is clear, but I cannot show it. I cannot show how there must be something eternal, and that only God is eternal, and respond to all these objections that have been raised from evolution and the problem of evil, etc.' Lack of understanding and faithful witness by the Church allowed Darwin and other views to leaven the culture. Remember, we are to seek first the kingdom of God; we are to take these thoughts captive.[43] If you cannot show it, then confess it. In other words, 'I have been a fideist, believing without understanding, and not having faith. I do not understand the meaning of the words I use. I use these words. I am misunderstanding the meaning of the first principles, the Seven Pillars.[44] I can recite it, but I do not understand it. If there is an objection raised, I do not know what to say.' Be transparent; confess it before God and before others.

If You Do Not Know What Is Clear, Step Back from Judging or Teaching Directly or Indirectly

If this is the case—if you do not have the basics in place—you have to step back from judging others and/or teaching, directly or indirectly. If you do not have the basics in place, you cannot teach; you should not teach; you should step back from it, according to Hebrews 5:12 and Moral Law 5.[45] 'I do not have insight. I have not built on historically accumulated insight. It does not show in my life. The fruit is not there, in many ways.'

Learn in Silence, Be Teachable

Be teachable. Do not just say the things that first come to your mind. Listen, think about it for a while—perhaps three days. Pray about it, and see whether you are hearing what is being said. Learn in silence—this applies to men and women in general and men and women in marriage.

---

43. *2 Corinthians 10:4–5.*

44. Gangadean, "Paper No. 36: The Pillar and Ground of the Truth," 201–206; "Paper No. 37: The Seven Pillars," in *The Logos Papers,* 207–210.

45. Gangadean, *Philosophical Foundation,* 221–229.

Submit to Oversight: Do Not Presume to Know—Be Examined to See If You Understand

Last of all, in terms of application—"Repent: for the kingdom of heaven is at hand"(Matt. 4:17)—you need to submit to oversight. Let them examine you in your understanding, to see whether you do understand. Do not just say, 'Well, I understand, I feel I understand, I am certainly persuaded. I have a sense of certainty in persuasion, but I cannot give reasons for it.' Do not presume to know; rather, be willing to be examined to see if you are in the faith, that is, have understanding, or whether you are using words without understanding their meaning and continuing to hold to positions that divide the body of Christ.

THERE ARE DIVISIONS AMONG US: Application to Current Disputes

Go back to apply this to the disputes about COVID, 5G, the deep state, education, what is God-centered education, eschatology, clarity, and inexcusability—whether you hold to what is clear and apply it consistently. Whether you understand what is going on in the culture wars right now, between cultural atheism and cultural theism. Whether you can deal with the underlying unbelief. There has been a lot of talk recently about 'social justice warriors,' 'truth,' 'reparations,' and the tearing down of statues in the name of 'justice' and 'righteousness,' without understanding the truth, without going back to the deeper sense of the kingdom of darkness versus the kingdom of God, including that the kingdom of darkness is teaching from Islam, spiritual monism, as well as critical theory—critical race theory, gender theory, and gender identity. We need to learn how to respond to these positions. This is part of seeking first the kingdom of God in all the relationships of life. It is part of the gospel: repent of root sin and seek first the kingdom of God and His righteousness in all the relationships of life. We are to teach it to our children. We are to teach it to our spouse (husbands to wives), and together, parents are to teach it to their children and be in unity concerning a God-centered education and not think blithely that we can add on some of these words to what we already have from our background.

Those who have come from a longstanding evangelical background did not get the teaching they should have received growing up. The default position is to go back to your background. You may have simply added on the teaching of Westminster Fellowship to what you have heard, and you are putting new wine into old wineskins. It does not and cannot work that way. You have to come through the door of repentance of root sin, and you have to deal with the question of conviction by the Holy Spirit after being regenerated: conviction of sin and death, the curse and the promise, repentance and faith, justification and sanctification, and then go on to baptism and calling in the Church, and to the end of the days, when there is the resurrection, and there is a reward.

"Sanctify them by the truth; your word is truth" (v. 17). **"That all of them may be one . . . that the world may believe"** (v. 21), that in all things God may be glorified.[46] Let us pray. Father, we thank you for your Word. Your Word is full, it is rich, it is sharper than any two-edged sword.[47] It works conviction in our hearts. May it indeed do so by the power of your Spirit, and may it bring us into the sanctification by which we can serve you, in all the relationships of life, starting in our own homes, in our congregation, in other congregations, and in the culture. Lord, help us to examine ourselves, to work with conviction as we stand in need. We ask and pray this in Jesus' name, amen.

46. *1 Peter 4:11.*

47. *Hebrews 4:12.*

14

Overcoming Divisions

Divisions in History—From the Garden to the Present

2020

1 Corinthians 1:10–13, 3:1–6, 11:17–19, 12:4–7

[10]I appeal to you, brothers, in the name of our Lord Jesus Christ, that all of you agree with one another so that there may be no divisions among you and that you may be perfectly united in mind and thought. [11]My brothers, some from Chloe's household have informed me that there are quarrels among you. [12]What I mean is this: One of you says, "I follow Paul"; another, "I follow Apollos"; another, "I follow Cephas"; still another, "I follow Christ." [13]Is Christ divided? Was Paul crucified for you? Were you baptized into the name of Paul?

[3:1]Brothers, I could not address you as spiritual but as worldly—mere infants in Christ. [2]I gave you milk, not solid food, for you were not yet ready for it. Indeed, you are still not ready. [3]You are still worldly. For since there is jealousy and quarreling among you, are you not worldly? Are you not acting like mere men? [4]For when one says, "I follow Paul," and another, "I follow Apollos," are you not mere men? [5]What, after all, is Apollos? And what is Paul? Only servants, through whom you came to believe—as the Lord has assigned to each his task. [6]I planted the seed, Apollos watered it, but God made it grow.

[11:17]In the following directives I have no praise for you, for your meetings do more harm than good. [18]In the first place, I hear that when you come together as a church, there are divisions among you, and to some extent

I believe it. [19]No doubt there have to be differences among you to show which of you have God's approval.

[12:4]There are different kinds of gifts, but the same Spirit. [5]There are different kinds of service, but the same LORD. [6]There are different kinds of working, but the same God works all of them in all men. [7]Now to each one the manifestation of the Spirit is given for the common good.

INTRODUCTION

OUR SERMON TOPIC IS OVERCOMING DIVISIONS, which Paul addresses in these four sections of readings. I would like to put this in context: divisions were not just in Paul's day, but they occur every day and throughout history. I would like to briefly mention events throughout history that show that there are divisions. The purpose of this is to help us to think soberly about ourselves, to see divisions among us, to learn to overcome them, and to learn from past suffering in the history of the Church—the history of redemption.

TWELVE PROMINENT DIVISIONS IN REDEMPTIVE HISTORY

I have a list of 12 prominent divisions. To cover all of history in 12 items requires a lot of selection, so expect just a highlight.

Division in the Garden between God and Man

Satan seduced man to his side against God.[1] Part of this seduction is to be understood as a division *within* the man, *within* Adam, because sin is first and foremost an act contrary to our nature as made in the image of God as a rational animal. It is a giving up of reason by not seeking diligently. This is a beginning sense of division: within ourselves and between God and man.

Divisions Among the Israelites Wandering in the Wilderness

Skipping over thousands of years of history, we find the Israelites wandering in the wilderness. As they came out of Egypt, they were cared

1. Gangadean, *The Biblical Worldview*, 37–54, 159–239.

for by God, but they did not understand or have faith. The Word that they heard was not mixed with faith/understanding,[2] and so they did not enter into the Promised Land. They perished in the wilderness. We could be believers, and be brought out of Egypt, but not come into the Promised Land because of a lack of faith/understanding from not diligently seeking.

Divisions in the Period of the Judges

We see a cycle of the priestly ministry after Moses and Joshua, and how that priestly ministry decayed to the point where the ark of the covenant was taken into captivity, the sons of Eli were killed, and Eli himself fell over and died. Scripture states that, "In those days *there was* no king in Israel: every man did that which was right in his own eyes" (Judg. 21:25 KJV).[3]

Divisions in the Period of the Kings

With the kings, there are many, many, many examples of division, beginning with the first kings: Saul and David. There is a contrast between the two; Saul sought to kill David, and Saul's heart was not right the way David's heart was. Saul wanted to honor himself; he built monuments to himself, and he envied David when they sang the praises: "Saul has slain his thousands, and David his tens of thousands" (1 Sam. 18:7). The Book of Psalms is filled with the conflict between Saul and David.

Divisions in the Period of the Prophets

Elijah, as the first of the prophets, called the people back. This call to repentance was based on the word of Moses the Prophet, which he received from God. It came to a head particularly in the conflict between Elijah and the prophets of Baal,[4] and on down to the slaying of Ahab and Jezebel. So, there are divisions *within* the people of God in Israel. Elijah was calling them back.

---

2. *Hebrews 4:2.*
3. Emphasis added.
4. *1 Kings 18:20–40.*

Divisions in Christ's Day

There were divisions between the leaders in Christ's day who lacked faith/understanding and took a literalist,[5] legalist[6] interpretation of things and, for that reason, they killed Christ.

Divisions Among the Apostles

In the Book of Acts, division came to a head in Acts 15, resulting in the first Church council. The Judaizers said, you must be circumcised to be saved.[7] Paul contended against this view, and the council concluded, "we gave no such commandment" (Acts 15:24b KJV), it is not necessary to be circumcised to be saved.[8] To have the sign is not the same as having the reality. In connection with this, we see Paul's conflict in the New Testament period. Paul came into conflict with Peter over Peter's vacillation concerning those who came from James. Peter left the Gentiles to go and sit with the Jews, and Paul rebuked him.[9] Among the Apostles, there were different levels of understanding and consistency.

Right after the Council of Jerusalem in the Book of Acts, at the end of chapter 15, we find the conflict between Paul and Barnabas.[10] These are persons who were very close during the first missionary journey. They had a difference in how to go about the second missionary journey. Barnabas wanted to take John Mark, and Paul said, 'No, it is not wise; he is not prepared.'[11] This conflict was very pointed since it was between two dear friends, and they parted asunder, and the Church commended Paul and Silas for the second missionary journey. We see how that worked out in Philippi as Paul and Silas were in the Philippian jail singing Psalms of praise to God.[12] We will come back to this pointed, acute division all the more because they were close friends.

5. *John 2:19–21, 3:4, 6:52.*

6. *John 5:16.*

7. *Acts 15:1.*

8. *Deuteronomy 10:16; 30:6; Jeremiah 4:4; Romans 2:29.*

9. *Galatians 2:11–14.*

10. *Acts 15:36–41.*

11. *Acts 15:36–41.*

12. *Acts 16:25–40.*

Divisions Throughout Church History

Historically, there were divisions, and Church councils and creeds responded to these divisions. This is the work of the Holy Spirit leading the Church into all truth,[13] and comes to be summed up in statements of faith or creeds. We saw it in Acts 15—the Council of Jerusalem—and then the Apostles' Creed versus Greek Gnosticism (a very different view of God and man).[14] In Nicea, concerning the Trinity: God is Father, Son, and Holy Ghost; we will focus on that today in **"I follow Paul . . . I follow Apollos . . . I follow Cephas"** (v. 12).

After Nicea and the doctrine of the Trinity, we have Carthage and the canon of Scripture, and then Chalcedon: the doctrine of Christ as fully God and fully man. Then, there was the Council of Orange (529 A.D.), where the sovereignty of divine grace was discussed, which came back into focus during the Reformation.

Divisions in the Reformation

Luther differed from Roman Catholicism in understanding Scripture, the Word of God. He understood: 'Repent, change your mind,' not, 'Do penance.' This sleight of hand plunged the Church into much ruin with the selling of indulgences. Luther nailed his Ninety-five Theses against indulgences to the door of the church in Wittenberg. This was the one main point concerning the Word of God from which the Reformation started and developed, and it included everything that we have done in the past and more.

Divisions between Science and Religion in the Modern Period

In the modern period—post–1648 (the end of the Westminster Confession) to 1948 (just after World War II)—there was a major conflict between science and religion that has not yet been responded to. It has been a significant division, especially with evolution, and the claims made in the name of science, which are not proper beyond the bounds of science, about the origin of the world and the origin of life. It is one thing to speak about how the world and life *operate,* but this is very different in kind from how they *originate.* To try to reduce origination

13. *John 16:13.*

14. Gangadean, "Paper No. 16: The Historic Christian Faith," in *The Logos Papers,* 103–114.

to how something operates is a major blunder of many in science,[15] and this is the work of the false prophet.

Divisions in the Postmodern World

There is conflict concerning Neo-Marxism, Critical Theory, Critical Race Theory, and all the jargon that goes with these. The main value is equality, particularly equality of outcome. They do not recognize equality at the most basic level with the image of God—equally created, equally fallen, equally redeemed—but base equality on secondary things, which is a major problem.

The conflict is raging between, first of all, the false prophet—the teaching in the academy and education without God; second, the harlot—the economic system of values without God; and third, the beast—politics without God, seeking to establish totalitarian rule over all according to man's law and the mark of that law.

Divisions in the Present Day

One step further, beyond Postmodernism (from 1950 to 2020), is in our day. Not just in our day but in our midst and in our church. Westminster Fellowship's distinctives begin with the opening words of the Westminster Confession: the clarity of general revelation and the inexcusability of sin, of unbelief, of root sin.[16] It is in our day, and in our midst, in this way: Recently, at Logos,[17] we had an extended discussion that got quite heated at points concerning the question: What is root sin? We will discuss this a little more and whether we have repented. Previously in Logos, we dealt with *existential hermeneutics:* how personality and background affect our interpretation of Scripture, how we hear one another, and the divisions that come through how we hear. Remember in 1 Corinthians 11:17–19 (this is about coming to the Lord's Table), Paul says, **"No doubt there have to be differences among you to show which of you have God's approval"** (v. 19). There *are* divisions among us.

15. Gangadean, *Philosophical Foundation,* 86–97.

16. *WCF. 1.1;* Gangadean, *The Westminster Confession,* 345–348.

17. Logos Theological Seminary.

We want to overcome these divisions, and there is a way to do so. Some are being asked to teach in Sabbath school, and teach the middle schoolers, and try to teach the dialectic, and not just *teach* the dialectic but really *do* the dialectic—there is a world of difference between these two. This has created significant division and turmoil, and we need to address it. All through last year and up to this day, we are dealing with the question: Have we repented of root sin? It is one thing to raise a question about it based on the amount of evidence one has. It is another thing to say, 'You have not yet repented of root sin.' These are two different things. The first question is much more nuanced. The second is making a judgment that we can and should make, but we make it on a certain basis.

How do we know if we have repented of root sin? We had a discussion, and this is one of the places—though not the only place—where it got heated: specifying root sin. To be brief, we made four points because we want to be clear about 'What is this root sin we are to specify?' and that we are not concocting this on our own. Paul speaks of it in Romans 1:20: "For since the creation of the world God's invisible qualities—his eternal power and divine nature"—both distinct but quite related, are clearly revealed—"have been clearly seen, being understood from what has been made, so that men are without excuse." This is one. We trace this back to Genesis 3. This is the second specification of root sin. Here, Adam failed to see the eternal power and the divine nature, and he blurred the distinction between God and man, and good and evil. How so? In the words of the temptation, "You [man] will be like God, knowing good and evil," or determining good and evil (Gen. 3:5). This is the root sin, and it was there in the original sin. It is also the first sin in the first commandment—not the seventh commandment, eighth commandment, or fourth commandment—but "You shall have no other gods before me" (Ex. 20:3). Man puts himself in the place of God in a particular way: to determine good and evil. Again, he came short of knowing God and man, and good and evil. So this is Romans 1:20, Genesis 3, and Moral Law 1.

Then, we discussed Psalm 19. 'How do we know the eternal power and divine nature?' Last time we preached, we brought this out, that nothing is hidden from the heat thereof, their language has gone into all the earth.[18] If men had heard this language, then they would have heard the gospel. General revelation is a preparation for the gospel. As they say, *praeparatio evangelica.*[19] If you cannot hear general revelation, you will have difficulty hearing the gospel.

We can add three more that are relevant to us: Job. We have read through the Book of Job recently. At the end of this book, Job said, "I have heard of thee by the hearing of the ear: but now mine eye seeth thee. Wherefore I abhor myself, and repent in dust and ashes" (Job 42:5–6 KJV). Sometimes, this conviction, where we come to abhor ourselves, is resisted. We feel ashamed; we feel we have come short. There is a lot of this in Adam in the Garden, and in us, too. We would say Job is repenting for failing to see what is clear about God because God spoke to him through many, many questions from general revelation, so he says, "now mine eye seeth thee. Wherefore I abhor myself."

This is the kind of thing we are dealing with in divisions within us, but we should also say this is true of David and Bathsheba. When David repented, he spoke of how God caused him to know truth in the inward part: "Surely you desire truth in the inner parts; you teach me wisdom in the inmost place" (Ps. 51:6). He came to a view of the good, a deeper understanding of the good, that would have given him pleasure in knowing, glorifying, and enjoying God. David would not have wanted to seek enjoyment with Bathsheba if this had been in place. This is another example of root sin operating.

Joseph's brothers sold him out of envy into Egypt, and yet, God preserved Joseph, and he kept his eye on God and God's purpose.

Last of all, in Aaron's rod that budded. The interesting thing about Aaron's rod is that it is placed in the Most Holy Place in the ark of the covenant. Aaron's rod that budded is a symbol to Israel for all their days. About 15,000 people died because of a rebellion by Korah against the authority of Moses and Aaron. Remember, in that same place, in the Most Holy Place, were the tablets of the law, given by God to Moses. The people should recognize that God was speaking through Moses in giving him the law, and they should recognize all the signs that came with the giving of the law.

18. *Psalm 19:1–6.*

19. *Praeparatio evangelica* means "preparation for the gospel."

Then there is the pot of manna, which shows God's care for them through the wilderness, yet they doubted. The Word spoken was not mixed with faith,[20] so although they came out of Egypt, they perished in the wilderness. Notice God's long-suffering symbolized in the pot of manna, under the leadership of Moses and Aaron. But Korah rose up, and with him, were others: Korah, Dathan, and Abiram, who directly challenged Moses. We are going to get back to the prophet, priest, and king distinction, and Korah and the priesthood. Many notable princes—250 of them—joined with them. Korah, Dathan, and Abiram perished in one way. Korah wanted to gather the congregation against Moses, not paying attention to what God had shown and said. Then the earth opened and swallowed them. The 250 princes were directly dealt with by God's fire coming down. The next day, the people continued to murmur, and a plague broke out, and 14,700 died. So 14,700 + 250, and Korah, Dathan, and Abiram, their families, and homes—it was probably around 15,000 that died. God sealed this before the Israelites by Aaron's rod that budded. It was placed in the Most Holy Place. When we come to worship, think of the types and shadows, the law of God, the pot of manna, and Aaron's rod that budded. There are divisions among us, and we need to learn how to deal with them.

HOW DO WE KNOW IF SOMEONE HAS REPENTED OF ROOT SIN?

If you understand what root sin is, and the examples we have just given in these four, plus another four (Job, David and Bathsheba, Joseph and his brothers, and Aaron's rod), we can see what we are to repent of. If we repent of not seeking and not understanding what is clear, then we will change our ways, and we will seek, and seek diligently. This is where they were coming short; they were not seeking diligently, and he that comes to God must believe that He is, with understanding, *and* that He rewards those who diligently seek Him.[21] If we repent of our sin, then we will bring forth fruit in keeping with repentance,[22] and the fruit will be seeking and understanding. How can we know if we have

20. *Hebrews 4:2.*

21. *Hebrews 11:6* KJV.

22. *Matthew 3:8; Luke 3:8.*

repented of root sin? It is by seeing and understanding what is clear; if we have repented of root sin, we will know what is clear.

Secondly, if we *know* what is clear, we can *show* what is clear. This is showing what is clear, over and against—in terms of how clear it is—*all* objections that have been raised. Over many decades, I have raised that question and asked, 'How do you know that God exists, and can you show it?' and time and again, it fell silent. Notable apologists who live in this area met as a group. Some former students at one point asked, 'Can you show what is clear?' There was an uproar: 'No, no, no, it is unfair. Do not ask that question.' It broke down there, just as it did on Covie forum,[23] after six months. 'Can you show how it is clear that God exists?' Everything fell silent. A similar thing goes on when persons are asked to show what is clear: they fall silent. This is the main fault line in the Church: the distinction between the prophet, the priest, and the king. The prophet begins with the foundation, which begins with clarity and inexcusability and showing what is clear. You must repent of root sin.

When change is needed in the Church—change as against growth; change is a function of the prophet: Apollos waters, Paul plants.[24] Sometimes, the prophet has to uproot before he plants. The main faultline in the Church is between prophet, priest, and king. This is what we encounter here: **"I follow Paul . . . I follow Apollos . . . I follow Cephas"** (1:12), or between Paul and Barnabas, in the prophetic and priestly ministry; we have already referred to this in Moses and Aaron, and we can go further. When change is needed in the Church, God uses the call to repentance. The call to repentance is a call to change your mind. It is not the same as a call to growth. Growth is to take place insofar as it builds on what has been planted, the way Apollos' watering builds on what Paul has planted. He says, **"I planted the seed, Apollos watered it, but God made it grow"** (3:6). The voice of a prophet is usually a single solitary voice, as in the case of Moses and Elijah, who appeared with the Lord on the mount. It comes as "The voice of him that crieth in the wilderness" (Is. 40:3a KJV). People can use that expression for other things, and it is often misused. Sometimes, it is a voice crying in the wilderness against the whole nation in terms

23. A record of Pastor Gangadean's interactions with other pastors and apologists are kept at The Surrendra Gangadean Memorial Library at the Logos Study Center.

24. *1 Corinthians 3:6.*

of numbers. We cannot appeal to numbers in a situation like that. We have to look at the doctrine. 1 Corinthians 3 speaks about having to speak at the level of milk because of immaturity: **"I gave you milk, not solid food, for you were not yet ready for it. Indeed, you are still not ready"** (3:2). This is repeated again in Hebrews 5. If the foundation is not in place or there is a wrong foundation, we are like infants, and we need milk and not meat,[25] and it has to be said again: "In fact, though by this time you ought to be teachers, you need someone to teach you the elementary truths of God's word all over again" (Heb. 5:12a).

Sometimes, we substitute our belief *without* understanding—involving words without meaning, fideism—for faith, which is belief *with* understanding, as Hebrews speaks about belief. Sometimes, this has to be engaged with, confronted, dealt with, and called to repentance.

Other disputes are going on. This week, I engaged in a discussion about COVID–19. I have mentioned this before, and we are dealing with it right now and have different attitudes. Also, we are dealing with 5G and how we are to deal with it. Here is a dispute; how do we settle it? We need to go back to the more basic. I do not think we would have to deal with COVID much if medication were available. The powers that be have clamped down on the most common ordinary means for that. This does not mean absolutely everyone, but it is the most ordinary means, and we do not have it. Here I am having to learn how to apply social distancing. It is one thing for a grandpa to apply it with his grandkids, and it is another thing for a grandma to apply it with her grandkids. These are different situations. How long do you get exposed? Two seconds or five seconds is better than four or seven seconds. You have to use a kind of social virtuosity to know how to apply social distancing, and likewise for 5G. I have been engaged in a lot of discussion. If we do something more basic and go for fiber optics, many of the questions of 5G would not be so pressing, and there is much more agreement about that. We can and should settle disputes. There are ways to settle them.

When you come to settle a dispute, come inquiring using Matthew 18.[26] Consider yourself first, but do use Matthew 18, and do not go behind someone's back and speak about them. Come inquiring rather

25. *Hebrews 5:11–14.*

26. Gangadean, *The Westminster Confession,* 391–395.

than confronting, teaching, and presuming that you know. Remember the situation with Korah, Dathan, and Abiram. Sometimes, when difficulties like this arise, we find Moses falling on his face. Sometimes, you can rip your garment to express very strong emotion because of the danger of what is going on. Come inquiring, using Matthew 18, not declaring.

We should say that the focus should be on church standards, not personal relationships and how they make one feel. It should be objective. The church standards are not going to change unless you address them directly and discuss them. The church standards will not change. The church standard that you must repent of your root sin will not change. The way in which we know that you have repented will only change if by discussion, you can show that it is not so. The door of the church is always open to repentant sinners. The sinners must change and those in the church must uphold the faith. Questions must be doctrinal and teleological versus personal and practical. This is part of what happened in the dispute between Paul and Barnabas. Paul said, 'No, given the work that is before us, John Mark is not ready.' Barnabas was a 'great guy,' someone you can very easily hang out with. He was the one who brought Paul in and encouraged Paul. They went on the first missionary journey together. But at the end of Acts 15, they reached a point where they had a dispute, and Barnabas was unyielding. Barnabas wanted to affirm the relationship and encourage the growth of John Mark. There is absolutely nothing wrong with that, but it was not to be on-the-job training. It would have ruined the work of the kingdom; it would have hindered it. You might say that the gospel going into Europe depended on this decision; our very conversions can be traced back to this decision. They went, and they came to Troas, and the voice said in Philippi, "Come over to Macedonia and help us" (Acts 16:9b). They had previously gone further eastward to Asia Minor, into Bithynia.[27] When they went into Philippi and spoke, they were taken and beaten, battered—their backs were beaten over and bloodied—and thrown into prison.[28] This is where Paul and Silas prayed, the earthquake came, and the door to evangelize Europe was opened.[29] This was what the decision was about.

27. *Acts 16:7.*

28. *Acts 16:23–24.*

29. *Acts 16:25–26.*

I want to underscore this because the dispute was so sharp between those who were so close that they parted. I am reminded that disputes between husbands and wives can also be so sharp that they part in divorce. What we want to say regarding Ephesians 5:21–33 is if you play around with this passage of Scripture and interpret it in light of your feminist background and your personal upbringing, you are going to play with fire, and it will be very likely that your marriage will end in divorce. "The wages of sin is death" (Rom. 6:23a). Do not treat lightly the Word of God. If your husband differs with you, 1 Peter 3:1–7 gives explicit instruction. You cannot say your husband is this or that and the other. Even if he is unbelieving, you win them without a word, expressing respect. Even if husbands do not teach, wives can still read the Scriptures, pray, and be encouraged. Husbands may contribute to divisions if they do not bring the Word of God to their wives and children. Husbands and wives bring it together for their children, nurturing them in the admonition of the Lord, keeping the goal in mind. Remember, the goal of marriage in the Garden of Eden was to "Be fruitful, and multiply, and replenish the earth, and subdue it: and have dominion" (Gen. 1:28a KJV). The purpose of this was to fill the earth with the knowledge of God.[30] Those who get married without this goal in mind are going to head into rocky territory, rapids, level 5 rapids. It will be a stormy thing. You must have the good in place, the goal of life: to glorify God, to fill the earth with the knowledge of God, beginning with knowing what is clear, to be able to show what is clear, to show it in the face of objections. If this is not in place, a lot of things will not be in place.

There can be a lot of discontent between two persons, within a marriage or within the Church. There can be murmuring and complaining as there was in the wilderness. We warned last week that perilous times will come. 2 Peter 3 also warns of this. Jude warns of this; also, he speaks about the gainsaying of Korah, spoken of in Numbers 16. I encourage you to read this and think about it. What we mentioned in Aaron's rod that budded was what it signified in the Most Holy Place.

In summary of what we have said so far, there *are* divisions regarding the Word of God. The divisions concern root sin, the clarity of general revelation concerning God and man, and good and evil, seen in the

30. *Isaiah 11:9; Habakkuk 2:14.*

Garden of Eden, Moral Law 1, Romans 1:20, Psalm 19, and all the others that I spoke of (Job, David, Joseph, and Aaron's rod). There are divisions.

Let us assume now that we are persuaded that there are divisions, and these are legitimate examples, and it is all through the history of the Church up into our day. While we are focusing on repenting of root sin, it is not only there but also how we approach other disputes like 5G and COVID. There are divisions. What is the solution?

SETTLING DISPUTES IN THE CHURCH

Recognize Diversity and Unity: Without the Good, Divisions Occur, and with the Good, Unity Occurs

The solution is, first and foremost, to recognize the diversity that God has created. The universe is extremely diverse and complex, and yet, it is a *universe*—it is one whole; it is a unity. We are to recognize in the creation the diversity and unity, and to recognize that every and all diversity, without the good, the goal of the knowledge of God—in marriage and in the Church, teaching children—all forms of diversity become a source of division. The distinction between male and female becomes a source of division; it has been a raging battle, especially in the 1970s and 1980s, in the post-Woodstock period, where there is a display of sex without love, supplemented with drugs, rock and roll, and the reaction to this in feminism, and then the further reaction in lesbianism and homosexuality. Now, it has come up to the Supreme Court. It has gone on to athletes, to the bathrooms, and into the kindergartens.

We will fall apart without the good. All the diversity without the good becomes a source of division, but contrary to this, all and any diversity with the good, the goal of the knowledge of God—understood really, concretely—becomes a source of unity. This is why 1 Corinthians 12:12 states that there is one body with many parts. We are to function together. We should say that there are several levels, or kinds, of unity: unity of the Spirit, unity of the faith, and functional unity of the body. If we had this, we would have ecclesiastical unity, where we would not have 50,000 denominations but one Church. If we had this, then the world would listen—"That all of them may be one . . . that the world may believe" (Jn. 17:21).

Recognize the Triune Personality as Rooted in God

We are to recognize the triune personality, and recognize this coming from the Triune God—we are made in the image of God: prophet, priest, and king. Christ is all three, and there is no division in Him. We must recognize the triune personality over and against all the other personality theories that we play around with. We may think, 'I can get different things from different personality theories,' without getting the more basic first, and then seeing whether we even need these other theories. We must recognize the strengths and limits of this diversity, and how diversity is to work together. First, recognize the principle of diversity and unity. Second, recognize the specific: **"I follow Paul . . . I follow Apollos . . . I follow Cephas"**(v. 12), prophet, priest, and king.

Recognize Your Own Personality Inclination

Recognize your own position: where are you on the spectrum? There are three main colors in the spectrum: red, green, and blue. There are a lot of shades in between. Which one is next to which, and how does that work out? It is a kind of spectrum: more one than the other. Recognize your own gift and personality, as well as your strengths and limits, and do not presume to go beyond it. Remember, Korah went beyond it; Korah directly challenged the Word of God coming through Moses. This is the third thing we could do: recognize our own gifts (prophetic, priestly, kingly), and I have got to say there is going to be a lot of discussion, a lot of misunderstanding, a lot of false starts, a lot of qualifications. You will have to go through much discussion to get it more, and more, and more into place. You have to be careful about presuming to know. Do not try to recognize other people's gifts unless it comes to a certain point in the discussion.

Recognize Your Own Background

Not only do we have personality differences according to these gifts, but we also have differences according to background, which has affected the personality factor. Reason is what distinguishes us from the animals. There is a distinction of diversity. People have failed to recognize this and have gone into an anti-rational position: 'Man is just within the animal class; he is not distinguished by reason.' We have had a lot of this for the last 150, 200, 300 years, more than that, but there has been a certain level of intensity, especially with evolutionary theory and Marxist theory. There is a lot of anti-rationalism. If you are raised in this background, you are going to reflect it. The kinds of discussions occurring in the '60s are not happening on college campuses today, and they are banning speech. Background contributes to the personality factor and makes it more intense. If you are priestly and you are raised more by your mom (rather than dad), who is priestly, this will accentuate it, and it will be more imbalanced.

Getting married in an age of feminism, men have been reluctant to make the point that 'this is my theology, this is where I stand,' and ask the woman whether she is there. This should have happened before marriage, but here is the problem: if you do this, you will find 'there is no one out there to marry,' and it cuts both ways (men for women and women for men). We have to recognize this problem, but it is not impossible. We accommodate it, be watchful of it, recognize we have to work on it, commit to working on it, and get assistance and encouragement in working on it.

We must reckon with our backgrounds, personalities, and how God has made us. It is not 'mutual submission' as some feminists try to speak of it. It is not, 'There is no difference between male and female in Christ.' With respect to particular things, yes. While men have abused women, the reaction is not to be 'the strong woman.' I have heard that again and again: 'I am woman, hear me roar!' This is different from what 1 Peter 3 says: "the unfading beauty of a gentle and quiet spirit, which is of great worth in God's sight" (1 Pet. 3:4b). This is what attracts a man to a woman. Without this, if you go the strong woman route, you are heading for destruction; you are heading for the destruction of your marriage, I assure you. Watch out. Recognize your background and recognize the gift.

Recognize God's Order

Sometimes, lip service is paid to equality under God. Of course, we are all equal and come out the same. As against saying, 'No, there is an order, and yes, it is prophet, priest, and king.' When it comes to the nitty-gritty, as it was with Paul and Barnabas, and with husband and wife, nurturing and relationship, emotions, and feelings are important, but they always stay within the context of the goal, the good. Men are much more goal-oriented, to the point of complaint: 'he gets the girl—he has gotten the goal—and now he is on his way,' and 'he has not courted me, he has not brought me flowers since.' This is how goal-oriented men can be. 'I did that, I have done that,' as against, 'No, the good is the knowledge of God.' You are supposed to have family worship every day and bring the Word to your wife so that both of you can bring it to your children. Otherwise, you are going to harm your wife *and* your children. You must commit to daily being in the Word. The wives are to conduct themselves in such a way that encourages their husband to do it, not demand of him, and the husbands are to do it. There is no excuse for not bringing the Word in family worship. This is basic ordinary means—recognize God's order.

IN SUMMARY

We have now, in summary, a significant discussion about divisions of many kinds and situations, up to our day and in our hour—down to this hour—and we have solutions to recognize diversity and unity and to recognize triune personality (Paul, Apollos, and Cephas). Remember how often this is put here in 1 Corinthians and elsewhere. The triune personality goes back to the Triune God, that we are made in the image of God.[31] Triune personality is part of the image of God. Male and female are also part of the image of God. They are ordered in God, just as the triune personality is ordered. Recognize your own gift, existentially, the strengths and limits of these, and where it may be in a spectrum. Recognize your background, in terms of general background, and the example, or lack of example, of your parents. Whether you had discipline as you should or did not have it, what are the limits of this in your life going forward? Do not try to treat things as needing *growth* when it needs *change*. Do not go from an evangelical background to add clarity to it. This is putting new wine into old wineskins. It is going to burst the bottle.[32] Consider this: there are many pastors in the Church with a priestly gift, but go out and find a church that teaches the foundation, starting with clarity and inexcusability. It has to build on the

31. Gangadean, *The Biblical Worldview*, 109–124; Gangadean, *The Westminster Confession*, 79–83; Gangadean, *The Westminster Catechisms*, 133–135.

32. Gangadean, "Paper No. 64: Aaron's Rod," 341–352; "Paper No. 65: Aaron's Rod (Outlined)," 353–358; "Paper No. 98: Faith and the Word of God," in *The Logos Papers*, 511–514.

foundation laid in Historic Christianity. If the foundation is bypassed, the priest is bypassing the prophetic office. So we have a problem. We are not affirming notable individuals, whether it is Augustine, Aquinas, Calvin, or Luther. We hold to the Historic Christian Faith, to what has been agreed on after much discussion. If you do not believe there is a Historic Christian Faith, spend time discussing this in light of the Scripture. You cannot ignore it. It is part of what we need to get the Word of God. Lastly, we are to pay attention to the order that there is. There are divisions, and there are solutions. We should have hope, but we must repent of our root sin, and we must be able to show what is clear in keeping with repentance.

Let us pray. Our Father in heaven, we thank you for your Word, for your gracious Word, for your love and kindness, your patience. Yet you by no means clear the guilty, whoever takes your name in vain. So we fear you and love you, and we bless your name for your grace and mercy. Now, bless us as we continue in closing this service, and keep your people safe by your truths.

15

FAITH, HOPE, LOVE, AND UNITY

Diversity of Gifts for the Good

2013

1 Corinthians 12:31b–13:13

[12:31]And now I will show you the most excellent way. [13:1]If I speak in the
tongues of men and of angels, but have not love, I am only a resounding
gong or a clanging cymbal. [2]If I have the gift of prophecy and can fathom
all mysteries and all knowledge, and if I have a faith that can move mountains, but have not love, I am nothing. [3]If I give all I possess to the poor
and surrender my body to the flames, but have not love, I gain nothing.

[4]Love is patient, love is kind. It does not envy, it does not boast, it is not
proud. [5]It is not rude, it is not self-seeking, it is not easily angered, it keeps
no record of wrongs. [6]Love does not delight in evil but rejoices with the
truth. [7]It always protects, always trusts, always hopes, always perseveres.

[8]Love never fails. But where there are prophecies, they will cease; where
there are tongues, they will be stilled; where there is knowledge, it will
pass away. [9]For we know in part and we prophesy in part, [10]but when
perfection comes, the imperfect disappears. [11]When I was a child, I talked
like a child, I thought like a child, I reasoned like a child. When I became
a man, I put childish ways behind me. [12]Now we see but a poor reflection
as in a mirror; then we shall see face to face. Now I know in part; then I
shall know fully, even as I am fully known.

[13]And now these three remain: faith, hope and love. But the greatest of
these is love.

CONTEXT:
Love in Unity of Diversity

THE SUBJECT OF THE SERMON COMES from the verse, **"And now these three remain: faith, hope, and love. But the greatest of these is love"** (v. 13). Love is magnified in a particular way, and we have our own thoughts about it. We magnify love, and in doing so, we often lift it out of the context in which it is spoken, but love does not thrive separated from this context. There are many other places where love is mentioned in Scripture, and in each of these, the manifold splendor of love is brought out in particular ways. We know, for example, our Lord's commandment teaches to "Love each other as I have loved you" (Jn. 15:12b). "Whoever has my commands and obeys them, he is the one who loves me. He who loves me will be loved by my Father, and I too will love him and show myself to him" (Jn. 14:21). "For he who loves his fellowman has fulfilled the law" (Rom. 13:8b). We are to love God with all of our hearts,[1] and the fruit of the Spirit is love, joy, and peace.[2] In 1 Corinthians, there is a particular context, and Paul immediately affirms it before and after. **"Love never fails. But where there are prophecies, they will cease . . . And now these three remain"** (vv. 8a, 13a). Then, he goes on to chapter 14 and speaks about tongues and how they are manifest. In chapter 12, he speaks about the diversity in the body including the various gifts. Going all the way back to the beginning of the book, he speaks about divisions and unity—there are divisions among the Corinthians.[3]

The focus is love in the context of our unity and diversity. We fail to reckon with this basic reality, and therefore we cease to love as we should. Paul says, **"these three remain: faith, hope, and love"** (v. 13a). Love is not to be separated from faith and hope. We will see that when love is separated, it does not stand by itself. Love builds on faith and hope and is their complete expression. Since love is a complete expression, it is spoken of as 'the greatest.' In this sense, we would like to bring into focus what Paul says about love.

Jesus said, "By this all men will know that you are my disciples, if you love one another" (Jn. 13:35). He says, "Greater love has no one

1. *Matthew 22:37–40.*

2. *Galatians 5:22–23.*

3. *1 Corinthians 1:10.*

than this, that he lay down his life for his friends" (Jn. 15:13). He says, "that all of them may be one . . . that the world may believe" (Jn. 17:21). Our love manifest in our unity is spoken of here. We can consider ways we have come short in our unity to see how we have come short in our love. We know that God is one and that there are three persons in the Godhead: Father, Son, and Holy Spirit.[4] There is unity in diversity. We know that Christ is prophet, priest, and king, and there is unity in this diversity.[5] We know that God is infinite, eternal, and unchangeable in his being, wisdom, power, holiness, justice, goodness, and truth,[6] and there is unity in this diversity. We know that all three persons of the Godhead are equal in power and in glory.

EPHESIANS 4:
Unity of the Spirit, of the Faith, and of the World

The Scripture has a lot to say about unity because it reflects God. Many of our dealings with each other are not what they should be because this basic reality of unity and diversity is not recognized. By God's grace, we hope to bring this into focus through this message. I will use two references and relate them in order to help focus it. There are a lot of parallels between what is being said in Corinthians and what is said in Ephesians—Ephesians 4, particularly, but the whole Book of Ephesians. That is, we are brought together—Jews and Gentiles—into one body. All of this is connected with the fullness that there is in God.

The first part of Ephesians 4 speaks about the *unity of the Spirit,* which leads us to the *unity of the faith* later on in that passage, "until we all reach unity in the faith" (Eph. 4:13a). This is another level of unity. We might speak about love as manifesting itself first in the unity of the Spirit and secondly in the unity of the faith. The unity of the faith is equally of the Spirit, as the Holy Spirit is the one who leads us into all truth,[7] through the work of the pastor-teachers,[8] after much discussion,[9]

4. Gangadean, *The Westminster Catechisms,* 123–127; Gangadean, *The Westminster Confession,* 56–60.

5. Gangadean, *The Westminster Catechisms,* 165–168.

6. Gangadean, *The Westminster Catechisms,* 119–122.

7. *John 16:13.*

8. *Ephesians 4:11.*

9. *Acts 15:7.*

summed up in the creeds and passed down to us, which we refer to as historically cumulative insight, which if we held to, there would be no divisions in the body of Christ—none whatsoever.[10]

We are to maintain the unity of the Spirit until we come into the unity of the faith, but it does not end there. The unity of the faith is the unity that Jesus spoke of: "that all of them may be one, Father, just as you are in me and I am in you . . . so that the world may believe (Jn. 17:21). The unity of the Spirit and the unity of the faith go further into the *unity of all mankind,* as a Church, as a credible witness, and can bring the nations into the house of the Lord. Why? That we might attain "to the whole measure of the fullness of Christ" (Eph. 4:13b); unto Christ, who fills the whole universe;[11] the fullness of him who fills everything in every way,[12] because all things were created by him and for him,[13] and to him be the glory forever.[14]

There is a broad scope to this prayer for love, manifest in unity in all of these senses. We will see that it really begins with us, in our being made in the image of God, and our observing the unity within our own individual being and achieving self-control through faith/understanding of our human nature made in the image of God. Every aspect of our being begins to fall apart because we have turned inward and become self-centered, and we are not God-centered in every aspect of our being. A common limitation where things fall apart is not just between our thoughts and feelings. It is *within* our thoughts, *within* our feelings, *within* our will. When unity in oneself, existential unity, is lacking, then we are to expect what is described by William Butler Yeats: "Things fall apart; the centre cannot hold; Mere anarchy is loosed upon the world."[15] Everything is held together in Christ. This question of unity of diversity is like life and death. Unity of diversity becomes mere differences where we are all going our own way because of our self-centeredness.

10. Gangadean, "Paper No. 16: The Historic Christian Faith," in *The Logos Papers,* 103–114.

11. *Ephesians 4:10.*

12. *Ephesians 1:23.*

13. *Colossians 1:16.*

14. *Ephesians 3:21.*

15. William Butler Yeats, "The Second Coming," Poetry Foundation, 1920, https://www.poetryfoundation.org/poems/43290/the-second-coming.

DIVERSITY IS SOVEREIGNLY GIVEN FOR THE COMMON GOOD

Paul speaks of the diversity of gifts. He speaks about it as the body in 1 Corinthians 12:7: "Now to each one the manifestation of the Spirit is given for the common good." Notice the unity principle:

> To one there is given through the Spirit the message of wisdom, to another the message of knowledge by means of the same Spirit, to another faith by the same Spirit, to another gifts of healing by that one Spirit, to another miraculous powers, to another prophecy, to another distinguishing between spirits, to another speaking in different kinds of tongues, and to still another the interpretation of tongues. All these are the work of one and the same Spirit, and he gives them to each one, just as he determines (1 Cor. 12:8–11).

This diversity originates in God, and these gifts come to us sovereignly as He determines. Toward the end of the chapter, in verse 28, he says:

> And in the church God has appointed first of all apostles, second prophets, third teachers, then workers of miracles, also those having gifts of healing, those able to help others, those with gifts of administration, and those speaking in different kinds of tongues.

Interestingly, he mentions the Apostles and says, 'First and second and third,' and by implication, spoke about tongues last. Somehow, we can reverse this order in our sin, since the Apostles are not present with us, and the Church is not heeding the teachings of the Apostles. "Are all apostles? Are all prophets? Are all teachers? Do all work miracles? Do all have gifts of healing? Do all speak in tongues? Do all interpret? But eagerly desire the greater gifts" (1 Cor. 12:29–31a). Then Paul says, "**But where there are prophecies, they will cease; where there are tongues, they will be stilled; where there is knowledge, it will pass away**" (v. 8b). Then he gives three reasons, and it culminates with, "**And now these three remain**" (v. 13a). This is the context in which he begins to speak about speaking in tongues.

Tongues seem to be very noticeable, and because of this, our attention focuses on them, but we should remember the context: why, how, and when tongues were given.[16] Then we remember the goal, the good. Paul referred to it here as a *common good* within the church or *common good* within mankind.[17] He also speaks of the diversity of gifts. "I am of Paul; and I of Apollos; and I of Cephas" (1 Cor. 1:12 KJV). We still have these divisions among us in the Church today. Every difference—*every* difference—has become an occasion of splitting because we do not keep the context in mind. What is the common good? What is the goal of life? What is it to love in relation to the good?

THE MEANING OF TONGUES: From Babel to Pentecost

Tongues originated about 2,200 years before Christ at Babel.[18] Mankind was in one place, with one language, and they had a project. The project was under Nimrod. They were building a tower to heaven, and within 400 years or so of the Flood, they had gone once again into apostasy. God, in His mercy, to restrain us from going as far and as quickly as we did in the Flood, scattered us. He increased strife to restrain us from evil by dividing our tongues. God's supernatural act was to scatter and restrain us from evil through intensifying the curse. As a consequence of these differences, we have strife. There are differences in our self-life; we maintain our identity, defined in so many different ways, our own ideas of God, our own idolatries, and we fight and live and kill and die for it—strife. We will not allow others to impose themselves on us.

God restrained us from going as far and as quickly into evil as we could by dividing us, or else we would have another judgment as in the time of Noah, but God said that would not happen again. It was understood and anticipated in the promise to Shem that mankind would be gathered. It was anticipated by Moses, in the Feast of Pentecost. Fifty days after coming out of Egypt, they received the law. They were constituted as a nation; they were the first fruits of the nations. All the other nations were to come to God, and all the other nations were to live under God. Israel was the *first* fruits, and so the harvest was anticipated. This is the beginning of the harvest. This is the Pentecost,

16. Gangadean, "Paper No. 122: Contra Charismatic Distinctive," in *The Logos Papers*, 651–653; Gangadean, *On Natural and Revealed Theology*, 223–228.

17. *1 Corinthians 12:7.*

18. *Genesis 11:1–9.*

the first fruits. It was anticipated that the Spirit would be given, poured out, and mankind would be gathered. Joel spoke about it,[19] and on the Day of Pentecost, after Christ died and rose again, He spoke to his disciples telling them to wait in Jerusalem until the Spirit comes,[20] the Spirit that would lead them into all truth.[21] He ascended, and on the Day of Pentecost, the Spirit came.

I will read this portion to you because the details are beautiful. If you put the details in context, they are really fascinating and significant.

> When the day of Pentecost came, they were all together in one place. Suddenly a sound like the blowing of a violent wind came from heaven and filled the whole house where they were sitting. They saw what seemed to be tongues of fire that separated and came to rest on each of them. All of them were filled with the Holy Spirit and began to speak in other tongues as the Spirit enabled them (Acts 2:1–4).

And it says, "there were staying in Jerusalem God-fearing Jews from every nation under heaven"(Acts 2:5), and they were hearing this.

> When they heard this sound, a crowd came together in bewilderment because each one heard them speaking in his own language. Utterly amazed, they asked: 'Are not all these men who are speaking Galileans? Then how is it that each of us hears them in his own native language?' (Acts 2:6–8).

This is the fascinating part. If we recall our geography, dimly or clearly, this is where it gets really interesting. We see how all of these trace back. "Parthians, Medes, and Elamites; residents of Mesopotamia, Judea and Cappadocia, Pontus and Asia, Phrygia and Pamphylia,"—Asia Minor—"Egypt and the parts of Libya around Cyrene,"—then through Africa— "visitors from Rome,"—going further west—"(both Jews and converts to Judaism); Cretans and the Arabs"—into the islands and back again to the Arabs (Acts 2:9–11a). "'We hear them declaring the wonders of God in our own tongues!' Amazed and perplexed, they asked one another, 'What does this mean?'" (Acts 2:11b–12). Then

---

19. *Joel 2:28–32.*

20. *Luke 24:49; Acts 1:8.*

21. *John 16:13.*

Peter stands up and explains. They were hearing them in their own language: the wonderful works of God. It was not a translation; it was an interpretation. In response, Peter begins speaking about this being the work of Christ, who was crucified, raised, magnified, and poured out. "Jesus, whom you crucified" (Acts 2:36b). He makes this the occasion of what God promised a long time ago: God has fulfilled His promise. This is the same Jesus Christ who has now sent the Spirit through whom the nations are to be gathered in.[22]

The nations that were scattered through tongues are now being gathered through tongues on the day of Pentecost, the first fruits, the beginning of harvest, anticipating the end of that process of the Feast of Tabernacles, of Booths, the end of harvest, where the harvest is complete. God spoke to the hearts of the people. However, they were slow to hear what was being said, as slow as hearing 'What does circumcision mean?' It was an inward reality of having a new heart, being born again.[23] However slow we are, God spoke objectively in this. He was gathering the people. We are to be one that the world might believe. This is part of our hope. This is part of our faith, our understanding, our hope, and what we are expecting.[24] This work that is to be done is corporate, cumulative, and communal. It is a historically accumulated insight, through the work of the pastor-teachers through the centuries, by which the Church comes into the unity of the faith. First, there is the unity of the Spirit, then the unity of the faith, and then the unity of all mankind: "that all of them may be one . . . that the world may believe" (Jn. 17:21). It is in this context, the call to unity, that Paul is speaking about love.

The point is made explicitly: "For we were all baptized by one Spirit into one body—whether Jews or Greeks" (1 Cor. 12:13a), whatever our different backgrounds. We can multiply this: Parthian, Medes, Elamite; Cappadocia, Phrygia, Pamphylia, Cyrene, Crete, Iranians; all baptized into one body. The same language is used in Ephesians 4: "one LORD, one faith, one baptism" (Eph. 4:5) and "one Spirit" (Eph. 4:4). We are to "Make every effort to keep the unity of the Spirit through the bond of peace" (Eph. 4:3), "until we all reach unity in the faith" (Eph. 4:13a).

---

22. *Acts 2:14–36.*

23. Gangadean, *The Westminster Confession,* 299–305.

24. Gangadean, "Paper No. 58: The Spiritual War (Church and World)," in *The Logos Papers,* 317–322.

"Then we will no longer be infants, tossed back and forth by the waves, and blown here and there by every wind of teaching" (Eph. 4:14a) but "grow up into him who is the Head, that is, Christ" (Eph. 4:15b) and we come into "the whole measure of the fullness of Christ" (Eph. 4:13b), "the fullness of him who fills everything in every way" (Eph. 1:23b). Maturity, fruitfulness, unity, and fullness; these go together.

UNITY OF DIVERSITY IS ROOTED IN GOD

This is how they go together: If the foundation is in place, we will go on to maturity. Paul speaks about foundation and maturity again and again. This is part of what happened in the earlier part of Corinthians; there is a disunity, with some saying, "I am of Paul; and I of Apollos; and I of Cephas" (1 Cor. 1:12 KJV). The triune personality in man, reflecting the Trinity in God, is not being regarded. Things are out of order. Each one puts himself first. Love **"is not self-seeking"** (v. 5). We put ourselves first and distort the others: "I don't need you!" (1 Cor. 12:21), and we go our own way, dividing the body of Christ. In this context, we may speak about Paul's fifteen characteristics of love.

Triune Personality: Order within Our Diversity

There is an order within our diversity. "I have planted, Apollos watered; but God gave the increase" (1 Cor. 3:6 KJV). Who is Paul? Who is Apollos? I am nothing.[25] **"It does not boast,"** (v. 4b), **"It is not rude, it is not self-seeking, it is not easily angered"** (v. 5a) in not recognizing the gifts and abilities of others, and saying, "I don't need you" (1 Cor. 12:21). Our theology, the theology that is dominant in the Church today, the otherworldliness of heaven, leaves us in a position where we say, "I don't need you" (1 Cor. 12:21). The whole idea of a body—something corporate, cumulative, and communal—is not there; it is broken. This is why faith and hope are important for love, understood in connection with the principle of unity of diversity in God. Paul rebukes them by saying, "Is Christ divided?" (1 Cor. 1:13a). These are perfectly united in Christ; He is prophet, priest, and king, and the one who gives this diversity. One of us cannot contain it all, but the body is "the fullness of him who fills everything in every way" (Eph. 1:23b).

25. *1 Corinthians 3:7.*

It is part of our loving God to recognize this diversity. Therefore, we are to love each other and not make God narrowly after our own image because we do not have our eyes on the goal: the glory of God that fills the earth.[26] We cannot love if we do not have the foundation or the goal in place as we should. We will go so far, to use the word, overuse it, distort it; we will use the word 'love' without the good in place. We may feel good about ourselves in our piety and may have a lot of zeal without knowledge, and we will have works that do not last.

Triune God: Order within God

There is an order within God, and there is an order among us: prophetic, priestly, and kingly. Paul says,

> I laid a foundation as an expert builder . . . But each one should be careful how he builds. . . . If any man builds on this foundation using gold, silver, costly stones, wood, hay or straw, his work will be shown for what it is, because the Day will bring it to light. It will be revealed with fire, and the fire will test the quality of each man's work (1 Cor. 3:10, 12–13).

When the priestly gets separated from the prophetic, love tends to become more sentimental, a feeling, not a commitment to God, to the good, and to each other.

Division occurs, and the giving of gifts and diversity is done to gather nations, most dramatically with tongues. This is how it dramatically began. Differences were not only just in language but also in culture, and reinforced in our DNA, in terms of which genetic element became dominant in us as we lived in relative isolation. It is in our very being, and that has become a big stumbling block in terms of 'the other'—how we regard the other, to what extent we understand the other, and to what extent we understand ourselves. Paul says that these differences are sovereignly given as God determines: "There are different kinds of working, but the same God works all of them in all men" (1 Cor. 12:6), and there are many parts in one body; we are not to reduce

26. Gangadean, *Philosophical Foundation,* 171–177, 208–211; Gangadean, *The Westminster Catechisms,* 109–111, 321–325; Gangadean, *On Natural and Revealed Theology,* 33–39, 127–139.

things to sameness and say everyone should be the eye.[27] We are not to have mere differences, where everyone is doing their own thing and going their own way. Both of these are equally abhorrent. We have to be careful about the one-size-fits-all mentality. We are to be equally careful about everyone doing their own thing. There are principles and applications. Principles cannot be changed, but we have difficulty and ask, 'Is that a principle, or is that an application?' If we understand the means and ends and keep these steadily in mind, we will not have difficulty discerning what a principle and a practice or application are, which may vary with each.

There Are Differences within Each Human Being

There are differences between male and female. We are to understand the differences and not try to say that one sex fits all, you cannot make up your mind, you are undecided, or you decide to change back and forth as in gender fluidity. 'Today, I feel like a nut, tomorrow I feel like a guy,' and then a day after, 'I feel a little more girlish today.' It is a bad way to go; it is not grounded in reality. There is also the body and soul, how these are related, and how these reveal God. The soul reveals God. The body reveals the soul, and there is an order between the two. The soul leads, but you cannot reduce the soul to the body or the body to the soul. There is real diversity and real unity. It is part of our work as children of God through the work of dominion to name the parts, understand the relation, and have rule over these things.

God originates diversity, and we are not to reduce it to one; we are not simply letting everyone go their own way. In addition, he has tempered everything so that "the parts that are unpresentable are treated with special modesty" (1 Cor. 12:23b). There are always people getting up on stage and sucking up all the oxygen and necessarily making a fool of themselves in order to get attention. It is ugly and obscene at times, as you saw what happened this week in the news.[28] 'Attention, attention, give me your attention. I just love attention.' Love is not proud; it does not envy.[29] Recognize diversity and unity; God has tempered each. Men and women kill for honor. 'Who is the richest?'

27. *1 Corinthians 12:14–20.*

28. A reference to a performance at the MTV Music Awards on August 25, 2013.

29. *1 Corinthians 13:4.*

'Who is the fairest?' How many stepmothers in fairy tales have beaten up their stepdaughters because they were a threat in terms of looks? Sometimes, we think we have power through our beauty. 'Beauty is truth, beauty is power, beauty is strength, beauty is everything.' That is it. We exalt one thing after another and come up with something hideous. It may look good, like Aphrodite, but how it plays out is horrible. It is present in the story between Athena and Aphrodite, where wisdom and love are in contest with each other in the Greek epics of *The Illiad* and *The Odyssey*. Remember, the golden apple was thrown in for the fairest, and the goddesses went at it. They bribed and connived. Guys do their own versions of this. No, we are not to take a particular excellence and make that into everything. "If the whole body were an eye, where would the sense of hearing be? If the whole body were an ear, where would the sense of smell be?" (1 Cor. 12:17). Where would the body be? It is not merely many differences going their own way. God has tempered and given honor in varying degrees as He sees fit. How wise of God is this?

Diversity Given for Equal Care within the Body

God gave diversity so that we might have equal care for one another. We are not saying, "I don't need you" (1 Cor. 12:21). Paul says that because we say it. Really, we have a hard time genuinely saying 'I need you' because of the way we think about the good: 'I don't really need you.' If the good is dying and going to heaven and being with Jesus, why do I need you for that? Tell me. I will give you $50 if you can come with an argument. I will make that $100. I am willing to lay down $5,000 on this if you can come up with an argument showing why I need you if the good is dying and going to heaven. That view is not corporate, cumulative, and communal as it was in the beginning: "Be fruitful, and multiply, and replenish the earth, and subdue it: and have dominion over the fish of the sea, and over the fowl of the air, and over every living thing that moveth upon the earth" (Gen. 1:28 KJV). A major point Paul is making here is that one part cannot say to another, "I don't need you" (1 Cor. 12:21). We can only say 'I need you' if we see what we are to do together over time—this is why the good is so important. Love is seeking the good for the other. Otherwise, you merely seek to please them and put forth some kind of flattery.

Paul gives all of these particulars in 1 Corinthians 12, and we come now to the passage on love.

You can have these gifts and diversity in a non-loving and empty way. **"If I speak in the tongues of men and of angels, but have not love, I am only a resounding gong or a clanging cymbal"** (v. 1)—*noise*—it is meaningless when our gift is separated from the good for the whole: each and every one. If I can figure out mysteries, I could have significant accomplishments of faith that can move mountains, but if I have not love, I am nothing.[30] I may excel in a particular area. 'In technology? No problem. I can do that.' Whether it is by supernatural or natural talent, 'I can do that.' People can 'move mountains,' can they not? In various areas? Whiz-kids. There are many of these whiz-kids, but all they have is 'whiz.' We can know in this sense and not have love. If I am not doing it for the good, I am doing it perhaps for my own glory. I may even give all I possess to the poor and, more than that, surrender my body to the flames. 'I am a martyr. I am one of the spiritual elite. I can do this,' and we can get ludicrous and sit up on a pillar for 37 years.[31] Grotesque. It does not have to be *that* grotesque, but 'I can do all kinds of "spiritual disciplines," minor flagellations of myself (or major), prayers, vigils, and fastings.' I may do this as a way to earn merit with God, not in service to others, as a living sacrifice. It is not a loving thing.

CHARACTERISTICS OF LOVE

Paul speaks about the characteristics of love. It may be helpful to look at them in clusters. The first characteristic of love is: **"Love is patient"** (v. 4a); it suffers long. Who would have put this as a first characteristic of love? Given the reality of sin—how slow things progress—and the reality of the curse, we have to be patient under the curse as we learn and patient with others as they learn. Parents have to be patient with their children. You all know that, right? They gradually come along, a gradual process that requires patience; God is patient with us.

"Love is kind" (v. 4). It is kind in simple acts of helping someone who may be in need or distress. A typical picture is helping an older

30. *1 Corinthians 13:2.*

31. "Saint Simeon Stylites," Encyclopædia Britannica, April 2024, www.britannica.com/biography/Saint-Simeon-Stylites.

woman walk across the street when there is traffic; a man giving his arm to a woman is symbolic of a certain kind of sensitivity, consideration, and help—opening the door for another so they do not have to struggle. Small acts of kindness, or it could be big acts. 'I was down and out, and this good Samaritan came and helped.' Kind, little ways, all kinds of ways. Instead of just passing another or harming, kindness is concern for the well-being of others in many, many ways.

"It does not envy" (v. 4). Someone else has ability, others notice it, and they seem to be happy, but we will say, 'I deserve that, too. I am just as good as the other person.' We are different, and God, in His own time and way, deals with us so we do not have to envy. When our focus is on what is good, we will see that these virtues and talents that are given are not the good. When we see someone using their talent to serve the common good, which is in place, there is no envy, but when it is used as an occasion to boast, and one expresses boastfully to others or is inwardly puffed up, that person does not have a clue.

Beauty used in the cause of truth, with humility, is admirable because it becomes a sign of a reality: the inward beauty. Beauty that is not used in this way but to aggrandize self is not love; this is self-life; this is not God-centered.

"It is not rude" (v. 5). It does not behave itself unseemly with words or actions. Rather than being rude, it is considerate. It is thoughtful to consider, get out of oneself, consider the other, and be sensitive to others. It is a kind of habit and disposition of our lives. Also, if some correction is needed, this person will not merely flatter you; that is no good, either. They may simply be silent and prayerful; perhaps you can pick up on something and realize that you need to be thoughtful about yourself. But it is not rude.

"It is not self-seeking" (v. 5). It is not seeking our own way. It is understanding unity and diversity and making room for others. It is not seeking our own way for ourselves. There may be agreement on principle, standards reiterated and reinforced from the beginning, and this is what we might insist on, but this is not 'our own way' after the fact. It is what *we* had agreed upon, and any of us may drift away from what was agreed upon. It does not mean it is wishy-washy and will not stand for anything, but it is not *our* way. It is more *the* way. Out of consideration, it is not 'the way, and I am putting this on you,' but it is the way that we have agreed upon, confirmed, professed, and rejoiced in; we are continuing in this.

"It is not easily angered" (v. 5) or easily provoked. It is not quick to take offense and is not touchy. It does not take the worst interpretation of things or use a self-centered interpretation, which makes us touchy. 'You looked at me wrong.' 'Did I do something wrong?' What is that? All of these come out of the tendency to be self-centered rather than God-centered and rather than centered on the good. Sometimes, we are so taken up with the self-centered interpretation that we are hardly aware of other things that may be going wrong. We should be mindful of other possibilities rather than interpreting everything from a self-centered perspective.

"It keeps no record of wrongs" (v. 5). It is in the context of forgiveness and cleansing that has been going on that wrongs will be brought up, but never unnecessarily, never in a non-relevant way, never to justify oneself by putting the other person down. This is the most common way of justifying ourselves. 'Well, you did it too. Don't you have errors yourself in this?' The focus is on moving ahead together, considering our own shortcomings first.

"Love does not delight in evil but rejoices with the truth" (v. 6). I have puzzled over this. I think I still have to figure this out. I am not sure what it is to delight in evil. I suppose some notable persons may do this—political figures that kill millions of people. Maybe it is like this: I am grieved where truth does not prevail and rejoice where truth prevails. I am not holding it against the other. This is in the context of continually seeking the good for others and with others, having first sought it for yourself.

"It always protects, always trusts, always hopes, always perseveres" (v. 7). This could be taken as a blank check and applied improperly and out of context rather than in the context of the good of others, unity and diversity, coming into the unity of the faith, and not doing anything that will hinder another person's growth or hinder another person's repentance. We are not to get in the way, injecting ourselves and our own attitudes. This is why we turn the other cheek. This is not about me and my insisting on it. Part of what is commended in the Beatitudes is "Blessed are the meek" (Matt. 5:5a). It is the lack of self-life that Jesus speaks about when he says, "If anyone would come after me, he must deny himself and take up his cross daily and follow me" (Lk. 9:23). This is what is being reflected in: "Follow me,"[32] "Learn of me,"[33] "Reflect me,"[34] and "Walk as I have walked."[35] This is what is being called for here. When we understand that love "**. . . always protects, always trusts, always hopes, always perseveres**" (v. 7), it is in the context of seeking the good for others. Paul is saying, this is what love is. This is that which never fails, at least in this context. Love is broader than this, but this is in this context. For example, "If you love Me, keep My commandments" (Jn. 14:15). Develop your talent in pursuit of the good in service to others.[36] Give honor to whom honor is due at every level: principles of honor, persons, and institutions, etc. The whole commandment of God is given to us to teach us love, the way to the good, to the knowledge of God. When these characteristics are brought, this certainly is love in this context, but it is broader and deeper than this. Paul speaks about the length, the depth, the breadth, and the height of the love of God that passes knowledge.[37]

THREE ARGUMENTS FOR THE CESSATION OF GIFTS

A division continues in Christendom, which begins in verse 8: "**But where there are prophecies, they will cease; where there are tongues, they will be stilled; where there is knowledge, it will pass away**" (v. 8b). Some say that tongues, prophecies, and miracles have not ceased. The Church is divided between those who say it has ceased and those who say it has not ceased. There are the cessationists[38] (literally called *the cessationists)* who say it has ceased, and then there are the continuationists. In the Pentecostal-charismatic churches, they say, 'It has not ceased; it continues.' Tongues continue, prophecy continues, and miracles continue. 'Who would want to limit God? And God does not change; we need it, and this is love. This is how love works.' All kinds of

32. *Matthew 4:19; 8:22;* and many other passages from Matthew, Mark, Luke, John.

33. *Matthew 11:29.*

34. *John 15:12; 13:13–17.*

35. *1 John 2:6.*

36. Gangadean, *Philosophical Foundation,* 259.

37. *Ephesians 3:18–19.*

38. O. Palmer Robertson, *The Final Word: A Biblical Response to the Case for Tongues and Prophecy Today,* (Edinburgh: Banner of Truth Trust, 1993).

arguments are given. We could say 'Yes' to all of these. We are to love, but we are also to grow up. When we grow up we leave childish things behind. **"When I was a child, I talked like a child, I thought like a child, I reasoned like a child. When I became a man, I put childish ways behind me"** (v. 11).

'God has not changed.' Yes, God did the same thing earlier. He gave supernatural gifts when the Church was coming into being out of Egypt. He fed them with manna from heaven, but the manna ceased. God does not change. It is a kind of sameness projected without seeing the circumstance. Someone might say, 'I had this experience,' but the experience must be interpreted. Can you distinguish ecstatic utterance from speaking in tongues? This appeal to experience is where we should ask: Does this tongue come as it did in the New Testament, with a language, as it did in the day of Pentecost? Because this seems to be the sense of it. If you speak in tongues when a stranger comes in, and he hears, he is convicted. There is a need for interpretation. The conviction did not occur until there was an interpretation by Peter.[39] It says, "When the people heard this, they were cut to the heart" (Acts 2:37a). Before that, they were saying, 'These men are just drunk. They are filled with new wine. These guys cannot hold their liquor early in the morning.'[40] The question is: Who is being edified and who is being magnified in this display?

Paul gives three reasons that tongues have ceased. First: **"when perfection comes, the imperfect disappears"** (v. 10). Tongues plus interpretation is revelation. When the revelation comes, is completed, the imperfect part is done away. The question is, does revelation come through the Scriptures, through the work of the Apostles and the Prophets? The Church's position historically has been, 'Yes, that has come.' Also, it was expected that certain things will be done away with, which is the second reason. **"When I was a child, I talked like a child, I thought like a child, I reasoned like a child. When I became a man, I put childish ways behind me"** (v. 11). There are some things that are appropriate for an infant stage, and it just naturally falls away. Training wheels on a bike. Can you see an adult using training wheels in the Tour de France? Cheering, 'Yay!' No, that would not be. There is an

39. *Acts 2:14–40.*

40. *Acts 2:13.*

expected growth process, and that we will go beyond childish ways. We are to go from spiritual infancy to maturity as we get the foundation in place. The third reason is the unclear and the clear: **"For now we see through a glass, darkly; but then face to face: now I know in part; but then shall I know even as also I am known"** (v. 12 KJV). Moses saw face to face.[41] This is not an expression reserved for the afterlife.[42] There are all kinds of problems when we think about seeing face to face, including seeing Jesus face to face, as though we had known Him after the flesh. "Wherefore henceforth know we no man after the flesh: yea, though we have known Christ after the flesh, yet now henceforth know we him no more" (2 Cor. 5:16 KJV). Think about the vision that John has of Jesus at the beginning of Revelation—that is Jesus. He fell on his feet like one dead,[43] in terms of the fullness of His glory. God, as He is in Himself, has no body; He is a spirit; He has no face, so "face to face" is an expression about seeing clearly. Things become clearer now that the Scripture has come. The prophets were designed to inquire about the time and place they were talking about. They earnestly desired this knowledge. The angels wanted to know.[44] Then Christ came and fulfilled the Scripture, which has been interpreted for us in the New Testament. Vision upon vision has been given to us of what to expect in the future, and we still miss it. We still struggle over the Book of Revelation. The rapture, the mark of the beast, and all of this wonderful, 'scary' content, but it is not the fear of the Lord. It is not as though these will be done away with at death, in the next life. It is being done away with here, in the course of history, as these things come. We are to grow to maturity.

LOVE NEVER FAILS

"Love never fails" (v. 8a). Tongues will cease, but faith, hope, and love will go on forever. Love is completed in our conduct and disposition.

41. *Numbers 12:8.*

42. Gangadean, *On Natural and Revealed Theology,* 9–39; Gangadean, "Paper No. 106: The Good and Heaven," 547–556; "Paper No. 116: The Knowledge of God vs. The Hope of Heaven," in *The Logos Papers,* 597–598; Gangadean, *Philosophical Foundation,* 40–41, 71–73.

43. *Revelation 1:17.*

44. *1 Peter 1:12.*

Our faith and hope will be completed in love, as it comes to expression. It is not that 'love is the greatest of these, so we can set aside faith and hope from love.' They are organically connected; there is a unity within them.

Paul calls us to love based on faith and hope, to unity in our being (at an individual person level), in the Church (the unity of the faith), hoping and working for the unity of all men—all men coming into the house of God. I have to confess that I often struggle with this: nobody is paying attention to this, nobody will pay attention to this, I am speaking into the air, I might as well stop. I struggle with hope, and when I do, my love is affected; how I think, act, and conduct myself is affected. I have to fight this.

Here are two things I heard. A notable philosopher says it will be a tall order to prove the existence of God. So he is saying it is not clear, and we are not inexcusable. Then, this next generation coming along is not listening. They think they know. I said, 'Okay, forget it.' I read this political commentator discussing an amendment for changing the Constitution. I Googled 'red and blue states,' and I started to count. I said, 'We do not have the votes. This is not going to happen. Forget it.' How do you deal with this struggle? Faith, hope, and love. Do not let your hands hang down. You have to fight against it, figure it out, pray, groan, meditate, go to bed sleeping on it, thinking about it, crying out in prayer, and wake up thinking about it. Then another piece will come in here, another piece there, and we say, 'Oh, yes, I see a way out.' It is like an avalanche of rocks has come down, but you see a little ray of light coming in here, or a little butterfly comes through a hole and flutters around, and you say, 'There is a way out.' Yes, keep going. Faith, hope, and love; it has to come to love. The greatest of these is love.

Let us sing concerning our unity in the Church from Psalm 133A, and then at the end of communion, we will sing concerning the unity of the world from Psalm 22I: "All ends of earth, remembering Him, shall turn themselves unto the LORD," and "The kindreds of the nations" will come.[45]

45. *Psalm 22:27, The Book of Psalms for Singing.*

16

SEVENFOLD MESSAGE TO THE CHURCH

Repent, for the Kingdom of Heaven Is at Hand

2022

Revelation 2:1–7

[1]To the angel of the church in Ephesus write:

These are the words of him who holds the seven stars in his right hand
and walks among the seven golden lampstands:

[2]I know your deeds, your hard work and your perseverance. I know that
you cannot tolerate wicked men, that you have tested those who claim to
be apostles but are not, and have found them false. [3]You have persevered
and have endured hardships for my name, and have not grown weary. [4]Yet
I hold this against you: You have forsaken your first love. [5]Remember the
height from which you have fallen! Repent and do the things you did at
first. If you do not repent, I will come to you and remove your lampstand
from its place. [6]But you have this in your favor: You hate the practices of
the Nicolaitans, which I also hate. [7]He who has an ear, let him hear what
the Spirit says to the churches. To him who overcomes, I will give the right
to eat from the tree of life, which is in the paradise of God.

INTRODUCTION:
The Church Is One

THE MESSAGE IS ON THE STATE OF THE Church. It is an occasional message. At the beginning of the new year, we might reflect on where we are, where we have been, and where we are going. In Revelation 2:1–7, we read the letter to the church at Ephesus. Seven churches are addressed in total in Revelation 2–3. We are reminded earlier that Christ is walking among the churches, which are represented as the candelabra.[1] It is actually one Church, one candelabra, though it has seven branches. By the working of the Spirit, we have the repetition of seven; there are many such repetitions, and the candelabra is saying 'one, yet seven.' Seven represents completion.

The message to the churches is one and the same, with different applications in each instance. It is the call to repent, for the kingdom of heaven is at hand.[2] Two letters explicitly speak of 'repent,' and in others, it is present, latent, at least to some in the church, but in some cases to all. The outcome of all of this, which is stated at the beginning of the Book of Revelation, is summed up in the Focus for the Week, the new Jerusalem: "And I John saw the holy city, new Jerusalem, coming down from God out of heaven, prepared as a bride adorned for her husband" (Rev. 21:2 KJV). Think of that word *adorned:* the bride's dress has been the focus of attention for many. Every bride is thoughtful and careful about the dress. It must be spotless; it must be fully prepared. It is an outward expression of an inward reality. There is no stain or wrinkle or any such thing; it is positively glorious. It is like the sun in its brightness, beautiful as the light of the moon and radiant with the life of Christ in her. We want to keep this in mind as we think about the message to the Church and the messages to the churches in Revelation 2–3. Throughout the rest of the book, there is a sevenfold vision, all saying again the same thing, of the conflict between good and evil, and that good will overcome evil, resulting in the fullness of the Church, the beauty of the Church, reflecting the beauty of the Lord.[3]

---

1. *Revelation 1:12, 20.*
2. *Matthew 4:17.*
3. Gangadean, *The Book of Revelation.*

I want to make some statements about the Church in general, the function of the Church, and thirdly, the Church as it is under the oversight of the elders. These are the three points. (1) *The Church.* (2) *The Church is for worship and discipleship.* (3) *The Church is under the oversight of the elders.* We will weave into this the message given to the churches in the Book of Revelation and throughout the Scriptures.

THE CHURCH IS THE BODY OF CHRIST, AND THE WORD OF GOD INCARNATE

The creation of man and woman in the beginning was to reflect this truth. Scripture says: "Husbands, love your wives, just as Christ loved the church and gave himself up for her" (Eph. 5:25), and "Wives, submit to your husbands as to the LORD. For the husband is the head of the wife as Christ is the head of the church, his body, of which he is the Savior" (Eph. 5:22–23). The husband-wife relationship, the covenant of marriage, reflects the covenant of creation between God and man, and specifically in Christ, in whom dwells all fullness through His body.[4] The Church is the body of Christ, and so much else follows from this.

The Incarnation Is for Redemption

Christ is the Word of God incarnate,[5] and the incarnation of Christ is for redemption. Man has sinned, turning away from the Word of God as it comes to him as light (reason),[6] as it comes in general revelation,[7] as it comes in Scripture,[8] and so He becomes incarnate. This Word continues to unfold in the Church historically—the Holy Spirit leading the Church into all truth[9]—and is applied to our hearts by the Spirit in regeneration[10] and continued in sanctification: to be sanctified through the truth, the Logos is truth.[11] The Word of God is incarnate

4. *Colossians 2:9.*

5. *John 1:14–18.*

6. *John 1:4.*

7. *John 1:3, 10.*

8. *John 1:11.*

9. *John 16:13.*

10. *1 Peter 1:23.*

11. *John 17:17.*

for redemption, and the fullness of this is in the sevenfold sense of the Word of God for redemption.[12]

Redemption Assumes the Biblical Worldview

Redemption in Scripture assumes the context and doctrine of the biblical worldview of creation–fall–redemption and should never be separated from these. These three go together: creation–fall–redemption, and we are not to think of the latter apart from the former (both creation and fall).

Creation–fall–redemption are the basic themes of biblical revelation. The latter assumes the former and is unintelligible without understanding the former. Redemptive revelation in the Scriptures assumes the existence of clear general revelation in the creation, as well as the existence of moral evil (sin) in the denial of clear general revelation. The movement in history is from good to evil to a restoration to what is good. The restoration from evil to good is gradual. Evil affects the understanding of good and evil itself,[13] and only gradually, through much conflict and suffering, do we overcome our denial of what is clear and come to understand the true nature of good and evil. The redemptive restoration to what is good, through long, intense conflict with evil, serves only to deepen the good in a way otherwise impossible. Good does not merely overcome evil but causes evil to serve the good.

Redemption Is Unfolded in the Scripture in Terms of a Spiritual War

Evil has come into the world. There is a conflict between good and evil, between belief and unbelief, and it is put this way in Scripture: God Himself says to Satan, the tempter, "I [God] will put enmity between you [Satan] and the woman" (Gen. 3:15a).[14] The woman had been seduced by the lie of the devil into unbelief and unrighteousness in eating of the forbidden fruit, the tree of the knowledge of good and evil. God is going to overcome this, and He does so according to His Word: "I will put enmity between you and the woman," that is,

12. Gangadean, *The Westminster Catechisms,* 113–114.

13. Gangadean, "Paper No. 103: The Noetic Effect of Sin," in *The Logos Papers,* 531–528.

14. Emphasis added.

between belief versus unbelief. Enmity is reflected in many ways. Even within believers and within churches, there is a conflict between belief and unbelief. Redemption is by this conflict, to the end that good will overcome evil, that belief will overcome unbelief.

Redemption Objectively Begins with Regeneration

When God said, "I will put enmity," He does so by bringing about regeneration, a new birth, sometimes spoken of as a re-creation, sometimes as a resurrection from the dead, spiritually speaking. Objectively, it begins with this reality. We might speak about regeneration as redemption objectively, ontologically, in our being. This is where the *ordo salutis* begins: with effectual calling of the believer out of sin and death to righteousness and life in Christ.

Subjectively, this redemption begins with repentance, with a conviction of sin and death based on clarity and inexcusability.[15] This is where the Call to Worship this morning comes from: "The stone the builders rejected has become the capstone" (Ps. 118:22). It is in Christ as He is revealed in creation, such that it is clear, so that there is no excuse for unbelief. The doctrine of clarity and inexcusability is what the builders refused. Throughout the world, in all the traditions of the world, we see that no one seeks and no one understands what is clear about God, and they deny clarity and inexcusability.

Call to Repentance Begins with the Curse[16]

The spiritual war is between belief and unbelief, so we must address this reality. We have to ask questions that concern conviction of sin and death. When man had fallen into sin, he was called back first inwardly by conscience. He was aware of his nakedness—no one had to tell him—and it caused him to seek to cover that which reminds him of the sin. Then God calls him a second time, outwardly: 'Where are you?'; and man justifies himself, excuses himself, by blaming God and the woman. It does not end there. Then comes the third call back, and this third call back is through the curse. The curse consists of toil

15. Gangadean, "Paper No. 102: The Clarity of General Revelation," 527–529; "Paper No. 41: What Is Clear About God," 225–229; "Paper No. 112: Why General Revelation Is Basic in the Christian Worldview," in *The Logos Papers*, 583–585.

16. Gangadean, *The Biblical Worldview*, 55–68, 219–294.

and strife, and old age, sickness, and death. It is imposed directly by God on man as a call back to restrain him from going into sin, to recall him from sin, and to remove sin that remains. This curse as a call back assumes the promise. The two are inseparable: curse and promise. They should not be separated in our thinking or in our speaking. The curse is, in this context, the third call back—after conscience and after the outward call back—and it is final; there is no more call back after this, and it is a continuing call back from sin and self-deception and self-justification. The curse is cumulative in a person's life and in history, as sin has been cumulative and has increased. It is recurrent in the believer through the trials of faith, it continues until it is completed, and it is not completed until death. In this life, it continues until death, and we pray that prayer, "deliver us from evil" (Matt. 6:13 KJV) from within us and from around us.

God's call to repentance through the curse is continued by the Church, the body of Christ. We continue to call men to repentance based on God's call, and our call should not be separated from God's call. We may not always speak of God's call, but we should always think about it, assume it, and understand it in this context. This is the Church as it is seen in the Word of God.

THE CHURCH IS FOR WORSHIP AND DISCIPLESHIP

The Church Is under the Word of God in Doctrine and Life

There are qualifications in order to be considered a church. In some cases, a church claiming to be a church may be so far gone that they are no longer a church. The Church is more or less pure in that it is more or less conscious and consistent in its belief versus unbelief. When we understand what is called for in discipleship and God's call, we will understand the work of the Church and how we must deal with remaining sin. It is very important that we understand and engage with this.

Worship Must Be in Spirit and in Truth

We say the Church is for worship as well as discipleship. Worship must be in spirit and in truth.[17] When we say it must be *in spirit,* we are speaking about the inward reality. When we say *in truth,* we are speaking of the outward, objective reality. For example, we are to use the Psalms only in our corporate worship, and we might say in our private worship (we cannot improve on the Psalms). We are to worship God in spirit and in truth. It is possible to sing the Psalms, which are objectively true, without understanding the meaning of it inwardly. Understanding the meaning inwardly is the subjective part, *in spirit,* and *in truth* is the objective. Both are to operate in worship. We are not to worship just in spirit and not just in truth, but in spirit *and* in truth. We are not to just sing the Psalms but also sing the Psalms with understanding/faith. We should not draw near to God with our lips but our hearts are far from Him.[18] Worship must be in spirit and in truth, and everything else follows if we worship in spirit and in truth. Nothing will follow if these are lacking; we will not get where we need to be. The Church is for worship and discipleship. It is in our standards. We are more or less conscious and consistent. Oversight must take this into account in our worship, individually and corporately.

The Church Is for Discipleship

Jesus said, "Therefore go and make disciples of all nations" (Matt. 28:19a). We are to make disciples—learners—and they must learn the basic truths. They must understand the law of God and how it applies to all of life. Jesus says, "teaching them to obey everything I have commanded you" (Matt. 28:20a). Discipleship has an objective aspect—the foundation and the law of God—and a subjective aspect in that the foundation is laid in our lives, not just in word, but in reality. It is understood, and it is being applied. Likewise, the law of God is not just the law of God spoken outwardly, in a minimal, legalistic sense, though that has certainly been the practice in the Church from time to time and has come to dominate the life of churches. It was there in

17. Gangadean, *The Westminster Confession,* 233–244; Gangadean, "Paper No. 134: Worship, the Sabbath, and the Church," 679–682; "Paper No. 135: On Worship," in *The Logos Papers,* 683–684.

18. *Matthew 15:8.*

Paul's life before his conversion. We are to work so that the foundation is not only stated but carefully laid in the lives of the people, in the hearts of the people. This requires a special working of the Spirit, but we watch to see that this work is going on.

Discipleship Is for the Unity of the Church

Discipleship, in laying the foundation and teaching the law of God, "to observe all things whatsoever I have commanded you" (Mat. 28:20 KJV), should result in unity in the Church. This unity is opposed to divisions, which are due to sin—unbelief in many forms as we are all going our own way, holding up our virtues as ends in themselves rather than a means to the end, and missing the mark by coming short in various forms of idolatry.

Discipleship is for unity. We may speak of unity in at least three senses, prominently, spoken of in Scripture. First, "That all of them may be one, Father, just as you are in me and I am in you . . . that the world may believe" (Jn. 17:21). That they might be one even as the Father and the Son are one. This is the unity in the Trinity, spoken of in the Council of Nicea. God is not one *simpliciter*. God is a Triune God: Father, Son, and Holy Spirit; three persons, one God, in unity. There is an order within the Trinity: the Father, and the Son is of the Father, and the Holy Spirit proceeding from the Father and the Son. This example of unity is held up explicitly in John 17:21. We are to be sanctified through the truth—the Word, the Logos, the sevenfold sense of the Word, is truth.[19]

A second sense of unity, versus division, is spoken of in 1 Corinthians 1:10–13. The Church was divided along personality lines. "I follow Paul . . . I follow Apollos . . . I follow Cephas" (1 Cor. 1:12). Some saying even, "I follow Christ." Paul's response: "Is Christ divided?" (1 Cor. 1:13a). The answer is, 'No.' The ministry of Christ as prophet, priest, and king, is not divided, and they are ordered, going from the prophetic to the priestly to the kingly. Personality difference is a recurrent problem in the history of the Church. It was there from early on, and it was manifest in the Corinthians. According to our gifts and our consciousness, which are various, we divide and emphasize our gifts and make them first, and we do not understand the order that there

19. *John 17:17.*

is within our being and which should be among us. We all have the same heart, a triune personality. We are to love God with our whole heart: our mind, our soul, and our strength.[20] Each person is to love God with our whole heart, understand the order, and pursue it. Just as there is order within the Trinity, there is order within our triune personality and in Christ.

This lack of unity is manifest when we come to the Lord's Table in communion. "When you come together as a church, there are divisions among you, and to some extent I believe it. No doubt there have to be differences among you to show which of you have God's approval" (1 Cor. 11:18–19). These things that are longstanding and deep-seated come to light during trials and become manifest, and they are further manifest as we seek to deal with them according to the Word of God. In doing so, we find out which view, which understanding, is approved—who rightly understands the Word of God and who does not.

The Book of Ephesians chapter 4 speaks of unity in terms of three forms. There is the *unity of the Spirit,*[21] which is basic: one Lord, one faith, one baptism.[22] We maintain humility of mind, meekness, and gentleness in our dealings with one another. There is the *unity of the faith.* We are to come into that unity. We are to preserve the unity of the Spirit until we all come into the unity of the faith,[23] as the Holy Spirit leads the Church into all truth.[24] It is to be manifest in the body, in *functional unity,* in the functioning of the body, in the Church, as each part does its work. The Church is to have this unity so that we might accomplish the work of redemption of Christ through His body, the Church, in our seeking to call men everywhere to repentance and to faith in Christ.

---

20. *Mark 12:30; Luke 10:27.*
21. *Ephesians 4:3.*
22. *Ephesians 4:5.*
23. *Ephesians 4:13.*
24. *John 16:13.*

THE CHURCH IS UNDER THE OVERSIGHT OF THE ELDERS

Other terms are used in Scripture. In Revelation 4, we see the 24 elders surrounding the throne of God and worshiping. The elders have a particular status in the context of the Church and the Church worshiping. God raises up the elders to lead the Church in doctrine and discipline. Elders are sometimes referred to in Scripture as *presbyters,* from which we get the name Presbyterian, or *episcopus,* from which we get the terms bishops, leaders, or elders.

Elders Must Meet Qualifications

Qualifications are in terms of the Word of God. Elders must be blameless, which is a general, broad claim. They are to walk in the light—all of the light that has been given to them, particularly as it has been summed up in the historically cumulative faith, which is the work of the pastor-teachers through the centuries.[25]

Many are in the position of elder but do not think much, say much, or affirm much about the historically cumulative faith as it is in the Westminster Confession of Faith, and certainly not in what we call the doxological focus.[26] The doxological understanding affirms the doctrine of the clarity of general revelation and the inexcusability of unbelief (WCF. 1.1), the use of reason (the light of nature and good and necessary consequence) to understand general and special revelation (1.1, 1.6), the doxological focus on the knowledge of the glory of God (SCQ. 1, 101; WCF. 4.1, 5.1), divine sovereignty in creation–fall–redemption, and the law of God for all of life. These are not things that are affirmed today as part of the historically cumulative faith. Or, if they are affirmed, they are affirmed outwardly, objectively, but it is not something subjectively worked into the innermost being of our lives. The elders must meet qualifications. They are to be blameless, living their lives under the Word of God, all the light that they receive.

---

25. Gangadean, "Paper No. 16: The Historic Christian Faith," in *The Logos Papers,* 103–114; Gangadean, *The Westminster Confession,* xix-xxix, 349–351.

26. Gangadean, *The Westminster Confession,* xxix-xxxii, 347–348; Gangadean, "Paper No. 115: Doxological Christianity," 595–596; "Paper No. 118: Eschatology (Seven Points)," in *The Logos Papers,* 603–607.

The Elders Are Given the Keys of the Kingdom

The keys open and close the gates. Those who are repentant can enter and continue as they grow in their repentance, or they may be removed, though they had entered at one time. Scripture says, concerning the Apostles and those who follow in that office, "If you forgive anyone his sins, they are forgiven; if you do not forgive them, they are not forgiven" (Jn. 20:23). The doors of the kingdom are open to the repentant and closed to the unrepentant. This has to be exercised, and we should say this has not always been the case. It has not often been the case; it is more often a repentance that is outward, in word, without looking for fruit in keeping with repentance, and not noticing repentance of root sin. We are being called as elders to repent of this and to exercise the keys: the authority to admit into the Church or to keep out of the Church. We have to come back to foundational truths and act accordingly. If we do not, we ourselves will be removed from this position.

The Elders Continue Aaron's Rod

The elders in the Church in the New Testament continue the work of the elders in the Old Testament. This is summed up under the teaching of Aaron's rod.[27] Aaron's rod was placed in the Most Holy Place. We will come back to this shortly. Aaron and the priesthood of the Old Testament were to teach holiness and the laws of cleansing determining the clean and the unclean. They were to understand the curse, its effect, what it means, and how it applies in our lives. They are to continually and repeatedly, day in and day out, year in and year out, make this teaching clear to the people. It is part of sanctification through the truth, beginning with the foundational doctrine. They are to teach holiness; Aaron, the high priest, had a gold band on his head that said, "Holiness to the LORD."[28] The priest focuses on holiness based on the teaching of the prophet, of knowledge, and it is to issue in righteousness, in our obeying the law of God in all of life.

Remember how Aaron's rod came into existence. There was a rebellion against the authority of the Word of God coming through Moses and Aaron. There was another rebellion in the case of Miriam and

27. Gangadean, "Paper No. 64: Aaron's Rod," 341–352; "Paper No. 65: Aaron's Rod (Outlined)," in *The Logos Papers,* 353–358.

28. *Exodus 28:36–38.*

Aaron against Moses. It was about the Word of God: "Has the LORD spoken only through Moses? . . . Hasn't he also spoken through us?" (Num. 12:2). And they found fault. It was a nitpicking fault, if it was a fault at all, in the Ethiopian woman he had married. We will see more of this as we go on further.

The Elders Prepare God's People for Works of Service

Elders not only admit persons into the Church, into the kingdom, based on their repentance—repentance of root sin and fruit in keeping with repentance—but they prepare God's people for works of service. The outcome of this preparation is the laying on of their hands on people, recognizing their calling in God. The laying on of hands is connected with calling; there is a specific call as in the priesthood and certain offices, but there are many callings. All the people of God are called in various ways to serve in the body. The elders prepare people for this whole range of work. It does not mean they teach them medical knowledge (congregants go to medical school for that), but they approach medical school based on the knowledge from the point of view of what is consistent with the foundation. We do not lay hands on ourselves, even in the secular world. Others recognize us in some position of authority and believe that we have achieved a certain level of understanding. The elders prepare all the members for works of service. The elders are the ones to say, 'Yes, you have been prepared. We bless you, in the name of the Lord, do this work.' We do not lay hands on ourselves and say, 'I believe I am called. I believe I am ready. Listen to me; I have the Word of God.' The elders are concerned to bring truth in holiness and sanctification (which are synonymous), to bring the truth into the inward part, the innermost part of our lives.

Know the Truth in the Inward Part

John 17:17 says, "Sanctify them by the truth; your word is truth." It is the truth that must come. John 8:31–32 says, "If you hold to my teaching, you are really my disciples. Then you will know the truth, and the truth will set you free." Romans 12:2 says, "Do not conform any longer to the pattern of this world, but be transformed by the renewing of your mind." The truth in the inward part. Think of David in the matter of Bathsheba: "Surely you desire truth in the inner parts;

you teach me wisdom in the inmost place" (Ps. 51:6). Think about Job: "I have heard of thee by the hearing of the ear: but now mine eye seeth thee. Wherefore I abhor myself, and repent in dust and ashes" (Job 42:5–6 KJV). Truth in the inward part. Think about Moses who lived 40 years in the backside of the desert. Think about Paul being brought low and having the affliction of God, the thorn in the flesh, that he might be humbled that the Lord may raise him up and reveal Himself to him.[29] Think about the fathers—Abraham, Isaac, Jacob, and Joseph—and how they were prepared over significant periods of time, through suffering, to get the truth in the inward part. Think of the prophets. This is the subjective side of it. The truth comes into the subject, into the person, into the actual experience, into the heart, into the innermost being; the truth that sanctifies and makes us holy.

Aaron's Rod versus the Gainsaying of Korah

Aaron's rod was a dead stick that was placed before God, chosen by God, upheld by God, and by the working of God, that stick came alive and budded and blossomed and bore fruit. This attested that the Word of God was coming through Aaron, by God's appointment and preparation, and the Word of God, the ministry, brought life. This is what the blossoming of Aaron's rod means. God had chosen Aaron. This was done in a particular context: the gainsaying of Korah, Dathan, and Abiram, and 250 princes, and about 25,000 people who had questioned the office of the elder saying, 'Why do you raise yourself above others?'[30] They were not raising themselves up; God raised them up and put them there. It was God's authority that was being manifest, and this was being denied in principle by saying, 'All are equal. Everyone is holy.' Remember Miriam and Aaron, too: they were caught in this. It is not recognizing the authority of the Word of God. Remember the sevenfold Logos.[31]

We will have to think about, 'What is this gainsaying?' It takes time for that which is deep within to become manifest. It may come in and lay dormant for years, for decades, but it does become manifest, and it is manifest in divisions among us. As 1 Corinthians 11 says, "there are divisions among you . . . No doubt there have to be differences among

29. *2 Corinthians 12:7–10.*

30. *Numbers 16:3.*

31. Gangadean, "Paper No. 30: The Word of God," in *The Logos Papers,* 179–180.

you to show which of you have God's approval" (1 Cor. 11:18b–19). It says there "have to be" (NIV) or "there must be" (KJV) divisions, "that they which are approved may be made manifest" (1 Cor. 11:19 KJV). Not only do divisions among us occur for this purpose, but the attempts to deal with the division are part of the manifestation. When we attempt to deal with it, and it is avoided and resisted, this is part of the failure to have truth deep within, in the inward part. I gave you seven examples of truth in the inward part in the words of Christ, David, Job, Moses, Paul, the fathers, and the prophets.

The Book of Jude mentions Cain: "Woe to them! They have taken the way of Cain; they have rushed for profit into Balaam's error; they have been destroyed in Korah's rebellion" (Jude 1:11). Cain could not answer why he needed Christ and Him crucified; he could not answer why he needed to bring the animal offering and why his offering was unacceptable. He lacked a conviction of sin and he lacked an understanding of what his father taught through the coats of skin they were wearing in the expulsion from the Garden. This teaching was available to Cain and Abel. Cain did not hear and receive it. Cain was a deist: he believed in 'God' of some kind, but not the God who is clearly revealed in general revelation. Jude says this is the religion of Balaam. He did it for profit. He thought gain was godliness.[32] Then they perished in the "gainsaying"[33] of Korah—Korah, Dathan, and Abiram, who denied the authority of God.

Gainsaying involves persistent objecting, and the objection is on the level of gnats versus camels.[34] The gnats would disappear if the camels were seen for what they are. If the log is taken out of our own eye, we can see clearly to take the speck out of our brother's eye.[35] If we do not, what will happen is that the distinction between gnats and camels will be denied; it will be all gnats, and worse yet, the gnats become camels because of a morbid consciousness: a micro-consciousness where there is a strain on small things and the big things are missed.[36] Legalism—trying to list all the outward manifestations of sin and missing the heart condition. This is a recurrent problem in the Church for many. Often,

---

32. *1 Timothy 6:5.*

33. *Jude 1:11* KJV.

34. *Matthew 23:24.*

35. *Matthew 7:3–5.*

36. *1 Timothy 4:2–3.*

objections come from legalism, and all the gnats become nitpicking, straining at gnats, and quibbles over a word,[37] and it is manifest in our lack of agreement. In the process of straining at gnats, when objections are raised, we fall silent without agreeing.

Jesus encountered this many times. He answered their objection, but they fell silent. They had nothing to say, but they did not agree with him. It comes from not glorifying God and develops into not enjoying God. The Book of Revelation starts with this, in the letter to the Ephesians: "You have forsaken your first love" (Rev. 2:4b). You are holding to the doctrine and willing to argue for the doctrine—orthodox in that sense—but not with a sense of the goal of knowing God and enjoying God forever. By the end of the letters to the churches, they were lukewarm—neither hot nor cold.[38] They went so far as to say they thought they were in a good state and did not realize their true state. I would like to read some of this for you. This is Revelation 3:15–16: "I know your deeds, that you are neither cold nor hot. I wish you were either one or the other! So, because you are lukewarm—neither hot nor cold—I am about to spit you out of my mouth." Remember, the letter to the Ephesians began with, "You have forsaken your first love" (Rev. 2:4b). You are starting to cool. You lost sight of the goal. You lost sight of what it was all about. Think about the first stage of love, in the early stages before and leading to marriage and the honeymoon, and we lose that—what that was all about. You might then try to regain it improperly.

In any case, the end of the letter says, "You say, 'I am rich; I have acquired wealth and do not need a thing.' But you do not realize that you are wretched, pitiful, poor, blind and naked" (Rev. 3:17). These are the successful churches that think they are rich and have it, but with regard to the goal of knowing God and making His glory known and enjoying Him, they have fallen far away. "As many as I love, I rebuke and chasten: be zealous therefore, and repent" (Rev. 3:19 KJV). Those who heed and overcome are given life. One reality of life is described in seven different ways.[39] One reality of Christ is described in seven different ways. One reality of the spiritual war, from the beginning to the end, is described in seven ways and seven visions. One Word of

37. *1 Timothy 6:4.*

38. *Revelation 3:15–16.*

39. *Revelation 2:7, 11, 17, 26, 3:5, 12, 21.*

God coming to us in a sevenfold manner.[40] If we do not repent, He will remove our candlestick.[41] We will no longer continue as a church. We are to repent of root sin and all the fruit that comes out of root sin. We are to be zealous and repent.

We may wonder sometimes, 'How do we regain our first love?' Whether it is true for all of us, it may be we never had truth in the innermost part. We had truth, but not in the inmost part. This is new territory. When the truth gets there, we believe it remains there. When you have ears to hear, and you hear inwardly and not outwardly, this tends to remain. This is the life that remains lastingly to those who overcome by faith.

CONCLUSION: Repentance under Oversight

The message to the Church is to repent in the context of the oversight given to the Church and be careful not to fall into the gainsaying of Korah and find objections, but submit, that there may be cleansing, that truth may come into the inmost part. Longstanding, deep-seated matters need to be taken care of, and the oversight needs to be watchful for this and see to it that this comes into practice.

The elders must be holy if they are to teach holiness. Malachi 3:3 says, "He will sit as a refiner and purifier of silver; he will purify the Levites and refine them like gold and silver. Then the LORD will have men who will bring offerings in righteousness." Because the priests had decayed, the Church decayed. 'Like priests, like people,' the elders are not doing what they should do. The priests must go through this process of cleansing themselves. The Word of God is described in the Psalms: "And the words of the LORD are flawless, like silver refined in a furnace of clay, purified seven times" (Ps. 12:6). The Word of God is pure. We are to cease from our own words. We are to meditate on the Word deeply and understand how it applies. The pastor-teachers are to do the work of applying the Word of God to the lives of the people of God, in all the details, and the people of God are to be submitted

40. Gangadean, *The Westminster Catechisms,* 113–114.

41. *Revelation 2:5.*

to their oversight and avoid falling into the trap of self-justification, of gainsaying, and objecting by not getting back to the more basic.

INDEX

About the Author

Dr. Surrendra Gangadean (1943–2022) was a Professor of Philosophy at Phoenix College and at Paradise Valley Community College for 45 years. Additionally, he taught from the pulpit at Westminster Fellowship for almost 30 years and taught courses at Logos Theological Seminary for over 25 years. Courses he taught include: Introduction to Philosophy, Logic, Ethics, Philosophy of Religion, Eastern Religions, World Religions, Introduction to Christianity, Introduction to Humanities, Philosophy of Art, The Great Books, Philosophical Theology, Biblical Worldview, Biblical History, Church History, Systematic Theology, Biblical Hermeneutics, and Existential Hermeneutics. He received an M.A. degree in Literature from Arizona State University, an M.A. degree in Philosophy from the University of Arizona, and a Ph.D. in Natural Theology from Reformed International Theological Seminary. He presented academic papers and public lectures on Natural Theology and the Moral Law. Dr. Gangadean was the organizing Pastor of Westminster Fellowship church, and President of The Logos Foundation, which serves academic education in Liberal Arts and Theology.

www.ingramcontent.com/pod-product-compliance
Lightning Source LLC
Chambersburg PA
CBHW020432130626
46549CB00001B/106

* 9 7 9 8 9 8 9 8 2 9 5 8 3 *